Foreign News on Television

This book is part of the Peter Lang Media and Communication list.
Every volume is peer reviewed and meets
the highest quality standards for content and production.

PETER LANG
New York • Washington, D.C./Baltimore • Bern
Frankfurt • Berlin • Brussels • Vienna • Oxford

Foreign News on Television

Where in the World is the Global Village?

Edited by Akiba A. Cohen

with António Belo | Joseph M. Chan | Knut De Swert
Elizabeth Godo | Abby Goodrum | Thomas Hanitzsch
Christine Heimprecht | Youichi Ito | Rasha Kamhawi
Francis L.F. Lee | Wan-Ying Lin | Ven-hwei Lo
Paolo Mancini | Marco Mazzoni | Constanza Mujica
Hong Nga Nguyen Vu | William Porath | Thorsten Quandt
André Sendin | Agnieszka Stępińska | Thilo von Pape
Jacques A. Wainberg | Tai-Li Wang | David H. Weaver
Jürgen Wilke | Lars Willnat | Ruud Wouters
Xiaoge Xu | Baohua Zhou

PETER LANG
New York • Washington, D.C./Baltimore • Bern
Frankfurt • Berlin • Brussels • Vienna • Oxford

Library of Congress Cataloging-in-Publication Data

Foreign news on television: Where in the world is the global village?/
edited by Akiba A.Cohen.
pages cm
Includes bibliographical references and index.
1. Foreign news. 2. Television broadcasting of news.
I. Cohen, Akiba A. editor of compilation.
PN4784.F6F685   070.4'332—dc23   2013003320
ISBN 978-1-4331-1690-2 (hardcover)
ISBN 978-1-4331-1689-6 (paperback)
ISBN 978-1-4539-1082-5 (e-book)

Bibliographic information published by **Die Deutsche Nationalbibliothek**.
Die Deutsche Nationalbibliothek lists this publication in the "Deutsche
Nationalbibliografie"; detailed bibliographic data is available
on the Internet at http://dnb.d-nb.de/.

The paper in this book meets the guidelines for permanence and durability
of the Committee on Production Guidelines for Book Longevity
of the Council of Library Resources.

© 2013 Peter Lang Publishing, Inc., New York
29 Broadway, 18th floor, New York, NY 10006
www.peterlang.com

All rights reserved.
Reprint or reproduction, even partially, in all forms such as microfilm,
xerography, microfiche, microcard, and offset strictly prohibited.

Printed in the United States of America

For my grandchildren Eli, Carmel, Romy and Ivri —
the next generation of news viewers

Contents

List of Tables ix
List of Figures xii
Acknowledgments xiii
Preface xvii
 Akiba A. Cohen

Part 1 The Project

1 Rationale, Design, and Methodologies 3
 Akiba A. Cohen, Thomas Hanitzsch, Agnieszka Stępińska, William Porath,
 & Christine Heimprecht

2 The Prevalence of News: Domestic, Foreign, and Hybrid 23
 Agnieszka Stępińska, William Porath, Constanza Mujica, Xiaoge Xu,
 & Akiba A. Cohen

Part 2 Contents

3 Topics in Foreign and Domestic Television News 41
 Knut De Swert, António Belo, Rasha Kamhawi, Ven-hwei Lo, Constanza Mujica,
 & William Porath

4 Countries of Location and Countries Involved 63
 Jürgen Wilke, Christine Heimprecht, & Youichi Ito

5 Actors in Foreign News 87
 António Belo, Elizabeth Godo, Knut De Swert, & André Sendin

6 Formal Features and Sources in Foreign News 107
 Jürgen Wilke & Christine Heimprecht

7 Foreign News on Public and Commercial Stations 129
 Joseph M. Chan & Francis L.F. Lee

Part 3 Viewers

8 Who Uses News, How Much, and Why? 153
 Lars Willnat, David Weaver, Agnieszka Stępińska, & Ven-hwei Lo

9 Interest in Foreign News 171
 Thomas Hanitzsch, Abby Goodrum, Thorsten Quandt, & Thilo von Pape

10 Countries of Interest 191
 Thilo von Pape, Thorsten Quandt, Thomas Hanitzsch, & Jacques Alkalai Wainberg

Part 4 Gatekeepers

11 Gatekeepers on Decision-Making in Foreign News 209
   Constanza Mujica & Thomas Hanitzsch

12 Self-Reflexivity of Gatekeepers on Content and Viewers of Foreign News 225
   Lars Willnat & Akiba A. Cohen

Part 5 Tying the Knots

13 Linking Content and Audiences: Topics in the News. 253
   Knut De Swert & Akiba A. Cohen

14 Linking Content and Audiences: Countries of Interest 269
   Francis Lee, Jürgen Wilke, & Akiba A. Cohen

15 Overall Conclusions for Individual Countries 293
   All Project Participants

16 Where in the World Is the Global Village?. 319
   Akiba A. Cohen

Methodological Appendixes 331

References. 353

Participants in the Project 371

Index. 377

Tables

Table 1.1	Television stations in the study	10
Table 1.2	Contextual variance in the countries of the study	17
Table 2.1	Countries in descending order of percentages of each type of news	30
Table 2.2	Mean duration (in seconds) of items by country and news category	32
Table 2.3	Lead items in newscasts by types of news (in percent)	34
Table 3.1	Main topic categories by country (in percentage of total news time)	44
Table 3.2	Main topic categories in domestic and foreign news by country (in percentage of total news time)	48
Table 3.3	Spearman rank correlations between time devoted to the 25 main topic categories of purely domestic (D), domestic with foreign involvement (DF), foreign with domestic involvement (FD), and purely foreign (F) by country	53
Table 3.4	Percentages and rankings of top 25 individual news topics by total news time of items in domestic and foreign news	55
Table 3.5	Hard, soft, and sensational news by country and news type (in percentage of news time)	57
Table 3.6	Shannon H entropy scores by country for all coverage, domestic news, and foreign news (based on 11-topic categorization)	60
Table 4.1	Number of countries of location in foreign news broadcasts and number of foreign news items	65
Table 4.2	Proportion of continental regions and countries in foreign news coverage on TV (in percent)	67
Table 4.3	Country Concentration Indexes (CCI) for the top 10 countries of location in the foreign TV news of all countries (in ascending order)	69
Table 4.4	Proportion of news featuring top 10 countries of location in countries of study	70
Table 4.5	Proportion of news featuring top 10 countries involved in countries of study	79
Table 5.1	Percentage of items with at least one actor and mean number of actors per item	93
Table 5.2	Status of the actors in foreign and domestic news by country (in percent)	95
Table 5.3	Percentage of internal and international politics, citizens, and social issues roles in foreign and domestic news items by country	96
Table 5.4	Percentage of items with at least one actor and mean number of actors for foreign and domestic news across all countries by topic	98
Table 5.5	Role status of actors in foreign and domestic news by topic categories (in percent)	99

Table 5.6	Gender of actors in foreign and domestic news by country (in percent)	100
Table 5.7	Female actors in female topics and other topics (in percent)	101
Table 5.8	Status of actors in foreign and domestic news by gender (in percent)	102
Table 6.1	Basic parameters of analyzed newscasts by country and station	109
Table 6.2	Overall distributions of formal features in the newscasts	111
Table 6.3	Percent of items with anchorpersons in newscasts	114
Table 6.4	Percent of foreign items mentioned in headlines, part of block, appearing live from location, and pre-recorded on location by country and type of broadcaster	115
Table 6.5	Percent of foreign items containing video news agency material, archive material, printed text, and tables and charts by country and type of broadcaster	118
Table 6.6	Percent of foreign items containing still photos, pictorial and graphic representation, animation, and maps by country and type of broadcaster	120
Table 6.7	Percent of foreign items containing flags and emblems, logos, background music, and slow motion by country and type of broadcaster	122
Table 6.8	Percent of overall use of formal features in domestic and foreign news	124
Table 6.9	Clusters of TV stations based on modes and tools (in percent)	126
Table 7.1	Soft news items, visual representation, and audio-visual effects in foreign news by country and public vs. commercial stations	137
Table 7.2	Mean length of sound bites and percentage of items containing conflict in foreign news and percentage of foreign news by country and public vs. commercial stations	139
Table 7.3	Percentages of concentrated countries, mean number of international organizations, and mean number of countries involved in foreign news by country and public vs. commercial stations	142
Table 7.4	Number of significant findings for each country	144
Table 8.1	News exposure to different media by country	156
Table 8.2	News exposure to different media by gender, age, and education (all respondents from all countries)	159
Table 8.3	Reasons for watching television news by country	160
Table 8.4	Reasons for not watching foreign news by country	162
Table 8.5	Demographic predictors of exposure to TV news, newspapers, and online news (minutes yesterday) by country	164
Table 9.1	Interest in foreign news (mean scores)	174
Table 9.2	Interest in domestic news (mean scores)	178
Table 9.3	Differences between interest in foreign and domestic news (mean score differences)	179

Table 9.4	Relationships between interest in foreign news and domestic news (Spearman rank correlations)	183
Table 9.5	Predicting interest in foreign news, pooled regression (standardized coefficients)	184
Table 9.6	Predicting interest in foreign news, country-wise regression (standardized coefficients)	187
Table 10.1	Mean number of countries mentioned per respondent and Country Concentration Index per sample country	194
Table 10.2	Interest in countries across the entire sample in percent	196
Table 10.3	Interest in continents across the entire sample in percent	197
Table 10.4	Ranked order of each sample country's mentioned countries of interest among the 30 most-mentioned countries overall	198
Table 10.5	Spearman rank correlations of countries of interest among all sample countries	199
Table 13.1	Rankings of domestic news topics and audience interest by country	255
Table 13.2	Rankings of foreign news topics and audience interest by country	258
Table 13.3	Percentage of high audience interest in most prevalent topic category of foreign news by country	260
Table 13.4	Comparison of foreign relations within foreign news content and audience interest by country	261
Table 13.5	Logistic regression for correspondence between the most prominent topic in the news content and respondents' evaluation of their interest in the topic	263
Table 13.6	Summary of significant variables in the logistic regression analyses by country	264
Table 14.1	Top 15 countries in foreign news and mentioned in surveys	272
Table 14.2	Summary of content-audience correspondence in countries of interest	274
Table 14.3	Content-survey correspondence as measured by Spearman rank correlations	277
Table 14.4	Predictors of country-level content-audience correspondence	281
Table 14.5	Content-survey correspondence in country concentration	283
Table 14.6	Regression on number of most prominent and less prominent countries mentioned (U.S. data)	286
Table 14.7	Summary of regression analysis on number of most prominently covered countries mentioned	287
Table 14.8	Summary of regression analysis on number of not prominently covered countries mentioned	288

Figures

Figure 1.1	General research design	9
Figure 3.1	Positions of countries regarding topics in all news items (based on multidimensional unfolding)	47
Figure 3.2	Positions of countries regarding topics in domestic news items (based on multidimensional unfolding)	51
Figure 3.3	Positions of countries regarding topics in foreign news items (based on multidimensional unfolding)	52
Figure 10.1	Distribution of the countries' interest in the overall sample	192
Figure 10.2	Top 20 countries of interest for the across-all-sample countries	201
Figure 10.3	Top 20 countries of interest in the Portuguese sample	202
Figure 10.4	Top 20 countries of interest in the U.S. sample	203
Figure 13.1	Graphic display of Chinese data: percentages of coverage and mean interest scores	260
Figure 14.1	Relationship between concentration in news coverage and concentration in audience interest	284

Acknowledgements

This project could not have been possible without the collaboration and cooperation of 30 participating scholars in 17 countries. Most of the participants contributed directly in the preparation of this book. Some, however, for a variety of reasons, were not involved in the writing process. As director of the project, I wish to acknowledge them at the top and their brief biographical statements appear with the others at the end of the volume: Paolo Mancini and Marco Mazzoni of the University of Perugia, who constituted the Italian team; Tai-Li Wang from National Taiwan University who worked together with Ven-hwei Lo while he was based in Taiwan; Wan-Ying Lin from the City University of Hong Kong who worked with Francis Lee; Baohua Zhou from Fudan University in China who collaborated with Joseph Chan; Ruud Wouters of the University of Antwerp in Belgium who worked with Knut De Swert; and last but not least, Hong Nga Nguyen Vu—better known to us as Angie—who while at the University of Zurich, was instrumental in organizing the data sets of the content analyses and the surveys.

In addition, the participating scholars in each of the countries wish to thank certain organizations and individuals for their help in making this study possible.

Belgium
Knut De Swert and Ruud Wouters wish to thank Stefaan Walgrave of the University of Antwerp for funding and providing resources for the project. Also, Marc Hooghe and his team at the Electronic News Archive Flanders for the use of their infrastructure and experience: Volkan Uce, Daniëlle Sadicaris, Anne Hardy and Julie De Smedt.

Brazil
Jacques Wainberg Alkalai wishes to thank his university, Pontifícia Universidade Católica do Rio Grande do Sul, as well as the the Conselho Nacional de Desenvolvimento Científico e Tecnológico (the Brazilian Council for Development, Science and Technology) for making the Brazilian segment of the project possible.

Canada
The Canadian team of Abby Goodrum and Elizabeth Godo wish to thank Richard Pope, Alex Hayter, Kathleen Chiappetta, and Ronak Ghorbani for their research support.

Chile
William Porath and Constanza Mujica wish to thank FONDECYT—Chile's National Scientific and Technological Fund (Project Number 1080047)—for funding the Chilean part of the project. Institutional support was also provided by the Faculty of Communications of the Pontificia Universidad Católica de Chile. They wish to recognize the support of their colleagues in the Faculty of Communications, especially Soledad Puente, who introduced us to the project. Finally, they thank Francisco Maldonado, their research assistant, and their student coders of the content analysis.

China
Baohua Zhou and Joseph M. Chan of the Chinese team thanks Miss Shuning Lu, Haiyan Zhou and Ying Yu, all master students from Journalism School of Fudan University, for their helping in coding media content, cleaning survey data, and making transcripts of gatekeeper interviews.

Egypt
Rasha Kamhawi would like to thank the College of Journalism and Communications at the University of Florida for partial funding of the Egyptian segment of the project. She would also like to thank Khaled Elghamry and Khader Abualhayjaa for coding the Egyptian data.

Germany
Two grants for the German part of the project were provided by the Deutsche Forschungsgemeinschaft (German Research Foundation). Jürgen Wilke received grant number WI 519/26-1 and Thorsten Quandt received grant number QU 260/7-1. Wilke wishes to thank Daniela Stelzmann who served as a research assistant. Quandt wishes to thank Sonja Kröger for conducting the interviews with the Tagesschau journalists.

Hong Kong
Francis Lee and Wan-Ying Lin would like to thank the City University of Hong Kong for an internal strategic research grant given to the team to support the content analysis and the survey. They also with to thank the journalist-interviewees for sharing their insights.

Israel
Partial funding for the Israeli segment of the study was provided by the Israel Science Foundation (Grant number 177/08). Cohen also wishes to thank his student

coders as well as Alon Kraitzman and Erez Marantz who served as able research assistants. Anat Oren helped in administering the survey and Yasmin Alcalay was instrumental in designing some of the data analysis.

Italy
Paolo Mancini and Marco Mazzoni wish to thank Fabiola Ciavarrini, Francesca Ferrara, and Cinzia Catalucci from the Università degli Studi di Perugia for their research support.

Japan
Youoichi Ito wishes to thank the following five researchers for their contribution to the Japanese content analysis and for the completion of the data set: Takeshi Kohno, Faculty of Law, Keio University; Hiromi Cho, Faculty of Foreign Studies, Bunkyo Gakuin University; Hongchun Lee, Faculty of Policy Management, Keio University; Yasuhiro Inoue, Faculty of International Studies, Hiroshima City University; and Milin Kim, the Institute for Media and Communications Research, Keio University.

Poland
All three stages of the Polish part of the project were sponsored by the Polish Ministry of Science and Higher Education (grant no. N N116 113534, years: 2008–2010). Agnieszka Stępińska would like to thank Szymon Ossowski, Bartosz Hordecki and Dominika Narożna who have been working really hard on collecting and coding the data.

Portugal
António Belo and André Sendin wish to invoke the memory of Joel Silveira (1953-2009) who was the main driving force behind the Portuguese participation in this project. Without him it would not have been possible. They also wish to thank School of Communication and Media Studies—Polytechnic Institute of Lisbon as well as its Research Institute ICML—Lisbon Institute of Communication and Media. Finally, Belo and Sendin thank MediaMonitor-Marktest, for generously providing the digital clips of the news items of the Portuguese sample, as well as Marcos Melo and Cristina Bettencourt who coded them.

Singapore
For the Singapore part of this study, we would like thank the Wee Kim Wee School of Communication and Information, Nanyang Technological University, Singapore, for providing a research grant to support the project. A big thank you also goes to our research assistants Adeline, Sahiyah, and Zheng Jiwen for their involvement in the project as coders and checkers. A special thank you goes to Emeritus Professor Eddie Kuo for his guidance and support.

Switzerland
The Swiss part of the study was generously funded by the Swiss National Science Foundation. Thomas Hanitzsch wished to thank Hong Nga (Angie) Nguyen Vu, Heinz Bonfadelli and Michael Bauer who were part of the Swiss team. Angie has been of especially great help and a wonderful resource during the work on the project.

Taiwan
Ven-hwei Lo and Tail-Li Wang would like to thank the Project for Excellence in Communication, College of Communication, National Cheng-Chi University, as well as the International Affairs Funds from the Graduate Institute of Journalism, National Taiwan University for the financial and professional support.

United States
Lars Willnat and David Weaver wish to thank the Roy W. Howard Chair held by Weaver and the School of Journalism at Indiana University-Bloomington for support of their work on this project. They appreciate very much the efforts of doctoral students Jacob Groshek, Bill Hornaday, Jason Martin, and Jihyang Choi in coding and analyzing data.

Preface

AKIBA A. COHEN

This book is about foreign news on television. It describes a multinational research project that was conducted in several stages from 2008 to 2011. It deals with the way decisions are made regarding what news about other countries should be presented to domestic (home) viewers. It analyzes the nature and content of such news in a variety of countries. It examines what viewers of television news think about foreign news, their interest in it, and what sense they make of it. And it looks into what gatekeepers of foreign news—journalists, producers, and editors—think about the content they produce and about their viewers. This comparative study does all this in two ways: first, across 17 countries around the globe; second, by comparing foreign news with domestic news as well as hybrid news—foreign news that is relevant to the country of broadcast and domestic news that is related to other countries.

In June 1988, nearly a quarter century ago, a small conference took place in Jerusalem with a score of invited scholars from Europe, the United States, and Israel, all of whom were then engaged in research on television news. At the conclusion of that meeting, the participants drafted a proposed research agenda that later appeared in the *American Behavioral Scientist* under the title "Where Did We Come From and Where Are We Going? Some Future Directions in Television News Research" (Cohen & Bantz, 1989). The basic idea behind that theme was that there was a growing need to study the interrelationship between the way journalists and editors control the selection and production processes as well as the dissemination of news, its content, and the way people think about it. The project described in this volume seems to fulfill this prescription, specifically in the area of foreign news.

This kind of multi-faceted research may also be referred to as a "start-to-finish" paradigm (Braman & Cohen, 1990). Such research examines all phases of the news, from producers through content to consumers, and not only how journalists think and work, or the nature of the content of news, or how people deal with the news, or a combination of any two of these topics. While it seems only natural to study news in this way, it is rarely done, mainly because of the complexity of the subject matter and its logistics, the need to bring together experts on the different phases, the need to use a variety of methods, and the high cost and the patience required on the part of scholars involved until such projects can be completed and their comprehensive findings published.

To make things even more complex, our approach to this project was somewhat unconventional. Rather than beginning with the journalists and editors who are responsible for providing news (or, as Gaye Tuchman [1978] long ago described it, as "making" news) both domestic and foreign, we began with the news content—that is, the product that these professionals make or create. In doing so, we conducted parallel content analyses of samples of newscasts in the 17 countries during the same time period. We then studied the audiences by means of opinion surveys. Only at the end did we interview the gatekeepers, the people responsible for deciding what appears in the news and how. We did this for two reasons. First, we assumed that we knew quite a bit—based on our own previous research and that of numerous other scholars—about how decisions are made regarding foreign news. Hence we didn't really need to go to the gatekeepers in order to find out from them about the basic issues involved in how and why they do what they do. Second, and more important, we wanted to see if they would be able to guess what our major empirical findings were regarding both the content of the news and what the audiences had to say. In other words, we wanted to get their reflections on some of the data that we presented to them in the course of the interviews. This inventive approach to studying journalism has not, to the best of our knowledge, been attempted before.

Why Study Foreign News, and Why News on Television?

Some laypeople, pundits, and even scholars may ask: Why study *foreign* news, and why *television* news? After all, they might say, it is well known—even without doing much research—that foreign news is but a small, often quantitatively insignificant part of the news repertoire, and that interest in foreign news among the viewing public is known to be of less interest than domestic news. They might also argue that since viewing television news (and reading newspapers) may be on the decline, mainly as a consequence of the Internet, that TV news is becoming less and less relevant.

We reject these arguments. We live in an age of globalization. Its advocates and its critics both agree that the phenomenon has increased interdependence among nations and economies, which is manifested in virtually all realms of production, marketing, and consumption of goods and services. Many products that were invented and developed in one country are manufactured, distributed, and serviced in other countries as well, sometimes *only* in other countries. Numerous companies have branches and outlets across the globe.

A central feature of globalization is that products and services that are available worldwide typically serve the same function for consumers wherever they are; they are used in the same manner; and they have the same denotations. Thus, for example, a Benetton T-shirt that can be bought in many countries is used as clothing everywhere; Ford, Toyota, and Volkswagen cars (and other brands as well) are vehicles driven on roads and highways everywhere; and ATM cards are used for cash withdrawal wherever such machines are found.

Seemingly, the same would be the case for cultural products. When files of popular music are downloaded from the Internet—legally or illegally—they are used by fans and music lovers for entertainment and enjoyment wherever they may be. When films are seen or books are read in countries other than those of their origin, all that is needed is for them to be translated into the local language. Beyond some possible loss of meaning, such films and books are enjoyed (or not) by filmgoers or readers worldwide. The same can be said of most other cultural products.

News, however, presents a different story. From a technical perspective, one of the manifestations of globalization is the instantaneous and simultaneous availability of media messages across the globe. Events taking place in Europe, for example, can be reported in Asia, Australia, and South America at the same time they are reported in the Middle East, Africa, and North America. From a purely technological perspective, Marshall McLuhan's well-known metaphor of the "global village" is a sign of our times. A network of global satellites with enormous footprints covers the world. Thus a signal uploaded in New York or Washington can be downloaded in Beijing and Shanghai, twelve time zones away, in real time.

Most foreign news is presented by domestic television stations—public, commercial, or state-owned—as part of their daily newscasts, relating to selected events that take place in other countries. Such items are often selected by editors because of their relevance to the country of broadcast. Such foreign news stories, then, are of potentially greater importance to citizens in the country of broadcast. In addition, these foreign events are often domesticated, that is, composed and presented in a manner that suits home viewers by making the stories more relevant to them (Cohen, Levy, Roeh, & Gurevitch, 1996). So foreign news is no doubt important!

There is another context for "foreign" news—news that is provided by global broadcasters such as CNN International, BBC World News, Al Jazeera, France 24, and China's CCTV, just to name a few of the growing number of such media organizations. They all send their signals around the globe, but the use that people can make of them, and particularly the meanings they convey in their content, are hardly the same (Cohen, 2002; Cohen & Roeh, 1992). These organizations disseminate news to gigantic yet heterogeneous audiences whose only common denominator is the language of the broadcast (most frequently English), but the topics being presented cannot inevitably be of equal interest to all. Also, a significant portion of the news aired by the global news networks deals with events in each respective network's country of origin: for example, American news on CNNI, British news on BBCW, Arab world news on Al Jazeera, and so on (Cohen & Atad, 2012), which may not be of interest to many people, even if they are able to pick up the broadcasts.

But to what extent is foreign news similar around the world? To what extent do the domestic broadcasters around the world provide news about the same topics, the same issues, or the same people? To what extent, thanks to communication technology, has the world really become a global village in terms of news? Surely some of the news is common across countries and broadcasters, especially when a major event occurs (a terror event such as 9/11, the election of the U.S. president, or the opening of the Olympic Games). But while the notion of the "global village" sounds intriguing, we have sought to determine to what extent this metaphor is grounded in reality. The voluminous data that we gathered in our multinational project has led us to the conclusion that this is far from the case.

So why should we still be studying television news, and why foreign news? Because, as noted above, even though there are additional platforms available for news (most notably the Internet) that are gaining in popularity, mostly among young adults in some countries, television is still clearly people's main source for news. This indeed was the case when our study commenced in 2008 (Pew Research Center for the People and the Press, 2008). We also know that there has been a significant decline in newspaper readership in many countries. In the United States, for example, the same Pew report indicated that from September 2007 to December 2008 television was still the main source for news, even though young adults (up to 30 years of age) tended to move toward the Internet as their top choice. And despite this trend, we strongly believe that television news is most likely to be with us for the foreseeable future and will be the main conveyor of information about what is happening in one's neighborhood, one's country, and even around the world.

A Brief History of the Project

This project was a collective effort. It was conceived by the current editor back in 2006. During the course of a year or so, various colleagues were sought from around the world. The formal beginning of the project took place at the annual conference of the International Communication Association in San Francisco in May 2007.

Throughout the project, coordination of activities was done from Israel, mostly through email and telephone. Over a nearly 4-year period until the completion of the project (and before the writing of this book began), the research teams met in various locations, mostly at international conferences (in Paris, Berlin, Montreal, Stockholm, Chicago, Taipei, Poznan, Tel Aviv, Perugia, Boston, and Lisbon) for the purpose of discussing theoretical and methodological issues, developing the research instruments, and analyzing the findings. In addition, several presentations were made at scientific meetings.

Each country's research team was responsible for obtaining its own funding. All 17 countries did the content analysis. However, the survey was done in only 13 of the countries, and the in-depth interviews with the gatekeepers were conducted in only 12 of the countries. All three phases of the study were completed by 11 of the 17 countries.

The Design of the Book

This volume describes our project from start to finish. It presents several theoretical issues that are germane to the understanding of the project. It presents voluminous cross-national data. And it attempts to integrate the three methodological approaches we have taken.

In thinking about how to present our findings, we considered the possibility of presenting "country chapters," that is, separate chapters on the findings from each of the countries. We ultimately decided not to proceed that way, because our focus is on the comparative aspects of studying foreign news on television, and, given limited space, we felt that it would be more important to show similarities and differences across countries in the various substantive areas rather than going into great detail about each country using a case-study approach. We also felt that writing separate chapters on 17 countries might lead readers to focus on a single country or on a few countries in which they are most interested, while skipping others, thereby missing the broader comparative perspective that we view as more critical.

The book consists of five parts. In the first part (Chapters 1 and 2), we describe the project and the methodologies used, while developing the concept of foreign vs. domestic news. Works such as this usually begin with a theoretical section that presents the rationale for the entire study as well as its research questions and/or hypotheses, but given the broad scope of this project, we decided to replace the traditional overall theoretical section and instead begin each chapter with specific theoretical overviews that are directly relevant to the questions and data that we present therein. The second part (Chapters 3 through 7) deals with various aspects of the content of the news: topics, countries, actors, formal features, and public vs. commercial stations. The third part (Chapters 8 through 10) presents the survey findings, including patterns of news consumption, interest in news, and countries of interest. The fourth part (Chapters 11 and 12) is based on what the gatekeepers told us—on how they make decisions in the foreign desk and what they know (or don't know) about the content they produce and their viewers. The fifth and final part (Chapters 13 through 16) integrates the findings. In Chapter 13 we link the content and survey data concerning the topics in the news, and in Chapter 14 we similarly link content and survey data about the countries of interest. Despite the fact that the book is not organized as individual country reports, Chapter 15 does provide a brief summary of the major findings in each of the 17 countries. Finally, Chapter 16 integrates those findings and suggests that, despite what many may believe, there is no global village.

While the various chapters in the book were led and written by different members of the international research team, it is important to consider this book as a single monograph that describes a complete and unified project. While all team members from the 17 countries were responsible for providing their respective country data and interpretations, in the end I am responsible for any overall flaws.

PART ONE

The Project

CHAPTER ONE

Rationale, Design, and Methodologies

AKIBA A. COHEN, THOMAS HANITZSCH, AGNIESZKA STĘPIŃSKA,
WILLIAM PORATH, & CHRISTINE HEIMPRECHT

Our decision to study foreign news implies, by definition, that we are engaged in comparative research, which itself is a rapidly growing area in the study of media and communication (Esser & Hanitzsch, 2012a; Gurevitch & Blumler, 2004). By delineating foreign news, we are *ipso facto* distinguishing it from domestic news. This suggests that there must be differences between foreign and domestic news, making the comparison worthwhile and important.

Studying how foreign news and domestic news may differ from country to country could be interesting, of course. However, the moment we speak of foreign news, it would also be natural to consider a broader worldwide perspective, because what is domestic news in one country would be foreign news in another country, or even in several or many countries. Indeed, some events seem to possess properties that prompt journalists and editors to report on them even if they have nothing to do with their own country. Thus, comparing how a variety of countries present news that has no bearing on them is a second dimension for comparison.

A third dimension for comparison is media ownership—that is, the difference between public service broadcasting, state-owned broadcasting channels, and private (or commercial) broadcasting. Major events taking place in a given country would likely be reported as foreign news by all media platforms and outlets, including television. And yet there is a sense that foreign news would be reported more often and in greater depth on public service stations. There are two possible reasons for this. First, public stations typically have a more clearly defined mandate—often by statute—to inform their publics of what is happening in the world. Second, since it is well known that people (quite naturally) express less interest in foreign than in domestic events, commercial stations often tend to provide more news that is in line with what people want and are interested in, which yields high ratings, while public stations are usually less dependent upon and hence less concerned with viewer ratings.

Clearly, then, this study lies squarely in the domain of comparative media research. There are many reasons for conducting comparative research: to clarify and verify theory and concepts in multiple settings, to establish the cross-cultural generality of findings and validity of interpretations, and to develop and contextualize the understanding of our own societies (Esser & Hanitzsch, 2012a; Gurevitch & Blumler, 1990; Kohn, 1989). There is growing consensus, argues Livingstone (2012), that it is no longer plausible to study a phenomenon in one country without asking whether it is common across the globe or distinctive to that specific context. Without comparison, national phenomena may become "naturalized" even to the extent that they remain invisible to the domestic-bound researcher (Blumler, McLeod, & Rosengren, 1992; Esser & Hanitzsch, 2012a).

We therefore believe that using a comparative design will ultimately provide us with a better understanding of foreign news in its multiple contexts. By examining domestic versus foreign news, we can get a better understanding of what news is all about and especially the criteria of newsworthiness and news selection. (A detailed discussion of this appears in Chapter 2.) By doing cross-national research and by looking at the news presented in one's country vis-à-vis the news in other countries, scholars can actually better understand why and how our own news is presented the way it is. And by comparing public and private television stations, we can also draw inferences as to how decisions are made in organizations that have different missions and goals.

Studying Foreign News in a Comparative Perspective

Several scholars (for example, Blumler, McLeod, & Rosengren, 1992; Livingstone, 2003) have discussed different models of comparative endeavors. In our present study, the most important—and surely the most complex—variable that we investigated was the country or the nation-state. Throughout the book we will use the concepts of "country" and "nation" interchangeably, although we are aware that in several cases the two notions might actually entail different meanings. Great Britain as a nation-state, for instance, consists of four nations: England, Scotland, Wales, and Northern Ireland.

In the field of communication research, the country—or nation, for that matter—is often treated as the "natural" default category for comparative analysis. This has come under criticism by those who consider "country" or "nation" as categories too under-theorized for academic research and too compromised by the undermining influence of globalization (Livingstone, 2012). Furthermore, countries may not always be proper units of comparison: far from being self-contained, they rather comprise multiple cultures (Livingstone, 2003). National borders do not necessarily correspond to cultural, linguistic, and ethnic divisions, nor do they correspond to a common sense of identity (Hantrais, 1999). On the other hand, nations offer convenient shorthand for comparative analysis, since they possess clearly defined boundaries and are often the only kinds of units available for comparison (Hofstede, 2001). Even more important, the country remains a valuable analytic category, as the nation-specific institutional arrangements serve as powerful explanatory contexts that account for cross-cultural differences (Esser & Hanitzsch, 2012a; Livingstone, 2012). News production is still strongly geared toward news agendas that prioritize domestic news, media coverage that champions national actors, and journalists who speak to national or local audiences.

Kohn (1989) was one of the first to explicate different models of comparative research with the "nation" as the key factor. Kohn refers to the nation as the *object* of the study where the focus of interest is on particular nations. This is not our objective, as we were not interested in any particular country. A second model offered by Kohn is one in which the nation is the *context* of the study, that is, by studying several nations it is possible to arrive at some kind of universal generalizations concerning the phenomenon of interest. This, too, was not our purpose, because we actually believe that there is less communality across nations than similarity. Kohn's third model considers the nation as a *component* of a larger international or transnational system. We were not examining nations in such a context, either.

The fourth and final model suggested by Kohn does fit our work. It considers the nation as the *unit of analysis*. While this approach could focus on similarities among countries, as in the second model, it can also focus on differences among countries. This model best fits the objective of our study; we believe that although there are some general similarities across countries in terms of how foreign news is produced, presented, and appreciated by viewers, we believe that disparity across and variability among the countries is more significant and more important. In a way this raises the question as to whether or not McLuhan's metaphor of the "global village" really exists. We shall return to this question later in the volume.

Conceptualizing Foreign News

The central idea behind this project was to comparatively and collaboratively investigate foreign news on television. Two issues need to be emphasized with respect to theory: comparison and collaboration. First, the centrality of theory in communication research can hardly be denied, and it is especially relevant to comparative research (Hanitzsch & Esser, 2012). Gurevitch and Blumler (2004) vehemently call for all comparative research to be situated in a theoretical or conceptual perspective. Norris (2009, p. 323) agrees and argues that without a theoretical map or conceptual compass, comparativists "remain stranded in Babel." At the same time, however, collaboration entails a tremendous challenge. It means that a research framework must be able to integrate a fairly diverse array of ideas and concepts contributed by the various collaborators who often have different academic backgrounds and theoretical-methodological preferences. On the one hand, there is a danger of ending up employing "least-common-denominator concepts that are so theoretically impoverished that they do not advance our understanding of communication phenomena in any meaningful ways" (Hallin & Mancini, 2012, p. 505). On the other hand, the general framework must keep enough flexibility to accommodate the often-particularistic interests of the participating researchers.

The study's *leitmotif* was foreign news, and although the concept of foreign news may seem rather straightforward, its particular definition for a content analysis or audience survey proves otherwise (Wouters, 2011). In general, one may recognize two major criteria used to define foreign news or to distinguish between foreign news and other types of news: the location of an event and a country's involvement in the event.

The simplest distinction between domestic and foreign news arose from the early news flow studies (Almaney, 1970; Gerbner & Marvanyi, 1977; Östgaard, 1965; Sreberny-Mohammadi et al., 1985; Wilke, 1987) and from a tradition in communication research that has later been termed "news geography" (Gasher, 2009; Gasher & Klein, 2008; Rantanen, 2003; Schulz, 1983). According to Rantanen (2009, p. 77), this concept conceived the question of "where" in terms of countries and followed the geographical borders of (nation-) states as they appeared on maps.

Using the traditional geography of news approach, Almaney (1970) provided an early example by combining both criteria—location and involvement—in an analysis of news reporting in the United States, drawing a distinction between "national" affairs (when events occurred within the United States); "international" affairs (when the United States and another country were involved); and "foreign" affairs (when events took place outside the United States and the country was not involved).

Such early proposals for a more complex classification of news categories with regard to location and involvement notwithstanding, most studies draw on a single indicator to serve as a criterion to categorize types of news. Hester (1978), for instance, defined foreign news as "news reported from outside the country of broadcast." Similarly, Weaver, Porter, and Evans (1984) identified foreign news in their American study as "news reported from outside the United States." In both cases, the key criterion was the *location* of the news event.

Larson (1982), on the other hand, adopted a broad though practical definition of "international" news from the perspective of the United States. In his view, the category of international news was made of stories that *mentioned* a country other than the United States, regardless of the location of the event. Consequently, stories mentioning international organizations were also classified as international news. Furthermore, Gonzenbach, Arant, and Stevenson (1992) attempted to differentiate within Larson's broad categories, distinguishing among "domestic news" (involving only the United States), "international news" involving the United States and a foreign country (regardless of geographic location), and "foreign news" with no reference to the United States. In these cases, the key criterion was the *involvement* of either the country of broadcast (in this case the United States) or a foreign nation and international actors (also see Wouters, 2011).

Tyndall (2008), in contrast, seems not to distinguish between these two criteria when considering foreign news. His first category, "foreign bureau," consists of stories filed by reporters in a foreign location. His second category, "foreign policy," refers to news items concerning the foreign policy of the United States (involvement), no matter whether the stories were filed from the United States or from the country involved. Finally, the third category, "international," includes stories focusing on events happening overseas, regardless of their location or the involvement of the United States in these occurrences.

As a general remark, it should be noted that the terms "foreign" and "international" are often used interchangeably, and, in some cases, they are even used in contradictory ways. Almaney (1970) and Gonzenbach, Arant, and Stevenson (1992), for instance, refer to international news when both the host country and other countries are involved, while they reserve the term "foreign" for news in which the country of broadcast is not involved. Tyndall (2008), on the other hand, does exactly the opposite: "foreign" refers to the foreign policy of the United States, whereas "international" refers to events located outside the country of broadcast, with or without its involvement. Additionally, Schulz (2001) used both terms without drawing a clear distinction between them.

In a strict sense, "international" refers to a relationship between nations, in which case the first application of the concept would appear to be more appropriate. However, if an event that occurs in one nation becomes news in another, it could also be said to have established a relationship between two nations, making the second concept appropriate, too. The dilemma is even more intricate if it is considered within the concept of "foreign" events that take place abroad without the involvement of the country of broadcast. This could also include (international) relations among two or more foreign nations. Given the complexity of this discussion, it seems appropriate to consider that the concept of "international news"—as an alternative concept to "foreign news"—as different from "international relations/politics," which is essentially a news topic. In our study, the term "international" was therefore used for the classification of news topics, but in some cases it was also pragmatically used as a proxy for "foreign" in order to avoid overly repetitive language.

At the same time, however, the present study incorporated yet another classification of news. The concept was based on a typology first put forward by Elliott and Golding (1974) and later used in the *Foreign Images* study of Sreberny-Mohammadi et al. (1985) and a follow-up study by Schmidt and Wilke (1998). Given the convergence of two main criteria mentioned above—location (within or outside country of broadcast) and involvement (domestic or foreign)—we created a matrix consisting of four types of news items, two "pure" and two "hybrid" categories. In so doing, we were able to incorporate a phenomenon that is often referred to as "domestication" or "glocalization" of news about foreign events. Domestication essentially means that foreign news events are increasingly framed and presented in a way that makes them more relevant to audiences in the home country (Cohen, Levy, Roeh, & Gurevitch, 1996; Shoemaker et al., 2012). Clausen (2003, 2004) has shown that both public service and commercial television stations give foreign news events a considerable national "spin"—a form of domestication. The four types of news that we distinguished in the present study were as follows:

1. *domestic news*: an event takes place in the country of broadcast with no foreign involvement;
2. *foreign news*: an event occurs in another country without any reference to the country of broadcast;
3. *domestic news with foreign involvement*: the event takes place in the country of broadcast but with a specific reference made to at least one other country;
4. *foreign news with domestic involvement*: the event occurs in another country but with a specific reference made to the country of broadcast.

Although this classification is still based on a traditional approach to the geography of news, it attempts to reconcile a conventional practice with calls for an alternative, more phenomenological approach, which Crang (1998, p. 11) refers to as "geography inside people's head." According to this approach, the study of "where" in news should not only be about geography in the traditional sense but also about the relationship between people and places (Relph, 1976). Indeed, the alternative approach emphasizes the fact that "the geographer's concern for an accurate description of the world may not coincide with goals of an individual agent concerned with acting in the world" (Entrikin, 1991, p. 13). Hence, in the present study, it seemed reasonable to use a well-recognized concept that included four categories in order to acknowledge that there are not only pure types of the news but also more complex scenarios, which we classified as "hybrid news" (see also Shoemaker et al., 2012).

The General Design of the Project

The project comprised three stages: a content analysis of a sample of newscasts, an opinion survey of adult respondents, and in-depth interviews with editors of foreign news on television. The idea was to arrive at a better and deeper understanding of foreign news by combining different kinds of evidence and by establishing links between the individual methodological steps. The study made use of quantitative methods (content analysis and audience survey) and qualitative methods (interviews with journalists). Furthermore, the design of the study was planned so that preceding methodological steps informed subsequent parts of the study (see Figure 1.1). For the audience survey, for instance, we used some material obtained from the content analysis for the construction of the questionnaire (Feedback 1). Moreover, during the qualitative interviews in the newsrooms, the gatekeepers were "confronted" with evidence from the preceding steps in the study. In so doing, the journalists were provided the opportunity to comment on the results from the audience survey (Feedback 2) and content analysis (Feedback 3). In the following pages we detail these methodologies.

Figure 1.1 General research design

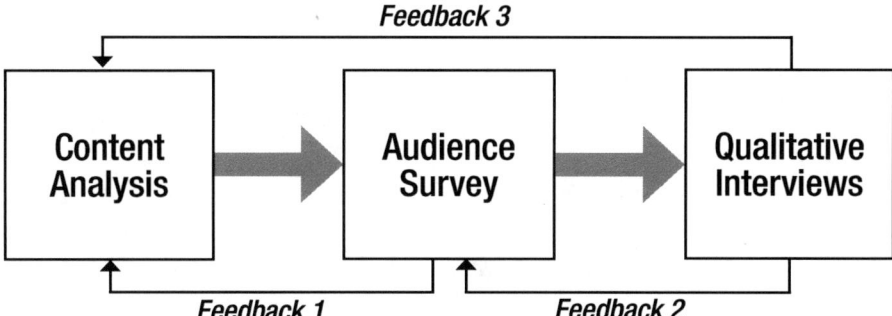

Following the principle of maximizing variance, the study included 17 countries: Belgium, Brazil, Canada, Chile, China, Egypt, Germany, Hong Kong, Israel, Italy, Japan, Poland, Portugal, Singapore, Switzerland, Taiwan, and the United States. They represent large and small countries, different geographical regions, as well as different cultures, ethnic groups, and religious denominations. We originally strove to incorporate even more nations, but we had to let go of a number of countries for various reasons at different stages of the project.

Content Analysis

SELECTION OF NEWSCASTS The first stage of the study was a large content analysis of a sample of news conducted in all countries of the study. In each, the research team recorded what were considered to be the main national evening newscasts, that is, newscasts that are broadcast across the respective countries. The goal was to record the main (usually the only) newscast of the country's public service broadcasting station as well as the most popular newscast of a privately owned (or commercial) station, based on viewership ratings. Table 1 presents the newscasts that were recorded and analyzed.

Table 1.1 Television stations in the study

Country	Public Service Channel	Name of Newscast	Private Channel	Name of Newscast
Belgium	EEN (Dutch)	Het Journaal	VTM (Dutch)	Het Nieuws
Brazil	Cultura	Jornal de Cultura	Globo	Jornal Nacional
Canada	CBC	The National	CTV	CTV News
Chile	TVN	24 Horas	Mega	Meganoticias
China	CCTV	Xinwenlianbo	—	—
Egypt	ERTU1	Nashret Akhbar al-Tasaeh	—	—
Germany	ARD	Tagesschau	RTL	RTL Aktuell
Hong Kong	—	—	ATV TVB	6:00 News 6:30 News
Israel	IBA	Mabat	Arutz 2	Hadashot 2
Italy	RAI 1	Telegiornale 1	Canale 5	Telegiornale 5
Japan	NHK	News 7 (Nyusu 7)	Terebi Ashai	Hodo Station (Monday-Friday) Super J Channel (Saturday-Sunday)
Poland	TVP	Wiadomosci	TVN	Fakty
Portugal	RTP	Telejornal	TV1	Jornal Nacional
Singapore	—	—	TV 5 (English) TV 8 (Chinese)	News 5 Tonight Wanjian Xinwen
Switzerland	SF TSR	Tagesschau Le Journal	Tele Züri	ZüriNews
Taiwan	PTS	Gong Shih Wan Jian Xin Wen	TVBS	TVBS Liu Chi Dian Xin Wen
United States	PBS	NewsHour with Jim Lehrer	NBC	NBC Nightly News

As can be seen, we analyzed the news of 33 stations. In 12 of the 17 countries—Belgium, Brazil, Canada, Chile, Germany, Israel, Italy, Japan, Poland, Portugal, Taiwan, and the United States—we had one public service and one private (commercial) station. In the other 5 countries there were some unavoidable deviations because of the inherent media structure of those countries. In China, where no private stations existed, we used CCTV, the only national state-run station (considered a public station). A similar situation existed at the time of our study in Egypt, where ERTU Channel 1 was the only Arabic-language, government-run television station aimed at the domestic Egyptian population that provided newscasts. In Hong Kong there was no public service television, only two privately owned free-to-air Chinese-language terrestrial television stations. We decided to use both ATV and TVB in order to get a broader scope of Hong Kong news. In Singapore, too, there was no public service station. Given the dominance of Chinese and English in Singapore, we decided to use the two main commercial stations: *Channel 5*, which broadcasts in English, and *Channel 8*, which broadcasts in Chinese. Both stations are run by MediaCorp, which is owned by the government of Singapore. Finally, Switzerland is a multi-language country. The dominant language is German with a smaller francophone population and an even less sizable Italian-speaking community (as well as a minute group that speaks Romansh). We decided to use the dominant German and the French public stations (SF and TSR, respectively) as well as *Tele Züri*, the most significant commercial station that operates from Zurich, in the German-speaking region of the country.

All news items and news commentaries in the newscasts were coded except for two types of items: standard stock market reports and weather forecasts. However, when a stock market story constituted a regular news item, and when the weather became an actual news story, such items were included. Also not coded were promotions for items that were to appear later in the newscasts or in some future television program. Advertisements and sponsorships were also not coded.

THE SAMPLE PERIODS The sample for the content analysis consisted of one newscast per station each day during 4 complete weeks in early 2008. Specifically, the following weeks were used in the sample: January 20–26, February 10–16, March 2–8, and March 23–29. The rationale was, on one hand, to use consecutive 7-day weeks in order to be able to deal with developing or continuing stories, and on the other hand to cover a broader period of time (nearly 3 months rather than a single month).

THE CODEBOOK The first stage in preparing for the content analysis was the development of the codebook. During the course of two face-to-face meetings—one in San Francisco in May 2007 and one in Berlin in November 2007—we decided on the main structure of the codebook and identified the main variables that would be included in it. This was followed by numerous telephone conversations and email exchanges in which details were worked out. Over the course of several months, discussions were held until we came up with what we agreed was a satisfactory version.

The codebook was prepared in English, the common language used by all the participants in the project. Rather than having it translated into the 12 dominant languages used in the countries of the study—Dutch (in Belgium), Portuguese (in Brazil and Portugal), English (in Canada and the United States), Spanish (in Chile), Chinese (in China, Hong Kong, Singapore, and Taiwan), Arabic (in Egypt), German (in Germany and Switzerland), Hebrew (in Israel), Italian (in Italy), Japanese (in Japan), Polish (in Poland), and French (in Switzerland)—we decided to use the English version throughout. Coders were typically students in departments of communication in the different countries who, in addition to their native language, also had a solid (sometimes almost native) knowledge of English.

Each variable was accompanied by a detailed explanation, and in some cases examples were provided. A pretest of the codebook was done in Israel using a sample of several news items. Based on insights obtained during the pretesting, modifications were made in the codebook, including the instructions and examples. Inter-coder reliability was also tested during the pretesting, and necessary changes were made in the codebook in order to enable optimum reliability. The final draft of the codebook was distributed to all the participating researchers, and additional comments and suggestions were solicited. The final version was confirmed following this round (for a list of the variables in the codebook, see Appendix A in the Methodological Appendix).

THE CODING PROCESS Prior to the beginning of the coding, the senior researcher in each country viewed each of the newscasts and created a list of all the items therein. The itemization log contained the station, date, time of broadcast, and the line-up listing each item by number with a brief caption pertaining to its subject. This list was presented to the coders for the purpose of identifying the start and end points of each item.

Once the coders were selected in each country, several training sessions took place led by the senior researchers. During the course of the training, the coders went over the codebook, variable by variable. The coders were instructed to code most of the variables based explicitly on what was said or seen in the news items. On some variables, however, the coders were told that they could exercise their judgment. These included the variables dealing with the scope of the event, its potential impact, and the variables pertaining to the conflicts.

The next step involved coding a series of items as examples. Reliability among the coders was established as a precondition for going ahead with the actual coding of the items. The recordings of the newscasts, along with specially prepared coding forms, were given to the coders. Since the number of coders in each country varied, the number of newscasts that each coder was given for analysis varied accordingly. Finally, the coders were instructed on how to record their codes into a computer data file using a specially prepared template. Each coder entered his/her data, and, when completed, all the files were combined into a single file for the country.

RELIABILITY OF CODING Although it is a matter of course to examine reliability for content analysis data, the way in which to proceed in comparative international projects is underexplored. Gudykunst (2003) refers to a very strong "patterning effect of culture" and thereby "different levels of reliability and validity… in different cultures." He concludes that "reliability and validity must be established within each culture studied separately. Pan cultural assessment of reliability and validity is meaningless" (p. 156). Peter and Lauf (2002) take the opposite view and claim that "it is necessary to assess reliability in a cross-national fashion" (p. 826) and that "as long as reliabilities in cross-national content analyses are suspect, the possibility remains that reported cross-national differences or similarities of media coverage are merely artifacts" (p. 827).

In our study, given the different languages of the newscasts and the diverse visual and formal depictions of the news in the different countries, the Peter and Lauf model is too rigorous, and its realization is virtually impossible. We therefore decided that each country team would determine the reliability of its own coders using rather stringent standards: 10% of the news material—or at least 30 items per variable—would be checked for each coder on all variables with the exception of identifications variables.

Given the logistical arrangements in each of the countries, as well as the finances available, the number of coders in each of the countries varied. Unfortunately, however, reliability data are available for only 14 of the 17 countries. In Canada one coder coded all newscasts, making inter-coder reliability impossible, and in Italy and Singapore technical difficulties hampered the teams in providing reliability scores. We are clearly aware of this lacuna, but given the relatively high reliability scores as well as similar patterns obtained in the 14 countries for which we do have relevant data, we can only assume that the reliability of the coding in the other countries was similar.

For the countries in which reliability was calculated, we used PRAM (Program for Reliability Assessment of Multiple Coders), which calculates several coefficients: Holsti, Scott's Pi, Cohen's Kappa, Pearson correlations, and Krippendorff Alpha. Holsti coefficients were calculated by hand for variables allowing for multiple coding (topics, countries of location, countries involved, and international organizations involved in the items).

Appendix B (in the Methodological Appendix) provides a glimpse of the reliability obtained for the coding. As noted, in some of the countries there were only two coders, while in others the number was higher. In cases with more than two coders, the mean coefficient for all pairs of coders is noted. The reliability across the entire set of variables is quite satisfactory. Across the board, of the 19 major variables reported for the 14 countries, a total of 266 coefficients was calculated. Of these, only 38 (14.3%) were below the 80% reliability level, including only 15 (5.6%) coefficients below 70%.

The variable with the lowest reliability was the determination of whether or not archive footage was used. This is quite reasonable, since it is often difficult to determine whether the footage being shown is from an archive or pre-recorded unless specifically indicated, usually by a caption on the screen.

The highest average reliability coefficients were found for the China and Hong Kong samples, whereas the lowest average reliability was in Poland and the United States. As noted, we are aware of the difficulty of not having reliability data for three of the countries, but given the highly satisfactory reliability in the 14 countries as well as the common meticulous training of the coders, using the identical codebook, we believe there is no reason to suspect much difference for the three missing countries.

Audience Surveys

As noted, the second phase of the project was an audience survey. Because of funding issues, audience surveys were conducted in only 13 of the 17 countries, excluding Belgium, Egypt, Italy, and Japan. The main objective of the surveys was to assess what people think about news in general and foreign news in particular along several dimensions.

THE SURVEY QUESTIONNAIRE After being designed in English by the various research teams and translated into the relevant languages, an identical questionnaire was used in all countries. The languages used for interviewing the respondents were Chinese (in China, Hong Kong, and Taiwan), English (in Canada and the United States), both Chinese and English in Singapore (respondents could chose the language of their choice), German (in Germany and Switzerland), Hebrew, Arabic, and Russian (in Israel), Polish (in Poland), Portuguese (in Brazil and Portugal), and Spanish (in Chile).

The questionnaire was designed for telephone interviews and carried 45 questions (see Appendix C in Methodological Appendix). It consisted of several parts: news consumption on television, newspapers, and the Internet; the perceived functions of news consumption; interest in selected topics of *domestic* news (politics, crime and violence, sports, relations with other countries, economics, accidents and disasters, and social issues); perceived present and desired amount of foreign news in a country's newscasts; general overall interest in *foreign* news and in the same selected topics concerning domestic news; countries in which respondents are interested; general characteristics of foreign news; perceptions of the world; and demographic variables (gender, age, education, and income).

SAMPLES AND FIELD WORK In each of the countries, the samples were representative of the respective adult populations. The sample sizes varied from country to country and ranged from 395 in Canada to 1,220 in Chile. This was attributable to financial and logistic considerations in each country.

As noted, the surveys were carried out by telephone except in the United States, where interviews were conducted online. In most of the countries the interviews were conducted by commercial firms commissioned for this purpose or by university-based public opinion research units. In Canada the country's research team conducted the interviews. The surveys were conducted at different points in time in the various countries, beginning with the survey in Chile that took place in September–October 2009 and ending with the survey that took place in the United States in June–July 2010. Details of the samples and field work appear in Appendix D of the Methodological Appendix.

Interviews with Gatekeepers of Foreign News

The third and final stage of the project was a series of face-to-face interviews with gatekeepers of foreign news on television, that is, with foreign news editors and the heads of the foreign news desks (sections) in the various television stations. The interviews were conducted by the lead investigators in each of the countries of the study.

Interviews were conducted in 12 countries: Belgium, Brazil, Canada, Chile, China, Germany, Hong Kong, Israel, Poland, Portugal, Switzerland, and Taiwan. Unfortunately, interviews could not be arranged in Egypt, Italy, Japan, Singapore, and the United States. Of the 49 interviews, 22 were conducted with gatekeepers in public service stations (including two in China's state-owned channel CCTV) and 27 in private stations. The number of interviews conducted in each country ranged from 2 in Belgium, Canada, China, and Taiwan to 8 in Chile (see Appendix E for details of the interviews). The interviews were conducted over a relatively long period, from May 2009 in Israel to March 2011 in Poland.

The interviews were conducted in a semi-structured fashion. A common list of questions was prepared for all the countries, and the interviews always began with the first question. An attempt was made to retain the order of the questions, but if an interviewee, in the course of his/her responses, went on to another topic that appeared on the list but was not yet reached, this was accommodated. In the interview, questions pertained to aspects such as the individual background and experience of the journalist, characteristics of his or her news organization, criteria for the selection of foreign news, news sources, the importance of visual material, proportions of foreign news, country preferences, and audience interest in foreign news.

Methodological Concerns and Caveats

In doing comparative research of this scope, various methodological concerns could arise (Cohen, 2012). Many of these concerns were dealt with in our project. What follows is a brief discussion of these issues.

Selection of Countries

Systematic selection of countries is unquestionably crucial for a comparative study. Hantrais (1999, pp. 100–101) very strongly argued that "[a]ny similarities or differences revealed by a cross-national study may be no more than an artifact of the choice of countries." And Geddes (2003) convincingly demonstrated how case selection can affect, or even render unreliable, outcomes of a comparative study. Whatever considerations serve as the rationale for case selection, the countries need to be chosen within a conceptual framework that justifies their selection (Chang et al., 2001; Esser & Hanitzsch, 2012a).

Since we were interested in the countries as the units of analysis, we followed the principle of maximizing variance. We therefore wanted to work in as many countries as possible that differ along crucial contextual dimensions. In fact, the project started out with 22 countries. During the course of the research process, however, 5 countries eventually ended their participation for a variety of reasons, mostly related to financial and logistical problems. These countries were Bulgaria, Finland, South Africa, Sweden, and the United Kingdom. Our experience shows that this is a common problem in comparative research. Oftentimes a systematic and sophisticated selection of countries is difficult to achieve in practice. There are many reasons for this: different research cultures, varying commitment to the study, conceptual and methodological disagreement, and the globally uneven distribution of resources for research. The countries included in the final selection nevertheless vary on several important dimensions, as Table 1.2 demonstrates.

Functional Equivalence

In the practice of comparative research, it often happens that various factors in the study are not identical in all the countries or cultures under investigation. Thus a fundamental requirement for comparative research to produce meaningful results is functional equivalence with respect to concepts, methods, and administration, as well as equivalence of language and meaning (Gurevitch & Blumler, 2004; Hanitzsch & Esser, 2012; Wirth & Kolb, 2004). In such cases it is necessary to find the optimal solutions in order to arrive at the best comparability. Holtz-Bacha and Kaid (2011, pp. 397–398), however, rightly note that "study designs and methods

Table 1.2 Contextual variance in the countries of the study

Country	Political system	Press freedom (Freedom House)	TV ownership	Development and media literacy	Region
Belgium	democratic	free	mixed (public and private)	high	Western Europe
Brazil	democratic	partly free	mostly private	medium	Latin America
Canada	democratic	free	mostly private	high	North America
Chile	democratic	free	mostly private	medium	Latin America
China	authoritarian	not free	mostly state-owned	low	East Asia
Egypt	authoritarian	partly free	mostly state-owned	low	Middle East
Germany	democratic	free	mixed (public and private)	high	Western Europe
Hong Kong	authoritarian	partly free	mostly private	medium	East Asia
Israel	democratic	free	mixed (public and private)	high	Middle East
Italy	democratic	free	mixed (public and private)	high	Western Europe
Japan	democratic	free	mixed (public and private)	high	East Asia
Poland	democratic	free	mixed (public and private)	high	Eastern Europe
Portugal	democratic	free	mixed (public and private)	high	Western Europe
Singapore	authoritarian	not free	mostly private	medium	Southeast Asia
Switzerland	democratic	free	mixed (public and private)	high	Western Europe
Taiwan	democratic	free	mixed (public and private)	medium	East Asia
United States	democratic	free	mostly private	high	North America

are often compromised by the inability to develop consistent methodologies and data-gathering techniques across countries." In the present study several issues related to functional equivalence required our attention. We dealt with all these issues by using what is commonly referred to as a committee approach (Harkness, 2003; Vijver & Leung, 1997) or assembly strategy (Hanitzsch, 2008). Theoretical concepts and research tools were collaboratively developed, capitalizing on the rich collective expertise of researchers involved in this project.

SELECTION OF TELEVISION CHANNELS As noted, our goal in each country was to compare the newscast of its public service television station—most countries have only one such station—with the newscast of the most heavily viewed commercial station, based on the country's rating system. Determining the most heavily viewed newscast in the private television sector did not raise any problem, since the definition of ratings is virtually the same everywhere, even though the specific parameters may differ slightly from country to country. However, the question of what constitutes a public service station is more complex. Some public stations are funded by government, some are financed by license fees, some are funded by sponsorships, while in some there is even some advertising. The rule we applied in selecting the station was based on each country's definition or some combination of these funding sources.

As noted above, some of the countries—China, Egypt, Hong Kong, and Singapore—deviated from the one public and one commercial station model. Nevertheless, since we did not wish to lose these countries, we compromised by using only one type of station. In China and Egypt we had one government-run station; in Hong Kong we used two Chinese-language commercial stations; and in Singapore we also studied two commercial stations, one broadcasting in Chinese and one in English.

SELECTION OF MAIN NEWSCAST Here, too, countries differ in terms of what they define as the main newscast of the day, or rather the evening. In countries that broadcast only one news program per day on a particular station, there was, of course, no problem. However, in some countries there are more options to choose from. Our rule of thumb was to select the newscast that had the largest viewership, based on ratings. It should also be noted that in some countries the public service and commercial newscasts were aired at the same time of day, while in other countries the schedules were different. This did not create a problem, however.

DEMOGRAPHIC CHARACTERISTICS The survey questionnaires contained questions on the respondents' demographic data. Obtaining information on one's education and income could be problematic across countries, since the categories used and peoples' perception of these factors is not uniform. Attempts made to standardize these data for comparative analyses remain problematic.

SEEKING "NORMAL" TIMES Since the focus in the study was on news in general and not on the coverage of any specific event, we wanted to use "normal" times, that is, not any event that might dominate or "distort" other news. We set the dates for the content analysis several months ahead after carefully scrutinizing anticipated forthcoming events. We also had contingency plans to halt the recording of the newscasts if some "world-shattering" event were to take place. Fortunately, we did not encounter any significant problem. A few events did receive relatively more attention, but no single event overshadowed the others. These included the primaries in the United States for the 2008 presidential elections, unrest in Kenya and in Zimbabwe, clashes between Palestinians and Israelis, and protests surrounding the torch-lighting ceremony for the Beijing Olympic Games. But basically those were "normal" times. An exception was the earthquake in Haiti, which may have been a problem in some countries where the survey was conducted around the time the event took place.

Missing data in content analysis During the course of the sample period for the content analysis, there were some problems concerning missing data. For example, in the public service station in the United States there were no broadcasts on weekends. The same was the case in Brazil. One evening in Israel, a major terror event took place in Jerusalem a few minutes before the newscast went on the air. As it happened, it occurred a few blocks from the public station's building. As a result, the entire newscast was devoted to the event with live coverage, mostly unedited, almost like an unending item that could not be itemized. It was decided to exclude that newscast altogether.

Translation of instruments Two main instruments were used in the study: the codebook for the content analysis and the survey questionnaire. Both instruments were developed in English, which was the common language used by all the international research team members.

The identical codebook and its related appendixes were used in all the countries. However, each country's research team also prepared certain documents and examples in the local language in order to assist the student coders in their training, as well as in the actual coding of the news items. And yet some variables might have been interpreted in an idiosyncratic manner in the various countries. For example, items were coded for the presence of "gory" images. This notion, like some others, may be differentially loaded in various cultures.

On the other hand, the translation of the survey questionnaire into the various languages had to be as accurate as possible. To do this, the English version of the questionnaire, once completed, was translated by a completely bilingual person in each relevant country and then was re-translated—from the non-English language back into English—in order to be sure that the newly obtained English version was identical to the original English version. Corrections were made as needed until the country teams were satisfied that the questionnaire was a perfect translation of the original English version.

PRACTICAL ISSUES There are several ways of organizing internationally collaborative research projects of this magnitude. Esser and Hanitzsch (2012b) have recently outlined several ideal-typical models of scientific collaboration, including a "centralized model," a "correspondent model," a "coordinated cooperation model," and a "coordinated, fully comparative cooperation model." Of these, the last model is viewed to be the most advanced, as it entails a great deal of intellectual freedom for all partners involved in the project. The approach used for this study squarely falls within this category of scientific collaboration.

Research in this model is carried out by a network of scholars whose positions within the project are generally considered equal, except for the fact that one person serves as project coordinator. The main advantage of this model is that that all participating scholars can bring in their intellectual capabilities and cultural expertise at any stage of the project. Ideally, all collaborators participate equally in the development of theories, concepts, research designs, and research methods, though in reality it is generally a few individuals who are the main "drivers" of the project. The coordinated, fully comparative cooperation model also entails collaborative exploitation of a project in terms of publications and academic reputation. The practical challenges associated with this way of collaboratively doing research can be so manifold that researchers may easily become disillusioned at various stages in the process.

SYNCHRONIZATION OF RESEARCH STAGES IN ALL COUNTRIES A study of this complexity, both in terms of the number of participating countries and the three phases, required an elaborate scheme for synchronizing the work. Ideally, every step along the way should take place at precisely the same time and under identical conditions. Of course, this is not entirely feasible.

The time frame of the sample for the content analysis consisted of exactly the same 28 days in all countries, with only marginal deviations resulting from different time zones across the globe. The coding of the content, however, took different amounts of time in the various countries. Some of the quickest country teams completed the coding within approximately six months, while the slowest took slightly over a year. These differences, however, had no impact upon the findings.

The design of the survey questionnaire was completed in July 2009. However, as noted, the interviews were conducted in the 13 countries over an 11-month period beginning in September 2009 (in Israel) and ending in July 2010 (in the United States). These differences were the result of logistic as well as financial constraints in the various locations. There is a possibility, of course, that the time gaps may have had an impact on the responses, but it is impossible to estimate such an effect.

A similar potential problem existed regarding the in-depth interviews with the gatekeepers. These conversations took place, as noted, from August 2009 (in

Honk Kong) to March 2011 (in Poland). Getting the gatekeepers to agree to be interviewed was quite a difficult task in some of the countries, and the specific scheduling was also not easy. In some cases the researchers, who personally conducted the interviews, had to travel hundreds of miles in order to meet with their interviewees. We are aware of the possibility that some of the information obtained during these interviews may be tainted, especially concerning the interviewees' responses concerning the data that were presented to them. This could be due to the request of the interviewees to relate, in retrospect, to the content that was analyzed from a sample drawn as long as 3 years previous, from January–March 2008. Significantly shorter time gaps existed between the time that the surveys were conducted and the in-depth interviews. This, in our view, was a minor potential problem.

Funding Under ideal circumstances, a project of this kind should be funded by one central source. An attempt was made to obtain such funding, but it did not materialize. Therefore, each of the participating countries was obliged to obtain its own funding. Some of the grants were abundant, some were definitely ample, and some were quite meager. This resulted in our early loss of 5 countries as well as the inability of 4 teams to do the survey and 5 teams to do the interviews with the gatekeepers.

Collaboration Our project was quite ambitious. It required much collaboration with and coordination among 17 country teams over a period of nearly 5 years. It is doubtful that it could have been accomplished without the amazing technologies of email and the Internet that researchers now have at their fingertips. But the most important ingredient by far was the nature of the collaboration among the 30 or so scholars. Organizing and supervising such a project could be extremely difficult.

Especially in broad-scope collaborative endeavors such as ours, one has to consider the vast amount of time and effort that goes into communication and coordination. International scholarly networks often consist of researchers have been socialized into different schools of thought, epistemologies, and methodologies. Collaborators may vastly disagree even on the focus of a given or planned study. Participants in these projects thus may find themselves spending valuable time in lengthy, and sometimes pointless, discussions (Hanitzsch & Esser, 2012).

It is often said that the methodological and procedural habits of collaborators who come from different academic cultures often produce frustration and disillusionment (Jowell, 1998; Livingstone, 2003) Differences do regularly occur with respect to preferred epistemologies (most notably quantitative vs. qualitative), modes of data collection, sampling methods, and uses of visual cues, to name just a few. Several of these problems may require long hours of discussion until a feasible solution is found. And yet these solutions still have the unfortunate tendency not to make everybody happy. Furthermore, conceptual knowledge and methodological skills are far from evenly distributed across participants from the various regions. And collaborators may disappear for no obvious reason, or they may decide to drop out of the project at any time.

Clearly, this study had to deal with all these problems more or less extensively in the course of our research. We often struggled in endless meetings to find common ground. Many compromises—in conceptual and methodological terms—have been made. The different cultural backgrounds of the collaborators in this study clearly played out in many respects, and the differences in theoretical and methodological preferences sometimes loomed large—perhaps larger than they actually were. And yet very few instances of serious disagreement occurred. Despite a long and sometimes difficult journey, we have completed what we think is a valuable and important study. Unlike other examples (Livingstone, 2012), this study has not collapsed under its own weight. With many tasks to accomplish, coupled with the need to maintain rather uniform procedures and schedules, we think that we have worked at an optimal level.

CHAPTER TWO

The Prevalence of News

Domestic, Foreign, and Hybrid

AGNIESZKA STĘPIŃSKA, WILLIAM PORATH, CONSTANZA MUJICA,
XIAOGE XU, & AKIBA A. COHEN

From the 17th through the 19th century, as Wilke (1987) demonstrated in his historical study of foreign news in German, French, English, and American newspapers, there was steady growth in the amount of foreign news coverage. Today, with the increasing globalization of news organizations (Chalaby, 2005) and the greater political and economic interdependence among nations, one could assume that the role of foreign news has increased in importance. As Marshall McLuhan's concept of the global village seems to have been realized, information from abroad should be more significant and relevant to audiences than ever before. In addition, the recent and rapid dissemination of new technologies enables broadcasters to gather, produce, and distribute without delay news from all over the world.

Some studies, however, conclude that there is a shrinking foreign news hole (see, for example, Moisy, 1997; Norris, 1995; Riffe, Aust, Jones, Shoemaker, & Sundar, 1994). Even historically, the growth in the amount of foreign news coverage was accompanied by an increase in attention to domestic news that put greater limits on the space available for foreign news (Wilke, 1987). Nevertheless, several scholars (Biltereyst, 2001; Riffe et al., 1994; Stacks, 2004; Wouters, 2011) warn about a certain bias in analyzing the decline of foreign news by pointing to the overly episodic, "snapshot" nature of the evidence supporting foreign news' long-term decline.

On the other hand, according to Shanor (2003), increasingly competitive media markets put the share and quality of foreign news under pressure. Since foreign news is expensive to produce and is often considered irrelevant by general audiences, it generally does not create revenue for media organizations.

The aim of this chapter is to present overall findings regarding the nature of television news based on the comparative content analysis of the news in the 17 countries participating in our project. The chapter addresses two main research questions. First, how much coverage is given to foreign news in the various countries in terms of the overall percentage, duration, and placement of these items within the newscasts? Second, what type of foreign news—with or without relevance to the country of broadcast—is presented to the viewers?

Determinants of Domestic and Foreign News Selection

Since David Manning White's classic study of "Mr. Gates" (White, 1950), numerous researchers have examined how editors define and classify news. In general, the classification or categorization of various news types involves value judgments as to which stories are worthy of inclusion and which should be discarded. The actual process of news selection was analyzed in the 1970s and the 1980s in various detailed studies on news-making and news production (Epstein, 1973; Gans, 1979; Schlesinger, 1987). The findings showed that journalists' decision-making should be regarded as a complex process that is influenced by multiple factors, including time or space available, editorial policy, economic goals, and the perceived interests of news consumers.

Today, news theory is divided into several main groups such as news values, functional, critical, and normative professional models. Gatekeeping theory, based on Lewin's (1947) metaphor of the gatekeeper as well as White's study (1950), was expanded and developed by Shoemaker (1991) and provides a structure for the factors that influence the selection of the events to be reported by the news media. These consist of the individual journalist's and the editor's preferences, routines in the news organizations, organizational factors, and social factors. Thus, most of the research in this area is devoted to recognizing the existence of a hierarchy in the significance of different factors during the selection process of either domestic or foreign events to be covered by the media.

As Gans (1979) concluded in his study of domestic news in the U.S. media, the selection of stories begins with substantive consideration. Accordingly, stories to be covered must be either "important" or "interesting." Judgments of importance are applied to both actors and actions: actors should preferably be known rather than unknown (the latter often get media attention by protesting, rioting, striking, and being victims), and actions should be negative, disruptive, and event-oriented rather than prolonged processes.

Regarding the importance of news, according to Gans, domestic U.S. news judgments are usually determined by four considerations: (1) rank in governmental and other hierarchies (the federal government and its activities are always important, and stories about the president and the Congress are of the highest importance); (2) impact on the nation and the national interest; (3) impact on large numbers of people (the most important story of all is the one that affects every American); and (4) significance for the past and future. The general rule is that the more considerations are satisfied by an event, the more important it is.

As for "interesting" stories, Gans's second category, these are typically "people stories." Such stories have traditionally been presented in the media for two reasons. First, important news is often negative and must be balanced by interesting stories that either report "good" or "light" news. In addition, interesting stories are often timeless, and thus they can be used when last-minute replacements are needed. Gans indicated six types of "interesting stories," usually involving ordinary people, heroes, victims, or "important" people in extraordinary or anecdotal situations.

In contemporary scholarship, this kind of news may be termed "soft" news in contrast to "hard" news. Hard news is characterized by Tuchman (1978) and others (Shoemaker & Cohen, 2006; Smith, 1985; Whetmore, 1987) as domestic and international politics, economics and social matters—all usually demanding immediate publication. On the other hand, "soft news" does not necessitate timely publication and has a lower level of substantive information value. This definition is based on two dimensions, topicality and timeliness. Patterson (2000), on the other hand, shows the multi-dimensional character of news. He refers to public policy components, sensationalism, human-interest elements, crimes, and disasters as news subjects, and the use of collectives and self-references as indicators of softening of news.

Subsequent studies in this area on topics (Baum, 2003), actors (Baum, 2005; Prior, 2003), types of the media (Baum, 2003), and programs (Brewer & Cao, 2006) led Lehman-Wilzig and Saletzky (2010) to a revision of Tuchman's seminal categorization of "soft" and "hard" news. They not only altered criteria for these two types, but also introduced a third category of "general" news—such as recent economic, social, or cultural news that should be published but not immediately, and important news relevant only for a specific group. Furthermore, they suggested that "discrete categorizations are no longer the best way to describe and measure the types of news being produced in the contemporary age; a multi-point spectrum might be more realistically descriptive" (Lehman-Wilzig & Saletzky, 2010, p. 51). Thus, they offer eight subcategories: very soft news, soft news, weak general news, general news, strong general news, weak hard news, hard news, and strong hard news.

Reinemann, Stayner, Scherr, and Legnante (2011), in their review of concepts, operationalizations, and key findings of 24 studies on "hard" and "soft" news conducted since the 1990s identified five dimensions used exclusively or in varying combinations to define these two types of news. These dimensions refer to five different stages in the news production and news reception processes: (1) topic/event, (2) news production, (3) news focus, (4) news style, and (5) news reception.

One of the areas that meets most news criteria is social conflict. In their five-nation study of social conflict in television news, Cohen, Adoni, and Bantz (1990) found that foreign conflicts that take place outside the country of broadcast usually appear on the news as more severe than domestic conflicts, that is, they are presented as more complex, more intense, and more difficult to solve than domestic conflicts. This is because such events must pass a higher editorial threshold of newsworthiness.

In studying factors that explain the output of foreign news in specific media and in specific countries, one may follow Hjarvard (2002), who distinguished between two traditions in the analysis of the content of foreign news reporting: studies of newsworthiness and the perspective of the international news flow. While the former emphasizes the factors that explain the criteria used by gatekeepers in the selection of foreign news, such as in the seminal study by Galtung and Ruge (1965), the latter focuses on news geography or on describing which regions or countries receive more attention and what representations are constructed of each region (Sreberny-Mohammadi et al., 1985). This global-level research generally assumes that international news coverage reflects the structure of power among nations (MacBride, 1980).

The structural theory of international news flow proposed by Östgaard (1965), Galtung and Ruge (1965), and Galtung (1971) has become some of the most frequently cited literature of this research stream and in an important way has dominated the scene since the 1960s. Östgaard (1965) developed a complex theory that condensed different components of news into three factors: simplification, identification, and sensationalism. He actually blamed these factors for the prevalent bias in the international news flow. His theory was further developed by Galtung and Ruge (1965), whose study was also the first to point out that the news that journalists deliver is shaped by a mixture of both internal and external constraints. Consequently, foreign news might be considered in two ways: either as a product of journalistic professional definitions combined with internal organizational constraints or as a product of external—political, economic, and technological—factors.

Subsequent studies have sought to map the features and factors that render a foreign event newsworthy (Rosengren, 1974a; Schaap, 1998; Sreberny & Stevenson, 1999; Staab, 1990; Stevenson & Cole, 1984; Wu, 2000). Other research has focused on journalistic and editorial decision-making processes (Chang & Lee, 1992; Westerståhl & Johansson, 1994). Shoemaker and Reese (1996) proposed a hierarchical model suggesting that influences on news result from individual news workers: the routine practices whereby news is collected, transformed, and disseminated; the media ecology; and the social system, its ideology, and values. Chang, Shoemaker, and Brendlinger (1987) proposed a set of conditions that make people or events more newsworthy—namely, novelty or oddity, conflict or controversy, interest, importance, impact or consequence, sensationalism, timeliness, or proximity. Finally, Harcup and O'Neill (2001) offered a revised set of the Galtung and Ruge (1965) factors, which they claim represent a contemporary set of values: the power elite, celebrity, entertainment, surprise, bad news, good news, magnitude, relevance, follow-up, and newspaper agenda.

Based on much of this literature, Shoemaker and Cohen (2006), in their ten-nation study examining both the content of news in newspapers, radio, and television, as well as the perception of news by audiences, focused on two more general global factors: deviance and social significance of events. Deviance was defined as a characteristic of people, ideas, or events that sets them apart from others in their region, neighborhood, and family. This variable covers previously distinguished features such as novelty, oddity, conflict, controversy, and sensationalism. They distinguish between three dimensions of deviance: normative deviance (a case of breaking norms and laws); social change deviance (in which ideas, people, or events challenge the status quo of the social system); and statistical deviance (in which an idea, person, or event is very different from the statistical average, thereby being odd, unusual, or novel).

In that study, Shoemaker and Cohen also explicate four dimensions of social significance. They refer to political significance (the extent to which the content of a news item has potential or actual impact on the relationship between people and government or between governments); economic significance (the extent to which the content of the news item has potential or actual impact on the exchange of goods and services); cultural significance (the extent to which the content of a news item has potential or actual impact on a social system's traditions, institutions, and norms); and public significance (the enhancements or threats a news item represents for the public's well-being). Their general assumption is that news items rated as highly deviant and socially significant would receive relatively more news coverage. It should be noted, however, that the cultural context is also important; thus, certain events may be highly deviant and socially significant in one culture but not so in another culture.

In line with the notion of international news flow, the content-based study by Gerbner and Marvanyi (1977) analyzed foreign news coverage in selected newspapers in nine countries and showed that variation in the amount of foreign news is correlated with political system variables. Kim and Barnett (1996) reported that economic development is the most important determinant of a country's place in the network of international news flow. This conclusion was also supported by Wu (1998b), who conducted a meta-analysis of 55 studies investigating the determinants of international news flow, mostly from the 1980s and the 1990s. The following components were found to be embedded in the world structure: gross national product per capita, an index of economic development, the size of the population or the nation, cultural proximity, former colonial ties, ideological groupings, language factors, regionalism, geographic proximity, elite status, media facilities and equipment, communication access and technologies, and international news services.

In the case of foreign news, part of the process involves a relatively small number of journalists who act as gatekeepers, coordinating the flow of foreign news. Indeed, a large proportion of the gatekeeping process that determines international news coverage is performed by journalists and editors at international news agencies (Boyd-Barrett, 1980, 2001; Fenby, 1986; Paterson, 1998; Boyd-Barrett & Rantanen, 2000, 2002, 2004). These journalists and editors are highly instrumental in deciding the amount of coverage a country receives, or determine the topics and issues that are emphasized if that country is covered at all. As studies conducted since the 1970s show, this results in a quantitative imbalance in the flow of news, with much more attention paid to "continual coverage of the global centres of the industrial world which contrasts with the intermittent images of the South in some form of crisis…" (Sreberny & Paterson, 2004, p. 7).

The development of international satellite televisions news services as well as online media has partially eclipsed the role of news agencies. They are still a significant source of foreign news for media organizations, but their actual share among sources of foreign news is difficult to determine because of the editors' reluctance to reveal such sources to the audience (Boyd-Barrett, 1980; Boyd-Barrett & Rantanen, 2004). In fact, one of the many variables in our study dealt with television news agencies and international broadcasters as sources of materials in foreign news. Interestingly, very few of the news items were clearly identified as having come from these sources.[1] And yet, based on the number of stations that subscribe to the agencies, we may assume that actual use of their materials and their impact on the newscasts is significant, even if not clearly identified.

In his subsequent study, Wu (2000) reviewed foreign news in 38 countries and suggested that the coverage is primarily determined by economics and the availability of news sources. However, in one of Wu's previous studies (1998a), as well as in earlier research by Robinson and Sparkes (1976), it was found that international trade played a key role in shaping foreign news in some countries, but was not a significant factor in the United States. In addition, it was suggested that the crafting of news reports dealing with foreign events is also subject to local or domestic influences. This includes the local community's power structure, as well as organizational factors and corporate characteristics. These influences are likely to affect not only the type of foreign news that appears in the media, but also the quality and depth of the coverage.

Furthermore, Vilanilam (1983) and Riffe (1996) provided evidence supporting the sway of national interest in foreign press coverage on former or concurrent ideologically and politically congruent partners in the 1980s. On the other hand, Ito (2004), using data from the 1990s, found this factor to be less relevant in Central European countries. Instead, he found that the existence of an international news agency was the most important factor in international news flow in that region. Ito's findings proved that the amount of news coming from the United States, the United Kingdom, and France—countries with international news agencies—was greater than the amount of news that would have been expected based on these three countries' other attributes such as population, per capita GDP, size of defense budget, size of the army, geographical distance, common ideology, and their volume of trade. Finally, several studies (Chang & Lee, 1992; Kim & Barnett, 1996) found that ethnic bonds and shared language had an impact on the amount of information traffic across national boundaries.

In sum, one may distinguish among several major groups of factors that determine the amount of foreign news in the media: (1) political predictors, including domestic factors such as the political regime as well as past and present international relations; (2) economic indicators, including features of the national market and labor as well as international economic relations, a country's power position, and interdependence with other nations; (3) geographic proximity affecting political and economic relations among neighboring countries, regional cooperation, or conflicts; (4) cultural proximity—language, tradition, and heritage; (5) population size, minorities, and immigration; and (6) sources of information, including international news agencies and language of the media. Thus one may expect that media in countries that have strong political, economic, and cultural ties with other countries would pay more attention to what is happening abroad, while media of political, economic, and military superpowers might be focused mostly on domestic issues. At the same time, media in democratic regimes would be expected to freely cover both domestic and foreign issues, while political actors in non-democratic regimes might distract the public's attention to domestic issues by focusing more on foreign events.

Predominant Type of News

We begin our presentation of the news by showing the distribution of all the news items in the 17 countries by distinguishing between the two "pure" types—domestic and foreign—and the two hybrid types—domestic with foreign involvement and foreign with domestic involvement (see Table 2.1). Across the entire sample, 55% of all the items dealt with purely domestic events. Furthermore,

Table 2.1 Countries in descending order of percentages of each type of news

Purely domestic		Domestic with foreign involvement		Both domestic categories		Foreign with domestic involvement		Purely foreign		Both foreign categories	
Taiwan	87	Canada	23	Taiwan	86	Germany	17	Egypt	56	Egypt	56
Japan	71	Chile	21	Hong Kong	79	Poland	17	Singapore	42	Germany	46
United States	68	Hong Kong	21	Japan	79	Chile	16	Switzerland	33	Singapore	45
Italy	67	Germany	18	Italy	78	United States	15	Canada	31	Canada	44
Portugal	67	Israel	17	Portugal	74	Israel	14	Germany	29	Switzerland	43
China	65	Belgium	16	China	73	Canada	13	Brazil	25	Belgium	36
Brazil	58	Egypt	16	United States	73	Belgium	12	Belgium	24	Poland	35
Hong Kong	58	Poland	16	Chile	70	Switzerland	10	China	21	Israel	33
Israel	50	Switzerland	16	Brazil	68	Egypt	9	Israel	19	Brazil	32
Chile	49	Italy	11	Israel	67	Japan	8	Hong Kong	18	Chile	30
Poland	49	Brazil	10	Poland	65	Portugal	8	Poland	18	China	27
Belgium	48	Singapore	9	Belgium	64	Brazil	7	Portugal	18	United States	27
Singapore	46	China	8	Switzerland	57	Italy	7	Italy	15	Portugal	26
Switzerland	41	Japan	8	Canada	56	China	6	Chile	14	Italy	22
Germany	36	Portugal	7	Singapore	55	Singapore	3	Japan	13	Hong Kong	21
Canada	33	United States	4	Germany	54	Hong Kong	3	Taiwan	12	Japan	21
Egypt	19	Taiwan	3	Egypt	35	Taiwan	2	United States	12	Taiwan	14
Total	55		13		68		10		22		32

when combining the purely domestic stories and the domestic stories with foreign involvement, the data indicate that 68%, or two-thirds of the items, deal in one way or another with domestic issues. At the other end of the continuum, nearly one-quarter (22%) of the news items were concerned with purely foreign events, while 10% of the items were characterized as foreign events with domestic involvement of the country of broadcast. Thus 32%, or one-third of all the items, dealt in one way or another with foreign issues. Finally, nearly one-quarter (23%) of all the news items were coded as hybrid news (either domestic with foreign involvement, or foreign with domestic involvement).

Of the 17 countries, 16 presented more purely domestic news than purely foreign news. There was one exception, however: in Egypt there were more purely foreign news items than purely domestic items. The countries with the highest percentages of domestic news were: Taiwan (87%) and Japan (71%), with China, Italy, Portugal, and the United States showing 65%–70%. Other than Egypt, the countries with the lowest percentages of purely domestic news were Canada and Germany (less than 40%). The countries with the highest percentage of purely foreign news, other than Egypt, were Singapore (42%) and Switzerland (33%), as well as Canada and Germany (each with around 30%).

Furthermore, in several countries there was a considerable amount of both types of hybrid news. Domestic news with foreign involvement was most prevalent in Canada, Chile, and Hong Kong, while foreign events with domestic involvement were relatively more prevalent in Germany, Poland, Chile, and the United States. The countries with the highest share of both hybrid types of news were Chile (37%), Canada (36%), and Germany (35%). On the other hand, in only two countries (the United States and Chile) did the amount of hybrid news of either type slightly exceed the amount of pure domestic or pure foreign news (in both cases there were more items of foreign news with domestic involvement than items of purely foreign news). At the same time, in some countries the hybrid categories were extremely rare. For example, in Taiwan, both hybrid categories appeared in only 5% of news items, while in Singapore and Hong Kong, foreign news with domestic involvement was negligible (3%).

Duration of News Items

The absolute numbers of news items in each news category do not tell the whole story, however. We therefore also considered and analyzed the duration of the items and relative placement in the line-up of the newscasts, both serving as indicators of newsworthiness from the perspective of the editors.

Table 2.2 presents the mean duration of the news items of all the countries as well as breakdowns into the four news categories. The data reveal that, on average, in 15 of the 17 countries, domestic news items (both purely domestic and domestic with foreign involvement) were longer than foreign news items. For each country, a t-test was calculated between the mean duration (in seconds) of the domestic and foreign news items. In 14 of the countries the differences were significant at the $p < .01$ level, with domestic items being longer than foreign items. In Belgium the difference was significant at $p < .05$. In Portugal, while domestic items were longer than foreign items, the difference was not significant. In Japan,

Table 2.2 Mean duration (in seconds) of items by country and news category

Country	Total	Purely domestic	Domestic with foreign involvement	Both domestic categories	Foreign with domestic involvement	Purely Foreign	Both foreign categories	N
Belgium	83	83	93	85	94	73	80	1,420
Brazil	85	89	110	92	88	63	68	784
Canada	134	129	179	150	167	92	114	749
Chile	99	105	116	109	94	58	77	1,506
China	60	72	54	70	57	26	34	784
Egypt	106	126	129	145	135	88	95	709
Germany	70	72	87	77	72	58	63	742
Hong Kong	103	100	137	110	76	74	74	798
Israel	90	97	95	96	94	64	77	1,128
Italy	75	76	85	77	76	61	66	1,365
Japan	123	119	151	122	137	123	128	895
Poland	140	145	159	149	138	110	124	540
Portugal	109	111	102	110	115	100	105	1,707
Singapore	71	77	73	76	80	64	65	992
Switzerland	78	82	94	85	73	66	68	1,380
Taiwan	109	110	119	110	120	98	100	1,346
United States	141	146	275		131	70	104	654
Total	96	100	114	103	102	74	82	17,501

foreign items were slightly longer than the domestic items, but the difference was not significant.

This finding, along with the data presented in Table 2.1, supports the conclusion that, not surprisingly, there was a clear preference for domestic news in the newscasts. In other words, domestic news plays a much more important role in news coverage, presumably because that is what the target audience is primarily interested in (see Chapter 9).

The findings also show that for most of the countries, purely domestic news items tended to be longer than the average news item. The exceptions to this were Belgium, Canada, Hong Kong, and Japan. At the same time, purely foreign news items in all the countries were shorter than the other three types of items as well as the average duration of all the news items. This phenomenon was most apparent in the United States and Chile, where the average foreign news item was about half the overall length of all the news items (these countries, as noted earlier, had a relatively low level of purely foreign news).

As indicated above, Table 2.1 shows that only 23% of all the items were of the hybrid type. And yet, in most of the countries, news items concerning domestic events with foreign involvement were, on average, the longest. The exceptions to this were the items in Belgium, China, Portugal, and Taiwan, while in Israel and Singapore both types of domestic news (pure and hybrid) were of almost equal duration.

At the same time, foreign news items with domestic involvement were longer than average in most of the countries in the study, with the exception of China, Chile, Hong Kong, Switzerland, and the United States. Furthermore, in Belgium, China, Portugal, Singapore, and Taiwan, an average news item covering foreign events with domestic involvement was longer than items covering a domestic event with foreign involvement. One must bear in mind that two of these countries (Portugal and Taiwan) generally only feature a small proportion of foreign news. Therefore, if newscasts in these countries cover foreign countries at all, their own involvement would tend to be emphasized.

Interestingly, newscasts in Canada, Hong Kong, and Chile not only devoted relatively large portions of their news to domestic events with foreign involvement—more than 20%—(see Table 2.1), but these items were relatively short in comparison with some of the other countries (see Table 2.2). A similar observation may be made regarding Germany and Poland. The other interesting case is the United States, where only 4% of the items (see Table 2.1) were dedicated to domestic events with foreign involvement, but when such stories were reported, they tended to be extremely long (275 seconds on average). At the same time, in Belgium, Portugal, Singapore, and Taiwan, although the proportion of items of foreign events with domestic involvement was not significantly high (12% in Belgium and 9% in Portugal) and even much lower (only 3% and 2%, respectively) in Singapore and Taiwan, their mean duration was the highest of all four types of news items in those countries (see Table 2.2).

Placement in Line-Up

Table 2.3 Lead items in newscasts by types of news (in percent)

Country	Lead items				Total
	Purely domestic news	Domestic news with foreign involvement	Foreign news with domestic involvement	Purely foreign news	
Belgium	61	21	9	9	100
Brazil	76	13	11	0	100
Canada	36	29	11	25	100
Chile	71	14	14	0	100
China	75	25	0	0	100
Egypt	11	42	19	27	100
Germany	43	30	5	21	100
Hong Kong	53	45	2	0	100
Israel	36	25	35	4	100
Italy	62	5	11	21	100
Japan	71	14	7	7	100
Poland	54	18	18	11	100
Portugal	62	12	11	14	100
Singapore	70	9	11	11	100
Switzerland	56	19	10	15	100
Taiwan	91	4	2	4	100
United States	85	4	11	0	100
Total	60	19	11	10	100

Another way to scrutinize the significance of stories in the newscast is to examine their placement in the line-up, and particularly the news category of the lead item in the newscast. We assume, of course, that invariably the event with the highest newsworthiness according to the organization's standards is placed as "number one" in the main evening newscast. The findings presented in Table 2.3 show that, in total, 21% of the lead news items were either purely foreign events (10%) or foreign events with domestic involvement (11%), while in 60% of the cases purely domestic news items were most frequently selected to begin the newscasts, and an additional 19% of the lead items were domestic with foreign involvement.

In Canada, Egypt, Germany, and Israel, less than 50% (and, in the case of Egypt, only 11%) of lead items were of the domestic category. At the same time, in Egypt 27% of the lead items were purely foreign; in Canada 25%, and in Italy 21% were purely foreign. In Israel, as many as 35% of the lead items were foreign items with domestic involvement.

Finally, among the countries with the relatively highest percentage of purely foreign news items leading their respective newscasts, we find those with an overall high number of foreign news items (Canada, Germany, and Egypt). An interesting exception here is Italy, where 15% of the items were purely foreign, but as many as 21% of the leading items were dedicated to this type of news. On the other hand, in Singapore, where 42% of the items were purely foreign, only 11% of the leading items covered a purely foreign event. Also, in the countries in which there was a prevalence of domestic news stories—such as Taiwan, the United States, Japan, and China—more than 70% of the lead items were domestic news, while in Italy and Portugal—the other countries with a high percentage of purely domestic news (67%)—more than 60% of the leading items covered purely domestic news.

News Distribution: Similarities and Differences

In a comparative study such as ours, the first and foremost goal is to identify patterns of similarities and differences across countries. We thus sought to determine if there exist certain distributions of the four categories of news across the countries. In broad terms, we were able to distinguish among three major groups of countries, ordered from those that aired more domestic news to those that aired more foreign news. As often happens, there was also an exception.

The first group consists of seven countries, Taiwan, Japan, the United States, Italy, Portugal, Hong Kong, and China, all of which are characterized by their dedication to purely domestic news (from 87% in Taiwan to 65% in China) and the related fact that they featured a low level of purely foreign news (from 21% in China to 12% in the United States and Taiwan). The similarities among these countries were even more visible when we combined Table 2.1's "both domestic" and "both foreign" categories. It is also noteworthy that in the United States and China, not only was the percentage of domestic news items relatively high, but the purely domestic stories were twice as long as the purely foreign items (see Table 2.2).

In order to understand the high proportion of domestic news stories in these countries, we must also recognize differences between them. While Japan and China may be considered economic powers with long traditions of political and cultural isolation, Taiwan may be seen as a country with rather little involvement in international politics. In this subgroup of three Asian countries, a small proportion of items dedicated to foreign events may also result from little perceived need or interest among their respective journalists and audiences in having information about other countries. In the other subgroup of countries, while a relatively large number of domestic news stories were presented, journalists may have had certain reasons to look more to other countries than their colleagues in the first subgroup. The reasons for this may vary, such as traditionally strong ties to former colonies (as in the case of Portugal), one of the most politically powerful states in the EU (as in the case of Italy), and political, military, and economic connections (as in the case of the United States).

The second group of countries consists of Brazil, Chile, Israel, Poland, and Belgium. Although these countries do present significant amounts of both categories of domestic news, they feature less purely domestic news than the previous groups (around 50%). On the other hand, they air a higher proportion of domestic news with foreign involvement (from 10% in Brazil to 21% in Chile) and purely foreign news (from 14% in Chile to 25% in Brazil).

The third group consists of Canada, Germany, Singapore, and Switzerland. These countries featured a higher proportion of foreign news (more than 40% in both foreign categories) and a lower presence of purely domestic news (from 46% in Singapore to 33% in Canada). Within this group, Canada was distinguishable from all the other countries in the sample: it is the only country that presents similar proportions of purely domestic news (33%) and purely foreign news (31%).

Singapore was another exception within the group. When considering the general levels of foreign and domestic news by group, Singapore appeared to fit in. However, there were differences in the distribution of the intermediate categories, that is, Singapore presented quite a bit of purely domestic news (46%) and a very low level of domestic news with foreign involvement (9%). A similar situation was found when disaggregating the foreign news category: there was a stronger presence of purely foreign news (Singapore had the second-highest figure in this category with 42%), while only 3% of the items were of foreign news with domestic involvement. Thus, there was a polarization between purely domestic news and purely foreign news, with a higher proportion of the latter than the overall sample mean.

The countries in the third group featured the lowest proportions of domestic news in the sample, or, to put it another way, the highest proportions of foreign news. Once again, very different or contradictory factors may explain these similar findings. First, television broadcasters in European countries (except for Italy) seemed to pay more attention to foreign events in Europe than to events on other continents. This may be explained by geographic and cultural proximity (see Chapter 4 for a detailed discussion of the geography of foreign news), a long-standing tradition of political and economic relations, including both conflicts and cooperation (alliances), and strong public service media systems that have traditionally perceived foreign news as part of their mission. Furthermore, historical factors that led to the establishment of the European Economic Community as well as contemporary interrelations between members of the European Union should be taken into account here.

The second and third groups, however, also included non-European countries. Chile, Brazil, and Canada represent countries with strong cultural (linguistic), economic, and political ties with the United States and some countries in Europe, as well as with other countries within the region, while Israel's geopolitical position requires it to pay special attention to the events taking place in all countries in its region. As for Canada and Poland, they both have neighboring countries that have been affecting them for centuries.

Finally, we classify Egypt as a separate case because of its unusually low level of purely domestic news (19%) and its high proportion of purely foreign news (56%). It should be recalled that the sample of our newscasts was drawn in early 2008 when Egypt was still under the Mubarak regime.

From earlier and contemporary history, it is known that dictatorships or authoritarian regimes with limited (if any) press freedom tend to prefer foreign news items over domestic news, because the former would be less likely to cause internal political problems than the latter (Haynes, 1984; Wilke, 1987). In the present case, this may be true not only for Egypt but also for China, a country with a high degree of internal control. On the other hand, a strong interest in foreign news may be due to a country's large and imposing neighbors and relations with other countries (as was the case with most of the European countries in our sample as well as in Israel).

Conclusions

Our comparative analysis of the different types of news clearly indicates that foreign news remains smaller in volume, shorter in length, and lower in line-up placement than domestic news in the majority of the 17 countries of our study. The relatively low status of foreign news on television provided further evidence and support for what Schulz (1983) has referred to as "universal regionalism." In terms of the distribution of foreign news, however, a highly mixed situation exists in the 17 countries. At one end of the spectrum lies the lowest percentage of foreign news as evidenced in Taiwan and Japan. At the other lies the highest percentage of foreign news as evidenced in Egypt and Singapore. Between these two extremes we find two major groups of countries that differ from each other in terms of their respective distributions of foreign news.

The crux of the issue is that there are many local factors in each country that impact on the way news is presented, and that render sweeping generalizations across countries meaningless. In an age characterized by globalization in almost every aspect of life, we suggest that this trend is less pervasive in the world of news. There are some inherent limits to globalization, especially in the realm of media products crossing borders (Cohen, 2002). While television signals can indeed reach every corner of the globe at the same instant, thanks to the gigantic footprints of orbital satellites, the uses that people make of the content and the meanings they ascribe to them are not necessarily the same.

Even though countries may be grouped according to their distribution of domestic, foreign, and hybrid news, the rationales and attempted explanations for these trends seem to be idiosyncratic for each case. This suggests that, in interpreting data, one needs to consider contextual variables such as size and political, military, and economic status of the countries, their historical and cultural links to other countries, and the characteristics of their respective local television systems. In Chapter 15 we provide some country-specific remarks that deal with this perspective.

Summary

The aim of this chapter was to present our overall findings regarding the nature of television news based on the comparative content analysis in the 17 countries participating in our project. The chapter addresses two main research questions: (1) How much coverage is given to foreign news in the various countries in terms of the overall percentage, duration, and placement of these items within the newscasts? and (2) What types of foreign news—with or without relevance to the country of broadcast—is presented to the viewers? The findings clearly (and not unexpectedly) demonstrate the predominant position of domestic news: of the 17 countries, 16 presented more purely domestic news than purely foreign news (the only exception being Egypt). The findings also show that for most of the countries, purely domestic news items tend to be longer than the average news item (the exceptions to this were Belgium, Canada, Hong Kong, and Japan). At the same time, purely foreign news items in all the countries were shorter than the other three types of items as well as the average duration of all the news items. Finally, in 60% of cases, purely domestic news was most frequently selected to begin the newscast.

Note

1. Only 2.5% of the news items in the entire sample were specifically identified as originating from news agencies, while in as many as 38.9%, the source could not be identified. Interestingly, there were no significant differences among the countries except for Brazil, where 25.4% of the foreign news items were identified as agency materials. Also, only 10.6% of the items were identified as originating from sources such as CNN, BBC, and Al-Jazeera.

PART TWO

Contents

CHAPTER THREE

Topics in Foreign and Domestic Television News

KNUT DE SWERT, ANTÓNIO BELO, RASHA KAMHAWI, VEN-HWEI LO, CONSTANZA MUJICA, & WILLIAM PORATH

Comparing television news around the globe is a challenge, especially regarding topics in the news. On any given day, a government may collapse in one country, an earthquake may hit another country, and still another may celebrate its greatest sports event of the year. News reports differ from day to day and from country to country. However, beyond the particularities of the day, two factors make it well worthwhile to compare topics in the news: the importance of the news selection process and the existence of news that is often relevant beyond the borders of the country where the event took place.

Comparative studies of television news go beyond the individual journalist and editor and thus are highly enlightening about the influence of higher-level situational factors such as countries and media systems. Our main interest in this chapter is to reveal structural differences or similarities in the selection of news across countries, while focusing mainly on the topics of foreign as well as hybrid news.

We begin by providing a general overview of the topics in the news in all countries of our study using broad topic categories. We present this general overview along with a more detailed analysis of the topics in foreign news only. Next, we look for patterns in the thematic content of the news broadcasts. Here we ask two questions. First, do (some) countries cluster when examining their preferred topic selections? Second, do thematic preferences of broadcasters transcend foreign/domestic news differences, or do domestic, foreign, and hybrid news coverage differ substantively on the topics they deal with? We proceed by looking at the relationships between the amounts of coverage of the different topics by the various broadcasters regarding domestic, foreign, and hybrid news. We then attempt to determine whether foreign news is "harder," "softer," or more "sensational" than domestic news in each of the countries. Finally, we look at topic diversity of television news by creating an index of news entropy for each broadcaster in the countries of our sample. We do this in order to determine which countries have the highest diversity or diffusion of topics and whether or not such diversity is the same for foreign and domestic news.

Despite growing attention to framing and formal features of television news items, the issue of topic content of the news remains one of the main research domains for communication scholars. This is because what is *in* the news (and what is *not*) is not without consequences. For example, agenda-setting researchers (McCombs & Shaw, 1972; Weaver, 2007) focus primarily on topics when they study macro-level media effects on politics and public opinion. Scholars of priming work with issue coding of television news media. Even researchers interested in framing sometimes limit their measurements of frames to topical attributes of news stories, thereby staying close to what is referred to as second-level or attribute agenda-setting .

There is considerable variation in what happens in the real world. Ideally, television news would consist of all stories that matter for a particular audience on any given day. However, in the daily practice of news work, this is not the reality. A typical news broadcast cannot be stretched much longer because many things may have happened that day, nor can the newscast be shortened because it was a poor news day. Either way, choices must be made—in this case regarding story selection. An extensive research field has specialized in news selection studies or "gatekeeping." Seventeen years ago, Shoemaker and Reese (1996) synthesized existing research and developed a theory of news content selection. Shoemaker and Vos (2009) recently updated the theory in the specific context of gatekeeping. These authors have noted that many factors within and outside media organizations affect news content, including individual media workers, media routines, and organizational constraints.

News is always produced within a context of numerous internal and external pressures. According to Shoemaker and Reese (1996), the personal values and professional background of news workers have important impact on the production of news content. As far back as White's (1950) classic study, research has shown that the process of defining what is and what is not news is often highly subjective. Studies have also demonstrated that personal preferences of journalists unavoidably enter into the process of selecting and constructing news (Gans, 1979; Shoemaker, 1991; Patterson & Donsbach, 1996).

Another important influence on media content comes from media owners. Shoemaker and Reese (1996) state that "the personal attitudes and values of news media owners may be reflected not only in editorials and columns, but also in news and features" (p. 223). They believe that media owners have the ability to set news policies and thereby control media content. Bagdikian (1989), for example, argued that owners shape media operations and content. His study found that Rupert Murdoch repeatedly used his newspapers to support Margaret Thatcher and Ronald Reagan. Recently, Durante and Knight (2009) showed a similar pattern in Silvio Berlusconi's Italy.

Following Tuchman (1973), Shoemaker and Reese (1996) contend that news is also influenced by media routines and the economic goals of the organization. News organizations must make a profit on news programs. Media routines are practical responses to the needs of both the organization and news consumers. The focus on the need to maintain audience levels leads to restricted sets of topics and content. Thus, media organization favors certain kinds of news content and topics. Stories featuring politics, conflict, internal order, human interest, and disasters tend to be over-represented, while many other topics are under-represented (Shoemaker & Cohen, 2006; Lin, Lo, & Wang, 2011). In fact, there is a long tradition of research that assesses media performance by examining whether media content reflects a true or a biased picture of society (Asp, 2007).

Finally, Grabe and her colleagues (2003) argued that individuals should have access to a broad range of stories, since people are interested in different topics. Thus, the news media should serve diverse groups of citizens. Past research, however, indicates that only a few topics receive frequent and prominent news coverage.

Overview of Topics in Television News

As noted in Chapter 1, we coded the news topics using an extensive list of specific topics, based on an array of 25 major topic categories. Each news item could be coded for as many as three specific topics. This approach enabled a detailed and precise coding, as numerous news stories deal with multiple topic areas. For example, a story about an internal government disagreement on fiscal policy would be coded as "internal politics" as well as "economic policy."

However, given the large variance across the topics, it became necessary for the presentation of the findings to recode the topics and condense them into eleven main categories. The grouping of the topic categories was done on the basis of inherent conceptual relatedness of the broader list of categories. Table 3.1 presents the percentages of the newscasts based on the weighted total amount of time devoted to the 11 major topic groups in all countries in our sample. Across the countries, social issues, internal politics, internal order, economic issues, and international politics were the most prevalent news topics. The least prevalent

Table 3.1 Main topic categories by country (in percentage of total news time)[3]

Country	Social issues	Internal politics	Internal order	Economy	International politics	Culture, religion, and ceremonies	Fashion, human interest, weather	Sports	Environment, energy, science	Accidents and disasters	Military and defense	Time in hours
Belgium	25	16	21	14	8	10	9	13	8	4	2	32.9
Brazil	32	16	14	21	15	14	6	5	12	3	1	18.4
Canada	22	29	24	12	18	10	18	9	6	9	8	27.9
Chile	21	9	22	14	4	11	13	27	6	8	2	41.5
China	36	36	7	17	8	7	4	5	12	19	4	13.1
Egypt	12	15	9	15	49	8	6	11	4	1	7	22.1
Germany	23	27	22	26	14	8	13	14	10	8	5	14.5
Hong Kong	26	22	17	28	5	8	12	5	6	12	2	22.7
Israel	24	20	31	9	27	12	9	6	5	3	13	28.1
Italy	12	34	26	10	5	11	10	5	5	5	1	28.4
Japan	18	20	23	29	8	2	10	9	8	9	2	30.7
Poland	26	32	22	17	13	12	5	7	4	7	9	21.0
Portugal	34	26	32	23	11	9	6	15	3	3	4	51.5
Singapore	34	16	13	26	5	12	11	11	9	4	1	19.6
Switzerland	24	27	24	18	10	19	15	14	7	7	3	29.8
Taiwan	19	36	13	14	2	9	14	1	4	6	2	40.6
U.S.	26	40	6	29	16	5	5	3	4	2	12	25.7
Mean	24	25	19	19	13	10	10	9	7	6	5	468.5

topics were stories about environment and science, accidents and disasters, and military and defense.

In general, each of the two most prevalent topic categories—social issues and internal politics—took up about one-quarter of the newscasts. Social issues is a heterogeneous topic category, an amalgamation that includes several specific topics such as health, welfare, social services, education, housing, social relations, transportation, and communication. Although this category was highly represented in the news in all the countries, prevalence was not the same in all the countries. Social issues were covered most frequently in China (36%), Portugal and Singapore (34% each), and Brazil (32%), and least frequently in both Egypt and Italy (12% of the news).

The variability within the category of internal politics was considerably greater. On this topic, the United States (40%), China and Taiwan (each with 36%), and Italy (34%) stand out with very broad coverage. In the case of the United States, this was attributable to the primary elections that were taking place during the sample period. Chinese CCTV is the official news channel of the government and is thus obliged to pay a high level of attention to official government business. In Taiwan, presidential elections took place during the last period of our sample, and Italy was going through a major government crisis. In the case of Italy and Taiwan, this high level of internal politics coverage was achieved while the coverage of international politics in both countries was very low. Internal politics were less evident in television news in Chile (only 9%), Egypt (15%), Belgium, Brazil, and Singapore (16% each).

As for international politics, not surprisingly, this topic was very prominent in Israeli television news (27%), probably because of Israel's ongoing conflict with the Palestinians. This conflict and the U.S. involvement in the region seem to have contributed to a great emphasis on international politics in Egyptian news (49%), which complements the very high level of foreign news in general in Egyptian news (see Chapter 2). Several countries—Taiwan, Chile, Hong Kong, Italy, and Singapore—offer very little coverage of such stories (ranging from 2% to 5%).

News concerning internal order issues, such as crime, judicial decisions, demonstrations, and terrorism, played a particularly important role in television news in Israel and Portugal. The prominent coverage in Israel was partly due to the prevalence of terrorism, with three major events taking place during the time of the analysis: an attack on students in a Jerusalem yeshiva (religious school) on March 6th; the assassination of a high-ranking member of Hezbollah, Imad Mughniyah, in which Israel was claimed to be involved; and numerous Palestinian rocket attacks on Sderot, a town close to the Gaza strip.

Another important topic with substantial coverage was the economy. The high level of attention paid to economic issues by American newscasts (29%) can be traced back to a number of in-depth analyses of the slumping economic situation, developments in U.S. stock markets, and the positions expressed by the candidates in the primary elections on how to deal with the situation. Hong Kong and Singapore, two countries highly dependent on the finance sector, naturally scored high on this factor as well (28% and 26%, respectively). Finally, Japan and Germany, both major economies, also devoted much news to economic issues (29 and 26 issues, respectively). In contrast, Israeli and Italian television paid relatively little attention (around 10%) to economic issues, possibly because of other, more pressing issues in those countries at the time of the study.

Sports as a news category received very different amounts of coverage across the countries. Chilean television news stands out with a remarkable share of more than one-fourth of the newscasts dedicated to sports alone. As the Chilean newscasts in the sample were comparatively long (43 to 45 minutes), this means that in each evening newscast, around 10 minutes were devoted to coverage of sports results, reports about athletes, and so on. One possible reason for this is the desire of Chilean television channels to provide Chilean viewers, who are geographically quite far from the world's main sports arenas, a sense of participation in global sporting events. Other countries in which sports coverage also played an important role in television news—but not as prominent as in Chile—include Belgium, Germany, Portugal, and Switzerland. In contrast, sports as a news topic was hardly covered by news editors of U.S. and Taiwanese channels.

Sports coverage does present a special problem, however. In many countries, sports news typically appears in special programs rather than in the main evening newscast. Also, the question of which stations hold the rights to sporting events also has an impact on sports coverage. In Belgium, for example, the amount of coverage of sports differs significantly according to which channel owns the rights to cover the first soccer league and/or cycling events. The channel holding the rights for broadcasting these events will usually include more sports in its newscasts.

Finally, news items about military and defense issues seem have been reserved for countries with an active military agenda. In the United States, a country involved in multiple military activities, and in Israel, a country with a long-standing conflict with Palestine, this topic was represented much more prominently in the news than in the remaining countries, in which these issues played a rather marginal role.

Given the complex picture of both similarities and differences among the newscasts in the 17 countries, we present a supplementary visual analysis of the topics using multidimensional scaling. This procedure presents a visual representation of two sets of objects (in this case countries and topic coverage). The distance between single countries or clusters of countries indicates the degrees of similarity or dissimilarity.[1] For example, in Figure 3.1, Chile stands out from most of the other countries, close to the topic of sports, which is the topic that gets relatively more attention in Chile than in the other countries. In this sense, Chile is an outlier. The United States, on the other hand, is located in the centre of the cluster, very close to internal politics (with a high level because of its election coverage) but also not far from topics such as the economy, social issues, and so on, and not far from most of the other countries.

Figure 3.1 Positions of countries regarding topics in all news items (based on multidimensional unfolding)

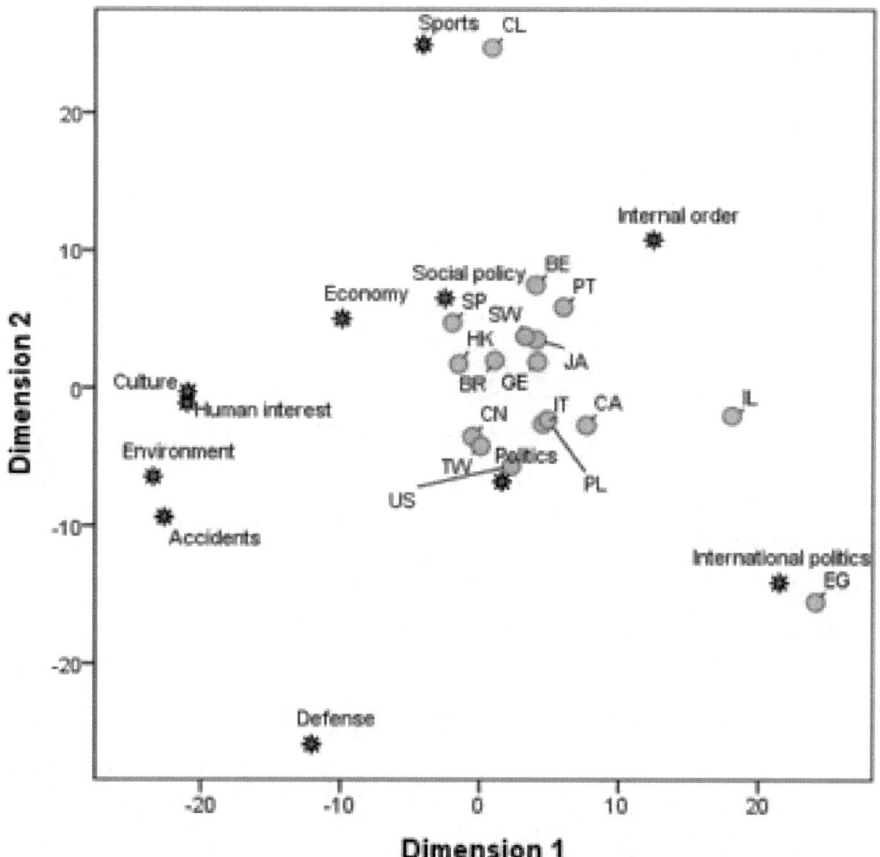

Legend: Belgium (BE), Brazil (BR), Canada (CA), Chile (CL), China (CN), Egypt (EG), Germany (GE), Hong Kong (HK), Israel (IL), Italy (IT), Japan (JP), Poland (PL), Portugal (PT), Singapore (SP), Switzerland (SW), Taiwan (TW), United States (US). "Politics" refers to internal politics.

The picture drawn by this analysis is quite clear. Regarding the topics, most countries shared about the same news content, with some relatively small variations here and there. There were no larger clusters or groups of countries separating themselves from the rest. Two countries, however, distinguish themselves as special cases. The first is Egypt. This North African country distinguishes itself from the others with a specific topic pattern. Especially when the topic of international politics is concerned, Egypt showed higher levels than any other country. Israel is the only country that comes close, but the difference is that in Israel much attention was paid to internal order, whereas in Egypt that was not the case. These findings may appear as a regional effect where the salience of the Israeli-Palestinian conflict is very high. For Israel, of course, this is not only an international conflict, but also an issue of internal order, which explains the different impact for each country.

Table 3.2 Main topic categories in domestic and foreign news by country (in percentage of total news time)

Country	Social issues		Internal politics		Internal order		Economy		International politics		Culture, religion, & ceremonies	
	D	F	D	F	D	F	D	F	D	F	D	F
Belgium	31	13	14	20	18	27	18	7	2	18	11	7
Brazil	39	14	19	8	17	6	20	24	2	53	18	3
Canada	24	18	26	33	22	28	14	8	14	26	12	8
Chile	25	10	10	5	24	13	14	14	0	17	12	8
China	40	14	41	12	6	13	17	13	3	31	5	14
Egypt	22	4	20	10	3	13	19	12	28	64	16	3
Germany	25	19	30	22	21	23	38	8	5	27	7	10
Hong Kong	29	5	19	36	16	23	31	7	3	15	7	9
Israel	28	12	16	28	36	18	10	6	22	38	12	11
Italy	13	9	37	20	28	19	9	16	2	19	10	15
Japan	19	16	21	16	24	19	32	20	1	32	2	1
Poland	29	19	32	29	24	17	21	8	7	25	12	11
Portugal	42	13	28	20	29	40	25	16	2	39	8	11
Singapore	48	14	4	34	13	13	31	19	2	10	13	10
Switzerland	27	19	20	38	24	25	22	10	5	20	23	13
Taiwan	20	13	38	20	13	16	15	12	0	10	8	12
United States	30	12	48	8	3	20	34	9	6	56	5	2
Total	29	13	25	22	20	21	20	12	5	29	11	9

Fashion, human interest, weather		Sports		Environment, energy, & science		Accidents and disasters		Military & defense		Total time in hours	
D	F	D	F	D	F	D	F	D	F	D	F
12	5	11	17	7	9	4	5	2	2	21.6	11.3
7	5	4	7	14	5	4	2	0	1	13.6	4.8
22	12	12	5	7	5	10	8	8	7	17.6	10.3
13	11	21	45	7	3	10	1	1	4	31.9	9.7
4	5	3	18	12	11	22	3	4	4	11.1	2.0
12	1	10	12	6	3	1	1	1	11	9.9	12.2
13	11	10	20	9	12	11	5	3	9	8.5	6.0
12	13	5	3	6	7	12	7	1	7	19.3	3.4
10	7	4	11	5	4	4	2	15	8	20.2	7.9
9	13	4	8	5	6	6	1	0	3	23.0	5.3
12	3	9	11	5	18	10	4	1	3	23.8	6.8
3	10	8	7	2	8	8	4	11	5	14.6	6.4
6	7	16	10	3	3	3	5	2	10	38.4	13.0
11	12	8	16	10	6	2	7	0	3	11.6	8.0
19	7	13	15	9	4	8	6	2	3	18.7	11.1
14	14	1	7	4	7	6	8	1	4	35.5	5.2
5	3	3	2	3	7	1	4	6	36	20.5	5.1
11	8	9	14	7	6	7	6	3	6	339.8	128.7

Another outlying country, as noted above, is Chile, mainly with regard to sports. One-quarter of Chilean television news was about sports. This occurs at the expense of topics such as internal politics, international politics, and military/defense. The remaining countries seem to cluster together, with average values for most topic categories similar to the entire sample. Only one additional small cluster can be distinguished, and that is internal politics, which groups the United States, Taiwan, Poland, China, and Italy. But the other countries are not placed far away. Taken as a whole, considering both domestic and foreign news together, other than the Middle East, there is no indication of a regional or other grouping of countries around topics.

Topics in Domestic News versus Foreign News

Looking separately at the distributions of the topics for domestic and foreign news is important in order to determine whether the patterns for these different types of news are similar or dissimilar. In order to present the data in a more concise fashion, we collapsed purely domestic news and domestic news with foreign involvement into one category (herewith domestic news) and purely foreign news and foreign news with domestic involvement as the second category (herewith foreign news).

Table 3.2 contrasts the percentages of news items dealing with the main topic categories between domestic and foreign news. News items dealing with social issues present the largest differences: there is a much greater prevalence of social issues in domestic news than in foreign news in all the countries in our sample. Given that social issues includes health, welfare, social services, social relations, housing, population, education, transportation and communication, the fact that they are more dominant in domestic news is virtually self-evident. Regarding news items dealing with economic issues, the picture is quite similar, although in Brazil and Italy this topic is more prominent in foreign news, while in Chile both types of news present the same level. As for internal politics, there are large cross-country differences. In the United States, Italy, Taiwan, and China, domestic news was largely dominated by internal politics, whereas internal politics of foreign countries was covered less frequently. In contrast, in Hong Kong, Singapore, and Switzerland, foreign news was dominated by internal politics. International politics, in turn, is a topic category that was almost only covered in foreign news, with the exception of Canada, Egypt, and Israel, where some domestic news items were about international politics.

These findings are also clearly noticeable in figure 3.2, a second multidimensional graphic presentation as in figure 3.1, but based only on domestic news items. Egypt stands out once again, but this time the country is less of an eremite, since it is in relatively close proximity to Israel and Canada. Another cluster consists of countries strongly focusing on their internal politics, including the United States, Italy, Taiwan, Poland, and China. More interestingly, there is also a third group visible in the graph—countries with a particularly high amount of coverage of economic news, including Brazil, Germany, Japan, and Hong Kong. In fact, Singapore, which appears quite remote, could be considered part of this group, since its news reported on a relatively large number of economic issues. Singapore appears far apart from the other countries, however, because of the remarkably low amount of attention paid to internal and international politics in its domestic news (4% and 2%, respectively). The other countries appear close together in the main group, focussing mostly on the largest category in domestic news, namely, social issues.

Figure 3.2 Positions of countries regarding topics in domestic news items (based on multidimensional unfolding)

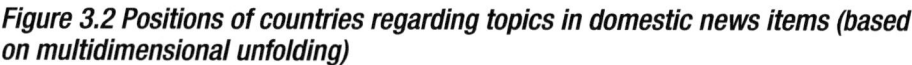

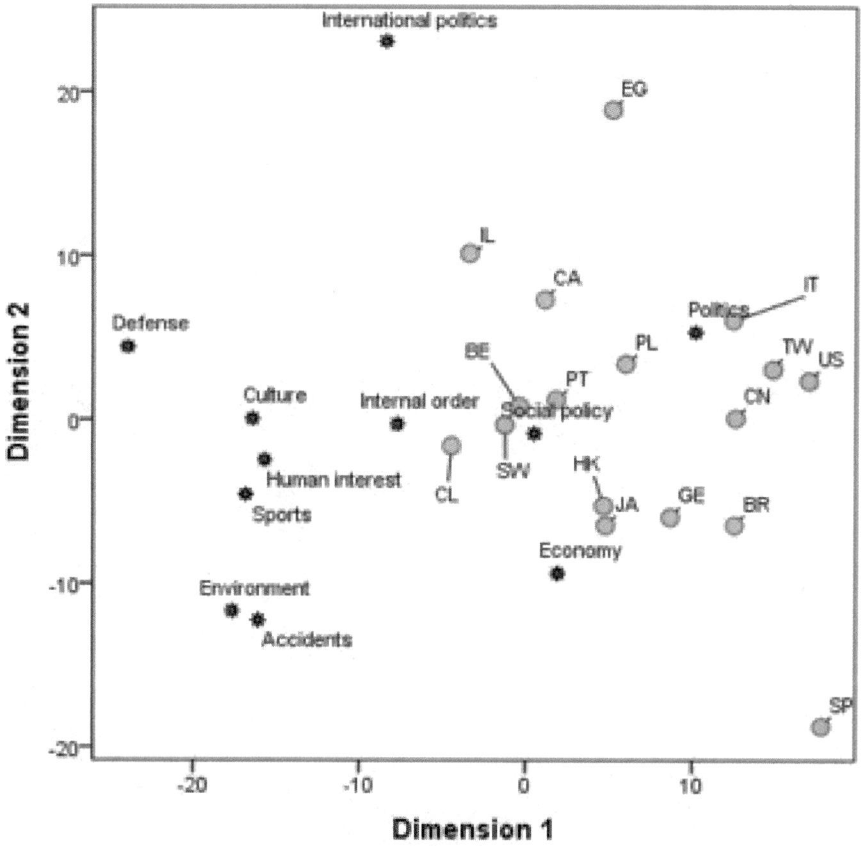

Legend: Belgium (BE), Brazil (BR), Canada (CA), Chile (CL), China (CN), Egypt (EG), Germany (GE), Hong Kong (HK), Israel (IL), Italy (IT), Japan (JP), Poland (PL), Portugal (PT), Singapore (SP), Switzerland (SW), Taiwan (TW), United States (US). "Politics" refers to internal politics.

The question is, of course, whether the same patterns of topics can be found with regard to foreign news. Figure 3.3 shows that this is generally not the case.

Once again, Chile's position is distinguished from the other countries, with about one-third of its foreign news about sports (for example, Spanish soccer). In addition, a new strong cluster appears. Instead of Egypt standing alone with a high level of attention to international politics, in foreign news there is a group of countries—Brazil, China, and the United States—with a higher percentage of foreign news devoted to international politics. It is probably not a coincidence that because

Figure 3.3 Positions of countries regarding topics in foreign news items (based on multidimensional unfolding)

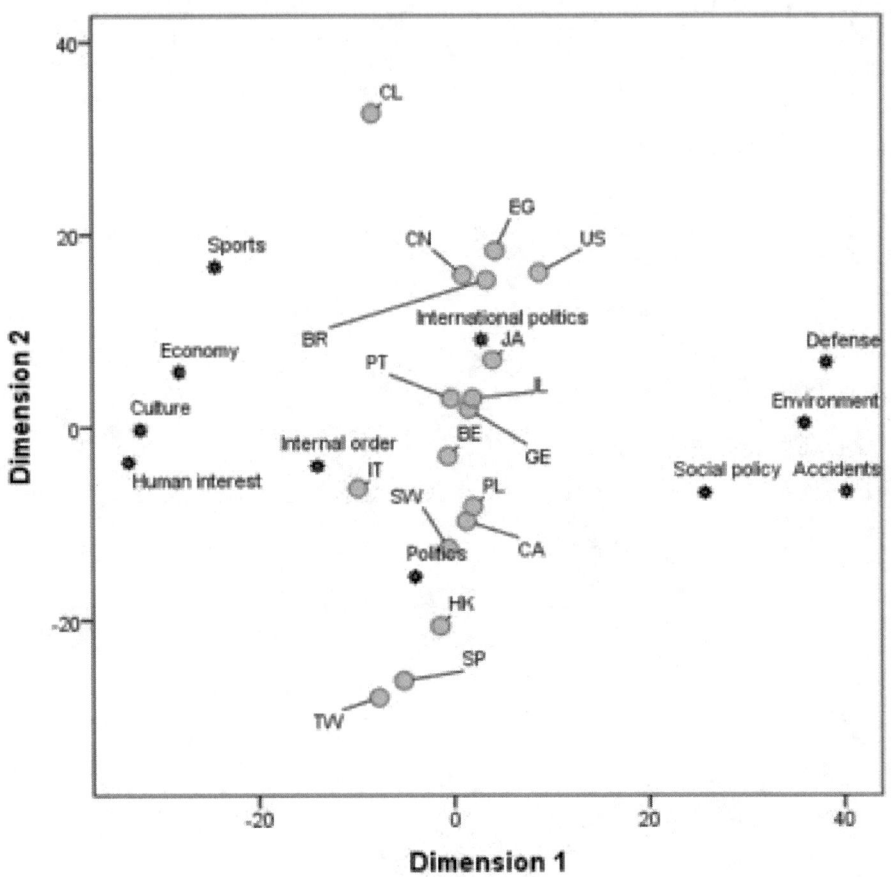

Legend: Belgium (BE), Brazil (BR), Canada (CA), Chile (CL), China (CN), Egypt (EG), Germany (GE), Hong Kong (HK), Israel (IL), Italy (IT), Japan (JP), Poland (PL), Portugal (PT), Singapore (SP), Switzerland (SW), Taiwan (TW), United States (US). "Politics" refers to internal politics.

these three large countries are economically and politically powerful, not only in their respective regions but in the world, domestic issues of other countries were of less interest and relevance to them, and therefore the foreign news they did present was oriented toward major international issues. There is also a cluster of numerous countries that gave prominence to internal politics (of other countries) in their foreign news: Belgium, Canada, Hong Kong, Poland, Singapore, Switzerland, and Taiwan. In several of these countries, the thrust of this coverage was the American primary elections; thus, at least part of this cluster may be explained by the interest (of the gatekeepers) in these countries in U.S. politics. Interestingly, there is no trace of a strong group of countries focusing on economic issues, as was the case with domestic news. None of the countries, either in domestic or in foreign news, seem to distinguish themselves by devoting clearly more or less attention to topics such as human interest, culture, or accidents and disasters.

Correlations between Topics According to Nature of the News Event

Our next objective was to determine whether the television channels in the 17 countries of our study held similar or different criteria for selecting news occurring inside or outside their territory according to purely domestic, purely foreign, and hybrid news types. To achieve this we calculated for each country six Spearman rank correlations—for all permutations of the four types of news—between the rankings of the amount of time devoted to each of the 25 main topic categories.

Table 3.3 Spearman rank correlations between time devoted to the 25 main topic categories of purely domestic (D), domestic with foreign involvement (DF), foreign with domestic involvement (FD), and purely foreign (F) by country

	D & DF	D & FD	D & F	DF & FD	DF & F	FD & F
Belgium	.65 ***	.48*	.37	.65***	.70***	.64***
Brazil	.51***	.31	.42*	.74***	.60**	.61***
Canada	.51***	.45*	.68***	.83***	.74***	.69***
Chile	.75***	.17	.36	.40*	.59**	.54**
China	.27	.02	.49*	.60**	.67***	.31
Egypt	.62**	.30	.51**	.70***	.67***	.67***
Germany	.49*	.35	.34	.63**	.59**	.74***
Hong Kong	.61**	.36	.33	.61**	.51**	.78***
Israel	.62**	.61**	.65**	.74***	.66***	.69***
Italy	.66**	.38	.37	.57**	.41*	.73***
Japan	.58**	.44*	.53**	.70***	.83***	.73***
Poland	.51**	.35	.41*	.65**	.57**	.74***
Portugal	.56**	.53**	.43*	.78***	.78***	.70***
Singapore	.76***	.55**	.53**	.80***	.63***	.81***
Switzerland	.61**	.39	.45*	.84***	.70***	.70***
Taiwan	.61**	.36	.70***	.62**	.70***	.77***
United States	.37	.53**	.53**	.16	.48*	.65***

*** $p < .001$; ** $p < .01$; * $p < .05$.

Table 3.3 shows that the correlation coefficients are generally high. This means that largely the same issues received prominence in the news for most countries, regardless of type of news concerned. Yet relatively speaking, the correlation between "the two extremes" (purely domestic news and purely foreign news) is often the lowest, and in some countries not even statistically significant (for example, Belgium, Chile, Germany, Hong Kong, and Italy). This means that the editors in these countries showed interest in different topics according to the type of news. For some others, such as Canada, Israel, Taiwan, the United States, and Japan, news topics were remarkably the same for domestic and foreign news. Even if they were not reporting on the same events and cases, they did seem to select them based on the same topic preferences. For example, when editors detected a certain interest on the part of their public for news about accidents or sports, they selected the same topics in foreign news as an indirect form of domestication. Foreign news was thus selected in terms of similar domestic thematic interests.

We must consider, though, that this analysis is slightly biased: the topic "international politics" tends to have only little relevance in purely domestic news and is bound to be more visible and more relevant in the other types of news. This trend tends to favor correlations between the types of news involving some degree of foreign news, which is exactly what Table 3.3 shows. The correlations with the purely domestic news type are structurally lower. However, regardless of this unavoidable handicap, the correlations are still remarkably high, which only strengthens the conclusion that topic patterns are rather dependent on a country or broadcaster-specific pattern of topic preferences, and that the type of news seems to have only a very limited influence on this topic selection for most countries in our sample.

Top 25 Individual Topics

Most of the analyses in this chapter have so far dealt with major topic categories that were created by collapsing the original long list of specific topic codes. It is interesting, however, to get at least a glimpse of some of the details within these larger categories. Thus, Table 3.4 presents a list of the 25 most frequently identified individual topics in the news across all countries in our sample, calculated on the basis of the amount of time devoted to the items. The table also specifies separately the relative rankings of these most prevalent topics among the domestic (including domestic with foreign involvement) and the foreign (including foreign with domestic involvement) news types, based on the complete list of over 200 topic codes.

The two broad topic areas highlighted most across all the countries were politics and sports. In the first case, the most prevalent specific news topics were elections, statements and activities of individual politicians, and international tension

Table 3.4 Percentages and rankings of top 25 individual news topics by total news time of items in domestic and foreign news.

	All News		Domestic		Foreign	
	Percent	Rank	Percent	Rank	Percent	Rank
Elections	9.0	1	7.0	2	14.2	1
Statements and activities of individual politicians	7.3	2	8.2	1	4.9	7
International tensions and disagreements	4.7	3	1.3	28	13.5	2
Individual athletes/coaches/teams	4.6	4	4.1	5	6.0	3
Crime investigation	4.2	5	4.5	3	3.3	13
State of economy	4.1	6	4.3	4	3.4	11
Sports results	3.3	7	2.4	11	5.7	4
Sports championships	3.0	8	2.3	14	4.9	6
Murder	3.0	9	2.7	9	3.6	9
Legislative activities	2.9	10	3.9	6	0.5	75
Business activities	2.9	11	3.5	7	1.4	27
Executive activities	2.7	12	3.2	8	1.3	32
Stock market situation	2.3	13	2.3	13	2.7	21
Judicial decisions	2.1	14	2.4	10	1.4	28
Celebrities	2.1	15	1.8	16	1.1	39
Military activities	2.1	16	1.0	48	5.0	5
Inter-party relations	2.0	17	2.4	12	1.1	40
Diplomatic visits	1.9	18	0.8	70	4.7	8
Non-celebrities	1.7	19	2.1	15	0.7	55
Wars between countries	1.7	20	1.0	47	3.5	10
Peaceful demonstrations	1.6	21	1.6	20	1.8	25
Internal party relations	1.6	22	1.8	17	0.9	46
Terrorism	1.5	23	1.0	54	3.0	15
Violent demonstrations	1.5	24	0.9	62	3.0	16
International terrorism	1.4	25	0.8	66	3.2	14

and disagreements. As for sports, the most prevalent topics reported on were individual athletes, coaches or teams, and results.

Elections dominated the list of both domestic and foreign news, but for foreign news the gap between elections and the other topics was much larger than for domestic news. This suggests that it was mostly the prominence of foreign elections, such as the U.S. primaries, that made this topic so dominant across all 17 countries during our sample period. And yet elections were also reported in other countries: presidential elections took place in Russia; in Italy a snap general election was held following the fall of the government coalition; and the aftermath of the election in Kenya received considerable attention because of a major crisis that occurred.

Indeed, elections were clearly the most dominant topic in the newscasts of 11 of the countries. Considering only the news about elections in foreign countries, nearly half of the items (48%) were about the U.S. primaries, and 12% referred to the Russian elections. There were also a considerable number of news items about elections in Malaysia, most of which, however, were reported in Singapore.

In domestic news, the predictable category of "Statements and activities of individual politicians" was the only topic that was more prominent than elections. The findings indicate that event-based news—in this context news on elections and international tensions—constituted a significant part of the daily foreign news diet, while on the other hand, in terms of domestic news, there was much prevalence of routine news content, that is, topics covered on a regular basis such as statements and activities of politicians, sports results, crime investigations, as well as legislative and business activities.

Major international conflicts that appeared in the news during the sample period were those between Israel and Palestine concerning the Gaza Strip, tensions among Colombia, Ecuador, and Venezuela, as well as the wars in Afghanistan and Iraq. Obviously, some topics that are clearly related to relationships between countries (such as wars, military activities, and diplomacy) were more prominent in foreign news, as well as in sports. Sports news seemed to be very international, unlike human-interest news about celebrities, which was more prominent in domestic news.

Hard, Soft, and Sensational News

So far, our analysis has been concerned with broad topics codes and specific topics. In recent years, there has been considerable debate within and outside the academy concerning the seeming decline of "hard" news in favor of "soft" and "sensational" news (see, for example, De Swert, 2007; Reinemann et al., 2012). This discussion has been growing along with the increasing commercialization of the media in general and the news industry in particular. However, little or no attention has been devoted to the question of whether these hard and soft news topics are equally prevalent within domestic and foreign news. In other words, does foreign news generally contribute to a higher level of hard news in television newscasts, or is soft news more dominant in news from abroad?

Table 3.5 Hard, soft, and sensational news by country and news type (in percentage of news time)

Country	Hard news		Soft news		Sensational news		Number of cases	
	Domestic	Foreign	Domestic	Foreign	Domestic	Foreign	Domestic	Foreign
Belgium	64.7	63.4	27.8	24.0	21.6	31.0	912	508
Brazil	78.0	85.8	23.1	13.9	20.4	7.7	532	252
Canada	74.1	78.3	32.9	17.6	31.1	35.9	423	326
Chile	52.5	43.1	40.7	57.4	33.1	10.6	1,056	450
China	85.0	70.8	27.8	31.4	26.0	13.8	569	215
Egypt	82.4	85.1	25.5	14.7	3.9	10.5	245	465
Germany	80.0	72.2	23.5	33.6	27.1	26.0	401	341
Hong Kong	82.1	72.2	17.9	17.2	23.6	28.0	633	165
Israel	76.0	76.4	22.1	25.1	33.1	18.1	757	371
Italy	59.6	73.1	20.3	25.3	32.5	17.2	1,073	292
Japan	65.4	79.6	17.9	13.1	32.7	22.3	703	192
Poland	82.4	76.3	16.9	24.1	30.6	19.1	353	187
Portugal	74.9	74.8	27.5	21.7	29.0	41.0	1,258	449
Singapore	82.7	73.5	24.6	31.9	13.1	18.1	545	447
Switzerland	67.6	76.3	41.5	28.1	31.1	28.9	789	591
Taiwan	73.2	62.5	21.3	29.7	17.5	21.1	1,161	185
U.S.	96.0	93.7	11.5	5.4	4.1	19.7	475	179
Total	72.9	73.5	25.3	24.8	25.3	23.2	11,885	5,615

There are several approaches to distinguishing between hard, soft, and sensational news. Hard news topics are more likely to be about policy or policy-relevant issues (Scott & Gobetz, 1992), including defense, financial news, social security, international politics, and so forth. Soft news topics, on the other hand, are included in newscasts in order to make the news lighter and easier to digest, and mostly lack immediate policy relevance (Baum & Jamison, 2006; Graber, 2003; Langer, 1992; Servaes & Tonnaer, 1992). Soft news is often considered as crucial in keeping the audience interested and on track with society (Zelizer, 2000). In addition, from a policy perspective, soft news items lack urgency (Tuchman, 1973). Besides, in line with what Fiske (1992) referred to as "tabloid news," sensational topics are events that appeal to the emotions and instincts of the audience. In our study, sensational news topics include items dealing with crime incidents (as part of internal order) and traffic accidents and disasters. Soft news includes sports, popular culture, fashion, ceremonies, weather, human-interest stories, and celebrities. Finally, hard news includes all other policy-related topic categories: internal politics, international politics, social issues, economy, military and defense, environment, energy, and sciences, as well as sports policy and crime policy. Of course, it is not impossible to find soft or sensational news items that are also partly policy related. In such cases, our coding procedure resorted to including an additional hard news topic code for the same news item. Thus, the sum of the percentages of the three columns in Table 3.5 may exceed 100%.

Taking all countries together, Table 3.5 shows that hard news overwhelmingly dominates the newscasts with about 73% of all broadcast time. In addition, the proportions of soft and sensational news were nearly equal (about 25% for soft news and 24% for sensational news). Moreover, for all three categories—hard, soft, and sensational—the overall percentages across all the countries were nearly identical between domestic and foreign news.

However, when examining the 17 countries within each of the three categories, significant differences emerge pointing to considerable variability. In the case of domestic hard news, the range is from 96% in the United States to nearly 53% in Chile. Between these two extremes lie China, Egypt, Germany, Hong Kong, Poland, and Singapore with 80–90%; Brazil, Canada, Israel, Portugal, and Taiwan with 70–80%; and Belgium, Italy, Japan, and Switzerland with less than 70% domestic news. As for foreign hard news, the percentage was notably greater than for domestic hard news in Brazil, Italy, Japan, and Switzerland, while it was notably lower in Chile, China, Germany, Hong Kong, Poland, Singapore, and Taiwan. In Canada, Egypt, Israel, Portugal, and the United States, there were virtually no differences.

Regarding soft news, there was also considerable variability across the countries. As for domestic soft news, the highest levels were in Switzerland and Chile (both around 41%) and Canada (33%), and the lowest was in the United States (4%). As for foreign soft news, the highest level was in Chile (57%), which, as noted earlier, presented considerable amounts of sports news. The lowest levels of foreign soft news were in the United States (5%); Brazil, Canada, Egypt, Hong Kong, and Japan (10–20%); and Belgium, Israel, Poland, Portugal, Switzerland, and Taiwan (20–30%). In contrast, China, Germany, and Singapore exceeded 30% foreign soft news. Comparing the percentage of soft news in domestic and foreign coverage, there was (1) notably less soft domestic news in Chile, Germany, Poland, Singapore, and Taiwan; (2) notably more soft domestic news in Brazil, Canada, Egypt, Portugal, Switzerland, and the United States; and (3) little or no difference in Belgium, China, Hong Kong, Israel, Italy, and Japan.

Finally, regarding sensational news, there were also some differences between the domestic and foreign domains. Sensational domestic news was highly evident in Canada, Chile, Israel, Italy, Japan, Poland, and Switzerland (all slightly more than 30%). The lowest levels were in Egypt and the United States (4%), and in the remaining countries, the range was from 13% in Singapore to 29% in Portugal. Sensational foreign news, on the other hand, was most prevalent in Portugal (41%) and in Canada (36%). The lowest levels of sensational foreign news were in Brazil (8%) and in Chile (11%). In the remaining countries the range was from 11% in Egypt to 31% in Belgium. Comparing the percentage of sensational news in domestic and foreign coverage, there was a higher level in foreign news in Belgium, Egypt, Portugal, and the United States. In addition, there was a lower level in Brazil, Chile (with a 23% difference), China, Israel, Italy, Japan, and Poland. Finally, in Canada, Germany, Hong Kong, Switzerland, and Taiwan, the differences were no greater than 5%.

In sum, while a first glance suggests much similarity across the 17 countries of the study between domestic and foreign news in hard, soft, and sensational news, these data seem to mask quite profound differences between domestic and foreign news in several countries. In addition, the differences among the counties were generally far greater than those between domestic and foreign news within a single country.

Entropy and Topic Diversity

Even if there is no formula for an ideal newscast, one could expect a television news broadcast to provide information to the public about a variety of issues, so that in the end, the public is informed about most topics relevant for society in a relatively equal manner. In order to get a grasp on the extent of diversity of television news in the countries of our study, we used Shannon's H entropy measurement as an indicator.

Shannon's H Information Entropy

$$Entropy = -\sum_{i=1}^{n} p(x_i) * \log_n p(x_i)$$

Where x represents a topic; $p(x_i)$ is the proportion of total attention the topic receives; $\log_n p(x_i)$ is the log of the proportion of attention the topic receives, using the total number of possible topics as the base of the log.[2]

Shannon's H entropy increases as the spread of attention across all topics is closer to equality. In other words, as more topics are treated in similar proportions, the higher Shannon's H value becomes. Thus, for example, a broadcaster that devotes half of the newscast to sports will have a lower entropy value, since it is most likely that fewer topics can be covered in the remainder of the newscast, and because the attention to sports will be disproportionately high compared to all the other topics. On the other hand, a newscast that devotes (roughly) equal attention to all possible topics—which of course is but a hypothetical situation—would receive a high entropy score.

Table 3.6 presents the topic entropy scores for all countries in the sample, based on the attention given to the 11 main topic categories. We present three values for each country: one for the diversity of all news items in the sample, one for domestic news, and one for foreign news.

Table 3.6 Shannon H entropy scores by country for all coverage, domestic news, and foreign news (based on 11-topic categorization)

Country	N of items (all coverage)	All coverage	Domestic coverage	Foreign coverage
Belgium	1,420	3.22	3.12	3.17
Brazil	784	3.12	2.94	2.66
Canada	749	3.29	3.34	3.15
Chile	1,506	3.18	3.09	2.92
China	784	3.04	2.86	3.22
Egypt	711	2.94	3.05	2.54
Germany	742	3.29	3.13	3.30
Hong Kong	798	3.14	3.05	3.10
Israel	1,128	3.17	3.15	3.06
Italy	1,365	3.01	2.85	3.20
Japan	895	3.13	2.96	3.06
Poland	540	3.19	3.10	3.20
Portugal	1,707	3.06	2.88	3.09
Singapore	992	2.93	2.75	3.22
Switzerland	1,382	3.26	3.23	3.13
Taiwan	1,346	2.92	2.80	3.35
United States	654	2.91	2.61	2.72
Total	17,502	3.26	3.18	3.23

From this table, it becomes clear that there were striking differences in issue diversity between countries, and also between domestic and foreign news coverage. Overall, German and Canadian television news was most diverse—Germany mainly because of its highly diverse foreign news, while in Canada it was because of relatively great domestic news diversity. Egypt and the United States presented the least topically diverse newscasts. In the United States, this was mainly due to its great emphasis on primary election news. In Egypt, it was attributable primarily to the overall low level of diversity of foreign news.

While across all countries foreign news seemed to be slightly more topically diverse (3.23 vs. 3.18), this was certainly not the case for all countries in the sample. In Brazil, for example, where topic diversity was generally low, domestic news was more diverse than foreign news. Other countries where foreign news was less diverse than domestic news were Canada, Chile, Egypt, Israel, and Switzerland. In most cases, this may have been due to one or two topics disproportionately attracting much attention.

Conclusion

In this chapter, we have discussed the topics in the newscasts of our study. We can draw several major conclusions. First, local factors appear to dominate the specific topic agendas in each country. For domestic news, this should be quite self-evident; but it is also the case for topic selection of foreign news differing among the countries. Similarities among countries were not dominant regarding foreign news. This is the case even though the greater world abroad is essentially the same vis-à-vis the various countries in the sample, compared with the obvious particularities of domestic news. Although we did identify some clustering of specific topic preferences, we were unable to discern any particular rationale or logic that would explain them. This brings us to the conclusion that very specific country situations (such as the high level of international politics in Egypt and the unusually heavy coverage of sports in Chile) are the driving force behind the clusters. In addition, some clustering may be due to specific events in certain countries. For example, Italy and the United States devoted significant broadcast time to their respective and upcoming elections, thus increasing the prominence of internal political news.

At the same time, there is another possible way of looking at the findings, one that emphasizes similarities. Apart from the countries mentioned above, most of the countries in our sample appear to be on the same page when aggregating the specific topics. When we use the three broad categories of hard news, soft news, and sensational news, the similarities between countries seem to outweigh the differences. Hard news was the bulk of the newscasts in all countries (other than Chile), and levels of sensational topics in the news were remarkably similar for all the countries, even if many of the systemic factors influencing levels of sensationalism across the countries are quite different.

Apart from discovering how gatekeepers in the various countries dealt with comparable topics in the news, our focus was to learn how similar or how different the domestic and foreign news agendas were. Beyond the fact that some topics are inherently either domestic or foreign, there are few indicators used by broadcasters as differential selection criteria. The aggregation of topics confirms this. Taking all broadcasters together, the differences between foreign and domestic news appear to be limited. The only difference was that foreign news coverage appeared to be slightly less sensational than domestic news. Yet the comparison between levels of hard, soft, and sensational news within the foreign and domestic news of each broadcaster revealed some further variation. What are notable are the low correlations between the levels of sensational topics in domestic and foreign news, thus suggesting that within broadcasters, sensational news is often treated differently in domestic and foreign news.

Finally, the entropy measures provided us with insight on how diverse the selection of the different topics by the various news organizations was. If we accept the normative perspective that in a democracy, high-quality and frequently watched newscasts are a key to public sense making, it is important to understand that a broad spectrum of topics—even including soft and sensational news—is a positive feature of television news. Even though some differences in entropy among the countries do exist, they are arguably small, thereby indicating that television news is relatively diverse all over. Yet even if we consider small differences, it appears that foreign news is generally more diverse than domestic news.

In this chapter, the analysis of the topics did not deal with the important distinctions between public and commercial broadcasters, specifically regarding hard, soft, and sensational news. These issues are presented and discussed in Chapter 7 of this volume.

Summary

This chapter focused on the topics covered by domestic and foreign news in the 17 countries of the study. The main finding across the various broadcasters revealed that not only domestic, but also foreign news coverage, is mostly driven by local, country-specific preferences and situations. Foreign news topics covered in one country are quite different from foreign news topics covered in another. And yet the picture is not entirely eclectic. First, a more general analysis of hard, soft, and sensational news indicated more similarities than differences: hard news remains dominant everywhere. Second, the amount of diversity among news topics appeared to be rather similar in most countries, with greater variability of foreign news topics compared with topics of domestic news.

Notes

1   The multidimensional procedure used was PREFSCAL in SPSS, with the relative amount of coverage for the 11 topic categories as a basis in each country in this study. See Heiser and Busing (2004) for a description of the procedure.
2   For examples of the use of this measurement in political science, see Boydstun (2008) and Sheingate (2006).
3. he columns in the table (from left to right) are presented from the most prevalent topics (social issues) across the 17 countries to the least prevalent (military and defense) As each news item could be coded for as many as three topic categories, the total values may exceed 100%.

CHAPTER FOUR

Countries of Location and Countries Involved

JÜRGEN WILKE, CHRISTINE HEIMPRECHT, & YOUICHI ITO

In this chapter we present two aspects of our findings from the content analyses conducted in the 17 countries. The main question here is which countries and regions of the world are presented as foreign news in the newscasts (from the perspective of the countries of broadcast) and to what extent are they represented? We answer this question in two ways. Our main focus is on where the reported events occurred (countries of location). In addition, we examine which countries were involved in the events, assuming that foreign news often refers to countries beyond the country of location.

The question of which countries are covered by foreign news is one of the most venerable and established in communication and media research. As early as the 1930s, Woodward (1930) counted the amount of news in the American press dedicated to different countries. The focus of that research was extended in post-World War II studies to include all the countries in the world (Kayser, 1953; IPI, 1953). Since the 1960s, the issue has received further attention in the context of the debate over the New World Information and Communication Order (Sreberny-Mohammadi, 1984; Sreberny-Mohammadi et al., 1985; Stevenson & Shaw, 1984; Schenk, 1987).

In the 1980s the term "geography of news" was coined by Schulz (1983) and used by Kamps (1998) in order to describe which countries or regions of the world are represented in the news. Others have used the terms "map" or "mapping," suggesting that people construct mental maps on the basis of the news they receive (Atwood & Buillon, 1982). In this respect, the study by Gerbner and Marvanyi (1977) was very impressive, as they compared, based on 60 newspapers from 9 countries, a "real" map of the world with the maps (the "worlds") created by the news coverage in newspapers in the United States, Western Europe, Eastern Europe, the Soviet Union, and several third world countries. Their study was based on the "necessarily arbitrary assumption that each region has equal chance of newsworthiness" (Gerbner & Marvanyi, 1977, p. 57), which is obviously not the case.

Number of Countries of Location

We use the term "news geography" to describe the extent to which the foreign news coverage from our 17 countries featured content relating to other countries and territories in the world. In no country are the media able to comprehensively report news from all over the world, nor would that be in the interest of their audiences. Moreover, the basic task of journalists is to decide which countries they wish to cover and thus determine the "world view" that the media convey.

Our codebook for the content analysis included a list of 244 countries, territories, and regions around the world. The list contains many more entities than the 192 current members of the United Nations, as it includes territories that are attached or incorporated into other countries, but have governing bodies of their own (for example, Tibet, which is claimed by the People's Republic of China as part of its territory). The list also contains regions of the world (for instance, Europe, Asia, Southeast Asia, the Middle East, South America, and so on), used when items made reference to regions rather than (or in addition to) specific countries.

News geography can basically be captured in terms of two characteristics: (1) countries of location of the events and (2) countries involved. Each news item was coded for the countries/territories/regions of location of the event being reported—as specifically indicated in the item—as well as the countries/territories/regions reported to be involved in the story (without necessarily using the term "involved"). Sometimes an event could take place in more than one location (say, a war on the border between two countries, or meetings taking place simultaneously in several places). Also, several countries could be referred to in an item as being involved in the event, even though it takes place elsewhere. The codebook allowed for coding up to three countries of location and five countries involved (we always included the country of location as a country involved, hence the number of countries involved could be minimally equal to the number of countries of location or larger). In 90% of news items, only one location was identified; in 7.4% there were two locations; and in 2.6% of the cases three locations were specified.

When looking at all 17 countries (see Table 4.1), we found that during the 4 weeks in our early 2008 sample, 132 sovereign and internationally recognized states were identified at least once as a country of location. In addition, two non-recognized states (by the United Nations)—Abkhazia and Kosovo—were identified as the location of events. In six cases, independent governing bodies affiliated with other states (Hong Kong, Macao, and the Netherlands Antilles), were identified. This means that, altogether, slightly more than half of the potential countries and territories in the world (56%) were dealt with by at least one country's news, while slightly less than half (46%) were not covered even once during this 4-week period.

Among the countries not identified at all were Albania, Bulgaria, Slovakia, and Slovenia in Europe; Burkina Faso, Eritrea, Gambia, Liberia, and Zambia in Africa; Kazakhstan, Kyrgyzstan, and Laos in Asia; and Belize, El Salvador, and Paraguay in Central and South America. Another 22 countries or territories ap-

Table 4.1 Number of countries of location in foreign news broadcasts and number of foreign news items

Country of TV broadcast	n of countries covered	n of foreign news items	Share of foreign news in percent	Average n of foreign news items per country
Egypt	70	464	65	6.6
Switzerland	70	591	43	8.4
Belgium	67	508	36	7.6
Germany	63	341	46	5.4
Israel	63	371	33	5.9
China	58	215	27	3.7
Italy	52	292	21	5.6
Chile	49	450	30	9.2
Canada	49	326	44	6.7
Portugal	48	449	26	9.4
Brazil	45	252	32	5.6
Taiwan	43	185	14	4.3
Singapore	40	447	45	11.2
Poland	39	187	35	4.8
Hong Kong	37	165	21	4.5
United States	36	179	27	5.0
Japan	28	192	22	6.9
Average	50	330	33	6.5

peared in only one news story, and 17 appeared in only two stories in the 4-week period. The countries in sub-Saharan Africa in particular were not represented at all in the foreign coverage in the time frame we studied. Of course, no single country dealt with all the countries that were in the news, and the variability—as we shall soon describe—was tremendous.

The greatest number of countries featured in the foreign news coverage during the period of analysis was found in Egypt and Switzerland (70 each), with the lowest in the United States (36) and Japan (28). Basically, three groups emerged: one in which the number of countries covered was rather high (Belgium, Germany, Israel, and China, in addition to Egypt and Switzerland); a second group that covered a smaller number of countries in their newscasts (Italy, Chile, Canada, Portugal, Brazil, and Taiwan); and finally, a third group of nations that covered a low number of countries (Singapore, Poland, Hong Kong, the United States, and Japan).

When relating the number of countries covered to the total amount of foreign news coverage, a distinct dispersion in the average number of newscasts emerged. The 40 countries featured in the foreign news coverage in Singapore appear quite often, on average in 11 newscasts each. On the other hand, in Taiwan, Hong Kong, and Poland, where the number of foreign TV broadcasts was generally low (and the number of countries covered was similar to that of Singapore), all countries appeared quite rarely (no more than in four or five news reports each). A great deal of foreign news about many different countries was found in Switzerland and Belgium, two small European states, in which television seems to cast a wide glance at the outside world.

Continental Regions

Countries from five continental regions are represented in our study: five from Asia, six from Europe, two from North America, two from South America, and two from the Middle East. This enables us in the next step of our analysis to describe to what degree countries within these regions are covered in foreign news.

The most-covered continent/region worldwide was Europe (33%), followed by North America (24%), the Middle East (20%), Asia (19%), South America (12%), and Australia/Oceania and Africa (3% each). However, the most striking observation is that newscasts in each country (with the exception of North America) focus primarily on their own continent. This confirms that regionalism was the most universal feature in news selection.

However, this was the case in differing degrees. As Table 4.2 indicates, television journalists in European countries seem to favor their home continent (55%) (Wilke & Heimprecht, 2011). The home continent bias was weaker in the other regions: Asia was covered in 46% of Asian foreign TV news, South America in 40%, and the Middle East in 38% of their respective newscasts. The relatively

Table 4.2 Proportion of continental regions and countries in foreign news coverage on TV (in percent)

Coverage in:		Coverage of:								
		Europe	North America	Asia	Middle East	South America	Australia/ Oceania	Africa	Antarctica	Total
Asia		25	26	46	5	2	5	1	1	111
	China	47	17	30	8	6	3	6	1	118
	Hong Kong	23	42	26	8	3	3	0	1	106
	Japan	15	47	35	4	0	4	1	3	109
	Singapore	22	13	62	3	0	9	0	0	109
	Taiwan	22	35	50	5	5	3	1	1	122
Europe		55	18	12	14	4	4	4	0	111
	Belgium	57	16	9	15	3	5	4	0	109
	Germany	48	18	13	20	3	3	6	0	111
	Italy	50	26	16	17	3	1	2	1	116
	Poland	72	21	9	6	3	2	0	0	113
	Portugal	50	14	15	11	9	3	7	0	109
	Switzerland	58	16	11	16	3	5	2	1	112
North America		18	36	18	37	8	2	6	2	127
	Canada	20	54	17	21	4	3	5	1	125
	United States	14	5	19	65	15	2	6	3	129
South America		34	21	8	5	40	2	1	1	112
	Brazil	36	30	14	9	23	1	2	0	115
	Chile	33	16	5	4	49	2	0	1	110
Middle East		31	19	11	38	4	3	6	0	112
	Egypt	36	15	11	34	4	2	8	0	110
	Israel	25	24	10	42	4	4	4	0	113

* For each news item, up to three countries could be coded. The news reports are weighted by their length in relation to the duration of the newscast

lowest margin for the home continent was North America (36%). Of course, this region consists of only two countries, Canada and the United States, which are quite different in their orientation. While in Canada more than half of the stories were located in the United States, only one-twentieth of the American stories were located in Canada. This was, once again, an indicator of the asymmetrical, one-way flow in which the United States predominates.

Europe was the second most covered continent in South America and the Middle East, and the same was true of North America in Asia and Europe. However, the proportions of the Asian newscasts dedicated to Europe and North America were almost equal (25% and 26%, respectively). The same was the case for Europe and Asia in the North American news (18% each). In TV news in the

Middle East, North America was the third most covered continent. The other three continents were more or less underrepresented in the foreign news of the 17 countries. The low percentage of news from Africa and Australia, of course, results from the fact that no TV newscasts from these continents were included in our study, and that the Australian continent is essentially one country. However, an examination of South America shows that Chilean TV newscasts have a stronger preference for stories from South America (49%) than do those of Brazil (23%), which seem to focus more on Europe and North America as compared to Chile. If one looks at the individual countries from each continent (see below), we note that Singapore was the most Asian-centric country (62%), Poland was the most Euro-centric (72%), and the United States was the most Middle Eastern-centric (65%).

The Most-Covered Countries

We now shift our focus to the presence of individual countries and territories in the newscasts. Relatively few countries tend to make up the bulk of foreign news coverage. In order to determine their geographic (and political) concentration, it is useful to analyze what portion of this coverage can be attributed to no more than the 10 most-prevalent countries.

For this we calculated a Country Concentration Index (CCI). The CCI indicates the percentage of all the foreign news coverage for each of the 17 countries based on the 10 most-prevalent countries. Table 4.3 presents each of the 17 countries in ascending order of their CCI scores. The data show that there was much variability among the countries.

The highest CCI score—that is, the lowest dispersion rate—was found in the foreign news coverage by Japanese television. In Japan, 96% of all news items dealt with 10 countries or territories (whereas 83% of all the items dealt with no more than 5 countries). The lowest CCI score was found in Germany, where only slightly more than half of the foreign news items focused on 10 countries. In other words, a considerable number of the foreign news reports from the two German TV stations covered additional countries.

How can these differences in the share of foreign news be explained? It seems that in several countries, foreign news reporting as a whole might be of relatively little importance; and when such reports do appear in the news—as in the case of Japan, the United States, Hong Kong, Israel, and Singapore—they were limited to a few countries. In other cases, the amount of foreign news was not exactly very low, but only a few countries were ever the center of attention. This seems to be typical of Israeli news, for example. The countries with relatively low concentration fell into two groups: those with many foreign news reports (for example, Egypt and Switzerland) and others with relatively few foreign news reports (for example, China).

Table 4.3 Country Concentration Indexes (CCI) for the top 10 countries of location in the foreign TV news of all countries (in ascending order)

Country of broadcast	CCI (10)
Germany	54
China	58
Egypt	59
Switzerland	62
Belgium	64
Italy	66
Portugal	67
Poland	68
Brazil	71
Chile	71
Taiwan	72
Canada	72
Singapore	74
Israel	74
Hong Kong	74
United States	76
Japan	96

We now move on to a more detailed analysis of the 10 most-covered countries and territories in the newscasts of the 17 countries. The country that was featured most in television news around the globe was the United States. Across all countries, more than one-fifth of all the foreign news was located there. Five of the other 10 most-covered countries were European, with the United Kingdom (UK) at the top of the list, followed by France, Spain, Russia, and Germany. The European countries together represented 21.5% of the coverage. The crises and the military actions in the Middle East may be the reason why three countries from that region—Palestine, Israel, and Iraq—were among the 10 most-covered. The fact that China was the only Asian country among the 10 most-covered may reflect its growing political and economic significance in the world.

When examining these data for the individual countries (see Table 4.4), we get an even more impressive picture of the outstanding position the United States takes in the foreign news of the world. In 10 of the 16 countries (not including the United States itself, of course), the United States was the most-covered country in the news in Belgium, Brazil, Canada, Germany, Hong Kong, Israel, Italy, Switzerland, Taiwan, and Japan. In the six remaining countries, the United States

Table 4.4 Proportion of news featuring top 10 countries of location in countries of study

Country of broadcast	Country of location	Percent of all foreign news items	Country of broadcast	Country of location	Percent of all foreign news items
Belgium	United States	15	Brazil	United States	32
	France	13		Colombia	10
	United Kingdom	7		France	8
	Netherlands	6		Ecuador	7
	Australia	6		Venezuela	5
	Europe	5		United Kingdom	5
	Spain	5		Spain	5
	Italy	4		East Timor	4
	Israel	4		China	4
	Palestine	4		Germany	3
	Others	39		Others	34
	CCI (10)	64		CCI (10)	71
	N of countries	67		N of countries	45
	N (foreign news)	508		N (foreign news)	252
Canada	United States	49	Chile	Argentina	21
	United Kingdom	8		United States	16
	Israel	7		Brazil	9
	Afghanistan	4		Spain	8
	Cuba	4		Colombia	7
	Pakistan	3		Ecuador	4
	China	3		Italy	4
	Palestine	3		United Kingdom	3
	Italy	3		Israel	3
	France	3		Venezuela	3
	Others	35		Others	32
	CCI (10)	72		CCI (10)	71
	N of countries	49		N of countries	49
	N (foreign news)	326		N (foreign news)	450

was the second most covered country. This dominance, which can be found in all continents and has also been established in previous studies, can be attributed to the fact that the United States is the only remaining superpower in the world. The intensive coverage in early 2008 focused mainly on the primary elections leading to the general election later that year. In addition to its internal politics, however, America's political and military power and geopolitical position, its economic strength, its trading volume, and social and cultural life (including sports) also help to create its news value.

Country of broadcast	Country of location	Percent of all foreign news items	Country of broadcast	Country of location	Percent of all foreign news items
China	Greece	14	Egypt	Palestine	16
	United States	12		United States	10
	United Kingdom	11		Syria	8
	Japan	7		Iraq	7
	Russia	6		Lebanon	5
	South Korea	6		Kosovo	4
	Algeria	5		Pakistan	4
	Germany	4		United Kingdom	3
	Belgium	4		Russia	3
	Mauritania	4		Israel	3
	Others	51		Others	44
	CCI (10)	58		CCI (10)	59
	N of countries	58		N of countries	70
	N (foreign news)	215		N (foreign news)	464
Germany	United States	17	Hong Kong	United States	44
	United Kingdom	7		Russia	7
	Italy	6		United Kingdom	5
	Palestine	5		South Korea	4
	Russia	5		Japan	4
	Israel	5		Palestine	4
	Norway	4		France	3
	Egypt	4		Iraq	3
	Sweden	4		Malaysia	2
	Spain	4		Pakistan	2
	Others	52		Others	27
	CCI (10)	54		CCI (10)	74
	N of countries	63		N of countries	37
	N (foreign news)	341		N (foreign news)	165

There are different reasons behind the fact that, in six of the countries analyzed, states other than the United States featured more frequently as foreign news. Generally speaking, neighboring countries were covered more intensively: Argentina in Chile; Russia in Poland; Spain in Portugal; Malaysia in Singapore; and Palestine in Egypt. Here, the predominance of regionalism that had been observed in previous studies (Schulz, 1983; Sreberny-Mohammadi et al., 1985; Schenk, 1987; Wilke & Heimprecht, 2011) is established once more.

The only deviation in this pattern can be seen in news broadcasts on Chinese television. In China, in early 2008, Greece was the most-covered country (14%). This can be explained by the fact that the Olympic torch was lit in Olympia,

Country of broadcast	Country of location	Percent of all foreign news items	Country of broadcast	Country of location	Percent of all foreign news items
Israel	United States	25	Italy	United States	24
	Palestine	19		Vatican City	8
	Egypt	8		United Kingdom	7
	Lebanon	7		France	7
	Syria	7		Palestine	6
	United Kingdom	7		Spain	6
	France	4		Europe	6
	Germany	3		Germany	4
	Australia	3		ASIA	4
	Russia	2		Israel	3
	Others	30		Others	39
	CCI (10)	74		CCI (10)	66
	N of countries	63		N of countries	52
	N (foreign news)	371		N (foreign news)	292
Japan	United States	40	Poland	Russia	23
	China	21		United States	18
	South Korea	5		Germany	7
	Germany	4		United Kingdom	7
	Bahrain	3		Ukraine	7
	ANTARCTIC	3		France	4
	OUTER SPACE	3		Switzerland	3
	Russia	2		Serbia	3
	United Kingdom	2		Italy	3
	Guam	1		OUTER SPACE	3
	Others	16		Others	37
	CCI (10)	96		CCI (10)	68
	N of countries	28		N of countries	39
	N (foreign news)	192		N (foreign news)	187

Greece, at the time of analysis, and set out on its way to Beijing, where the Olympic summer games were to take place several months later. Thus, the Chinese interest in Greece at this point in time was clearly triggered by ethnocentric motives. Greece did not occupy a position among the 10 most-covered countries in the foreign news in any of the other countries.

Not only in Europe, but also across the board, the second most important country in terms of foreign news coverage, following the United States, was the United Kingdom. In 15 of the 17 countries analyzed, the United Kingdom was among the most-covered countries. This might be more a consequence of its long-

Country of broadcast	Country of location	Percent of all foreign news items	Country of broadcast	Country of location	Percent of all foreign news items
Portugal	Spain	21	Singapore	Malaysia	20
	United States	14		United States	15
	East Timor	11		China	11
	United Kingdom	5		Japan	7
	Kosovo	5		Taiwan	7
	Iraq	4		United Kingdom	6
	Brazil	4		Australia	5
	Italy	3		Hong Kong	4
	Mozambique	3		Thailand	3
	France	3		ASIA	3
	Others	36		Others	28
	CCI (10)	67		CCI (10)	74
	N of countries	48		N of countries	40
	N (foreign news)	449		N (foreign news)	447
Switzerland	United States	16	Taiwan	United States	35
	France	12		China	19
	Germany	7		Hong Kong	8
	United Kingdom	7		South Korea	5
	Italy	6		Europe	4
	Israel	5		Australia	4
	Palestine	5		United Kingdom	3
	Australia	5		ASIA	3
	Kosovo	4		Germany	3
	Serbia	4		Japan	3
	Others	43		Others	34
	CCI (10)	62		CCI (10)	72
	N of countries	70		N of countries	43
	N (foreign news)	591		N (foreign news)	185

term historical importance than its current political and economic significance. It is also possible that this was not only because the United Kingdom plays an important role in the European context, but also because of its past colonial ties and linguistic commonalities with North America (Canada and the United States) and Asia (Hong Kong, China, and Singapore). Britain is home today to many immigrants and working people from many parts of the world, and as such there is much interest in what happens there. British sports were also of particular interest: 25% of all news regarding the United Kingdom had to do with this topic. France, another European country in the list of most-covered countries, appeared

Country of broadcast	Country of location	Percent of all foreign news items	Country of broadcast	Country of location	Percent of all foreign news items
United States	Iraq	37	Average of all 17 countries	United States	21
	Palestine	10		United Kingdom	6
	China	9		France	5
	Israel	8		Palestine	5
	Colombia	7		Spain	5
	Venezuela	6		China	4
	Ecuador	6		Russia	3
	Bangladesh	5		Israel	3
	Afghanistan	5		Germany	3
	Kenya	5		Iraq	3
	Others	31		Others	57
	CCI (10)	76		CCI (10)	50
	N of countries	36		N of countries	137
	N (foreign news)	179		N (foreign news)	5,614

in about half of the countries analyzed. France was followed by Germany in 7 countries, as well as by Italy and Spain in 6 countries. Russia also was among the 10 most-covered countries in 6 countries in early 2008.

Other countries and territories were covered in foreign TV news even more than those mentioned above. Palestine ranked among the 10 most-covered countries in 9 of the 17 countries in question, and Israel appeared in eight of the top lists. This indicates that in the process of news selection there is another criterion apart from being a superpower and regionalism, namely, the news value of the long-smoldering crisis in the Middle East. Other trouble spots around the globe were deemed to be less important, such as the war in Afghanistan or the precarious situation in Iraq at the time.

We now take a closer look at the individual countries that have been the focus of our analysis. Every single European country shows the general pattern that has emerged so far. For example, the countries covered in German foreign news can be divided into three groups: (1) countries covered because of a shared Western European location (Italy, Norway, Russia, Sweden, Spain, and the United Kingdom); (2) the superpower factor (the United States); and (3) regions embroiled in conflict (Israel, Egypt, and Palestine).

The three countries that border on Switzerland—France, Germany, and Italy—are always the center of attention in Swiss foreign news. They are the so-called "next-door giant neighbors" (Liu & Gunaratne, 1972). In addition, the United Kingdom was also covered to a large extent. Only in Switzerland did the conflict between Serbia and Kosovo arouse relatively high interest and occupy a similar portion of the foreign news reports. One reason for this is probably the high number of Albanian refugees and emigrants from that region who form one of the largest foreign ethnic groups of Swiss residents.

The picture of Belgium's foreign news is very similar in this respect. The coverage there was not exclusively dominated by the United States, but also by European states that can be identified as Belgium's "giant neighbors." This coverage of European news was, of course, also due to the fact that Brussels, the Belgian capital, serves as the headquarters of the European Union (EU) and is used as a site for numerous meetings and summit conferences of other organizations. What happens there is foreign news for the other European member states. Accordingly, television news in Belgium seems to be interested in what happens in the individual states of the EU. Interestingly, the other European countries in our sample did not cover Belgian events very often. Another area of importance in Belgian news was the crisis in the Middle East.

Apart from similarities in the basic pattern, the other European countries had specific features of their foreign news broadcasts, which could be explained by their geographic location, political history, and culture. This can be said, for example, about Poland, where television news was unequivocally dominated by Russia. Not only do the vicinity and the shared border come into play, but possibly also the lasting anxiety as a result of former dependence on the Soviet Union. Therefore, the presidential elections in Russia were, at the time, well covered by the Polish newsmakers. On the other hand, the United States is considered a guarantor of independence from the former superpower in the East. The American missiles intended for installation on Polish territory resulted in a new controversy with Russia and led to the addition of "outer space" to the list of locations for foreign news.

As for Portugal, neighboring Spain was clearly the dominant force in Portuguese foreign news (21%). Also, East Timor, Brazil, and Mozambique—all former Portuguese colonies—still seem to have a certain news value. The news factor in such cases is proximity in terms of geography, history, and culture.

When looking at North America, a contrasting picture emerges. Foreign newscasts in Canada were dominated by its "giant neighbor," the United States. As we have already seen (and previous studies have demonstrated), the flow of news between the two countries was rather unbalanced and unilateral for decades (Hart, 1963). This has not changed. In none of our 17 countries did the United States play such an important role in foreign news as in Canada. Half of the foreign news reports in Canada covered events or people in the United States. The United Kingdom was in second place (8%), being the "mother country" of the Commonwealth of Nations to which Canada still belongs. The space for other countries was rather limited. It was, however, reserved for crisis regions (Israel and Palestine as well as Afghanistan and Pakistan) or European countries (Italy and

France). The fact that, despite the cultural and linguistic similarities, France ranks only 10th in terms of foreign news coverage in Canadian TV newscasts may seem surprising at first glance. However, this was likely to be linked to the fact that the content analysis was limited to two anglophone channels (CBC and CTV).

Foreign news broadcasts in the United States present a unique case. As has already been pointed out, not only was the amount of foreign news rather low, but also its composition was also quite different from anywhere else in the world. Regionalism, for example, was virtually not a factor for the United States. News selection was primarily dominated by the country's own international standing, especially regarding conflicts and crises in which it was directly or indirectly involved as a "global player." Iraq was the setting for events in more than one-third of foreign news reports in the United States because of its military involvement there. The conflict in the Middle East (Palestine and Israel) ranked second, while conflicts in South America were in third place (tensions among Colombia, Venezuela, and Ecuador). Compared to Iraq, Afghanistan received much less attention on U.S. television news in early 2008. The fact that China occupied third place among the most-covered countries—with reports about the Tibet conflict—points to the growing significance of this country in the United States. The previous state of alienation has transformed into competition. Bangladesh and Kenya, two countries that also ranked among the top 10 in American television news, could nowhere else attain such a position. The reasons for this were social protests and a plane accident in the first case and post-election sprees of violence in the second.

In both South American countries, our basic pattern reappeared. In both Brazil and Chile, foreign news was dominated by reports on the United States (ranked first in Brazil, second in Chile). Regionalism was indicated by the presence of numerous other countries located on the subcontinent (in Brazil: Colombia, Ecuador, and Venezuela; in Chile: Argentina, Brazil, Colombia, Ecuador, and Venezuela). The proportion of foreign news devoted to South America was considerably higher in Chile (44%) than in Brazil (22%). TV news in Brazil, however, tended to focus more on Europe (21%) than its Chilean counterparts (15%). The United Kingdom and Spain were among the most-covered countries in both countries. In Brazil, France and Germany were also in the top 10, as was Italy in Chile. Strangely enough, in both countries, none of the conflict regions in the Middle East or East Asia in early 2008 were among the 10 most-covered countries. These regions seem to be too far away and lacking in cultural ties. On the other hand, the newscasts of both countries did report the boundary dispute among Colombia, Venezuela, and Ecuador in their "relative backyard."

Our Middle Eastern countries, Israel and Egypt, were not engaged in confrontation with each other, but they were basically on opposite sides of that region's ongoing conflict. In their respective newscasts, six countries appeared in both: the United States and several other countries in the region, Israel in Egyptian news, Egypt in Israeli news, Palestine, Syria, Lebanon, and Iraq. In Israel, European countries made up the third-largest group of countries covered (the United Kingdom, France, and Germany, together comprising 14%). In Egypt, only the United Kingdom was among the 10 most-covered countries. Russia occupied the 10th place in Israel and the ninth place in Egypt among the most-covered countries. Considering the high number of immigrants in Israel from the former Soviet Union, one might have expected more news about Russia, but such news is available on a Russian-language Israeli channel (not studied here) and on several satellite channels from Russia that are available in Israel.

The five Asian countries included in our study also show similarities and differences in foreign news. As already pointed out, foreign news in Asia only comprises a small proportion of the totality of news (with the exception of Singapore). In three of these five countries, the United States was the most-covered country, with a considerable proportion of the overall share (Hong Kong with 44%, Japan with 40%, and Taiwan with 35%). Reasons for this may vary from country to country. America's political and economic supremacy also radiates into Asia. In China (following Greece) and in Singapore (following Malaysia), the United States occupies second place in the rankings, with considerably lower percentages (12% and 15%, respectively). In Taiwan, the maintenance of the status quo is much more dependent upon the United States, while the same does not apply to the People's Republic on the mainland.

In the Asian countries in our study, regionalism varied in its significance in terms of foreign TV news. It was most distinctive in Singapore: its neighbor Malaysia, where elections took place early in 2008, was in the top spot (20%), followed by five other Asian countries (with Asia as a non-specific location as well). Altogether, these countries make up 55% of the foreign news coverage in Singapore. This may be due to its multi-Asian population. In the case of Taiwan, five Asian countries were also among the 10 most-covered, making up about one-third of foreign news reports, with China, Taiwan's "big giant neighbor"—as Liu and Gunaratne (1972) noted decades ago—as the most prominent country (19%). This situation between the two countries may have led to very limited reporting. The figure of 19% translates to only 10 stories in 4 weeks. On the opposing side, in China's TV news, there were only two stories datelined in Taiwan.

Foreign news in the three remaining countries was less "Asian-dominated." This was the case for China, where European countries appeared fairly often because of long-term and current political-economic reasons, as well as other news in response to current events and developing interests (Algeria and Mauritania). As for Hong Kong, its rank order is somewhat different from China: the United States dominates even more (44%), followed by Russia (7%) and the United Kingdom, the former colony's ruler (5%) and with other European (France),

Middle East (Palestine, Iraq) and Asian (Malaysia, Pakistan) countries among the 10 most-covered. In Taiwan, the United Kingdom and Germany, two European countries, as well as Europe as a non-specific location, were found among the 10 most-covered countries.

Finally, Japan seems to represent a special case. With a limited amount of foreign news—as earlier studies had determined (Cooper-Chen, 1992; Cooper-Chen & Kanayama, 1998; Miller, 1994)—the United States and China account for three-fifths of the coverage. These two countries seem to represent the main objects of political, economic, and technological interest in Japan. They are followed by South Korea (because of a tragic fire) and Germany, the Antarctic (because of whaling protests), and outer space (because of a Japanese astronaut in an American space shuttle). Very few stories covered Russia, the United Kingdom, and the West Pacific island of Guam, the latter an American military base and a resort similar to Hawaii. Guam was in the Japanese news in early 2008 because of the "Miura affair" (a Japanese citizen was convicted in Japan for a murder committed in Los Angeles in 1981, but the conviction was overturned in 1998; nonetheless the man was arrested by American authorities when he arrived for a visit to Guam in 2008).

Apart from these basic patterns, several other specific observations can be made. Australia ranked among the top 10 countries in the news of five countries: Belgium, Israel, Singapore, Switzerland, and Taiwan. Three events in spring 2008 can be discerned as the causes for this: the death of the well-known actor Heath Ledger, the Australian Open tennis tournament, and the Australian government's apology to the Aborigines.

Looking back at past decades, it becomes obvious that Russia in particular has lost its former news value. As long as the Soviet Union existed and dominated Eastern Europe (and, tentatively, other regions in the world), it was a superpower along with the United States and thus had a considerable impact on the foreign news of many countries. China, on the other hand, has gained much news value in recent years. Furthermore, our data illustrate the continuing lesser role of sub-Saharan Africa (at least outside the African continent). Only very rarely could African countries be found among the most-covered countries: Kenya in the U.S. news and Mozambique in Portugal (for reasons already explained). Ghana received a limited amount of attention because of a soccer tournament (0.4% of foreign news), but more than Zimbabwe (0.3% of foreign news), or South Africa (0.2% of foreign news).

In summary, our findings show that there were countries and territories that were featured quite regularly in foreign news. In addition, their appearance in newscasts often depended on specific current events. For example, the fact that Algeria as well as Mauritania occupied the seventh and tenth places in China's TV news ranking during the period of analysis can be explained by diplomatic visits that took place on those days. Specific events can also be a reason for the re-actualization of former relations in TV news. For example, the coverage of East Timor by TV news in Brazil and Portugal was the result of a specific event: on February 11, 2008, José Ramos-Horta, East Timor's president, was shot and wounded by rebel soldiers.

Countries Involved

In our study we coded foreign news not only with regard to where the reported events occurred, but we also focused on the countries involved in these events. Thus, we also determined which countries "were mentioned and/or referred to directly or indirectly" in the news items. A maximum of five countries involved could be coded for each item, including the country of location, which we considered as being involved as well. Table 4.5 presents the hierarchy for all countries included in the analysis and the Country Concentration Index for the 10 most-involved countries.

The findings show a total of 174 involved countries for the 17 countries included in the analysis, that is, 30 countries more than the number of countries of location. Thus, the coverage included several more countries, irrespective of the location in which the events took place. By involvement (and beyond their role as location), the countries' presence in foreign news coverage tends to increase. The countries' values were consistently higher when taking into account involvement

Table 4.5 Proportion of news featuring top 10 countries involved in countries of study

Country of broadcast	Country involved	Percent of all foreign news items	Country of broadcast	Country involved	Percent of all foreign news items
Belgium	Belgium	39	Brazil	United States	36
	United States	24		Brazil	26
	France	17		Colombia	19
	United Kingdom	11		Ecuador	15
	Russia	9		Venezuela	14
	Netherlands	8		China	13
	EUROPE	7		France	10
	Australia	7		United Kingdom	8
	Spain	7		Spain	6
	Israel	6		Germany	6
	Others	84		Others	87
	CCI (10)	62		CCI (10)	64
	N of Countries	92		N of countries	67
	N (foreign news)	508		N (foreign news)	252

rather than merely event location. This is also true of the individual countries in our study.

The greatest number of involved countries was found in the foreign news in Egypt (107) and the smallest in Japan (32). Variability was quite large in Switzerland (96), Belgium (92), and Germany (81), and relatively small in the United States (39). Several other countries had a middle position with about 60 countries involved (Israel, Brazil, Canada, Portugal, Chile, Singapore, and Italy).

Furthermore, given our definition of involvement, it is obvious that the 17 countries of our analysis were highly involved in foreign news and in most cases held a top position in the ranking. This can be viewed as an indicator of national

Country of broadcast	Country involved	Percent of all foreign news items	Country of broadcast	Country involved	Percent of all foreign news items
Canada	United States	69	Chile	Chile	65
	Canada	41		Argentina	26
	China	12		United States	20
	United Kingdom	12		Colombia	14
	Israel	9		Brazil	11
	Afghanistan	6		Spain	10
	Iran	6		Ecuador	9
	Australia	5		Venezuela	9
	Palestine	5		Italy	7
	France	5		United Kingdom	7
	Others	79		Others	71
	CCI (10)	69		CCI (10)	72
	N of countries	65		N of countries	63
	N (foreign news)	326		N (foreign news)	450
China	China	39	Egypt	United States	34
	United States	19		Palestine	29
	Greece	14		Israel	25
	United Kingdom	8		Egypt	20
	Russia	8		Iraq	14
	Algeria	8		Russia	13
	Tibet	7		Lebanon	11
	Japan	6		Syria	10
	Germany	5		Kosovo	9
	France	5		Iran	8
	Others	77		Others	105
	CCI (10)	60		CCI (10)	62
	N of countries	67		N of countries	107
	N (foreign news)	215		N (foreign news)	464

interest or orientation in foreign news coverage. In 9 of the 17 countries—Belgium, Chile, China, Germany, Israel, Poland, Italy, Portugal, and the United States—the country of location was itself the country most highly involved. In three other countries—Canada, Brazil, and Switzerland—their involvement was only in second place. Foreign news coverage was less ethnocentric in Taiwan (third place), Egypt (fourth place), and Singapore (seventh place). Only Hong Kong did not appear at all among the 10 most-involved countries in its own foreign news. Thus, the rather lower-ranking role of Hong Kong and Singapore in the global political system and in foreign politics was confirmed.

Country of broadcast	Country involved	Percent of all foreign news items	Country of broadcast	Country involved	Percent of all foreign news items
Germany	Germany	42	Hong Kong	United States	56
	United States	28		United Kingdom	13
	United Kingdom	12		China	12
	Russia	11		Russia	10
	France	10		Japan	9
	Israel	8		Iraq	7
	China	8		South Korea	6
	Italy	8		Australia	6
	Norway	7		India	6
	Palestine	6		France	5
	Others	109		Others	82
	CCI (10)	56		CCI (10)	61
	N of countries	81		N of countries	49
	N (foreign news)	341		N (foreign news)	165
Israel	Israel	52	Italy	Italy	35
	United States	30		United States	34
	Palestine	22		Europe	13
	Egypt	10		France	11
	Lebanon	8		Israel	10
	Syria	7		United Kingdom	9
	United Kingdom	7		Palestine	9
	France	4		Vatican City	9
	Germany	4		Spain	7
	Iran	3		ASIA	5
	Others	41		Others	75
	CCI (10)	78		CCI (10)	65
	N of countries	69		N of countries	59
	N (foreign news)	371		N (foreign news)	292

The highest degree of national interest (if not ethnocentricity) was found in news coverage in the United States: the country was involved in 70% of its already-scarce foreign news coverage. Chile followed in second place with a comparably high level of 65%. The majority of countries were involved in one-half to one-third of foreign news coverage (Poland, Israel, Germany, Canada, Japan, China, Portugal, and Italy). The six remaining countries were even less involved in the news, that is, foreign news coverage appeared non-ethnocentric or cosmopolitan. This was the case for Brazil, Switzerland, Egypt, Taiwan, Hong Kong, and Singapore.

Country of broadcast	Country involved	Percent of all foreign news items	Country of broadcast	Country involved	Percent of all foreign news items
Japan	United States	48	Poland	Poland	53
	Japan	41		Russia	27
	China	29		United States	27
	Germany	7		Ukraine	10
	France	5		Germany	8
	South Korea	5		United Kingdom	7
	United Kingdom	5		France	6
	OUTER SPACE	4		Czech Republic	4
	Bahrain	4		OUTER SPACE	4
	Australia	4		Italy	4
	Others	27		Others	56
	CCI (10)	85		CCI (10)	73
	N of countries	32		N of countries	51
	N (foreign news)	192		N (foreign news)	187
Portugal	Portugal	35	Singapore	Malaysia	21
	Spain	23		China	20
	United States	20		United States	19
	East Timor	12		Japan	9
	United Kingdom	6		United Kingdom	8
	Europe	5		Taiwan	8
	Australia	5		Singapore	8
	Kosovo	5		Australia	6
	France	5		Hong Kong	6
	Brazil	4		India	4
	Others	63		Others	46
	CCI (10)	66		CCI (10)	71
	N of countries	65		N of countries	60
	N (foreign news)	449		N (foreign news)	447

Looking at the data from a different perspective, we see that in most cases the countries of location also dominate as countries involved. This is not surprising, of course. There were only slight variations in the rank ordering, and in some cases countries were even replaced by others in the list of the 10 most-covered countries. The dominance of the United States was even more evident: it was involved in almost every third foreign news item in the 17 countries. The share of other countries also increased when it came to involvement—about one-third of the items for both the United Kingdom and France, and double that for Germany and Italy. Iraq, which was among the 10 most-covered countries in terms of location, lost its relative standing when it came to involvement. Conversely,

Country of broadcast	Country involved	Percent of all foreign news items	Country of broadcast	Country involved	Percent of all foreign news items
Switzerland	United States	25	Taiwan	United States	43
	Switzerland	24		China	22
	France	19		Taiwan	13
	Germany	10		Hong Kong	9
	United Kingdom	9		South Korea	7
	Italy	8		France	5
	Israel	7		Europe	5
	Serbia	7		Japan	5
	Palestine	6		United Kingdom	5
	Kosovo	6		Australia	4
	Others	84		Others	48
	CCI (10)	59		CCI (10)	71
	N of countries	96		N of countries	50
	N (foreign news)	591		N (foreign news)	185
United States	United States	70	All countries	United States	30
	Iraq	37		United Kingdom	9
	Israel	14		Israel	8
	Palestine	11		China	8
	China	9		France	8
	Afghanistan	8		Germany	6
	Colombia	7		Palestine	6
	UK	7		Italy	6
	Venezuela	6		Spain	5
	Ecuador	6		Russia	5
	Others	51		Others	105
	CCI (10)	77		CCI (10)	46
	N of countries	39		N of countries	174
	N (foreign news)	179		N (foreign news)	5,614

Italy ranked among the 10 most-involved countries (but not among the 10 most-involved by location). When the involvement of Israel and Palestine is combined, this provides, once again, an indication for strong interest in the Middle East conflict. Ultimately, the assessment of involvement reinforces the basic pattern in foreign news on television: regionalism, the presence of economically and politically strong countries, and the world's crisis regions.

Summary and Conclusions

The findings of our study show a complex, multi-faceted picture of foreign news reporting on television around the world. We found many differences but some similarities, too. The differences began with the sheer amount of foreign news. The differences continue when we look at the geography of news. As we noted in Chapter 2 in dealing with the four types of news (purely domestic, purely foreign, and two types of hybrid news) we raise significant questions regarding the reality of globalization that is so often taken for granted. There are, of course, indicators of globalization in many areas, even in the cultural production industries, but foreign news reporting seems to be an exception, at least to a certain degree. Foreign news is clearly not the same everywhere (Cohen, 2002).

In some countries, news reports relate to events taking place in numerous other countries, while the array of events covered in other countries is quite limited. From a worldwide perspective, based on our 17-country sample, Europe seems to be the most-covered continent, followed by North America and the Middle East. But this does not negate wide differences among the individual countries. Across our 17 countries, the United States and the United Kingdom were the most heavily covered (and most involved), along with an assortment of other countries, in various ranked positions.

The picture is even more complex when considering each individual country. But even then, the four main areas of foreign coverage that have been found in earlier studies are confirmed once again as the most basic pattern almost everywhere: the significance of regionalism, the dominance of (a seemingly single) superpower, the attention to regions where crises are dominant, and, only then, other countries.

This order is sometimes different, however, due to specific events, even in non-political domains such as sports. It should be recalled that we analyzed the main evening newscasts in each of the countries and not special sports news programs. Some newscasts, however, provide more sports news than others. For example, reports on soccer were particularly evident worldwide. England's Premier League contributes to significant coverage. Another example: in the coverage of foreign news on German TV, Norway was among the top 10 countries; this was because of the European handball championship that happened to be taking place in January 2008.

The picture of the world is still uneven, particularly with respect to various geographic regions that are totally under-represented. This may be criticized as in earlier decades, but it is apparent that any attempt to change this would be difficult, because the world itself is uneven and journalism is, of course, not a perfect mirror of reality.

The multi-faceted picture of foreign news on television demands multi-causal interpretations. Several factors have been mentioned and may explain the findings. The nature of the countries' political systems and their degree of integration into the international system and trade relations must be taken into consideration. So, too, is the need to weigh the geopolitical structure of the world, such as the impact of neighboring countries, especially if they are characterized by high political power. History, culture, religion, and traditions comprise another set of factors that have an impact on the news-selection process. And last but not least, foreign news coverage may depend, at least to some extent, on idiosyncratic preferences of individual journalists who may have particular interests in certain countries and events. (We will say more on this in Chapter 11.)

Finally, news editors and journalists seem to be taking into account, at least to some extent, the perceived interests of their audience, especially in market-driven societies where ratings are an important factor. Later, in Chapter 10, we will report our survey findings regarding the interest expressed by news viewers concerning foreign (and domestic) news. And in Chapter 14 we will discuss the extent to which the various countries presented in the newscasts is related to peoples' interest in those countries.

CHAPTER FIVE

Actors in Foreign News

ANTÓNIO BELO, ELIZABETH GODO, KNUT DE SWERT, & ANDRÉ SENDIN

Following the analysis of the overall content of foreign news and their geographic origins, our next step was to investigate an equally interesting question: Who gets access to the news? In this chapter we refer to "actors" as the people or organizations that are mentioned or privileged with the opportunity to provide information and opinions to the public via the newscasts. In the following pages we discuss several issues related to the presence of actors in the news, including the identity of actors who appear most often and how they are portrayed. We do this separately for domestic and foreign news in order to discover whether or not differences exist in these two domains. In addition, as in the other chapters, we compare the 17 countries in our sample in order to determine whether certain phenomena related to actors are universal or can be attributed to the particulars of a specific country.

We begin by presenting a brief summary of previous studies on actors in television news, focusing primarily on the roles and the characteristics of actors. Next, we describe the procedure we adopted for coding over 30,000 actors identified in our sample of news items. Finally, we present the main findings regarding presence of actors in newscasts: their status, their role, and topics in which they appear and their gender.

Actors in the News

A common practice in television news is the use of persons of authority—experts, witnesses, politicians, and so forth—who are quoted or privileged to appear in newscasts. In addition to providing mere information, news is a form of representation of authority and "represents *who* are the authorized knowers and *what* are their authoritative versions of reality" (Ericson, Baranek, & Chan, 1989, p. 3). And, as Cottle (2000, p. 427) briefly states, "who gets 'on' or 'in' the news is very important."

Several studies examined the presence (or absence) of certain authorized knowers. Becker (1967) spoke of a "hierarchy of credibility" in which "participants take it as given that members of the highest group have the right to define the way things really are…. Thus, credibility and the right to be heard are differently distributed through the ranks of the system" (p. 241). Twenty years later, Ericson and colleagues (1989) approached the issue of authority from an institutional perspective, arguing that "through the process of displaying the place of authorized knowers in the knowledge structure of society, and conveying the type of knowledge that gives them that place, news organizations underscore their own authority" (p. 5). This manifests a symbiotic relationship, emphasizing the significant role that authority plays in mainstream news and the way in which those privileged to speak are able to benefit the news organizations as they are, in turn, benefited by them. It is not surprising, then, that Cottle (2000) and other theorists have found that practices of news access "routinely privilege the voices of the powerful and marginalize those of the powerless, whether as a result of media ownership, control and instrumental design; prohibitive costs of market entry, advertising pressures [or] the commodification of news" (p. 427).

The way authority plays out in terms of actors' roles has been investigated in a variety of contexts and by using a number of research methods. While much of this research to date has focused on American news media, our data fills this gap regarding the use of authority on a global basis. For example, in the Jordan and Page (1992) study of American foreign news, the authors concluded that "the president—and even more so administration officials and fellow partisans—have loud voices in TV broadcasts of foreign policy news" (p. 227). They found connections between public opinion and U.S. foreign policy through opinion surveys along with television news broadcasts. They also found that "reported statements and actions by media commentators, allegedly nonpartisan 'experts,' opposition party figures, and popular (but not unpopular) presidents had the largest effects [on public opinion], while the impact of other sources was negligible" (p. 227). These correlations with respect to the shaping of public opinion suggest the need for data from other countries in order to enable a comparative perspective, particularly as many of the specific roles they analyzed are mirrored in our study.

In addition, Danielian and Page (1994) looked at interest groups on TV news. They determined that "imbalances resulting from differential command of money and other resources seem to violate norms of equal access, representativeness, balance and diversity" (p. 1056). Using protests groups (and not individual actors) as an indicator, Berry (2000) found that news stories "commonly cast the citizen groups in an unfavorable light because they came across as unruly, rebellious, radical or simply just out of the mainstream" (p. 121).

Langer (1997) takes a somewhat different view on the selection of actors in tabloid television, arguing that "what journalists like to refer to as news sense has as much to do with priorities of 'form' as it does with institutionalized sanctioned content" (p. 133). Cottle (2000) explains how a limited repertoire of news narratives position "celebrities," "ordinary people," and "victims" symbolically to enact or perform standardized roles within the mythic structures of tabloid news stories. Although our data do not deal specifically with tabloid television, there are opportunities to differentiate between hard and soft news through the topic codes assigned to each item so that we can determine if similar "standardized" roles operate within the coverage of the same topics. Langer also explores the use of victims and witnesses, concluding that witnesses "lend truth value to the story, giving it validity in the realm of personal experience…enhancing the possibilities for a sympathetic response…" (p. 90).

In addition to the dominance of American research, however, several studies have taken a comparative perspective. The final report of the group of specialists on media diversity, presented to the Council of Europe (Ward, 2006), presents findings on newscasts in the United Kingdom, Italy, Croatia, and Norway, based on content analysis of television newscasts. In addition to the topics covered, the study also examined the actors that have direct access to the news by speaking in the items, concluding that a clear predominance of males exists, and that the general public and politicians were the main category of actors in the newscasts of these countries.

In a study of German, American, and Arab newscasts, Senokozlieva, Fischer, Bente, and Krämer (2006) assumed that television news is essentially a cultural phenomenon; hence formal and implicit characteristics of newscasts may be systematically related to culture-specific characteristics. They suggest, for example, that the fact that Arab newscasts presented large groups of people more frequently than did German and American newscasts "might be interpretable with regard to the Individualism/Collectivism divergence between these three countries/regions" (p. 6). Similarly, a study by Silveira, Cardoso, and Belo (2010) examined Portuguese prime-time newscasts between 2002 and 2006, paying particular attention to actors involved in the news, including their appearance, role, and gender in commercial and public stations. Their findings are similar to the German-American-Arab study but with lower percentages of items presenting at least one actor.

Finally, Dayan and Katz (1992)—in their conceptualization of the framework of "media events" and who applied them to a variety of "contests," "conquests," and "coronations" in several countries—spoke of those privileged to speak in the events in which the story determines "...the distribution of roles within each type of event and the ways in which they will be enacted" (p. 25).

An additional, highly salient issue relating to actors in television news is gender representation. Some research suggests that female news sources *ceteris paribus* receive less prominence and are not granted equal access to news, both in the print media as well as in television, compared with male sources (see, for example, Freedman & Fico, 2005; Spee & De Swert, 2005; Armstrong, 2006). Cohen's (1987) study of news interviews in three American television networks found 83% male interviewees. In Spain, Dièz (2005) found only 24% female interviewees in television news; and in Belgium, Vos and colleagues (2012) found only 22%.

Using a comparative international approach, the Global Media Monitoring Project (GMMP) measured the percentage of female sources in television news on several occasions, in a joint effort comprising television news from 71 countries (Spears & Seydegart, 2000). In 1995, no more than 21% of the actors in the news were female. Since then, this number has gradually increased (22% in 2000 and 2005, and 24% in 2010), but the proportion of men appearing in television news still largely outweighs that of women (Gallagher, 2006, p. 22; Gallagher, 2010, p. 7). While the GMMP cannot be praised enough for its truly broad comparative approach, its weakness lies in the very limited amount of coded material for each medium—only one day's worth. These data are therefore not sufficiently useful for comparing different aspects of the newscast, such as topics or foreign-versus-domestic news, which is the main focal point of our project.

Research on the relationship between foreign news and gender balance is scarce. When studying topics in the news, researchers often compare male-related vs. female-related topics, looking for the explanatory power these topics might have for the presence of female sources in the news (see, for example, De Swert & Hooghe, 2010). Typical foreign news topics (such as war, international economy, and natural disasters) are often attributed to "male" topics (Van Zoonen, 1998). This could lead to the notion that foreign news would show higher levels of gender imbalance than domestic news (see also Zoch & VanSlyke Turk, 1998), since news items about "male" topics tend to contain fewer female sources (De Swert & Hooghe, 2010) and are often presented in a "private" or at least lower-status public role compared with men (Van Craenenbroeck & De Swert, 2005). Thus the portrayal of women in typical "feminine" situations, and not in the general news, may be considered a form of "symbolic annihilation" (Tuchman, Daniels, & Benet, 1978).

However, journalists dealing with domestic news are more or less bound in their selection of sources to the gender division of relevant roles in their society, while for foreign news there is a wider variety of potentially relevant domestic and foreign news sources. Since the pool of potential news sources is so different, one could at least expect differences to occur in gender balance between domestic and foreign news. For countries where domestic news sources are almost exclusively male because women do not hold sufficient key positions in society, foreign news could be an opportunity for female news sources to enter the news, thereby increasing gender balance. Indeed, in the current international (political) scene, which is of course still predominantly male-dominated, there are indeed relevant female news sources, too (for instance, Hillary Clinton, Michelle Obama, and Angela Merkel). However, this could also mean that in countries where female actors are leaders in society and highly visible in domestic news, foreign news might decrease the overall gender imbalance.

In sum, in this chapter on the actors in the news, we examine five main research questions.

RQ1: What is the prevalence of actors in domestic and foreign news?

RQ2: In what format and language are the actors presented?

RQ3: What is the status and what are the roles of the actors?

RQ4: To what extent is there a gender imbalance in terms of actors in the news?

RQ5: Does foreign news increase or decrease the gender balance in television news?

The Method for Analyzing Actors

In the course of coding and analyzing our 17,502 news items across the 17 countries, we identified 30,898 "actors." We defined actors as people who appeared in the news items, either as individuals or as representatives of an entity such as a country, commercial firm, social group, and so on. Actors could be identified either as speaking themselves, or represented by a quotation. In the case of quotations, both direct (for example, "The Prime Minister said: 'we will make the right decision'") and indirect ("The Prime Minister said that his party would make the right decision") were coded equally.

All identifiable actors in an item were coded in the order in which they appeared, whether by a verbal reference to their name and/or with a visual caption on the screen, or as a well-known person such as a country's leader, even when no formal identification was provided. Individuals seen but not heard speaking or quoted—that is, not given authority or privileged to speak—were not coded. The actors were also coded for their role; gender; as an individual or as a representative of a group, country, or organization; language spoken; and the length of the sound bite. If more than one sound bite was given to an actor, the length of all the sound bites was combined.

The coding of the actor's role was based on the topic categories (see Chapter 3). Each actor was identified in connection with one topic code, such as internal politics, the economy, accidents and disasters, and so forth, as well as his or her function or profession and his or her status level within the function or profession. For each topic code several functions or professions were possible (for example, president, mayor, or voter for internal politics; economist, investor, or consumer for the economy; or a driver, rescue person, or victim for reports on accidents and disasters). Also, for each function or profession, a score of one to three was coded based on its specific status level. For example, in internal politics the president (or prime minister) was coded as 3 (highest), a minister was coded as 2 (middle level) and a member of parliament was coded as 1 (lowest level). This detailed coding scheme of roles enabled a variety of analyses across country/organizational affiliation, topic areas, functions and professions, status levels, and gender.

Findings

In the analyses that follow, as with the analysis of topics in the news (Chapter 3), we combined purely domestic and domestic items with foreign involvement; likewise, we combined purely foreign and foreign items with domestic involvement.

Frequency of Actors

As noted, the first question dealt with the frequency of actors. For each country and news type (foreign and domestic), Table 5.1 presents the percentage of items with at least one actor and the mean number of actors per item. A quick glance indicates much variance among the countries. Overall, 69% of the news items present at least one actor. Poland, Hong Kong, and Taiwan had the highest percentage of items with at least one actor, all with over 90%; Belgium followed with 82%. At the other end of the spectrum was China, the only country with less than half of the news items involving at least one actor (41%). Considering only foreign news, the overall is about the same. Although with lower values, the countries with higher percentages were the same, but now with percentages between 80 and 90, while China, Chile, Egypt, Germany, and Israel have less than 50%.

In all the countries combined, there were fewer foreign news items with at least one actor (mean of 59%) compared with domestic items (mean of 74%). The difference between the two news types was greatest—over 15%—in Chile, Israel, and Italy. The differences were not significant in Brazil, China, the United States, Belgium, and Japan. Note that in Belgium and Japan the percentage of news with at least one actor is slightly higher in foreign news.

As for the number of actors, overall there were 1.8 actors per item, indicating that it was quite common to present more than one actor in each news item. As with the percentages of at least one actor per item, the mean number of actors per item was higher in domestic items (2.0 actors) than in foreign items (1.5 ac-

Table 5.1 Percentage of items with at least one actor and mean number of actors per item*

	Percent of items with at least one actor			Mean number of actors per item		
	Foreign	Domestic	Total	Foreign	Domestic	Total
Belgium	83	81	82	2.2	2.4	2.4
Brazil	69	69	69	1.6	1.8	1.7
Canada	55	70	63	1.5	2.2	1.9
Chile	43	77	67	1.1	2.3	2.0
China	35	43	41	0.5	1.2	1.0
Egypt	49	62	53	0.9	1.3	1.0
Germany	44	57	51	0.9	1.5	1.2
Hong Kong	84	94	92	1.9	2.4	2.3
Israel	47	64	58	1.2	1.7	1.5
Italy	50	73	68	0.9	1.5	1.3
Japan	67	65	65	1.9	1.7	1.8
Poland	84	95	91	3.6	5.2	4.6
Portugal	64	77	73	1.4	1.7	1.6
Singapore	64	72	69	1.4	1.7	1.6
Switzerland	55	66	62	1.1	1.6	1.4
Taiwan	85	94	92	1.8	1.9	1.9
United States	64	68	67	1.5	2.0	1.9
Total	59	74	69	1.5	2.0	1.8

* Shaded cells indicate significant difference between foreign and domestic news at $p < 0.05$ (independent samples t-tests for difference between proportions for "percent of at least one actor" and independent samples t-tests for difference between means for "mean number of actors").

tors). In this case, too, we found the same tendency toward a significant greater prevalence of actors in domestic news than in foreign news. This was the case for all the countries in this study except for Belgium, Brazil, and Japan, where the differences were not significant. Moreover, Japan was the only country in which the mean number of actors per item was higher in foreign news, although, as noted, the difference was not significant.

Certain country-specific highlights were also observed. Poland not only presented the highest percentages of news items with actors, but also the highest number of actors per news item—a mean of 4.6, significantly higher than any other country. Only Belgium, Chile, and Hong Kong presented an average of more than two actors per item; the remaining counties in our sample ranged between one and two actors per item. The Chinese news presented an opposite picture: not only the lowest percentages of items with at least one actor but also, together with Egypt, a mean of just one actor per news item.

Format and Language of Presentation of Actors

The second research question dealt with the format of presentation of the actors by providing quotes, on-camera speaking sound bites, or both. Space does not permit a full discussion on the functionality and potential impact of presenting quotations by actors and/or on-camera speaking. Suffice it to say that across the 17 countries, the most prominent format was the combined use of quotes and on-camera speaking, about 50% of the actors. Exceptions to this were Canada, Chile, Egypt, Israel, Portugal, and Switzerland, where in the majority of cases actors were presenting as only speaking.

What about the distinction between domestic and foreign news items? Among actors who were only quoted—the least prominent of the three modes of presentation—the percentage of foreign items was double that of the domestic items (30 vs. 15, respectively), which is common in all countries. Only in Egypt, Germany, Israel, and Japan were these differences not significant.

In terms of the language spoken by foreign actors, there were substantial differences among the countries. While in Canada, Chile, Singapore, and the United States a large majority of actors typically spoke the language of the broadcast, in other countries such as China, Israel, Taiwan, and Hong Kong, fewer actors spoke the language of the broadcast, especially in the last case, where only 1% of actors spoke in the language of the broadcast.

Also, in the cases where the spoken language was different from the language of the broadcast, various options were used. In Switzerland, Germany, Egypt, and Poland, most of the sound bites were translated by voice-over dubbing. On the other hand, in Israel, Belgium, Hong Kong, Portugal, Taiwan, and Singapore, the text of the spoken languages was most often presented in subtitles at the bottom of the screen.

Status and Roles of Actors

The third question we examined concerns the status and roles of the actors. As mentioned above, the status of each actor was coded into three categories: high status (president, minister, etc.), medium (department coordinator, deputies, etc.) and low (citizens, students, etc.). An interesting finding is that the largest subcategory of actors (41%) was coded as high status, which may suggest an effort to increase the credibility of the news sources while reinforcing the elite's access to the media (see Table 5.2).

Considering all actors, Egypt clearly stood out as the country with the greatest prevalence of high-status actors (73%). The United States (55%) and Sin-

Table 5.2 Status of the actors in foreign and domestic news by country (in percent)*

	High			Medium			Low			Undetermined		
	Foreign	Domestic	Total	Foreign	Domestic	Total	Foreign	Domestic	Total	Foreign	Domestic	Total
Belgium	47	33	38	22	33	29	27	25	26	4	9	7
Brazil	64	29	40	10	18	16	22	44	38	3	8	7
Canada	41	32	35	20	26	24	31	32	32	8	10	9
Chile	48	33	35	20	29	28	28	32	31	4	7	6
China	74	35	40	13	34	31	9	23	21	4	8	8
Egypt	79	64	73	9	10	10	9	23	15	2	3	2
Germany	43	37	39	20	25	23	28	21	23	8	17	14
Hong Kong	65	28	34	8	30	27	9	24	21	17	18	18
Israel	52	29	35	16	25	23	27	37	35	5	8	8
Italy	43	46	45	23	23	23	31	30	30	3	2	2
Japan	49	40	42	23	26	26	21	26	25	6	8	8
Poland	39	30	32	19	31	28	28	24	25	14	16	16
Portugal	46	38	40	12	20	18	33	31	31	9	11	11
Singapore	52	47	49	11	11	11	19	22	21	18	20	19
Switzerland	49	33	38	16	27	24	25	28	27	9	11	11
Taiwan	27	27	27	22	18	19	23	23	23	28	32	32
United States	55	56	55	14	15	14	23	17	18	8	13	12
Total	51	37	41	16	24	22	23	27	26	9	12	11

* Shaded cells indicate significant difference between foreign and domestic news at $p < 0.05$ (independent samples t-tests for difference between proportions).

gapore (49%) followed, with moderate prevalence of high-status actors in their foreign news, while for the majority of countries this percentage was situated between 30% and 40%. Only in Taiwan was the percentage of high-status actors lower than 30%.

In all countries the percentage of high-status actors was clearly higher than that of low-status actors; the only exception was Israel, where the percentage was the same. Brazil, Canada, Chile, Poland, Portugal, and Taiwan were the only countries in which this difference was less than 10%.

This prevalence of high-status actors is clearly related to the type of items, since the use of high-status actors was significantly greater in foreign news, where more than half of the actors had high status. This gap between foreign and domestic news was found in almost all countries in the sample, particularly in Brazil, China, and Hong Kong. The exceptions were Germany (where this difference was not significant), Taiwan (with equal percentages), and Italy and the United States (where the percentage of high-status actors was higher in domestic news, although not significantly).

In foreign news across all the countries, as can be seen in Table 5.3, domestic politicians—in contrast to citizens and actors in the realm of social issues—were the most frequent actors in the newscasts (23%), but less than in domestic news (30%). In addition, in the realm of International Politics, 22% of the actors were foreign politicians, but only 2% were domestic politicians.

While this is not an exhaustive analysis of all 154 possible individual roles in this study, a pattern does begin to emerge with respect to who is given authority to speak in the news. Political representatives were most common: of the 10 most

Table 5.3 Percentage of internal and international politics, citizens, and social issues roles in foreign and domestic news items by country*

	Internal Politics			International Politics			Citizens			Social Issues		
	Foreign	Domestic	Total	Foreign	Domestic	Total	Foreign	Domestic	Total	Foreign	Domestic	Total
Belgium	20	19	19	13	1	5	14	11	12	7	15	12
Brazil	12	24	20	47	2	15	12	21	18	7	18	15
Canada	24	21	22	13	2	6	20	18	19	17	18	17
Chile	11	19	18	16	1	3	15	16	16	9	13	12
China	34	46	45	43	2	8	3	14	12	2	8	8
Egypt	7	40	22	81	20	54	2	12	6	3	8	5
Germany	21	31	28	11	1	5	20	13	16	7	11	10
Hong Kong	30	30	30	22	2	5	13	12	12	9	16	15
Israel	40	18	23	9	0	3	19	27	25	4	17	14
Italy	25	45	42	12	0	2	21	17	18	15	9	10
Japan	15	33	29	31	1	8	11	19	17	10	12	12
Poland	26	33	31	11	1	4	17	13	14	15	16	16
Portugal	17	27	25	19	1	5	26	21	22	8	16	14
Singapore	30	14	21	6	1	3	11	17	14	29	41	36
Switzerland	29	19	22	18	3	8	14	17	16	10	12	11
Taiwan	24	33	32	4	0	1	17	17	17	12	17	16
United States	27	48	43	22	1	6	10	5	6	21	24	24
Total	23	30	28	22	2	8	15	16	15	11	16	15

* Social issues includes transportation, health, welfare, social relations, population, education and communication. Shaded cells indicate significant difference between foreign and domestic news at $p < 0.05$ (independent samples t-tests for difference between proportions).

frequently coded individual actor roles, 5 were political (ministers, foreign and domestic heads of state, election candidates, and members of parliament or party leaders). This is in line with past research (Jordan & Page, 1992) and our current understanding of the types of individuals to whom journalists have relatively easy access (Herman & Chomsky, 1988; Hall et al., 1978). In some respects, this may also be accounted for by the types of stories that are considered newsworthy, with much emphasis on politics in national news. However, giving a voice to official sources is exacerbated when considering Cottle's (2000) notion of powerful members of society, which suggests that we look at political voices alongside business interests and those in the "internal order" topic category. Yet while there are individual roles within other categories that may be considered powerful, the combination of political, business, and enforcement actors represents a certain set of perspectives from which citizens, activists, and particularly working-class individuals are excluded. Combined with the absence of a feminine perspective, Becker's (1967) "hierarchy of credibility" was reflected by our findings, demonstrating the credibility that comes with rank and status, irrespective of rights or diversity.

The exceptions to this "dictatorship" of politicians were Chile and Portugal, where Sports Actors (25%) and Citizens (26%), respectively, were the most frequent category of actors.[1]

This tendency toward the predominance of internal politicians in foreign news was similar in 11 of the 17 countries in this study. The largest exception was found in Egypt's 7% of Internal Politics actors versus 81% in International Politics, but Brazil, Chile, China, Japan, and Portugal were also exceptions. On the other hand, Israel, Singapore, and Taiwan showed a strong prevalence of internal politicians over their international counterparts.

Besides Internal Politics, there were other categories of actors that proved to be less relevant in foreign news, such as Social Issues, tumbling from 16% in domestic items to only 11% in foreign news items. Curiously, newscasts in Italy showed the opposite tendency, with actors related to social issues shown more frequently in foreign news.

Interestingly, the category of citizens appeared much the same in foreign news as in domestic news, although in Brazil, China, Egypt, Israel, and Singapore, citizens tend to appear more in domestic news. On the other hand, in Belgium, Germany, Japan, Poland, and Portugal, citizens appear more in foreign news.

In the 10 most frequently coded individual actor roles across all countries, two others could also be considered as Citizens ("Man in the Street" and "anonymous people"). Somehow, this result presents some alignment with viewers' preferences, as audiences have been shown to prefer news about ordinary people over politics, economics, disasters, and so on (Hargrove & Stempel, 2002).

Table 5.4 Percentage of items with at least one actor and mean number of actors for foreign and domestic news across all countries by topic*

		Percent with at least one actor	Mean number of actors
Internal politics	Foreign	74	2.0
	Domestic	83	2.2
	Total	81	2.1
Internal order	Foreign	63	1.5
	Domestic	75	1.9
	Total	71	1.8
International politics	Foreign	72	1.6
	Domestic	77	1.9
	Total	73	1.7
Sports	Foreign	39	0.9
	Domestic	64	1.7
	Total	53	1.3
Health, welfare, social services	Foreign	70	1.8
	Domestic	83	2.2
	Total	81	2.2
Economy	Foreign	61	1.4
	Domestic	69	1.9
	Total	67	1.8
Business, commerce, industry	Foreign	53	1.3
	Domestic	74	2.0
	Total	69	1.8
Human interest	Foreign	58	1.4
	Domestic	81	2.2
	Total	74	1.9
Accidents and disasters	Foreign	40	0.8
	Domestic	63	1.6
	Total	57	1.4
Culture	Foreign	63	1.5
	Domestic	71	1.9
	Total	69	1.8

* Shaded cells indicate significant difference between foreign and domestic news at $p < 0.05$ (independent samples t-tests for difference between proportions for "percent of at least one actor" and independent samples t-tests for difference between means for "mean number of actors").

Table 5.5 Role status of actors in foreign and domestic news by topic categories (in percent)*

		High	Medium	Low	Unknown/Undetermined
Internal politics	Foreign	77	7	4	11
	Domestic	56	26	6	11
	Total	61	22	6	11
International politics	Foreign	73	15	9	4
	Domestic	59	18	18	5
	Total	70	15	10	4
Military and defense	Foreign	50	20	16	14
	Domestic	30	38	14	18
	Total	36	33	15	17
Internal order	Foreign	27	21	41	11
	Domestic	23	35	35	8
	Total	23	32	36	8
Economy	Foreign	46	22	16	15
	Domestic	44	24	18	13
	Total	45	24	18	13
Social issues	Foreign	47	22	24	8
	Domestic	36	28	24	12
	Total	38	27	24	11
Science and environment	Foreign	12	74	9	5
	Domestic	16	53	15	16
	Total	15	58	13	13
Sports	Foreign	57	32	7	4
	Domestic	40	41	13	6
	Total	45	39	11	5
Culture and religion	Foreign	23	35	31	11
	Domestic	22	27	38	13
	Total	22	29	36	13
Celebrities and royalty	Foreign	57	35	0	8
	Domestic	30	44	6	20
	Total	40	40	4	16
Citizens	Foreign	0	0	88	12
	Domestic	0	0	80	20
	Total	0	0	82	18

*Shaded cells indicate significant difference between foreign and domestic news at $p < 0.05$ (independent samples t-tests for difference between two proportions).

In terms of the mean number of actors per item (see Table 5.4), the most dominant presence of actors in foreign news is in Internal Politics (an average of 2.0 actors per item), followed by health, welfare, and social services (1.8) and international politics (1.6). At the bottom of the list are accidents and disasters (0.8 actors on average) and sports (0.9).

As for the status of the actors (see Table 5.5), the highest status was in items dealing with International Politics (70% of the news) followed by Internal Politics (61%), while the lowest status was that of ordinary citizens (82%).

Gender

As for gender balance, our study supports the findings of earlier studies. Our data show, once again, an explicit gender imbalance in the news across the globe.

Table 5.6 Gender of actors in foreign and domestic news by country (in percent)*

	Female			Male		
	Foreign	Domestic	Total	Foreign	Domestic	Total
Belgium	26	27	27	74	73	73
Brazil	23	31	29	77	69	71
Canada	25	30	28	75	70	72
Chile	16	24	23	84	76	77
China	9	16	15	91	84	85
Egypt	11	12	11	89	88	89
Germany	23	22	22	77	78	78
Hong Kong	22	21	21	78	79	79
Israel	22	24	23	78	76	77
Italy	24	20	21	76	80	79
Japan	15	13	13	85	87	87
Poland	25	22	23	75	78	77
Portugal	21	24	24	79	76	76
Singapore	29	39	35	71	61	65
Switzerland	22	26	25	78	74	75
Taiwan	32	27	27	68	73	73
United States	15	26	24	85	74	76
Total	21	24	23	79	76	77

* Shaded cells indicate significant difference between foreign and domestic news at $p < 0.05$ (independent samples t-tests for difference between proportions).

When considering the 24,020 actors who were privileged to speak in the newscasts in our sample and for whom we could quite confidently determine gender, we identified only 21% females in foreign news and 24% in domestic news (see Table 5.6). These figures are slightly higher than in the GMMP (2005) study (22%), but considering the fact that in most societies gender equality is increasing over time, a small increase in our 2008 sample figures would be quite normal (and very close to the data of the GMMP 2010 study). In any event, the obvious conclusion is that the large gender imbalance in television news remains.[2]

When we look at country differences we see that, regarding foreign news, most countries present between 20% and 30% women in the news. Only Taiwan (32%) is above this range, but even in this case it does not come close to a gender balance. On the other hand, China (9%), Egypt (11%), and Japan (15%) are the most male-dominated countries when it comes to actors speaking in the newscast.

Table 5.7 Female actors in female* topics and other topics (in percent)

	Female Topics			Other Topics		
	Foreign	Domestic	Total	Foreign	Domestic	Total
Belgium	35	41	40	24	21	22
Brazil	40	47	46	22	26	25
Canada	46	47	47	22	24	23
Chile	13	44	42	13	19	18
China	0	24	22	7	13	12
Egypt	50	24	25	10	8	9
Germany	29	40	36	18	16	17
Hong Kong	14	29	28	24	17	18
Israel	38	46	44	21	18	19
Italy	65	35	40	17	16	16
Japan	25	20	20	16	12	13
Poland	42	41	41	21	16	17
Portugal	41	44	43	18	16	17
Singapore	38	41	41	27	35	31
Switzerland	24	36	34	20	22	21
Taiwan	51	39	41	26	22	22
United States	44	44	44	13	23	20
Total	35	38	37	19	19	19

* Female topics are: Culture; Education; Health, Welfare, Social Services; Social Relations; Fashion and Human Interest. News items coded both as a female topic and another topic were not considered in this analysis—only exclusively female topics news.

Does foreign news make a difference in this perspective? Across the countries, there was slightly less gender balance in foreign news than in domestic news, but the difference was not statistically significant. When examining specific countries, however, some differences were noted. In several countries (Germany, Hong Kong, Italy, Japan, Poland, and Taiwan) higher percentages of female actors were counted in foreign news than in domestic news. In these countries, then, foreign news tended to increase the gender balance in the news, but this was statistically significant only in the case of Taiwan. In even more countries, however, foreign news seemed to be a hindrance to gender balance in the news: in Belgium, Canada, China, Egypt, Israel, Portugal, and Switzerland there were small but not significant differences; and in Brazil, Chile, Singapore, and the United States the differences were significant. In sum, there is no clear trend, but foreign news surely did not contribute to an overall decline in the gender balance.

According to Table 5.7, the so-called "feminine" topics present a higher proportion of female actors—37%, which was 14% higher than the general figure in Table 5.6. In some countries the difference was even higher, which leads us to the question we posed earlier: Are there any countries where female actors were reduced to (feminine) issue-specific illustrations rather than used as full voices in society about all issues? This difference is quite high, indicating that these feminine news topics are generally important in improving the gender balance. In terms of differences between foreign and domestic news, there is no general significant difference. In some countries, feminine news topics in foreign news contain significantly more female actors than the domestic ones (Italy, Egypt, and Taiwan), while in other countries the domestic items about feminine topics had clearly more female actors than the foreign ones (Germany, Chile, China, and Hong Kong).

Table 5.8 Status of actors in foreign and domestic news by gender (in percent)

		High	Medium	Low	Undetermined
	Foreign	16	17	36	27
Female	Domestic	16	20	37	27
	Total	16	20	37	27
	Foreign	84	83	64	73
Male	Domestic	84	80	63	73
	Total	84	80	63	73

As for the status of female and male actors, the findings in Table 5.8 clearly show that there is indeed a relationship between the two variables. Both high- and medium-status roles are dominated to a similar extent by male actors (between

80% and 84% male actors), while women are represented in only 16% to 20% of these roles. In the low-status category, on the other hand, female actors are featured twice as often as in the high- and medium-status roles.

Our last research question was about actors' speaking time. Our data show that, on average, male actors get to speak 18.5 seconds, while female actors only get about 16 seconds. These figures are virtually the same for both domestic and foreign news. While this difference is not very large, it is in line with the other findings, indicating the inferior position of women as actors in the news.

Conclusions

Our analysis of the presence of actors revealed several important differences between foreign and domestic news. But first—and perhaps the most important conclusion—is a more general observation that is related to the presence of actors in television news around the world. The findings in this study show a large presence of actors in the news, which confirms the findings of earlier studies (see, for example, Senokozlieva et al., 2006; Silveira et al., 2010; Dìez, 2005). Our study adds to their work by showing that actors in most countries are used more often in domestic news than in foreign news.

The use of actors may represent a form of identification with the viewer. As such, this may explain the fact that domestic news has relatively more actors, since it is easier for news viewers to identify with issues and people involved in domestic rather than foreign news stories, the latter of which are often unfamiliar and seen as irrelevant to them. This may lead news producers to include more actors in domestic reporting. For more discussion of how viewers relate to domestic versus foreign news, see Chapter 9.

Enabling identification with the viewer requires a calculated choice concerning who should be privileged to speak in the news: actors with high status (based on their authority) or common citizens (based on their proximity to the event). This may explain the sharp contrast between the two most prominent categories of actors and why almost half of the actors have high status, and at the same time the "Man in the street" (or should we say "Woman in the street"?) and anonymous people are also among the most prevalent roles in the news. This could indeed be a reflection of viewer preferences that bolster ratings and may recall the surveys conducted by Hargrove and Stempel (2002) that found that newspaper readers prefer news stories involving "ordinary people" rather than government officials and politicians.

This predominance of politicians and citizens was the case for both foreign and domestic news. Naturally, the proportion of international politicians was greater in foreign news items, while domestic politicians were featured more in domestic news. However, this "dictatorship" of politicians appeared especially in foreign news: in 13 of the 17 countries of our study, their presence was greater in foreign news. This phenomenon of politicians starring in television news concurs with other studies on actors in the news, such as Jordan and Page (1992), Silveira and colleagues (2010), Dìez, (2005), and Ward (2006). It must be remembered, however, that these studies considered news in general and did not distinguish between foreign and domestic news.

As for the second most prominent category of actors—citizens—we found no uniform picture. While in nine countries citizens appear more often in foreign news than in domestic news, the opposite tendency was found in eight countries. What is most interesting is the fact that, with the exception of China and Egypt, citizens do (also) have a significant presence in foreign news.

Another conclusion of interest is that the percentage of high-status actors is greater in foreign news, while the percentage of medium- and low-status actors is lower in domestic news. This is due mainly to the prevalence of international politicians like presidents and foreign ministers in foreign news, thereby increasing the overall status level of actors in foreign news.

Regarding the gender of actors, the findings of this study are generally in accord with others such as Gallagher (2006), Desmond and Danilewicz (2010), Dìez (2005), and Lobo and Cabecinhas (2008), which show an explicit gender imbalance in the news. In fact, all the countries showed a massive presence of male actors in foreign news—around 77%—and even in the countries where this tendency was less pronounced, almost two-thirds of the actors were male.

Finally, what to us is the most important overall conclusion is the absence of any trend or pattern among the countries. There is no group of countries that shares a set of common characteristics that clearly distinguishes them from others. Regarding the comparison between foreign and domestic news, it was possible to find some tendencies, like the presence of more (general) actors in domestic news, more high-status actors in foreign news, more quoted interventions in foreign news, and more speaking interventions in domestic news. However, we could not rank or classify the 17 countries in any common and systematic way that took into account all the dimensions of the analysis of the actors. This conclusion lends additional support to our suggestion that there is little, if any, universality in the way foreign news is reported.

Summary

The most significant overall conclusion of this chapter is the absence of a clear and systematic pattern among the 17 countries regarding the actors in the news. This is in line with our notion that there is little universality in the way foreign news is reported.

And yet, in general terms, we highlight the large presence of actors in the news, which confirms the findings of earlier studies. We conclude that in most countries actors appear more often in domestic news than in foreign news. This may be the case because actors represent a form of identification with viewers, and it is easier for viewers to identify with issues and people in domestic news compared with foreign stories. This identification may also explain the calculated choice of who is more frequently privileged to speak in the news: actors with high status (based on their authority) or common citizens (based on their proximity to the event). While politicians and common citizens were the most predominant actors in the news, this phenomenon was more evident in domestic news. The only exception was the significant presence of citizens in foreign news in China and Egypt. As for the gender of actors, the findings in this chapter are in accord with other studies showing an explicit gender imbalance in the news. In fact, all the countries showed a massive presence of male actors in foreign news.

Notes

1 In order to present readable tables, Table 5.3 presents only the four most prevalent actor categories across all countries; hence the Sports category does not appear in the table.
2 It should be noted that Desmond and Danilewicz (2010) found even lower values for the presence of women as sources—less than 20% of the news stories—although they identified 40% of "ordinary citizens" quoted, thus indicating that they were less likely to be contacted for expert opinion.

CHAPTER SIX

Formal Features and Sources in Foreign News

JÜRGEN WILKE & CHRISTINE HEIMPRECHT

Television is an audiovisual mass medium that transmits its messages with the help of different systems of semiotic signs and two perceptual channels. This is true for all types of program content, including news, which, according to Bourdon (2000), has taken on the form of a "specific genre." This newscast genre has universal characteristics, including a brief introduction with credits—often featuring a globe—and an anchorperson, who stares at the viewer and reports the world by "launching" reports of correspondents and interviewing guests in the studio and reporters live from the scene of the events.

As Bourdon (2000) observes, this genre developed in four stages. In the 1950s it was characterized by "marginality and uncertainty," being not yet a central genre or an essential slot of programming (p. 63). The 1960s saw stabilization: "The importance of television as a medium could no longer be denied. News found a specific location and duration in the schedule, establishing itself as a major, national ritual" (p. 81). The next stage, in the 1970s, emphasized the anchorperson, the journalist-presenter who was placed center stage, according to the American model. This was also the period of rapid technical development of video, satellite, and graphic packaging that "allowed for a better, slicker, visual offering; with the everlasting question of its television values or its journalistic value" (p. 81).

The 1980s and 1990s introduced deregulation and competition. This, according to Bourdon, "clearly showed in the format. Puritan anchorpersons gave way to anchorpersons as lively hosts. Mixed forms (infotainment, tabloid television) were (and still are) on the rise" (p. 81). Yet in the course of this development, which varied across countries, several factors needed be considered: the tradition of earlier media (print, newsreels, and radio); the semiotic and institutional characteristics of television; the change from a public service model to commercialization, with the United States as a role model ("Americanization"), and especially technical innovations, political circumstances, and journalistic orientations.

In contrast to the study of television content, the process of formatting television news, as outlined by Bourdon, has rarely been the subject of systematic examination in communication research. In the course of their analysis of 250 studies on television news from 1970 to 1998, Schaap, Renckstorf, and Wester (1998) could identify only 43 studies in which "formal features" had been examined. These, however, were mostly experimental (reception) studies on structural variations of news item formats and dealt with the complexity and combination of textual and visual information. Differentiated analyses of the highly complex design and presentation of television news were mostly lacking, however. One exception is a study by Heinderyckx (1993) that analyzed 17 European news programs (from 8 countries) with regard to a number of formal features. Kamps (1999) undertook a similar comparison of television news in Germany, the United States, and the United Kingdom. Finally, there are a few national studies on the presentational features of television news (Wix, 1996).

Taking this into consideration, one of the goals of our study was to identify and examine formal features of television news in the 17 countries of our study. This analysis is the subject of this chapter.

The objective of the analysis was achieved by conducting a detailed formal examination of television news in the 17 participating countries. For this purpose, a number of variables were included in the codebook of the content analysis. These categories ranged from the length of the items and their placement in the newscast to the forms of presentation and illustration. For each formal element, the coders indicated their presence or absence in the items. Overall, the goal was to determine whether similar or varying news formats exist around the world. We were also interested in possible differences among the state/public and commercial stations in terms of their formats. Assuming that the use of these formats may differ among the various TV systems, in what follows we will focus on their comparison and will not distinguish between domestic and foreign news as much as we did in the previous chapters.

Newscasts and News: Length and Duration

We begin with a detailed overview of the analyzed television newscasts (Table 6.1). Even though we analyzed the main newscasts aired during prime time, the length of the newscasts varied among the countries. Therefore, a distinction must be made between the overall duration of the various newscasts and the net amount of time actually devoted to the news segments.

At the newscast level, the commercial TVBS station in Taiwan was the longest newscast in our sample, running for 120 minutes, followed by TVI in Portugal (77 minutes) and TV Asahi in Japan (75 minutes, Monday to Friday). In several countries the newscasts are one hour long (Public: Canada, Chile, Portugal, Taiwan, the United States; State: China, Egypt; Commercial: Chile). The shortest newscasts were found in Germany: 15 minutes in the public service station and 18 minutes in the commercial station. The newscasts of other countries generally ranged from 30 to 40 minutes.

Table 6.1 Basic parameters of analyzed newscasts by country and station

Countries	Public/State	Mean duration of full newscast in minutes (mean net news in newscast in minutes)	Mean duration of item in seconds	Mean number of items per newscast	Private	Mean duration of full newscast in minutes (mean net news in newscast in minutes)	Mean duration of item in seconds	Mean number of items per newscast
Belgium	VRT	40 (35)	75	28	VTM	36 (35)	94	23
Brazil	Cultura	40 (31)	79	22	Globo	35 (29)	91	21
Canada	CBC	60 (39)	163	15	CTV	30 (21)	100	12
Chile	TVN	60 (43)	103	25	Mega	60 (46)	96	28
China	CCTV	60 (28)	60	28	—	—	—	—
Egypt	ERTU1	60 (49)	112	27	—	—	—	—
Germany	ARD	15 (14)	68	12	RTL	18 (17)	72	15
Hong Kong	—	—	—	—	ATV	45 (29)	112	29
					TVB	30 (19)	91	13
Israel	IBA	Sunday-Thursday: 40 (28); Friday & Saturday: 10-12	82	20	Arutz 2	Sunday-Thursday: 60 (43); Friday & Saturday: 10-12	97	21
Italy	RAI1	30 (16)	71	26	Canal5	30 (15)	80	23
Japan	NHK	30 (25)	100	15	TV Asahi	Monday-Friday: 75; Saturday-Sunday: 30 (41)	144	17
Poland	TVP1	30 (22)	134	10	TVN	30 (23)	147	31
Portugal	RTV	60 (50)	99	30	TVI	77 (61)	118	19
Singapore	—	—	—	—	Channel5	30 (19)	68	19
					Channel8	30 (23)	74	21
Switzerland	SF1	25 (23)	79	37	TeleZüri	20 (15)	70	13
	TSR	30 (26)	82	19				
Taiwan	TBS	60 (34)	105	19	TVBS	120 (53)	112	29
United States	PBS	60 (49)	198	15	NBC	30 (21)	94	13

The nominal newscast length is usually longer than the time assigned to the actual presentation of the news. Only about 53 of the 120 minutes on TVBS in Taiwan consist of real news. One of the reasons for this is the commercial breaks during the news broadcasts, which are customary in some countries, for instance, Chile, Hong Kong, Israel, and Taiwan, and apply not only to commercial stations. In Portugal there are commercial breaks on the public service news as well, because these are watched by a very large number of viewers and are thus quite attractive to advertisers. In Germany and Italy commercial breaks in television news are prohibited, even for commercial stations. In contrast to the Taiwanese station TVBS, the German public service news devotes 14 of every 15 minutes to actual news. In the other countries the difference between the duration of the newscast and the time assigned to news varies. Usually weather forecasts are added, although we did not code them in our study. This is also the case for separate sports news (Hong Kong and Poland) or movie reviews (Hong Kong). In two countries, newscasts on weekends were shorter: in Israel, on Fridays and Saturdays; in Japan, on Sundays. On average, however, there is no significant difference across all the countries between the duration of the newscasts on public, state, and commercial television stations.

Of course the overall length of a newscast has a bearing on the average length of individual news items. This is also reflected in our analysis. The largest number of items per newscast (37) was in SF1 in Switzerland, followed by TVI (31) and RTV (30) in Portugal, TVBS in Taiwan (29), ATV in Hong Kong (29), CCTV in China (28), and Mega in Chile (28). The fewest items per newscast were found in Poland (TVN: 9; TVP: 10), followed by Germany (ARD: 12; RTL: 15), Canada (CBC: 15; CTV: 12), and Hong Kong (TVB: 13). In most countries the number of news items in public and commercial television hardly differed. Television systems seem to converge in this respect. One exception was Taiwan, where the private channel TVBS (29) had significantly more news items than the public channel PTS (19).

A third finding can be derived from Table 6.1. The differences in the overall duration of the newscasts and the number of items per newscast mean that the individual news items are of different average length. In some countries the items were generally quite short, as in China (CCTV: 60 seconds), Germany (ARD: 68 seconds; RTL: 72 seconds), Singapore (Channel 5: 68 seconds; Channel 8: 74 seconds), Italy (RAI 1: 71 seconds), and Switzerland (Tele Züri: 70 seconds). In other countries television news items were of medium length (90 to 120 seconds), and in still others the channels offered comparatively long items, especially CBC in Canada (163 seconds), TVN in Poland (147 seconds), TV Asahi in Japan (144 seconds), and TVP (134 seconds) in Poland. The length of the item may be understood as a function of the degree of elaboration and information content.

The more time available, the more coherently the events can be structured and backgrounds provided.

Formal Features: Overall Distribution

Using our codebook, we analyzed 23 different formal features for each of the news items. The overall distribution of their occurrence (if at all) is presented in Table 6.2. Eleven features—fewer than half of all those analyzed—were found in all 17 countries: news anchor seen or heard; pre-recorded video; live reports; archive material; tables/charts; still photos; pictorial/graphic representation; animated representation; printed text; maps and flags. Some of these features, however, are rare, such as live reports in only seven countries (Brazil, Canada, Germany, Italy, Japan, Poland, and the United States). The same is true for tables/charts in two

Table 6.2 Overall distributions of formal features in the newscasts—Belgium to Israel

	Belgium		Brazil		Canada		Chile		China	Egypt	Germany		Hong Kong		Israel	
	P	C	P	C	P	C	P	C	S	S	P	C	C	C	P	C
Anchor seen or heard	x	x	x	x	x	x	x	x	x	x	x	x	x	x	x	x
Reporter report from studio	x	-	-	-	x	x	x	x	-	x	-	-	-	x	x	x
Anchor interview reporter in studio	x	-	-	-	x	x	x	-	-	-	-	-	-	-	x	x
Anchor interview reporter not in studio	x	x	x	x	x	x	-	x	-	x	-	x	-	-	x	x
Interview non-journalist in studio	x	-	x	-	x	x	-	-	-	x	-	-	-	-	x	x
Pre-recorded video	x	x	x	x	x	x	x	x	x	x	x	x	x	x	x	x
Live report	x	x	x	x	x	x	x	-	-	x	x	x	-	-	x	x
Archive material	x	x	x	x	x	x	x	x	x	x	x	x	x	x	x	x
Tables/charts	x	x	x	x	x	x	x	x	x	x	x	x	x	x	x	x
Still photos	x	x	x	x	x	x	x	x	x	x	x	x	x	x	x	x
Pictorial/graphic representation	x	x	x	x	x	x	x	x	x	x	x	x	x	x	x	x
Animated representation	x	x	x	x	x	x	x	x	x	x	x	x	x	x	x	x
Printed text	x	x	x	x	x	x	x	x	x	x	x	x	x	x	x	x
Maps	x	x	x	x	x	x	x	x	x	x	x	x	x	x	x	x
Flags	x	x	x	x	x	x	x	x	x	x	x	x	x	x	-	x
Logos	x	x	-	x	x	x	x	x	-	x	x	x	x	x	x	x
Background music	-	-	x	x	x	x	x	x	x	x	x	x	x	x	x	x
Slow motion	x	x	x	x	x	x	x	x	-	x	x	x	-	x	-	x
Speeded up motion	-	-	x	x	x	x	x	x	x	x	-	x	-	-	-	-
Soft focus	x	-	-	-	-	-	x	x	-	-	x	x	-	-	-	-
Color change	-	x	-	x	x	x	x	-	-	-	x	-	x	-	x
Digitization	x	-	x	-	x	x	-	-	-	-	x	x	x	-	-	-
Distorted human voice	x	-	x	x	-	-	-	-	-	-	-	-	-	-	-	-
Total	20	15	18	18	21	21	20	19	12	18	16	19	14	17	16	19

N= 5,614
x = present; - = absent
P = public station; C = commercial station; S = state station

Table 6.2 Overall distributions of formal features in the newscasts (continued)—Italy to United States

	Italy		Japan		Poland		Portugal		Singapore	Switzerland		Taiwan		United States	
	P	C	P	C	P	C	P	C	C	P	C	P	C	P	C
Anchor seen or heard	x	x	x	x	x	x	x	x	x	x	x	x	x	x	x
Reporter report from studio	-	-	-	x	x	x	-	-	x	x	-	-	-	x	x
Anchor interview reporter in studio	-	-	x	-	x	x	x	x	x	-	-	x	-	-	-
Anchor interview reporter not in studio	x	-	x	x	x	x	x	x	x	x	-	x	-	x	x
Interview non-journalist in studio	x	x	-	x	x	x	-	x	-	x	x	-	x	x	-
Pre-recorded video	x	x	x	x	x	x	x	x	x	x	x	x	x	x	x
Live report	x	x	-	x	x	x	x	x	x	x	-	x	x	-	x
Archive material	x	x	x	x	x	x	x	x	x	x	x	x	x	x	x
Tables/charts	x	x	x	x	x	x	x	x	x	x	x	x	x	x	x
Still photos	x	x	x	x	x	x	x	x	x	x	x	x	x	x	x
Pictorial/graphic representation	x	x	x	x	x	x	x	x	x	x	x	x	x	x	x
Animated representation	x	x	x	x	x	x	x	x	x	x	x	x	x	x	x
Printed text	x	x	x	x	x	x	x	x	x	x	x	x	x	x	x
Maps	x	x	x	x	x	x	x	x	x	x	x	x	x	x	x
Flags	x	x	x	x	x	x	x	x	x	x	x	x	x	x	x
Logos	x	x	x	x	x	x	x	x	x	x	x	x	x	x	x
Background music	x	x	x	x	x	x	x	x	x	x	x	x	x	x	x
Slow motion	x	x	x	x	x	x	x	x	x	x	x	-	x	x	x
Speeded up motion	x	x	x	-	-	-	-	-	x	x	-	-	x	x	-	x
Soft focus	-	-	x	x	-	x	-	-	x	x	-	-	x	x	x
Color change	-	-	-	x	-	x	-	-	x	x	x	-	-	-	x
Digitization	-	x	-	x	x	x	-	-	-	x	x	-	-	x	-
Distorted human voice	-	x	-	-	-	-	-	-	-	-	-	-	-	-	-
Total	17	18	17	20	19	21	16	17	19	21	19	14	18	15	17	19	19

N= 5,614
x = present; - = absent
P = public station; C = commercial station; S = state station

countries (Canada and Israel) as well as pictorial and graphic representation in three countries (Belgium, Chile, and Israel). Logos were rarely used in China and Brazil. The presentation of a distorted human voice was very rare; in several countries this feature was not employed at all in the newscasts of our 4-week sample. The remaining formal features were even less common or totally absent, especially interviews with non-journalists in the studio, soft focus, color change, distorted human voice, and digitization.

Almost all 23 formal features occurred in most of the 17 countries, although in some cases only rarely. Nevertheless, there are countries in which formal features can be found to a lesser degree than in others—such as in China (12 out of 23), Hong Kong (14 and 17 in the two channels, respectively), Israel (16 in the commercial channel), Belgium (15 in the commercial channel), Taiwan (15 in the public channel), and Portugal (16 in the public channel). A more precise picture emerges only when we look at the specific frequencies of occurrence for the different formal features, an examination to which we now turn.

In the following pages we present detailed analyses of the various formal features. Each table deals with one particular feature. Within each table the countries are presented in descending order based on the overall percentages.

Manner of Presentation

Television news broadcasts typically have a certain structure and use certain formats of presentation. A trailer featuring the program's title is generally used as an introduction. This often contains a preview of some of the items in the newscast.

News Anchors

Typical of the television news genre is the presence of a host, an anchorman/woman who appears on the screen and presents the news. These people welcome the viewers, relate the news, and connect with correspondents on the scene or with various interviewees. Such persons are found in all countries (see Table 6.3).

In Egypt's only channel and in both channels in Portugal, the anchor was seen in all items. This was also the case on the commercial stations in Taiwan and Brazil. As for the other countries, there was considerable variation. In some there were between 5% and 25% of items in which the anchor could be heard but not seen. An extreme case in this regard was China, where the anchor was seen in only 11% of the items and could only be heard in 89% of the items. Thus, the news presentation is less personalized. Finally, there was considerable variability in the percentage of items in which the anchor was not seen and not heard. This was most noticeable in the commercial channels of Switzerland and Germany (72% and 42%, respectively). Relatively high figures appeared in both Italian stations (around 25%), in the German public station (25%), and in the commercial stations in Israel and Chile (26% and 31%, respectively).

Headlines

Are news items mentioned at the beginning of the newscast in the form of headlines? Table 6.4 shows that in this regard each channel in the 17 countries takes a different approach. Headlines are most common in Poland, Brazil, and the United States (commercial channels 40% to 47%), and least common in Portugal, Taiwan, Hong Kong (commercial channels) and Germany (public channel). Taking the means, in 7 of the 17 countries two or three of ten news items are mentioned in the headlines; in other countries this is even less common. Public and commercial stations in this context are almost identical in some countries (the United States, Chile, and Belgium), but quite different in others. Whereas in Switzerland and Israel headlines are much more common in public television than in commercial TV, the opposite is true in Poland and Brazil. In Germany only RTL, the

Table 6.3 Percent of items with anchorpersons in newscasts (N=5,614)

Anchor is…		Seen	Only heard	Not seen or heard
Egypt	State	100	-	-
	Commercial	-	-	-
Portugal	Public	100	-	-
	Commercial	100	-	-
Hong Kong	Public	-	-	-
	Commercial	99	-	1
Taiwan	Public	92	-	8
	Commercial	100	-	-
United States	Public	92	8	-
	Commercial	92	4	4
Poland	Public	89	12	-
	Commercial	89	7	4
Singapore	Public	-	-	-
	Commercial	88	8	5
Canada	Public	91	8	1
	Commercial	84	16	-
Brazil	Public	75	25	-
	Commercial	100	-	-
Italy	Public	72	-	28
	Commercial	77	-	23
Switzerland	Public	92	-	8
	Commercial	28	-	72
Belgium	Public	76	13	11
	Commercial	93	-	7
Germany	Public	75	-	25
	Commercial	58	-	42
Israel	Public	71	23	6
	Commercial	57	17	26
Chile	Public	65	25	10
	Commercial	60	9	31
Japan	Public	79	14	7
	Commercial	78	5	15
China	State	11	89	-
	Commercial	-	-	-
Total	Public	80	14	7
	Commercial	78	7	15

Table 6.4 Percent of foreign items mentioned in headlines, part of block, appearing live from location, and pre-recorded on location by country and type of broadcaster

Country	n	Mentioned in Headlines		Part of Block		Live from Location		Pre-recorded on Location	
		Public/State	Commercial	Public/State	Commercial	Public/State	Commercial	Public/State	Commercial
Belgium	508	23	18	29	4	8	10	91	96
Brazil	252	19	44	36	0	3	58	96	98
Canada	326	18	19	26	34	31	37	51	58
Chile	450	14	26	43	56	6	5	95	95
China	215	10	-	29	-	4	-	20	-
Egypt	464	20	-	22	-	16	-	82	-
Germany	341	0	14	8	45	17	6	64	75
Hong Kong	165	-	3	-	18	-	1	-	98
Israel	371	23	13	33	34	4	12	74	79
Italy	292	31	36	20	9	17	41	75	73
Japan	192	37	10	26	19	7	8	62	52
Poland	187	29	47	14	18	39	34	59	55
Portugal	449	14	0	0	0	19	10	71	54
Singapore	447	-	20	-	42	-	9	-	69
Switzerland	591	35	6	16	79	17	1	82	94
Taiwan	185	16	0	18	0	0	9	81	100
United States	179	27	40	79	49	6	38	27	60

private channel, featured headlines in its newscasts at the time of analysis, as opposed to ARD, the public service station, and in Taiwan and Portugal headlines were found only in the public service stations.

Block Presentation

We defined a "block" of news as two or more items that are presented sequentially with some kind of link between them, sometimes merely a reference to "news from abroad." Many items are presented individually, but some are part of blocks. As can be seen in Table 6.4, there is much variability across the countries in this respect.

Overall, the United States and Chile presented the highest level of blocks (mean: 67% and 50%, respectively), and Portugal hardly presented any blocks. As for specific channels, presentation of news items as a block occurred most frequently in the commercial channel in Switzerland (79%), in public TV in the United States (79%), and in the commercial channel in Chile (56%). News as a block was also quite common in the commercial channels of Germany (45%) and Singapore (42%).

Reporters in the Newscasts

In presenting the news, reporters often appear in one of two guises: in a live "stand-up" at the scene of the event or in a recorded segment on location.

As Table 6.4 shows, a "stand-up" took place most frequently in commercial television in Brazil and Italy and in the Polish public channel. This was also the case in 38% of the items in the American commercial network. The majority of stations use the live stand-up less frequently, however, especially those in Chile, China, Taiwan, and Hong Kong. In the United States, Brazil, and Israel, the stand-up of reporters is typical only in commercial television; in Germany, Portugal, and Switzerland, it dominates the public channel.

The basic visual material for television news is composed of pre-recorded videos from the scene of the events. As Table 6.4 indicates, in Hong Kong, Brazil, Chile, and Belgium, more than 90% of all items present pre-recorded videos from the news scene. In most other countries the percentage of this feature is also quite high. On only two channels—the public channel in the United States and the state channel in China—less than one-third of the items contain pre-recorded videos. In fact, the Chinese state TV station is an extreme exception in using only a very small number of pre-recorded videos.

Comparing the prevalence of pre-recorded videos with live, on-the-scene reports, it appears that pre-recorded videos are by far more dominant than reporters in a live stand-up, except in the case of Poland, which—as noted—presents fairly frequent stand-up scenes.

Sources and Materials

Television news items originate in a variety of ways, the majority being produced by their stations' own journalists. But television stations often have only a few foreign correspondents across the globe because of the cost factor, and this is why (apart from the existence of the classic press agencies) several video news agencies have been established since the 1950s to provide television stations with images (Paterson, 2011). In our study we attempted to determine the prevalence of these sources, but we were only partly successful, because the identification of the source of the material is not always provided in the news items.

Only in Brazil—especially for its public channel—can the relevant proportion be determined (see Table 6.5). In most other countries the figure is less than 5%, and in some cases even less than 1%. In these countries, agency material seems to be identified only in exceptional cases. Thus, the source of the material remains unknown to the viewers, possibly giving the impression that the material originated from the station itself.

Material could derive from other sources as well. The exchange of television news is done through organizations such as the Eurovision News Exchange (EVN), administered by the European Broadcasting Union (Cohen, Levy, Roeh, & Gurevitch, 1996). The public service channels in several countries contribute a significant number of items to this organization. Similarly, several commercial channels established the European News Exchange (ENEX). The material provided by these organizations to the various stations is presented by them as their own. In addition, material from other stations is either not used at all, or its sources are not disclosed. We found very little use of clearly marked material from one station by another station—only one in three items in Chile, and one in ten items in Canada and Israel. In all other countries, there was very little use of other stations as sources. International broadcasters such as CNN International, BBC World, and Al Jazeera were also rarely used as source material during the period of investigation. Finally, only on rare occasions did the newscasts in the 17 countries feature what was specifically labeled "exclusive" visual material, most notably in Brazil (8%) and in Canada (4%).

Of course, television stations can also use material from their own archives. This seems a natural course of action when reporting on prior events or when historical context is provided. And archive material, since it is free of charge, has financial advantages.

As Table 6.5 shows, archive material was used quite a bit, most frequently in Chile (in 45–50% of the items) and in Japan and Canada (around 40% each). On the other hand, the lowest figures appeared in Switzerland, Belgium, and China (around 10–15%, each), and Singapore (10%). In the other countries there was moderate use of archive materials. In some (Japan [public], Poland, Germany, and Canada [commercial]), archive material was present in more than 40% of all items—in two countries more than 30% (Brazil and Italy [both commercial]), and in six countries more than 20% (Taiwan, Hong Kong, Portugal, the United States, Egypt, and Israel). Finally, there was little difference in the use of archive

Table 6.5 Percent of foreign items containing video news agency material, archive material, printed text, and tables and charts by country and type of broadcaster

Country	n	Video News Agency Material		Archive Material		Printed Text in Report		Tables and Charts	
		Public/State	Commercial	Public/State	Commercial	Public/State	Commercial	Public/State	Commercial
Belgium	508	0	2	8	15	19	11	2	2
Brazil	252	37	11	24	32	4	4	14	7
Canada	326	2	6	39	42	16	21	1	1
Chile	450	1	0	45	50	6	3	1	3
China	215	6	-	11	-	10	-	1	-
Egypt	464	0	-	24	-	5	-	2	-
Germany	341	0	1	13	46	6	14	5	5
Hong Kong	165	-	3	-	27	-	1	-	5
Israel	371	1	1	20	21	3	5	-	2
Italy	292	1	1	32	30	6	9	4	6
Japan	192	0	3	48	38	95	85	22	8
Poland	187	0	0	29	48	13	21	9	8
Portugal	449	3	7	27	22	2	1	2	3
Singapore	447	-	2	-	10	-	44	-	2
Switzerland	591	0	0	11	12	36	52	5	11
Taiwan	185	1	2	25	28	3	10	3	8
United States	179	2	0	21	29	38	44	8	8

material between public service and commercial channels in Canada, Israel, Italy, Switzerland, and Taiwan. The biggest differences were in Germany and Poland.

Modes and Tools

We now present data concerning the degree to which certain modes and tools are used in foreign television news.

Printed Text

Despite the fact that television news consists mostly of images and the spoken word, text and letters can be added to it. This serves to identify and interpret images or support the voiceover.

The use of printed text varies significantly across the 17 countries (see Table 6.5). This feature is used most often in Japan (in 85–95% of the items) and almost not at all in Hong Kong (1%). Apart from Japan, countries can be classified into three groups: (1) those that add printed text, on average, to every second or third item (Singapore, the United States, and Switzerland); (2) those that add text to every fifth to tenth item (Poland, Canada, Germany, Belgium, Taiwan, and China); and (3) those that do so in less than 10% of the cases (Egypt, Israel, Portugal, Brazil, and Chile). The second group consists mainly of Western countries, and the third group includes Asian, Southern European, Middle Eastern, and South American countries. It would not be incorrect to say that printed text is added more frequently in countries with a high percentage of newspaper readers (World Press Trends, 2010). In most of the countries the commercial stations use printed inserts slightly more frequently than do the public service stations.

Tables and Charts

Another means of illustrating television news is the use of tables and charts, which aid the presentation of numbers and other data.

Table 6.5 indicates that in most countries tables and charts are rarely used. To begin with, complex numbers are not very suitable for television, and tables often come across as abstract and difficult to decipher by viewers (Cohen, 1998). Their occasional use is especially fitting for economic topics or for presenting sports rankings. We found them to be used most often in Japan (22%) and Brazil (14%), in both cases in the public service stations.

Still Photos

Although television is primarily a medium of moving images, still photos are often presented in television news. Still photos can illustrate the spoken text, especially if no video material is available. In addition to portraits, documentary photos and icons are often used to symbolically express the content of a news item.

Table 6.6 Percent of foreign items containing still photos, pictorial and graphic representation, animation, and maps by country and type of broadcaster

Country	n	Still Photos		Pictures/Graphics		Animation		Geographical Maps	
		Public/State	Commercial	Public/State	Commercial	Public/State	Commercial	Public/State	Commercial
Belgium	508	9	13	1	1	2	5	5	24
Brazil	252	10	9	1	3	1	4	10	23
Canada	326	73	34	6	9	1	8	9	12
Chile	450	16	18	1	1	2	2	2	4
China	215	7	-	5	-	1	-	2	-
Egypt	464	23	-	1	-	0	-	8	-
Germany	341	49	47	0	29	4	13	27	12
Hong Kong	165	-	49	-	29	-	13	-	7
Israel	371	7	9	1	6	3	4	0	4
Italy	292	30	30	2	1	2	2	8	1
Japan	192	44	28	4	1	16	13	7	20
Poland	187	48	53	15	12	23	17	31	8
Portugal	449	7	5	11	10	16	4	8	1
Singapore	447	-	26	-	3	-	3	-	1
Switzerland	591	21	12	6	20	13	0	15	0
Taiwan	185	13	40	1	13	7	13	3	10
United States	179	63	39	59	38	26	33	65	35

As with other formal features, there is much variation in the use of still photos among the 17 countries (see Table 6.6). Newscasts are most often illustrated with still photos in Canada (73% in the public channel), and least frequently in Portugal (5–7%). Here, too, three groups can be identified: (1) countries in which approximately every second item contains a still photo (Canada, the United States,

Poland, Hong Kong, and Germany); (2) countries in which this occurs in two-fifths to one-third of the items; and (3) countries in which this occurs less frequently. In several countries there was little or no difference between public and commercial stations (Germany, Italy, Chile, and Brazil). In the other countries, public stations used many more still photos than commercial stations (Canada, the United States, Japan, and Switzerland).

Pictorial or Graphic Representation
The current technical means of TV production, especially the use of computer software programs, make it possible to use not only moving images and still photos, but other kinds of pictorial and graphic representations as well. This allows abstract issues to be visualized and made more comprehensible to viewers.

However, as Table 6.6 indicates, these features are not used very often in most of the countries of our study. Only in the United States (59%), Hong Kong (29%), and Germany (29%) does such usage occur very frequently. In Poland, Portugal, and Taiwan they were used in more than 10% of the items, and in the remaining countries even less frequently.

Animation
Another feature of news that is used these days is animation, which makes television news more lively and (according to some viewers) more interesting. Animation also helps to illustrate abstract issues or to make unobservable processes visible.

American television editorial rooms make substantial use of animation (see Table 6.6) in almost every third to fourth item. Ranked second in most intensive use of animations was Poland (every fifth news item), followed by Japan, Hong Kong, Portugal, and Switzerland, where animation appeared in more than 10% of the items. Among these countries using animation, all but the United States used it relatively more in their public stations. In Germany and Taiwan there was more use of animation in commercial stations. The remaining countries presented almost no animation at all.

Geographical Maps
Maps are used in television news to indicate where the reported events have (or are) taking place. In the course of this process, physical maps are transformed into cognitive mental maps, as it were. Usually shown are cities, countries, or continents. Some news programs actually feature a world map as a backdrop.

The newscasts in the 17 countries make differing use of this feature (see Table 6.6). It is most often used in the United States and least often in Singapore. In between these extremes lie two groups of countries: those that use maps in 10–20% of their newscasts, and those that use maps even less frequently. Both groups consist of countries from Europe, Asia, North America, and South America. The second group, however, includes more Asian countries, as well as the two from the Middle East (Egypt and Israel). On average, public service and state channels employ maps more often than do private stations. This is especially true for the United States, Poland, Germany, Italy, and Portugal, but there are also countries in which the opposite is the case (Brazil, Japan, and Belgium).

Table 6.7 Percent of foreign items containing flags and emblems, logos, background music, and slow motion by country and type of broadcaster

Country	n	Flags and Emblems		Logos		Background Music		Slow Motion	
		Public/State	Commercial	Public/State	Commercial	Public/State	Commercial	Public/State	Commercial
Belgium	508	21	27	26	30	0	0	1	5
Brazil	252	0	12	0	1	42	1	0	2
Canada	326	10	13	10	6	15	3	7	4
Chile	450	9	7	6	6	3	8	29	24
China	215	1	-	0	-	2	-	0	-
Egypt	464	20	-	4	-	0	-	0	-
Germany	341	29	18	14	13	1	26	5	13
Hong Kong	165	-	59	-	12	-	1	-	0
Israel	371	0	2	1	3	2	28	0	1
Italy	292	16	24	6	6	9	3	1	0
Japan	192	33	30	15	33	8	44	10	10
Poland	187	28	24	8	5	2	8	1	2
Portugal	449	8	5	4	1	1	1	1	1
Singapore	447	-	3	-	3	-	12	-	2
Switzerland	591	6	2	7	6	4	1	4	1
Taiwan	185	19	21	15	9	3	2	0	2
United States	179	72	36	8	8	6	14	12	11

Flags and Emblems

Flags and emblems can be used in television news to indicate countries and nations. They have symbolic meanings that exceed mere identification of a country. This is why flags are often used in international, political, and sporting events and are a common sight on television. However, this may be the case with only a few recognizable flags (and emblems), depending on how familiar the viewer is with them.

The use of flags differed greatly in the 17 countries (see Table 6.7). Hong Kong and China, two territories with close political connections, were surprisingly different from each other in this respect. In Hong Kong's commercial channels television, flags in the news appeared very frequently; in China's state channel, however, almost never. This may be because they are not well known by the general public. In the United States, flags commonly appear on news broadcasts as well (particularly in the public channel). A second group is composed of countries that use flags in one-fifth to one-third of the news; a third group does so only in every tenth item, if at all. Most countries (except for Switzerland) used flags (and emblems) more often than maps. In a relatively large number of countries, public service stations as well as commercial stations make use of flags about equally. Only in the United States and Germany did public service stations prefer them, as is the case for commercial stations in Belgium and Italy.

Logos

Organizations and corporations usually have logos that accompany their company names, symbols that represents them and embody corporate identity and with which they are associated. Such logos have a stand-in function; they not only offer the advantages of compression and briefness but also have a symbolic value. This is why they are also employed in television news. However, these logos, especially those that are well known, were relatively few.

It is thus not very surprising, as Table 6.7 reveals, that logos were used less often than maps or flags (in an average of 8.5% of news items in all the countries). In only two countries (Belgium, and Japan [both commercial channels]), logos were found in slightly more than every fourth item; in three other countries in more than every tenth item (Taiwan, Germany, and Canada); and in the remaining countries in less than every tenth item. The differences between public and commercial stations were minor, with the exception of Japan.

Background Music

Most of the information contained in television news is provided by the visual and spoken text. Sometimes, however, news items are accompanied by background music. This is usually used for the purpose of dramatization, which may influence reception by viewers. The use of music is frequently frowned on by journalists, as it tends to lessen neutrality and objectivity. Experiments have refuted the notion that the use of music in information programs increases the acceptance and retention of the presented facts. The interest may be increased slightly, but the retention of information could be hindered (Brosius, 1990).

Background music is used in quite different ways and to different degrees (see Table 6.7). It is most heavily used in Japan (commercial channel), where it can be heard in almost half of the items. Relatively speaking, it is also used quite frequently is Brazil, followed by Israel, Germany, and Singapore (more than 10–30%). In the other countries it is used less than in every tenth item—in fact, almost never. Most of the background music is heard in commercial stations (es-

Table 6.8 Percent of overall use of formal features in domestic and foreign news

	Domestic (N=11,886)	Foreign (N=5,614)	Total (N=17,500)
Item part of a block	20	26	23
Reporter in a "stand-up"	19	14	17
Pre-recorded video	72	75	73
Live report	5	5	5
Archive material	26	26	26
Anchor interview reporter in studio	2	2	2
Anchor interview reporter not in studio	3	3	3
Tables/charts	8	4	7
Still photos	23	24	23
Pictorial graphic representation	11	7	10
Animated representation	9	7	8
Printed text	22	18	20
Maps	5	10	7
Flags	7	15	9
Logos	12	8	11
Background music	6	8	7
Slow motion	4	5	4
Speeded-up motion	1	-	1
Soft focus	2	1	1
Color change	2	1	1
Digitization	2	1	1
Distorted human voice	<1	<1	<1
Mean	15	15	15

N=5,614

pecially in Japan, Israel, and Germany). In these instances, background music seems to be a tool to present news in a more entertaining manner. The exception is Brazil, where music is used predominantly in the public channel.

Slow Motion

Slow motion is a visual effect in which events and processes are artificially slowed down so as to be perceived as more detailed, dramatic, and sensational. Viewer perception is thereby altered, especially when news is charged with emotion.

Regarding this feature, Chile stood out, as more than one-quarter of its news items contained slow motion (see Table 6.7). This can be partly attributed to the high percentage of sports reports in Chile's foreign news. When it comes to sporting events and athletic performances, television makers tend especially to use slow motion sequences. This is a less common practice in other events and topics.

Other Features

In our content analysis we examined the use of several more formal features. These include the use of soft (blurred) focus and digitization of images, mostly of human faces, distortion of the human voice, and changes of color of images. We do not detail the relevant findings here, as their overall appearance was very rare (less than 5%, if at all; see Table 6.2).

Domestic and Foreign News

In this chapter we have thus far focused our analysis on comparing formal features in foreign television news in the newscasts of state/public and commercial stations. In concluding the chapter we wish to take a look to see if there are any differences in the use of formal features between foreign and domestic news items (Table 6.8).

As we had initially expected, there are no large differences in this respect between both types of news. That is primarily the case for the features that are generally less prevalent. Even the overall mean frequencies of the 23 formal features that we examined are quite similar for both types (15%). Nevertheless, there are some slight differences. While reporters in "stand-up," tables/charts, pictorial/graphic representations, and printed text and logos are used slightly more in domestic news than in foreign news, the opposite is true for items as part of a block, as well as maps and flags. The latter seem to be helpful particularly in illustrating news from other countries. On the other hand, sill photos are used equally in both types of news.

Types of Newscasts

As our analysis shows, the examined formal features appeared quite differently in the television news of the 17 countries. Some were found quite often, others only rarely. Of course, this depended first and foremost on the specific news items being reported, but also on the technical, financial, and professional options available at the different TV stations. The latter could also explain why formal features are used to such differing degrees in individual countries. In summarizing the findings, we can say that there are countries in which formal features appear frequently, whereas other countries hardly use them at all.

Table 6.9 presents a cluster analysis that provides an overall picture across the 17 countries in terms of the extent to which formal features were used. We included 10 formal features, particularly the modes and tools, in the hierarchical cluster analysis and put to test a different number of clusters. Finally, we decided to focus on five clusters, because this result provided the best possible contrast among stations. Even so, we obtained one large and four smaller groups. (Reducing the clusters to four would have made the largest group even larger.)

Table 6.9 Clusters of TV stations based on modes and tools (in percent)

	Group 1 "Sober" P & C in Belgium, Brazil, Chile, Israel, Italy, Portugal, Switerland; S in China and Egypt; C (English) in Singapore, and P in Taiwan	Group 2 "Photos" P & C in Canada, Germany, and Poland; C in Taiwan, C (Chinese) in Singapore	Group 3 "Flags" Both C stations in Hong Kong	Group 4 "Text" S & C in Japan	Group 5 "Playful" P and C in the United States
Tables/ charts	4	5	5	15	8
Still photos	14	48	50	36	51
Pictorial representation	4	11	29	2	48
Animation	4	11	13	15	30
Printed text	13	20	1	90	41
Maps	7	14	8	14	50
Flags	10	18	58	32	54
Logos	7	9	12	24	8
Background music	7	7	1	26	10
Slow motion	4	4	-	10	12

Note: P = public; C = commercial; S = state

The analysis illustrates that the 33 different stations can be best assigned to five clusters that differ in terms of the usage patterns of formal features, particularly their modes and tools. The two most diverse clusters may be dubbed "sober" newscasts and "playful" newscasts.

The "playful" newscasts (Group 5) are those of the two U.S. stations in our sample. They make use of all the tools to a comparatively high degree. In no other group do so many photos, pictorial and graphic representations, animations, maps, and slow motion material appear. In about every second report, on average, the American television viewer sees visual elements such as illustrations, photos, flags, maps, printed texts, and animations. The "sober" newscasts, in contrast, are in Group 1. Consisting of 19 stations, it is the largest cluster and includes all the stations from Belgium, Brazil, Chile, Israel, Italy, Portugal, Switzerland, the single Chinese and Egyptian stations, the English-language station in Singapore (Channel 5), and the public station in Taiwan (TBS). The "sober" newscasts can be described as reluctant to use the examined formal features. These stations rarely use the various tools in their newscasts, with still photos being the most dominant feature at an average level of only 14%.

Group 2 consists of eight stations that rarely—or only moderately—use most of the formal features. This group consists of the stations in Canada, Germany, and Poland, and the commercial channel in Taiwan and the Chinese-language channel in Singapore. An exception to the general low-to-moderate pattern is the number of photos in the newscasts, seen on average in every second report. These photos typically appear behind the anchor during his or her delivery. Although the percentage of photos in two other groups (3 and 5) is quite high, the photos are not as predominant as in the "photo" group, where they are by far the most characteristic element.

The third cluster, dubbed the "flags" group, uses the formal features to quite varying degrees. In the reports of the two stations from Hong Kong, we found the greatest use of flags and a comparatively high number of photos and pictorial or graphic representations. On the other hand, these stations did not use slow motion at all and make nearly no use of background music, text, maps and tables, or charts.

The fourth cluster, the "text" group, consists of the two Japanese stations. The most striking feature of this group is that text is presented in nearly every report (averaging 90%). Apart from that, there are similarities to the two U.S. stations that shape the "playful" group, as the two Japanese stations also take full advantage of the other formal features and use most of the tools frequently.

By using squared Euclidian distance as a measure, we can say that Group 5 ("Playful") and Group 3 ("Flags") are the most dissimilar, while Group 1 ("Sober") and Group 4 ("Text"), like Group 2 ("Photos") and Group 4 ("Text"), are more similar to each other. Group 2 ("Photos") and Group 3 ("Flags"), as well as Group 2 ("Photos") and Group 5 ("Playful"), differ from each other, too, though to a lesser degree.

It is remarkable that in most cases all the examined news programs of a country—including the public service and commercial stations—are found in the same group. The only exceptions are Singapore and Taiwan. Thus, there is no group that is composed predominantly of public service or commercial stations. Generally speaking, these channels differ from each other only in their formal features. As for regional clusters—that is, the concentration of stations in one group from a certain region of the world—these are not identified here, either.

Summary

Formal features may be considered a kind of "global language" in television news and include central elements that are inherent in most stations and other elements that occur only rarely. What Heinderyckx (1993) discovered for Western Europe 20 years ago may be extended beyond this region. As he noted, though many features are ubiquitous, "significant nuances exist between different channels" (p. 448). All these elements indicate that modern television (like other media) has moved to a complex multimodal format, integrating different semiotic and technical resources (Jewitt, 2009; Bucher, Gloning, & Lehnen, 2010).

In our study as well, there were significant differences across the countries and stations in terms of the use of formal features. Even though the highly sophisticated state-of-the-art technology that enables many of these features is generally available all over, we believe that the extent to which the features are used varies from country to country. The respective usage "profiles" seem to depend on the existing "national" traditions and viewers' expectations, but perhaps most influential are the organizational, financial, technical, and editorial ramifications. The larger the budget and the professional staff, the more facilities can be applied. Besides, the use of formal features also depends on journalists' understanding of their task and the formal design possibilities, as well as the idiosyncratic preferences they have for their programs. Furthermore, formal features also depend on the type of news itself, on the events, on the topics, on the locations, and on the available material upon which the television producers can rely.

CHAPTER SEVEN

Foreign News on Public and Commercial Stations

JOSEPH M. CHAN & FRANCIS L.F. LEE

In an article outlining the ideal media system for a democratic society, Curran (2000) envisions a model in which public service television constitutes the core of the media system, complemented by a professional sector, a civic sector, a social market sector, and a private enterprise (that is, commercial) sector. The model, in other words, involves the co-presence of commercial and public broadcasting. Public service television should be the core because, governed by the norms of fairness and equal access, it remains "the best way of establishing an open public forum" (p. 143). Commercial broadcasters, on the other hand, can "make the media system as a whole more responsive to popular pleasures" (p. 146).

Many contemporary societies are indeed marked by a mixed or dual broadcasting system in which public and private broadcasters co-exist. This situation was created mainly through a wave of "deregulation" in the broadcasting arena, especially in European countries, in the 1980s and 1990s (Holtz-Bacha & Norris, 2001). However, it does not mean that Curran's vision is achieved. His model resides on two interrelated presumptions that may deviate from reality. First, the value of having both public and commercial broadcasters can be realized only if the two retain their respective characteristics. Especially important is for the public broadcaster to remain true to its mission of providing people with what they need instead of merely what they want. Second, the rise of commercial broadcasters cannot result in a situation in which they so dominate the ratings that the public broadcaster becomes marginalized or is pressured to abandon its mission.

Against such a background, this chapter examines the differences between the foreign news offered by public and commercial television stations in 13 countries. Specifically, it examines whether foreign news on public television is more cosmopolitan, analytically deeper, and less sensational than foreign news on commercial television. While the public-commercial differential (hereafter PC differential) can be expected, based on the supposed nature of the two types of broadcasting, there is also the possibility of convergence. Accordingly, this chapter also examines whether commercialization of public television would affect the size of PC differential at the country level of analysis. Overall, the analysis examines whether the economic nature of news organizations could explain the characteristics of foreign news content they provide. The findings should give us insights into the underlying concern about how the structure of broadcasting affects the quality of news and public communication.

Public vs. Commercial Television: Differentiation or Convergence?

Since the 1980s and 1990s, when the wave of broadcasting deregulation in Europe began, numerous studies of television news have incorporated in them an analysis of the differences between public television (PTV) and commercial television (CTV). Such studies typically begin with the expectation of a PC differential based on the presumed nature of the two types of broadcasters. PTV, because of its public service ideals, is often expected to offer more news and public affairs programming, report hard news topics to a greater extent, and/or present news in less sensational ways. Putting it generally, PTV is expected to provide the news on which the formation of an informed citizenry depends. In contrast, CTV is expected to do the opposite, driven by its presumed tendency to prioritize ratings over news quality. In other words, the differences in the news content of PTV and CTV are explained by the presumed differences in their editorial policies following their respective economic nature.

Indeed, some studies have revealed such PC differentials in news content. Vettehen, Beentjes, Nuijten, and Peeters (2011), for instance, analyzed the use of "arousing news characteristics" in Dutch television news. They found that PTV employed four arousing news characteristics—close-ups, laypersons, music, and frequent camera shots—to lesser extents. Similarly, Stromback and Dimitrova (2011) found that in Sweden, PTV's political coverage was more likely than CTV's to employ the issue frame and less likely to employ the horse-race frame (also see Bek, 2004; Pfetsch, 1996; van Praag & van der Eijk, 1998).

Consistent with such findings from content studies, research on the effects of news consumption has also found that people's preference for commercial or public television does matter. Aarts and Semetko (2003), for example, found that preference for news on PTV related positively to political knowledge, efficacy, and voter turnout in the Netherlands. Hooghe (2002) found a positive relationship between preference for CTV and feelings of powerlessness in Belgium. Holtz-Bacha and Norris (2001) found a positive relationship between preference for PTV and political knowledge in 10 of 14 European countries.

However, the empirical findings are not always clear-cut. The above-mentioned study by Stromback and Dimitrova (2011) also found that Swedish PTV and CTV did not differ on a number of other indicators of journalistic intervention in political communication. Other studies have also found either mixed or null findings regarding the PC differentials. Klijin (2003), for instance, argued that certain visuals about violence raise comprehension, and he hypothesized that PTV would employ comprehension-raising visuals to a larger extent. Yet his findings did not support the hypothesis. Similarly, Uribe and Gunter (2007) did not find discernible differences between Britain's BBC (public) and ITV (commercial) broadcasters in their use of emotionally arousing elements in news.

In the case of the United States, Kerbel, Apee, and Ross (2000) found that the PBS (public) and ABC (commercial) networks were similarly likely to employ the horse-race frame when covering the 1996 presidential elections. Esser (2008) examined sound bites and image bites in television news in the United States, Germany, France, and the United Kingdom. He found that there were more cross-national differences than differences between PTV and CTV. De Swert and Hooghe (2010) even came up with the counter-intuitive finding in Belgium that, despite the diversity policy adopted by the PTV station, news on PTV used female sources to a lesser extent than did news on CTV (see also Cottle & Rai, 2008; Hoynes, 2002; Leon, 2008).

The above-referenced studies by no means constitute a comprehensive review of empirical evidence about the PC differentials in news, but they should be adequate for giving us a sense of the findings in the literature. On the whole, the expected PC differentials in news content exist only in some contexts and on some dependent variables. There are even cases of counter-intuitive findings, with CTV exhibiting some indicators of "good journalism" to a larger extent.

The absence of across-the-board differences between the two types of broadcasters is understandable, though. In many countries that originally had only public broadcasting, the emergence of CTV has led to a form of competition that could generate convergence between the two types of broadcasters. Theoretically, as Pfetsch (1996) explicated, the convergence hypothesis can be derived from a Downsian analysis of the rational decisions made by competitors in a two-horse race. As both sides want to capture the largest audience, both will move toward the provision of "a convergent middle-of-the-road program" (p. 434). Empirically, scholars from various countries have reported that the rise of CTV has pressured PTV to redesign its news and public affairs programming to attract a larger audience (Comrie, 1999; Machill, 1999; Neveu, 1999; Stevenson, 2010).

Notably, the convergence hypothesis points not only toward the commercialization of PTV but also the tendency for CTV to adopt some of the values and practices of PTV. If PTV newscasts sometimes commercialize in order to boost ratings, CTV may also adopt part of the format and style of PTV newscasts to boost credibility. Sanders and Bale (2000), for instance, found that the U.K. commercial satellite broadcaster Sky expended a great deal of effort in covering the 1997 general elections. They argued that a "symbolic agenda" was driving the broadcaster's coverage: the coverage was meant to build reputation and respect. Also pointing toward the influence of public broadcasting on commercial broadcasters, Kolmer and Semetko (2010) argued that CTV in Germany tended to report a substantial amount of foreign news in part because the strong public service broadcasting tradition in the country could have "initially raised the bar for private channels" (p. 712).

Certainly, convergence is a matter of degree. There are, after all, significant PC differentials found in some studies. As these PC differentials vary in size across contexts, an important question would be: What factors can explain the variations? Here it should be noted that PTV stations in different countries are embedded in different media systems (Hallin & Mancini, 2004). They may differ from each other in a number of key ways, such as revenue sources, the amount of market competition they face, the strictness of relevant regulations, and so on. Meanwhile, CTV stations in some countries may also operate under regulations requiring them to provide a substantial amount of news and public affairs programming (Curran, Iyengar, Lund, & Salovaara-Moring, 2009). To our knowledge, whether and how structural and contextual factors may shape the PC differentials in news content remains an unexplored question in the literature. The present comparative project provides us with the data to tackle this question, and this would be a major contribution of the present analysis.

Sensationalism, Analytical Depth, and Cosmopolitanism in Foreign News

As the above discussion shows, the available literature has already provided both theoretical arguments and empirical findings regarding whether and what kinds of PC differentials exist. This chapter, therefore, is not merely an exploratory analysis of possible differences between PTV and CTV. Rather, the analysis is more theory-driven. Specifically, it will focus on three key concepts: sensationalism, analytical depth, and cosmopolitanism. A number of research questions are set up to guide the analysis.

First, when compared to CTV, PTV is expected to feature news with a lesser degree of sensationalism, which can be defined as the attempt to strengthen the sensual appeal of the news product so as to attract a larger audience. Sensationalism has long been regarded as a hallmark of market-driven journalism (McManus,

1994). The specific methods used by news organizations to strengthen sensual appeal can range from an emphasis on soft news or sensational news topics (such as disasters and human interest stories) to the adoption of presentational techniques that make news more audio-visually appealing and emotionally arousing (for example, the use of background music, animation, and so forth). In other words, sensationalism can be manifested in both content and presentational style (Grabe, Zhou, & Barnett, 2001).

More concretely, a number of indicators in the current data set are pertinent to the concept of sensationalism. As shown in Chapter 3, news topics can be differentiated as hard news, soft news, and sensational news. For the present chapter, the most important distinction is the one between hard news and the other two types of news topics. PTV's public service ideal should lead them to place more emphasis on policy-related hard news, whereas CTV's concerns with ratings and market appeal should lead them to emphasize soft and sensational news topics. Besides, CTV's tendency to sensationalize news may imply a stronger tendency to employ attention-grabbing audio and visual elements. Hence we may expect CTV newscasts to contain visuals of violence and various types of audio-visual effects more frequently. However, given the aforementioned mixed findings in the literature, the "expectable" PC differential may or may not exist in different contexts. Hence we put forward a research question as follows:

RQ1: Do CTV and PTV differ in the extent to which their foreign news stories focus on hard news topics, contain visuals of violence, and employ various kinds of audio-visual effects?

Second, based on the presumed nature of the two types of broadcasters, PTV newscasts may be expected to present news with more analytical depth when compared to CTV newscasts. Analytical depth can be defined as the extent to which news reports present a large amount of both current and background information and organize them coherently so that the audience can understand the broader social and political significance of the events being reported. This definition is in line with the Hutchins Commission's definition of responsible journalism in the 1940s as journalism that gives readers "a comprehensive and intelligent account of the day's events in a context which gives them meaning" (Commission on the Freedom of the Press, 1947, p. 21).

It is difficult to measure analytical depth directly. However, researchers have pinpointed a number of phenomena that can be taken as indicators of analytical depth (or the lack thereof). For example, many scholars have criticized the episodic and fragmented character of news (Bennett, 1988; Iyengar, 1991). Directly relevant to the empirical analysis of this chapter is the fact that researchers have also criticized the tendency of personalization (Bennett, 1988). A focus on the personal instead of the social can represent a lack of emphasis on analyzing the broader social and political significance of the events being covered. Moreover, many scholars have commented on how speeches made by political leaders are often decontextualized and edited into short sound bites (Adatto, 1990; Hallin, 1992). Analytical depth is arguably sacrificed when more elaborate statements and arguments are not presented. With personalization and length of sound bites as indicators of analytical depth, we posed the following research question:

RQ2: Do CTV and PTV differ in the length of sound bites and relative emphasis on personal conflicts over social conflicts in their foreign news stories?

Cosmopolitanism constitutes the third conceptual focus of the analysis. Degree of cosmopolitanism can be defined as the extent to which the newscasts or news stories connect a local audience to a wide and diverse global community. Theorists of globalization point out that we are living in an era of increasing global interconnectedness, a world in which local happenings are influenced by far-away events and vice versa (see, for example, Giddens, 1991; Robertson, 1992). A "global perspective" should become more and more important to contemporary world citizens. Here, providing a global perspective means first and foremost the provision of more foreign news. Besides, decades of research on international news has repeatedly shown that not all countries are equally newsworthy (see Galtung & Ruge, 1965; Chang, 1998). Foreign news often focuses on a small group of elite nations. A truly global perspective, however, should be based on a more diverse "world map."

Moreover, in the age of increasing global interconnectedness, events and issues in one country often have implications and effects on other countries. To the extent that many issues (for instance, global warming) cannot be resolved by a single national government, international organizations are playing increasingly important roles in international affairs. Lee (2010) argued that the presence of international organizations in news and the prominence of "multi-national stories," that is, stories concerning more than a single country, can be taken to represent the extent to which foreign news is presenting a picture of the globally interconnected world to its audience.

Therefore, degree of cosmopolitanism can be indicated by proportion of foreign news, degree of concentration of foreign news on a small number of countries, proportion of stories featuring international organizations, and proportion of stories featuring more than one foreign country. Given these indicators, the third research question is as follows:

RQ3: Do CTV and PTV differ in the amount of foreign news being provided? Do they differ in the range of countries covered in foreign news, the extent to which their foreign news stories feature international organizations, and the proportion of multi-nation stories?

In sum, the three research questions address the PC differential in terms of degree of sensationalism, analytical depth, and cosmopolitanism. Theoretically, one might expect PTV news to be analytically deeper, more cosmopolitan, and less sensational when compared to CTV news. But as pointed out earlier, the PC differentials are unlikely to exist in all contexts. Characteristics of existing public and private broadcasters vary. Hence the performance of the two types of television stations in different countries is likely to vary depending on certain contextual characteristics, such as the strength of the tradition of public broadcasting, the type of media regulations in place, the degree of market competition, and so forth.

It is not easy to examine the influence of many of these contextual characteristics, given the lack of information or the difficulty in quantifying them. More important, a more meaningful analysis could be undertaken with a clearer conceptual focus. This chapter thus focuses on the implications of the commercialization of public broadcasting. Theoretically, as PTV becomes more commercialized, its behavior and content are likely to become similar to those of CTV. As a result, the PC differential will diminish.

In terms of concrete indicators, we now examine how the revenue source of public broadcasting and number of competitors in the media market affect the PC differentials. In some countries, deregulation of the broadcasting system has led to the appearance of advertising on public channels. Reliance on advertising revenue, which varies across countries, is a good indicator of degree of commercialization of PTV.

Besides advertising revenue, the pressure for a public station to commercialize may also come from the strength of the existing competition in the market. Without getting into the complexities of how market competition should be measured, this analysis adopts the basic assumption that competitive pressure rises with the number of competitors in the market. PTV in markets with more competitors is likely to be more commercialized.

Theoretically, our expectation is that commercialization of PTV would reduce the size of the PC differential. But to maintain presentational consistency, we set up a research question instead of hypotheses to guide the analysis:

RQ4: At the country level, does the size of the PC differential relate to degree of commercialization of PTV?

Some Notes on Method and Data

The following analysis includes data from only 13 of the 17 countries involved in our comparative project. China and Egypt are not included because there are no purely commercial stations in either country. Also, Hong Kong and Singapore were excluded because they have only commercial television stations.

The analysis focuses only on foreign news (with the exception of the analysis of the ratio of foreign news to domestic news in the newscasts). Presumably, the concerns and arguments underlying the research questions are largely applicable to domestic news as well. However, we deal only with foreign news in the following analyses partly because of space limitations and partly because of the core analytical interest of this chapter. Foreign news in the analyses in this chapter, as in several other chapters, consists of items coded as "pure" foreign news as well as hybrid items consisting of foreign news with domestic involvement.

Tackling the research questions is straightforward. Each relevant indicator is examined in turn, using bivariate analytical approaches, after clarifying the operationalization of the variable involved. One methodological issue is whether the 13 countries should be pooled together, or if the analysis should be conducted country by country. We opted for the latter approach for two reasons. First, the 13 countries do not constitute a representative sample of countries in the world. Hence what the pooled data set may represent is unclear. Second, this chapter emphasizes the possibility of a varying extent of PC differentials across contexts. A country-by-country analysis allows us to discern the cross-national variations more clearly. In a sense, such an analysis is also similar to conducting "replications" across countries.

Analysis and Findings

Sensationalism

The research questions can be tackled in turn. For sensationalism, the first relevant indicator is the proportion of stories focusing on "hard news" topics. Following the conceptual distinctions as well as operational definitions explicated in Chapter 3, in some of the analyses every news item was treated as addressing either a hard news topic, a soft news topic, or a sensational news topic. As outlined earlier, hard news topics are those that are highly likely to be about policy or policy-relevant issues. Sensational topics are those about events that are likely to be covered in ways that appeal to people's emotions and instincts. Soft news topics are those that do not have policy implications but are covered because of their appeal to curiosity and human interests. But for the purposes of the present chapter, as indicated above, we grouped soft news and sensational news together to simplify the analysis. The statistical analysis, therefore, consists of cross-tabulating the dichotomous PTV vs. CTV variable with the dichotomized "hard news vs. soft or sensational news" topic variable.

The left side of Table 7.1 summarizes the findings. The χ^2 values derived from the cross-tabulation analysis are statistically significant in 9 of the 13 countries.[1] All significant findings point to the same conclusion: PTV newscasts feature hard news more frequently than CTV newscasts. For example, 41% of the foreign news items in CTV newscasts in Germany concerned hard news topics, whereas 73% of the news items in PTV newscasts treated hard news. These findings are

Foreign News on Public and Commercial Stations | 137

Table 7.1 Soft news items, visual representation, and audiovisual effects in foreign news by country and public vs. commercial stations

Country	n	Soft News				Visual Representation				Audiovisual Effects			
		Public	Commercial	χ^2	Confirm	Public	Commercial	T	Confirm	Public	Commercial	T	Confirm
Belgium	508	55	46	3.43*	Yes	0.20	0.29	1.51	NS	0.03	0.06	1.10	NS
Brazil	252	78	75	0.21	NS	0.11	0.11	0.11	NS	0.43	0.05	7.75***	No
Canada	326	59	56	0.41	NS	0.43	0.42	0.09	NS	0.28	0.14	2.38**	No
Chile	450	28	34	2.00	NS	0.18	0.24	1.24	NS	0.48	0.47	0.14	NS
Germany	341	73	41	34.03***	Yes	0.21	0.44	3.09**	Yes	0.07	0.56	8.31***	Yes
Israel	371	69	60	3.38*	Yes	0.13	0.14	0.21	NS	0.03	0.30	7.72***	Yes
Italy	292	69	64	0.66	n.s	0.11	0.14	0.49	NS	0.10	0.04	1.79*	No
Japan	192	78	61	6	Yes	0.11	0.17	0.75	NS	0.26	0.86	5.75***	Yes
Poland	187	71	58	34*	Yes	0.37	0.28	0.67	NS	0.04	0.18	2.46**	Yes
Portugal	449	60	51	3.61*	Yes	0.19	0.19	0.08	NS	0.02	0.02	0.26	NS
Switzerland	591	57	41	3.21*	Yes	0.19	0.22	0.44	NS	0.12	0.06	2.09*	No
Taiwan	185	67	46	8.11**	Yes	0.08	0.15	1.07	NS	0.04	0.25	3.49***	Yes
United States	179	93	76	7.58**	Yes	0.66	1.01	1.79*	Yes	0.22	0.35	1.46	NS

*** $p < .001$; ** $p < .01$; * $p < .05$ (one-tailed)

Notes: For each variable, cell entries in the first two columns are either mean scores or percentages. Statistical significance of the difference between public and private stations was tested either with independent-samples t-tests (for mean scores) or χ^2 tests in cross-tabulations (for percentages). In the right column, "Yes" indicates that the difference between public and commercial stations confirms the theoretically expected differences; "NS" indicates non-significance; and "No" indicates that the difference between public and commercial stations is contrary to the theoretically expected difference between them.

consistent with the presumed difference between PTV and CTV—that is, PTV should be less sensational.

The second indicator of sensationalism is use of visuals of violence. In the content analysis, every news item was coded in terms of whether it showed physical violence, killing, wounded persons, physical damage, and other consequences of violence. The coding thus resulted in five dichotomous variables. For simplicity, the five items were added together to form a 0-to-5 index. T-tests for independent samples were then conducted to see if PTV and CTV news stories scored differently on the visual violence index.

As the middle third of Table 7.1 shows, the number of significant findings is much smaller. The differences between PTV and CTV are statistically significant in only two countries, yet in both cases the results are consistent with the theoretically expectable difference between PTV and CTV: in Germany and the United States, CTV news items, on average, contain more visual representations of violence than do PTV news items.

Use of audiovisual effects constitutes the third and last indicator of sensationalism. In the content analysis, as reported in Chapter 6, coders recorded whether or not each news item involved the use of background music, slow motion, speeded-up motion, repetition of same visuals, soft focus, color change, and digitization. Similar to the analysis of visual violence, the seven dichotomous items related to audio-visual effects were added together to form a 0-to-7 audiovisual effects index. Here, too, independent-samples t-tests were conducted to see if PTV and CTV news stories scored differently on the index.

The right side of Table 7.1 shows the results of the analysis, which are more mixed and complicated when compared to the findings regarding soft news and visual representation. Significant differences between PTV and CTV exist in nine countries, but the differences vary in directions. In four cases, PTV newscasts were more likely than CTV newscasts to employ various audiovisual effects when reporting news. In the other five cases, PTV newscasts were less likely than CTV newscasts to employ audiovisual effects. Notably, when the significant difference is consistent with theoretical expectation (in other words, when CTV is more sensational), the actual nominal difference between PTV and CTV is usually extremely large (for example, in Germany, Israel, Japan, and Taiwan). In contrast, when the significant difference is contrary to theoretical expectation, the nominal PC differential is often very small, as in Switzerland and Italy. Yet it remains true that, on the whole, the findings do not show even a general tendency for PTV to use audiovisual effects to a lesser extent than CTV.

Analytical Depth
We now turn to analytical depth, for which length of sound bites is the first indicator. In the content analysis, the length of the sound bite of each speaking actor

Table 7.2 Mean length of sound bites and percentage of items containing conflict in foreign news and percentage of foreign news by country and public vs. commercial stations

Country	n	Mean Length of Sound Bites in Seconds				Percentage of Items Containing Conflict				Percentage of Foreign News			
		Public	Commercial	T	Confirm	Public	Commercial	χ^2	Confirm	Public	Commercial	χ^2	Confirm
Belgium	508	20.1	18.6	0.85	NS	7	30	20.13***	Yes	42	28	28.60***	Yes
Brazil	252	48.6	12.2	1.98*	Yes	7	14	0.74	NS	34	31	0.92	NS
Canada	326	26.9	9.8	2.25*	Yes	18	30	3.92*	Yes	41	47	3.00	NS
Chile	450	14.4	16.6	1.41	NS	52	44	0.51	NS	30	30	0.10	NS
Germany	341	10.6	10.4	0.20	NS	3	18	10.82***	Yes	46	46	0.00	NS
Israel	371	15.0	16.5	0.79	NS	3	0	1.95	NS	28	37	10.24**	No
Italy	292	22.7	21.4	0.21	NS	11	14	0.33	NS	24	18	6.56**	Yes
Japan	192	14.2	15.7	1.02	NS	5	10	0.73	NS	18	25	7.03**	No
Poland	187	10.9	10.2	0.78	NS	34	36	0.02	NS	37	32	1.79	NS
Portugal	449	23.7	29.8	1.79*	No	1	1	0.09	NS	30	22	14.63***	Yes
Switzerland	591	19.9	9.4	1.65	NS	13	28	6.20**	Yes	49	25	64.56***	Yes
Taiwan	185	13.7	9.9	3.91***	Yes	2	14	3.22*	Yes	22	8	48.30***	Yes
United States	179	66.6	11.3	3.57***	Yes	1	0	0.61	NS	36	20	20.07***	Yes

*** $p < .001$; ** $p < .01$; * $p < .05$ (one-tailed)

Notes: For each variable, cell entries in the first two columns are either mean scores or percentages. Statistical significance of the difference between public and private stations was tested either with independent-samples t-tests (for mean scores) or χ^2 tests in cross-tabulations (for percentages). In the right column, "Yes" indicates that the difference between public and commercial stations confirms the theoretically expected differences; "NS" indicates non-significance; and "No" indicates that the difference between public and commercial stations is contrary to the theoretically expected difference between them.

was recorded. The score of a news item on the length of sound bite variable is simply the average of all the sound bites appearing in the news item. Independent-samples t-tests were conducted to test the hypothesis.

As the left side of Table 7.2 shows, significant differences in lengths of sound bites exist in 5 of the 13 countries. In four cases the PC differential is in the theoretically expected direction, that is, sound bites in PTV newscasts are generally longer. In fact, the PC differential in length of sound bite can be very substantial in individual countries. In the United States, the average length of a sound bite on the PTV station is more than one minute, whereas the average length of a sound bite on the CTV station is only 11.3 seconds. Portuguese television news exhibits the opposite: the average length of a sound bite in CTV news items is 29.8 seconds, which is about 6 seconds longer than the sound bites in PTV news.

Besides length of sound bites, we are also concerned with relative emphasis of personal conflicts over social conflicts in foreign news. Conflict is a fundamental news value. Social, political, and international conflicts such as wars, elections, and protests are all important news events. Knowing about and understanding these conflicts is key to an understanding of a foreign country and/or the world at large. Yet there are conflicts that are less socially significant. Divorce litigation between two individuals is a personal conflict that usually has no broader social significance. In the content analysis, a news item was coded in terms of whether it involved conflicts or not. If it involved conflict, the coder had to decide whether the conflict was personal or social. In the analysis, all the news items not including any conflicts were excluded. The dichotomous PTV vs. CTV variable was cross-tabulated with the dichotomous personal or social conflict variable.[2] This allowed us to discern the relative prominence of the two types of conflicts in television news.

The middle third of Table 7.2 summarizes the findings of the analysis. A significant difference between PTV and CTV exists in five of the 13 countries, and the pattern is consistent with theoretical expectation in all five cases, with PTV newscasts paying relatively more attention to social conflicts. In Belgium, for example, 30% of the news items involving conflicts on CTV concerned a personal conflict, whereas only 7% of the conflict items on PTV concerned personal conflicts.

Cosmopolitanism

RQ3 asks whether PTV and CTV exhibit different degrees of cosmopolitanism in their coverage of foreign news. The first indicator of cosmopolitanism is simply the proportion of foreign news itself. The relevant analysis involves cross-tabulating the PTV vs. CTV variable with a dichotomized foreign vs. domestic news variable. As Chapter 2 discussed, the importance given to foreign news can be measured in terms of percentage of items, length of items, and ranking of items in the newscasts. However, for the purpose of this chapter, it is not necessary to examine all three types of indicators. For simplicity we examined only proportions of foreign and domestic news items. As the right side of Table 7.2 shows, the proportions of foreign vs. domestic news on PTV and CTV do differ significantly in eight countries. The differences in six cases are consistent with the theoretical expectation that PTV would exhibit a higher degree of cosmopolitanism than CTV. In Belgium, for example, foreign news constituted 42% of the news items from the PTV station, whereas only 28% of the news items on CTV were foreign news. Yet a contrary pattern appeared in Israel and Japan. In Israel, for instance, 37% of the news items from CTV were foreign news, while the corresponding figure for PTV was only 28%.

Besides proportion of foreign news, a higher degree of cosmopolitanism is also indicated by the coverage of a more diverse range of countries, or a lower level of concentration on a few prominent countries. The content analysis coded the location of the event being reported in a news item. A measure of country concentration can be derived from this variable. For example, in Belgium, 73 of the 508 foreign news items from the two news stations concerned events in the United States, 52 items concerned events in France, 36 items concerned events in the United Kingdom, and 32 concerned events in the Netherlands. These were the four most frequently covered countries in Belgium, and together they accounted for 38% of all foreign news items. The last figure can be taken as a measure of country concentration of foreign news in Belgium.

This Country Concentration Index (CCI) is analogous to the notion of "concentration ratio" (Albarran, 2002; Hoskins, McFadyen, & Finn, 2004) used by media economists to measure market concentration. It is calculated in the same way as the CCI reported in Chapter 4. The only difference between the CCI employed here and the CCI in Chapter 4 is that this chapter focuses on the four most frequently covered countries, whereas Chapter 4 examined the proportion of items accounted for by the 10 most frequently covered countries. While four is admittedly an arbitrary number, we adopt it instead of 10 because the differences between PTV and CTV in terms of country concentration are more discernible when a smaller number of most frequently covered countries are being examined.

As the left side of Table 7.3 shows, a significant PC differential on country concentration in foreign news is found in five countries. In Taiwan, for example, as much as 79% of the foreign news items on CTV concerned an event occurring in one of the four most frequently covered foreign countries. On the PTV channel, however, only 48% of the foreign news items related to one of those four countries. The finding is therefore consistent with the expectation that PTV newscasts would be more cosmopolitan than CTV newscasts. In fact, all of the significant differences regarding country concentration are in this direction.

Table 7.3 Percentages of concentrated countries, mean number of international organizations, and mean number of countries involved in foreign news by country and public vs. commercial stations

Country	n	Percentage of Concentrated Countries				Mean Number of Int'l Organizations				Mean Number of Countries Involved			
		Public	Commercial	χ^2	Confirm	Public	Commercial	t	Confirm	Public	Commercial	T	Confirm
Belgium	508	35	45	4.68*	Yes	0.12	0.09	1.03	NS	2.11	2.06	0.53	NS
Brazil	252	39	52	4.50*	Yes	0.22	0.33	1.53	NS	1.96	2.07	0.71	NS
Canada	326	55	62	1.61	NS	0.16	0.11	1.23	NS	2.14	1.86	2.16*	Yes
Chile	450	51	51	0.01	NS	0.04	0.05	0.35	NS	2.21	2.08	1.22	NS
Germany	341	29	38	3.34*	Yes	0.29	0.16	2.42**	Yes	2.45	2.09	2.62**	Yes
Israel	371	45	49	0.61	NS	0.22	0.12	2.35*	Yes	1.92	1.58	3.26***	Yes
Italy	292	47	42	0.75	NS	0.19	0.23	0.81	NS	2.05	2.03	0.08	NS
Japan	192	71	77	0.65	NS	0.49	0.27	2.77**	Yes	1.74	1.67	0.51	NS
Poland	187	44	61	5.48*	Yes	0.20	0.05	2.82**	Yes	2.03	1.83	1.30	NS
Portugal	449	41	47	1.41	NS	0.11	0.10	0/30	NS	1.83	1.82	0.02	NS
Switzerland	591	37	42	0.79	NS	0.15	0.05	3.42***	Yes	1.93	1.58	3.85***	Yes
Taiwan	185	48	79	17.68***	Yes	0.11	0.03	2.25*	Yes	1.71	1.40	2.50**	Yes
United States	179	60	53	0.87	NS	0.20	0.22	0.38	NS	2.15	1.97	1.24	NS

*** $p < .001$; ** $p < .01$; * $p < .05$ (one-tailed)

Notes: For each variable, cell entries in the first two columns are either mean scores or percentages. Statistical significance of the difference between public and private stations was tested either with independent-samples t-tests (for mean scores) or χ^2 tests in cross-tabulations (for percentages). In the right column, "Yes" indicates that the difference between public and commercial stations confirms the theoretically expected differences; "NS" indicates non-significance; and "No" indicates that the difference between public and commercial stations is contrary to the theoretically expected difference between them.

Next, our analysis addressed whether PTV news would feature international organizations more than CTV news, and whether PTV would provide more multi-nation stories when compared to CTV news. In the content analysis, up to two international organizations appearing in every news item were recorded. A 0-to-2 index can therefore be derived, representing the number of international organizations involved in a foreign news item. In addition, as discussed in Chapter 4, the content analysis also registered up to five countries mentioned in a news item. The relevant dependent variable for the analysis regarding multi-nation stories is simply the number of countries involved in a news item. Independent-samples t-tests were conducted to see if PTV and CTV scored differently on these two dependent variables.

The middle and right side of Table 7.3 summarize the findings. For reporting of international organizations, the table shows that PTV and CTV did differ from each other significantly in 6 of the 13 countries, and in all cases the differences are in the same direction. PTV news in Germany, Israel, Japan, Poland, Switzerland, and Taiwan featured international organizations more frequently than CTV news, which suggests that PTV news exhibits a higher degree of cosmopolitanism. Similarly, the right side of Table 7.3 shows that PTV and CTV differed in the average number of countries involved per foreign news item in five countries, and in all five cases the differences are in the same direction and suggest a higher degree of cosmopolitanism on the part of PTV news, since foreign news on PTV in Canada, Germany, Israel, Switzerland, and Taiwan was more likely to feature multi-nation stories.

Summary of Public-Commercial Differentials

Before tackling RQ4, it would be useful to first summarize the findings up to this point. We have examined three research questions with a total of nine indicators. Given the presence of 13 countries in the analysis, there were a total of 117 separate statistical tests conducted. Putting all the findings reported in the earlier tables and texts together, there are a total of 54 significant findings. Forty-seven of the significant findings are consistent with theoretical expectations that PTV newscasts would be less sensational, analytically deeper, and more cosmopolitan than CTV newscasts, while there are only seven findings contradicting such expectations. The findings are statistically insignificant in the remaining 63 cases.

In one sense, these results are consistent with the findings in the literature on the PC differential. On one hand, significant PC differentials are not found in the majority of cases. It seems that PTV and CTV newscasts are quite similar to each other in many places and in many respects. But on the other hand, to the extent that differences do exist, those differences still largely correspond to the presumed nature of the two types of broadcasters.

At the same time, the findings can also be summarized by country. Table 7.4 shows the number of significant findings for each country. A couple of points can be noted. First, the seven significant findings that contradict the hypotheses are spread over seven individual countries. In other words, in none of the 13 countries does PTV consistently exhibit the presumed characteristics of CTV even more strongly than CTV itself. This suggests that the seven "theory-defying" findings are idiosyncratic results with little general significance. In fact, given the number of statistical tests involved and the adoption of one-tailed significance level, a few "significant findings" defying theoretical expectations could have been expected merely due to chance. Hence it is not necessary to take such findings too seriously and further analyze them.

Table 7.4 Number of significant findings for each country

	Supporting conventional theoretical expectation	Contradicting conventional theoretical expectation
Belgium (N=508)	3	0
Brazil (N=252)	2	1
Canada (N=326)	3	1
Chile (N=450)	0	0
Germany (N=341)	7	0
Israel (N=371)	3	1
Italy (N=292)	1	1
Japan (N=192)	3	1
Poland (N=187)	3	0
Portugal (N=449)	1	1
Switzerland (N=591)	5	1
Taiwan (N=185)	8	0
United States (N=179)	4	0
Total	43	7

Second, and more important, numbers of significant theory-confirming findings do vary substantially across countries. At one end is Taiwan, where eight of the nine hypotheses about the PC differential in news are supported. Germany follows closely behind, with seven of the hypotheses receiving support. At the other end of the spectrum, none of the nine hypotheses is supported in Chile, and only one hypothesis is supported in Italy.

One methodological issue to note here is that the actual sample sizes differ across countries. Technically, significant findings are more likely to emerge when the actual sample size is larger. However, Table 7.4 shows that the number of significant findings appearing in a country is by no means driven by sample size. Taiwan, the country with the largest number of theory-confirming significant findings, actually has the second-smallest actual sample size among the 13 countries. Similarly, the actual sample sizes for Chile and Portugal are comparatively larger than many other countries in the analysis, but between the two countries there are only two theory-confirming significant findings. In fact, the Spearman rank correlation between number of significant findings and actual sample sizes among the 13 countries is statistically insignificant and even negative in sign ($\rho = -.17$). Therefore, the between-country variation in the numbers of theory-confirming significant findings is not a methodological artifact. The key question, then, is what explains the variation.

Media Characteristics and Public-Commercial Differentials

RQ4 questions if, at the country level, the size of the PC differentials would vary with the degree to which the public broadcaster relies on advertising revenues and with the number of competitors the public broadcaster has to face in the television market. To tackle the question, measures of the PC differentials at the country level, PTV's reliance on advertising, and number of competitors in the market are needed. For size or prominence of PC differentials, one possible measure is simply the number of significant and theory-confirming findings in each country, that is, the numbers in the first column of Table 7.4. This should constitute a useful indicator since, as just discussed, the numbers are not heavily influenced by differences in actual sample sizes.

In addition, another index of size of PC differential was generated from the findings behind Tables 7.1 to 7.3. The nominal difference between PTV and CTV on each indicator for each country was first calculated and then standardized. The difference between PTV and CTV was calculated in such a way that a larger number represents a larger PC differential corresponding to the hypothesis. For example, on prominence of soft news, Belgium had a PC differential of 8.6%; Brazil had a PC differential of 2.5%, and so on. The average PC differential is 11.27%, and the standard deviation is 9.56%. The standardized scores for Belgium and Brazil, then, are −0.28 and −0.92, respectively (in other words, the country differential minus the average and then divided by the standard deviation). Applying the procedures for the findings behind Tables 7.1 to 7.3, nine sets of standardized scores were derived. The size of the PC differential for each country is the average of the nine standardized scores for the country.[3] This indicator, as expected, correlates very highly with a number of significant findings at the country level ($r = .93, p < .001$).

For the two context characteristics, information was provided by the research teams from the respective countries. The reliance on advertising revenue variable is a three-category item such that: 1 = advertising revenues constitute 25% or less of the PTV station's income; 2 = advertising revenues constitute 26% to 50% of the PTV station's income; and 3 = advertising revenues constitute more than 50% of the PTV station's income. Number of competitors is a ratio scaled variable about "number of newscasts competing for the same audience in the same market." It ranges from 0 to whatever number of competitors there are in the market, and in the actual data set it ranges from 0 for Switzerland to 10 for Taiwan.

Because of the small number of cases involved (N = 13) and the fact that reliance on advertising revenue and number of competitors in the market do not correlate with each other at all ($r = .18, p > .55$), the hypotheses were tested simply by bivariate correlation analysis. Given the small number of cases, Spearman rank correlation coefficients are used to represent the relationship between variables. The analysis shows that the number of theory-confirming significant findings is indeed negatively and significantly correlated with PTV's reliance on advertising revenue ($\rho = -.54, p < .03$, one-tailed). That is, the more advertising-reliant a country's PTV is, the less prominent the PC differential is. This finding supports H4a. However, the correlation between the number of competitors and the number of theory-confirming significant findings at the country level is not statistically significant ($\rho = -.24, p > .20$, one-tailed).

Nevertheless, a look at the raw data for the country-level analysis shows that Taiwan arguably constitutes an "exceptional case" that may have exerted undue influence in the analysis. Taiwan is an outlier on the number of competitors variable: while the PTV stations in nine of the 13 countries have two to four competitors in the market, Taiwan had 10. Besides, PTV in Taiwan does constitute a special case in a more substantive sense. Different from the other countries where the PTV station has existed for decades, the PTV station in Taiwan formally began broadcasting only in 1998, at a time when Taiwan already had a fully developed and highly commercialized television broadcasting system.

Given these considerations, the correlation analysis was conducted again by removing Taiwan from the data set. The results show that, when the other 12 countries were analyzed, the relationship between PTV's reliance on advertising revenues and the prominence of PC differentials, measured in terms of the number of theory-confirming significant findings, remains statistically significantly negative ($\rho = -.52, p < .05$, one-tailed). At the same time, the relationship between number of market competitors and number of theory-confirming significant findings also becomes statistically significantly negative ($\rho = -.60, p < .02$, one-tailed).

The pattern of findings remains basically the same when size of PC differential replaces number of theory-confirming significant differences in the analysis, but the correlation coefficients are generally weaker. The correlation between size of PC differentials and reliance on ad revenue is at $\rho = -.61$ ($p < .02$, one-tailed) when all 13 countries are analyzed, and at $\rho = -.60$ ($p < .02$, one-tailed) when Taiwan is excluded. The Spearman ρ coefficient for the correlation between size of PC differentials and number of competitors is $-.17$ when all 13 countries are analyzed, and it becomes $-.43$ ($p < .09$, one-tailed) when Taiwan is excluded. In other words, the findings are weaker when size of PC differential is used. But, overall, the analysis has consistently shown that the PC differential is smaller when the public broadcaster is more reliant on advertising revenue. There also seems to be a relationship between the PC differential and the number of competitors in that the PC differential becomes smaller when the number of competitors is larger. Yet this relationship is admittedly less robust as it emerges only when the analysis is conducted in specific ways.

Conclusions

This chapter has provided a systematic analysis of the differences between foreign news offered by PTV and CTV in 13 countries. PTV newscasts, because of their public service ideal, can be expected to offer foreign news that is less sensational, analytically deeper, and more cosmopolitan. The analysis generated a substantial number of significant differences between PTV and CTV that are consistent with such expectations, but there are an even larger number of "null findings." As already pointed out, the results, when taken together, are actually similar to the findings in the literature: while some studies have found significant differences between PTV and CTV that are consistent with the presumed nature of the two types of broadcasters (e.g., Bek, 2004; Pfetsch, 1996; van Praag & van der Eijk, 1998), many studies have found little or even no PC differentials at all (e.g., Esser, 2008; Kerbel et al., 2000; Klijin, 2003).

Part of the reason for the lack of across-the-board significant findings may reside in whether some of the indicators can capture the supposed differences between the two types of broadcasters. For example, the analysis on the use of audiovisual effects has come up with the most mixed findings throughout the chapter. CTV news used audiovisual effects more frequently in five countries, but PTV news used such effects more frequently in four countries. Here one may need to reconsider whether the use of audiovisual effects necessarily indicates a concern for audience ratings. In a study on how working journalists actually think about the reporting of emotions in news, Pantti (2010) found that journalists from both public and private broadcasters did not simply equate the reporting of emotions with sensationalism. Rather, journalists regard emotions as having an important place in many news stories. The question is when and how emotions are incorporated and/or highlighted in news. By the same token, it is plausible that PTV journalists also see audiovisual effects as useful in aiding audience comprehension of news stories, as long as such effects are used properly and not excessively. It can help explain why PTV news may feature audiovisual effects to an even greater extent in some countries.

Despite the possible weaknesses of some of the individual indicators, the absence of across-the-board significant differences is certainly also due to the reality of convergence, at least in some countries, between PTV and CTV. In Europe, many commercial broadcasters gained immediate market success as they entered the broadcasting scene in the 1980s and 1990s. The situation created pressure on public broadcasters to commercialize their own programming and content in order to win back the audience. On the other hand, public television can also affect commercial television in at least two major ways. First, the presence of a strong public broadcasting tradition in a society may lead to a public service culture that even commercial broadcasters cannot completely ignore. Second, commercial television is also likely to have the incentive to gain respect from the public, political actors, and other media organizations (Sanders & Bale, 2000). Therefore, commercial television stations may also adopt some of the values and styles of public television. The mutual influence between public and commercial television thus leads to similarity rather than differences.

Nevertheless, the most important findings in this chapter are really the variations across countries in terms of the prominence of the PC differentials. At one end, some countries show a large number of findings that confirm the differences between PTV and CTV (for example, Germany and Taiwan) that one would anticipate. At the other extreme, none of the theoretically expectable differences between PTV and CTV appears in Chile. One approach to explaining these differences is to look into the individual countries for country-specific explanations. Germany, for example, is widely regarded as having a strong public broadcasting tradition (Kolmer & Semetko, 2010). The importance of freedom of broadcasting was even explicitly enshrined in the country's constitution—Article 5(1) of the Basic Law of the Federal Republic of Germany states that "Freedom of the press and *freedom of reporting through audiovisual media* shall be guaranteed" (emphasis added). Meanwhile, although public broadcasters in Germany are allowed to derive part of their revenue from advertising, they remain reliant on license fees as their major income, and advertising on public television is also subject to strict regulations. These background characteristics can help explain why the PC differential remains prominent.

Similarly, the prominence of PC differential in Taiwan can be explained in terms of the country's specific context. As noted, Taiwan has long enjoyed a well-developed commercial broadcasting system and a very strong cable television system. The commercial broadcasters, however, have long been criticized for providing highly sensationalized news to the public. Therefore, when the public television station began broadcasting in 1998, public television was deliberately introduced as a substantially different type of broadcaster. This could explain why, despite the presence of a large number of commercial broadcasters as "competitors," the PC differential remains very prominent in Taiwan. The commercial broadcasters do not constitute new challengers to established public broadcasters, as in the case of many European countries. Instead, PTV itself constituted the new challenger endowed with the mission of providing an alternative to the audience.

Space does not allow us to discuss each country in turn. More important, discussing the countries individually may not be the best approach if we are concerned with generating general theoretical explanations of the cross-national variations in the prominence of the PC differentials. In the analysis in this chapter, therefore, we opted to examine empirically if two characteristics of the media system can explain the size of the PC differentials. The findings generally support the expectations. In a dual broadcasting system, commercialization of PTV may be likely, but not inevitable. A key consideration is whether the set-up and organization of PTV would encourage or discourage commercialization. One arrangement that is likely to encourage PTV to commercialize is to require it to obtain its own funding partly through advertising. In this chapter we indeed show that countries where PTV is more reliant on advertising, such as Chile, are much less likely to exhibit substantial PC differentials in news.

Moreover, there should be a greater chance for public television to commercialize itself if market competition is fierce. Here it should be conceded that the present chapter does not have an ideal measure of market competition. A good measure of degree of competition should take into account the actual distribution of audience shares among the broadcasters in a market. In the present chapter we use the sheer number of competitors as our measure. Yet the measure does allow us to come up with the result that, when the "exceptional case" of Taiwan is removed, countries where PTV has more competitors are less likely to exhibit substantial PC differential in news.

These findings thus illustrate that the presence or absence of PC differentials in foreign news is indeed something that can be explained by referring to contextual factors. In one sense, this chapter has arguably opened up a new line of research. While it focuses only on two media system characteristics due to the lack of available information and the conceptual focus on the impact of commercialization of PTV on the PC differential, future cross-national analysis can examine other contextual factors that may also affect whether PTV and CTV would converge. Possible factors to examine include, among others, presence of regulation of commercial broadcasting, audience shares of the public television stations, and citizens' level of political interest and participation.

Returning to the normative concern raised at the beginning of the chapter, our findings suggest that the structure of the broadcasting system does have an impact on the type and range of information citizens will get from the media. But the co-presence of public and commercial television in a media system does not by itself guarantee diversity and choice for the audience. It is important to ensure that specific media "sectors," employing the term used by Curran (2000), are organized in ways that the presumed benefits of having the sectors can be realized. On one hand, this chapter's findings can be taken to mean that the presence of commercial broadcasters does not necessarily result in the commercialization of the public broadcaster. But on the other hand, the findings show that public broadcasters are likely to retain their unique characteristics and public service ideal only under certain conditions that insulate them from commercial pressures.

Summary

Overall, this chapter sought to determine whether the economic nature of news organizations could explain the characteristics of foreign television news. It examined the differences between the foreign news offered by public (PTV) and commercial television stations (CTV) in 13 countries. Specifically, it asked if foreign news on public television is more cosmopolitan, analytically deeper, and less sensational than foreign news on commercial television. The chapter also examined whether media convergence caused by the commercialization of public television affects the size of the differential between public and commercial broadcasters (PC differential). The analysis generated a substantial number of significant differences between PTV and CTV in the expected direction, but a larger number of "null findings" as well. The most important finding is the variations in the prominence of the PC differentials across countries. While some countries witness many findings confirming the expected differences between PTV and CTV, these differences fail to appear in certain countries. In addition to contextual factors, an important reason for the lack of across-the-board significant findings is the convergence between PTV and CTV. Our analysis demonstrates that countries in which PTV is more reliant on advertising are much less likely to exhibit substantial PC differentials in news. We also found that countries in which PTV has more competitors are less likely to exhibit substantial PC differential in news. This lends support to the observation that public television is more inclined to commercialize itself if market competition is fierce.

Notes

1   Since the actual sample sizes can be small in some countries, and given the directional nature of the hypotheses, one-tailed tests were used in determining whether a hypothesis is supported in a country or not. Two-tailed tests were adopted for testing H3a, however, since the test of H3a includes domestic news items and hence the actual sample sizes are large.
2   In cases where the coders could not determine whether the conflict being reported was personal or social, the item was grouped together with "social conflicts." Specifically, this means that the dichotomous variable refers to personal conflict vs. non-personal conflict. This procedure was followed so as not to exclude the conflict items with undetermined nature. The logic of the hypothesis is not affected, though: the expectation remains that CTV newscasts should provide more items focusing on personal conflicts.
3   Cronbach's α for the nine sets of scores = .65. The reliability coefficient is not very high but is acceptable.

PART THREE

Viewers

CHAPTER EIGHT

Who Uses News, How Much, and Why?

LARS WILLNAT, DAVID WEAVER, AGNIESZKA STĘPIŃSKA, & VEN-HWEI LO

This chapter focuses on the audiences for and possible predictors of media exposure and interest in foreign news coverage by television, newspapers, and online news media. Despite the obvious importance of news media as sources of information about world events, particularly during periods of crisis, there has been relatively little empirical research into the demographic characteristics of foreign news audiences and the reasons why people do or do not pay attention to foreign news (Biltereyst, 2001; Elvestad, 2009). We need this kind of research to better understand the audiences and possible effects of foreign TV news coverage.

Although there is much research from Western nations, particularly from the United States, examining predictors of media exposure and its political and social impact, very little research has been done comparing the predictors of media exposure among citizens across different countries. Our study was designed in part to fill this gap in media use research by exploring patterns and predictors of exposure to various news media—television, newspapers, and the Internet—among citizens in 13 different countries.[1]

Even though the main focus of our study in general and the current survey in particular is the analysis of *television* news consumption, we decided to include in the survey comparable questions on newspaper reading and online news exposure in order to provide a broader picture of news consumption. While television is the main source of news for people in most nations, printed newspapers still play a role, albeit in a somewhat declining fashion, while online news has been playing a growing role in shaping people's overall news consumption. Moreover, the relative importance of each medium as a news source differs slightly from nation to nation. Thus, studies such as ours that compare television news consumption across nations must include measures of exposure to print and online media to provide the necessary context.

Previous studies suggest that greater news exposure and attention to foreign news is associated with increases in knowledge about foreign affairs (Korzenny, del Toro, & Gaudino, 1987; McNelly & Izcaray, 1986; McNelly, Rush, & Bishop, 1968; Perry & McNelly, 1988; Perry, 1990; Snyder, 1993). More recently, Beaudoin (2004) demonstrated a positive association between international knowledge and international news attention with data collected in a telephone survey conducted in 2000 with a sample of 422 adult Americans. Attention to foreign news was measured with a composite index that combined people's attention to international news in newspapers, television, and the Internet. The author also found that respondents with higher levels of education and interpersonal discussions of foreign affairs were able to expand their foreign affairs knowledge more than those with less education and fewer discussions of international affairs.

In a similar telephone survey of 467 adult Americans conducted one year later, Beaudoin (2008) found that especially people's attention to international news on the Internet contributed to a better understanding of international affairs. While attention to foreign news in newspapers, cable television, and the Internet all correlated positively with international knowledge, attention to Internet news was by far the best predictor of more knowledge about foreign affairs. Especially relevant to the present study was the finding that interest in international affairs (measured with four items, involving the geography, economic conditions, histories, and political happenings of other nations) was a strong predictor of more international knowledge as well.

Beaudoin's findings were supported by another survey conducted in 2003 among a sample of 389 adults (Kwak, Poor, & Skoric, 2006). The authors found that exposure (not attention) to international news in newspapers, television, and the Internet were positive predictors of international political knowledge and international engagement. Interestingly, younger users of the Internet tended to benefit more than older users from reading international news online with respect to international knowledge and international engagement. The opposite was true for exposure to international news on television. Among those who watched international news on television, older rather than younger respondents were more likely to gain international knowledge.

Another objective of our study was to examine the role of television news as a main source of foreign news in different countries.[2] There is considerable evidence that television news plays an important role in political learning, including international knowledge (Chaffee & Frank, 1996; Chaffee, Zhao, & Leshner,

1994; Norris & Sanders, 2003). A study by Lo and Chang (2006) revealed that television news made a significant contribution to knowledge about the 1991 Gulf War, and that the respondents learned as much about the Gulf War from television news as from newspapers. These findings support the role of television news as a key source of information about politics and international affairs.

Although television has been and still remains the main source for news in many countries, the rapid development of new technologies has changed the news acquisition habits of many people. Since the mid-1990s, the Internet has emerged as a new channel for political information (Johnson, Braima, & Sothirajah, 1999; Kaye & Johnson, 2002). The availability of online news, the multifaceted nature of its delivery, and its interactive nature suggest that the Internet can be an important source of news for many people. Displacement theories assume that the more time a person spends using new media, the less time that person will devote to traditional media (Mutz, Roberts, & van Vuuren, 1993), because "its users must reallocate their limited amount of time" (Waal & Schönbach, 2010, p. 479). As more people turn to the Internet as a source of information (Drew & Weaver, 2006), it is worthwhile to examine exposure to the Internet as well as to television and newspapers as sources of foreign news.

Therefore, in this chapter we present patterns and predictors of exposure to foreign news in television, newspapers, and online news media among citizens in 13 different countries. Specifically, this chapter addresses the following questions: What is the frequency of exposure to foreign news among respondents from the 13 countries in different news media? What are the major news sources? What are the main reasons for watching or not watching news on television? What are the socio-demographic and other predictors of exposure to TV news, newspapers, and online news? Are there any similarities and differences among respondents from the 13 countries?

The data for this chapter come from the 13-nation telephone survey that was conducted in late 2009 and early 2010 with a total of 10,305 respondents. All surveys were based on identical questionnaires to ensure cross-national comparability and relied on representative samples of the adult population (18 years or older) in each nation: Brazil (N=468), Canada (N=395), Chile (N=1,220), China (N=1,128), Germany (N=998), Hong Kong (N=599), Israel (N=760), Poland (N=800), Portugal (N=500), Singapore (N=501), Switzerland (N=1,010), Taiwan (N=1,141), and the United States (N=785).[3] The questionnaire assessed people's overall exposure to news in minutes per day (television, newspapers, online), their reasons for consuming television news, and their reasons for not watching foreign television news. In order to evaluate how well these reasons for watching (or not watching) television news might predict overall exposure to television news in each country, we present a series of regression analyses that control for the effects of demographic variables such as gender, age, education, and income.

Table 8.1 News exposure to different media by country

Country	N	Number of days/week watched TV news	Minutes watched TV news yesterday	Minutes read newspaper yesterday	Minutes got online news yesterday
Brazil	325	5.59 (2.02)	52.18 (59.17)	7.71 (21.02)	19.55 (53.87)
Canada	395	5.02 (2.40)	46.95 (49.35)	17.25 (22.66)	16.03 (34.29)
Chile	1,220	5.90 (1.75)	32.90 (31.74)	9.43 (20.53)	6.43 (16.06)
China	1,118	5.30 (2.60)	32.03 (46.24)	15.24 (29.39)	19.04 (45.79)
Germany	995	5.16 (2.44)	21.70 (29.56)	23.99 (32.09)	7.81 (21.14)
Hong Kong	595	5.62 (2.10)	43.17 (45.79)	24.63 (33.70)	16.74 (34.38)
Israel	760	4.12 (2.81)	24.19 (38.35)	15.58 (28.14)	13.56 (27.77)
Poland	800	5.81 (2.06)	55.25 (54.96)	13.56 (34.54)	20.17 (52.74)
Portugal	500	5.93 (1.99)	47.54 (43.00)	9.74 (21.28)	11.44 (34.46)
Singapore	501	4.21 (2.59)	27.09 (37.05)	25.41 (26.96)	20.02 (44.27)
Switzerland	1,006	4.53 (2.45)	18.81 (23.27)	24.24 (24.90)	6.83 (19.65)
Taiwan	1,131	5.95 (1.96)	46.32 (47.14)	16.82 (29.99)	12.47 (28.56)
United States	683	5.30 (2.17)	41.32 (48.87)	14.67 (22.09)	22.23 (36.05)
Overall Mean		5.31 (2.35)	36.00 (43.88)	16.81 (28.04)	13.91 (35.00)
Eta Squared		.066	.070	.040	.025

Note: Standard deviations in parentheses. Questions asked: During a typical week, on how many days do you watch at least some TV news?; About how much time in hours and minutes did you spend watching TV news yesterday?; About how much time in hours and minutes did you spend reading a newspaper yesterday?; About how much time in hours and minutes did you spend getting news from the Internet yesterday?

Exposure to News

Table 8.1 presents the findings regarding time spent with various types of news, including television, newspapers, and online news media. Beginning with television, we find that, on average, respondents from the 13 nations included in this survey watch television news about five days per week. The most exposure to television news was recorded in Taiwan and Chile (both about 5.9 days per week), while respondents in Israel (4.1) and Singapore (4.2) watched the least.[4] The average exposure to television news per day is about 36 minutes, but differs significantly from country to country. News audiences in Poland (55 min.) and Brazil (52 min.) watch the most television news per day, while audiences in Switzerland (19 min.), Germany (22 min.), Israel (24 min.), and Singapore (27 min.) watch the least. Of course, the daily exposure to television news is partly determined by the length of local news broadcasts. The most popular evening news shows in countries such as Poland and Brazil, for example, last 60 minutes, while the most often viewed evening news broadcasts in Germany and Switzerland last only 15 minutes. Thus, the format of television news in each country is an important determinant of the amount of exposure to televised news and information.

A more consistent measure of news exposure across nations is the amount of time spent reading newspapers and online news. Since the availability of newspapers and online news is less determined by format issues, exposure to these types of media more likely reflects the personal preferences and motivations of individual news users. The findings indicate that respondents across all 13 countries spent about 17 minutes per day reading newspapers and 14 minutes reading or watching online news. As with television news exposure, time spent with newspapers and online news varies greatly from country to country. While respondents in Portugal (10 min.) and Brazil (8 min.) spend the least amount of time reading newspapers, audiences in Hong Kong, Singapore, Germany, and Switzerland (between 24 and 25 min.) spend the most. Exposure to online news also turned out to be fairly diverse, with the most exposure found in the United States (22 min.), Singapore, Poland, and Brazil (all about 20 min.), and the least in Switzerland, Germany (both about 7 min.), and Chile (6 min.).

Thus, despite the rapid development of online media in most industrialized nations, television news still represents the most relied-on source of information for most respondents. Only respondents in Germany and Switzerland indicate that they spend more time reading newspapers than watching television—a likely result of the short main evening news in these two countries. It should be noted, though, that online news exposure has surpassed the time people spend reading newspapers in some of the nations analyzed here. As our findings show, news consumers in Brazil (+12 min.), the United States (+7 min.), Poland (+6 min.), China (+4 min.), and Portugal (+1 min.) spend more time reading online news than more traditional newspapers. On the other hand, newspaper consumption still trumps online news consumption in Switzerland (+17 min.), Germany (+16 min.), Singapore (+5 min.), Taiwan (+4 min.), Chile (+3 min.), Israel (+2 min.), and Canada (+1 min.).

Overall, then, audiences around the world show distinct patterns of news consumption that partly reflect the structure of the news environment in each country (for example, short newscasts in Germany), long-held traditions of news consumption (for example, strong newspaper readership in Switzerland), and other factors that determine media use (for example, a fast-developing preference for online news in the United States).

In addition, these consumption patterns across nations seem to fit fairly well media models developed around the idea of newspaper-centric and television-centric audiences (Hallin & Mancini, 2004; Shehata & Strömbäck, 2011). Based on the findings of our survey study, it seems reasonable to argue that nations such as the United States, Taiwan, Portugal, Poland, Chile, Canada, and Brazil are more television-centric nations, while countries such as Switzerland and Germany belong to the few remaining newspaper-centric nations. It is also clear, however, that there are some nations where newspaper and television news exposure is more balanced. In China, Singapore, Hong Kong, and Israel, for example, news exposure is dominated by television news, but it is clear that the consumption of newspapers and television news in these nations is more balanced than in the other countries mentioned above.

Because gender, age, and education are likely to have an important influence on how much news people consume and which media they use to do so, Table 8.2 provides a closer look at the relationship among these variables. The findings indicate that men and women consume about the same amount of television news—they both watch television news five days per week for about 36 minutes each day. However, men spend about five more minutes each day reading the newspaper (19.5 min. vs. 14.5 min.) and about six more minutes each day consuming online news (17.0 min. vs. 11.2 min.). Overall, then, male respondents in our samples spend slightly more time with newspapers and online news than our female respondents.

While the relationship between gender and news exposure is relatively weak, the breakdown of news consumption by different age groups clearly shows that there is a linear relationship between age and news consumption. As age increases, so does the number of days people watch television. The same is true for time spent reading newspapers and watching television news. Exposure to online news, on the other hand, is negatively related to age. Younger respondents tend to spend more time consuming online news than do older respondents.

As Table 8.2 shows, the difference in news exposure between the youngest and oldest age group in our sample is quite substantial. While those who are between 18 and 25 years old watch about 26 minutes of news per day and spend about 10 minutes with newspapers, this increases to almost 47 minutes spent with television news and 27 minutes spent with newspapers among those who are 65 years or older. Time spent with online news, however, is much higher among the youngest news users (26 min.) than the oldest (6 min.). Thus, it is safe to conclude that age is a significant predictor of news exposure around the world.

The relationship between education and news exposure is less linear than that observed between age and news exposure. As Table 8.2 shows, respondents with higher levels of education actually spend slightly fewer days per week, on average, watching television news than those with more education. Respondents with the least formal education (5 years or less) report 5.4 days of average television news exposure per week, while those with the most education (17 years or more) say that they spend 5.1 days per week watching the news.

Table 8.2 News exposure to different media by gender, age, and education (all respondents from all countries)

	N	Number of days/week watched TV news	Minutes watched TV news yesterday	Minutes read newspaper yesterday	Minutes got online news yesterday
Male	4,795	5.29 (2.33)	36.43 (43.83)	19.43 (30.28)	16.97 (37.72)
Female	5,425	5.32 (2.36)	35.64 (43.93)	14.50 (25.69)	11.21 (32.12)
Age					
18–25	1,212	4.11 (2.57)	26.47 (36.95)	10.15 (21.21)	25.87 (53.18)
26–35	1,643	4.61 (2.48)	28.55 (37.94)	10.76 (21.26)	20.81 (42.51)
36–45	1,993	5.09 (2.39)	31.21 (39.30)	13.83 (23.49)	13.81 (30.01)
46–55	2,005	5.62 (2.19)	36.83 (40.93)	17.19 (26.53)	11.38 (31.26)
56–65	1,571	6.04 (1.87)	45.48 (51.33)	21.27 (30.60)	8.56 (22.86)
65 and older	1,605	6.09 (1.90)	46.86 (51.06)	27.06 (37.89)	6.18 (23.43)
Education					
0–5	388	5.46 (2.40)	42.03 (48.30)	9.84 (24.35)	5.38 (43.39)
6–12	3,789	5.54 (2.27)	38.40 (45.92)	15.82 (29.10)	8.38 (25.84)
13–16	4,210	5.16 (2.36)	33.51 (40.96)	18.49 (27.58)	17.26 (36.91)
17 or more	1,642	5.12 (2.40)	35.55 (44.79)	16.42 (27.26)	19.55 (42.45)
Overall Mean		5.31 (2.35)	36.00 (43.88)	16.81 (28.04)	13.91 (35.00)

Note: Standard deviations in parentheses.

This slightly negative correlation pattern is also reflected in the average time our respondents spend watching television news each day. While those with the lowest level of education spend about 42 minutes per day watching the news, respondents with the most education report only about 36 minutes of television news exposure per day. Newspaper and online news exposure, on the other hand, is found to be significantly higher among those with more education. Exposure to newspapers jumps from about 10 minutes per day in the lowest education group to about 16 minutes in the highest education group. Similarly, online news exposure soars from about five minutes among those with the least education to almost 20 minutes among those with the most education. Overall, these findings indicate that global news audiences with more education tend to watch slightly less television news but spend significantly more time with newspapers and online news each day.

Table 8.3 Reasons for watching television news by country

Country	N	Something to talk about with people	Keep up with national affairs in own country	Keep up with events in foreign countries	TV news can be entertaining
Brazil	451	4.24 (0.88)	4.73 (0.52)	4.62 (0.61)	3.47 (1.30)
Canada	365	3.79 (1.17)	4.69 (0.62)	4.59 (0.69)	3.24 (1.29)
Chile	1,175	3.97 (1.22)	4.34 (1.06)	4.19 (1.16)	3.50 (1.33)
China	987	3.82 (1.02)	4.29 (0.84)	4.03 (0.97)	2.99 (1.21)
Germany	918	3.77 (1.14)	4.56 (0.73)	4.39 (0.88)	3.08 (1.23)
Hong Kong	575	3.36 (0.97)	4.15 (0.75)	4.09 (0.71)	2.98 (1.05)
Israel	590	3.79 (1.29)	4.57 (0.82)	4.11 (1.14)	2.66 (1.33)
Poland	759	3.62 (0.96)	4.30 (0.67)	4.21 (0.72)	2.97 (1.11)
Portugal	480	4.32 (1.02)	4.72 (0.67)	4.69 (0.63)	3.25 (1.51)
Singapore	439	3.75 (1.06)	4.43 (0.82)	4.32 (0.87)	3.48 (1.09)
Switzerland	892	3.71 (1.09)	4.31 (0.82)	4.26 (0.84)	2.99 (1.17)
Taiwan	1,079	3.97 (1.08)	4.47 (0.78)	4.12 (1.09)	2.78 (1.36)
United States	751	3.59 (1.06)	4.42 (0.83)	4.17 (0.94)	3.64 (1.05)
Overall Mean		3.82 (1.11)	4.43 (0.82)	4.25 (0.94)	3.14 (1.27)
Eta Squared		.039	.036	.038	.053

Note: Standard deviations in parentheses. Questions asked: It gives something to talk about with other people; It helps keeping up with current events and issues in "country"; It helps keeping up with current events in other countries; TV news can be entertaining (1 = strongly disagree, 2 = somewhat disagree, 3 = neither agree nor disagree, 4 = somewhat agree, 5 = strongly agree).

Reasons for Watching News

In order to learn more about why people might watch television news, we included a set of questions in our survey that probed respondents' motivations for consuming television news. The questions broadly reflect the three main categories of motivations identified by earlier uses-and-gratification studies conducted by Blumler and Katz (1974) and Rosengren, Wenner, and Palmgreen (1985): learning, social interaction, and entertainment.

To assess whether people watch television news to learn more about current events that happen in their own country or abroad, respondents were first asked whether they thought that "TV news helps keeping up with current events in my country" and that "TV news helps keeping up with current events in other countries." The social and entertainment functions of television news were measured by the extent to which respondents agreed with two statements: "TV news gives something to talk about with other people," and "TV news can be entertaining."

Agreement with these four statements was measured on a scale ranging from 1 ("strongly disagree") to 5 ("strongly agree").

As Table 8.3 shows, most respondents indicate that they follow television news primarily to keep up with national ($M = 4.43$) or international affairs ($M = 4.25$). While agreement with these two motivational factors differs only slightly between nations, respondents in Brazil, Canada, and Portugal especially valued the informational role of television news for both national and foreign events. Respondents in all nations, however, considered keeping up with national affairs slightly more important than keeping up with international affairs. The fact that television news can provide something to talk about ($M = 3.82$) or might be entertaining ($M = 3.14$), on the other hand, is rated less highly by respondents as an important motivational factor for watching television news. While respondents in Brazil ($M = 4.24$) and Portugal ($M = 4.32$) especially value the social function of television news, audiences in the United States ($M = 3.64$) are the most likely to agree that television news can be entertaining.

Reasons for Not Watching Foreign News

Due to the focus of our study on foreign news consumption, we were especially interested in the reasons why people do *not* watch foreign news. The decline in international news coverage in the United States, for example, is often attributed to the lack of audience interest in foreign news (Gitlin, 1980; Hallin, 1996; Hess, 1996; Moisy, 1997; Schudson & Tifft, 2005). A survey by Pew (2008) found that most Americans (53%) track international news only when major developments occur, while far fewer (42%) are consistently engaged. Other studies have found that U.S. audiences "show only a narrow interest in a limited category of news stories and are generally inattentive to events outside their immediate environment, especially those in the remote setting" (Tai & Chang, 2002, p. 262).

In order to shed more light on the possible reasons why global audiences might *not* watch foreign news, we adopted a set of questions that were originally developed by Pew for a 2002 survey on news consumption in the United States (Pew, 2002a). The Pew survey found that almost six in 10 respondents (58.5%) thought that they didn't have enough background to understand foreign news, and almost half (45.2%) said that nothing ever seems to change. In addition, slightly more than one-third said that events in other nations do not affect them (38.5%) and that there is too much emphasis on wars, violence, and disasters in foreign news coverage (37.8%).

While these percentages indicate a fairly negative view of foreign news, such perceptions might be characteristic only of an American news audience. We therefore decided to include the original four questions in our own survey to see how widespread these perceptions actually are. Respondents were asked how strongly they agree with the statements that: "events in other countries do not affect me," "there is too much reporting of wars, violence and disasters," "I don't have enough background to understand events in other countries," and "it seems that the same things happen all the time and nothing changes." As before, agreement with these four statements was measured on a scale ranging from 1 ("strongly disagree") to 5 ("strongly agree").

Table 8.4 Reasons for not watching foreign news by country

Country	N	Events in other countries do not affect me	There is too much reporting of wars, violence, and disasters	Don't have enough background to understand events in other countries	It seems that the same things happen all the time, and nothing changes
Brazil	468	2.76 (1.42)	3.78 (1.32)	3.40 (1.35)	4.03 (1.31)
Canada	391	1.78 (1.10)	3.31 (1.32)	2.63 (1.34)	3.36 (1.34)
Chile	1,147	2.56 (1.43)	3.90 (1.41)	2.95 (1.47)	3.65 (1.53)
China	1,057	2.95 (1.27)	3.26 (1.10)	3.30 (1.19)	2.96 (1.15)
Germany	977	2.16 (1.14)	3.01 (1.30)	2.61 (1.18)	3.06 (1.36)
Hong Kong	580	2.45 (0.95)	3.01 (0.93)	2.99 (1.01)	2.86 (0.97)
Israel	690	2.68 (1.43)	3.18 (1.42)	2.66 (1.49)	2.86 (1.43)
Poland	791	2.87 (1.12)	3.33 (1.15)	2.89 (1.11)	3.04 (1.15)
Portugal	493	2.05 (1.38)	3.93 (1.37)	3.18 (1.56)	3.88 (1.38)
Singapore	493	2.35 (1.25)	2.96 (1.22)	2.68 (1.22)	2.70 (1.25)
Switzerland	999	2.23 (1.13)	3.51 (1.18)	2.59 (1.18)	3.19 (1.20)
Taiwan	1,084	2.71 (1.36)	2.63 (1.29)	3.35 (1.35)	3.09 (1.42)
United States	780	2.20 (1.18)	2.96 (1.19)	2.58 (1.18)	3.10 (1.19)
Overall Mean		2.49 (1.30)	3.27 (1.31)	2.92 (1.32)	3.19 (1.35)
Eta Squared		.059	.090	.052	.066

Note: Standard deviations in parentheses. Questions asked: Events in other countries do not affect me; There is too much reporting of wars, violence, and disasters; I don't have enough background to understand events in other countries; It seems that the same things happen all the time, and nothing changes (1 = strongly disagree, 2 = somewhat disagree, 3 = neither agree nor disagree, 4 = somewhat agree, 5 = strongly agree).

As Table 8.4 shows, the findings of our 13-country sample do not match those obtained in 2002 in the United States. The most important reason cited by our respondents for *not* watching foreign news is too much reporting of wars, violence, and disasters (M = 3.27). This reason is closely followed by the perception that "nothing ever changes" (M = 3.19). Overall, respondents in Brazil, Chile, and Portugal are the most likely to agree with the idea that foreign news tends to emphasize the negative and that nothing ever changes, therefore making foreign news less interesting.

Unlike the U.S. respondents in the 2002 Pew survey, our respondents do not seem to think that they lack the background to understand events in other countries ($M = 2.92$) or that these events do not affect them ($M = 2.49$). Surprisingly, Americans are among the least likely to agree with these two last statements—a possible indicator that foreign news consumers have become more sophisticated and demanding—even in the United States. Respondents in Brazil, China, and Taiwan, on the other hand, have the least confidence in their understanding of foreign events and also tend to think that foreign events do not affect them.

Overall, then, the most important reasons for not watching foreign news are associated with the perception that international news tends to focus on negative events and generally does not present enough new information that might warrant attention by an already-overtaxed news audience. While it is certainly understandable that news audiences around the world perceive foreign news as mostly negative, it is somewhat surprising to learn that audiences in many countries do not agree that there has been a lot of change in the international sphere.

Predictors of Foreign News Exposure

Prior research (Bogart, 1981; Mindich, 2005; Weaver & Buddenbaum, 1979) has found consistently that gender, age, and education are good predictors of news exposure, and we expected to find the same in our international sample of news users. In order to evaluate how well respondents' demographic backgrounds predict their exposure to news, their gender, age, education, and income were entered into a regression model that tests these relationships for each nation and for the entire sample. Respondents' daily exposure to television news, newspapers, and online news were used as the dependent variables. The goal of this analysis is to track the most consistent demographic predictors of news exposure in our 13 countries.

As the first block in Table 8.5 shows, age is a fairly strong and consistent predictor of television news exposure in all 12 countries except Brazil. Thus, older respondents in most nations tend to watch more television news. The strongest correlations between age and television news exposure are found in Canada, China, Germany, Israel, and Poland. The analysis also shows that women in Germany, Switzerland, Taiwan, and the United States are somewhat less likely to watch television news. Surprisingly, the respondents' level of education was not associated with television exposure, except for a negative correlation found in Switzerland. The same was true for income, which only showed a weak positive relationship in Israel, and a weak negative relationship in Germany.[5] Overall, demographic factors explain the range between zero (Brazil) and 18% (Canada) of the variance in this regression model, indicating that, other than age, demographics are relatively weak and inconsistent predictors of television news except for age.

Table 8.5 Demographic predictors of exposure to TV news, newspapers, and online news (minutes yesterday) by country

	Brazil	Canada	Chile	China	Germany	HK	Israel	Poland	Portugal	Singapore	Switzerland	Taiwan	United States	All respondents
TV News Exposure														
Female	-.01	.08	.04	-.04	-.11***	.04	.06	-.01	-.03	-.05	-.07*	-.07*	-.08*	-.03*
Age	-.03	.40***	.09**	.34***	.28***	.24***	.28***	.27***	.16**	.17**	.21***	.14**	.23***	.19***
Education	—	.06	.03	.09	.06	-.07	-.06	-.08	.12	-.10	-.12***	-.02	.02	-.05***
Income	.05	-.06	.04	.06	-.08*	.01	.10*	—	-.06	.07	-.05	-.01	-.03	.06***
R Square (percent)	.00	17.7***	1.1***	10.0***	9.6***	7.6***	8.2***	8.2***	2.1	4.1***	7.6***	2.8**	6.1***	4.2***
Newspaper Exposure														
Female	-.05	-.01	-.10*	-.06	-.12***	.08	-.02	.01	-.22***	-.18***	-.14***	-.07*	-.13***	-.10***
Age	.09	.32***	.14***	.34***	.45***	.30***	.23***	.13***	.12*	.17***	.38***	.24***	.19***	.25***
Education	—	.23***	.13***	.17***	.10***	.01	.06	.14***	.12	-.02	.10***	.04	.01	.11***
Income	.11*	-.02	.11**	.06	.01	.10*	.08	—	.05	.11*	.03	.04	.06	.03**
R Square (percent)	2.1*	12.8***	5.9***	11.1***	22.3***	9.3***	5.4***	3.2***	7.1***	7.4***	17.1***	6.2***	6.4***	7.7***
Online News Exposure														
Female	-.03	.02	-.12***	-.06	-.14***	.02	-.09*	-.10***	-.09*	-.16***	-.08*	-.08**	-.11***	-.07***
Age	-.24***	-.18***	-.05	-.21***	-.18***	-.13**	-.14***	-.21***	-.05	-.03	-.09**	-.11**	-.08*	-.13***
Education	—	.02	.18***	.08*	.14***	.19***	.03	.18***	.31***	.21***	.11***	.20***	.06	.12***
Income	.09	.18**	.12**	.05	-.08*	.06	.17***	—	.03	.04	.02	.07	.05	.08***
R Square (percent)	6.7***	7.3***	10.4***	7.8***	7.5***	9.3***	7.1***	9.6***	14.4***	9.2***	3.4***	9.0***	2.5***	6.1***
N	410	286	1,008	919	841	506	501	796	374	408	847	867	737	8,500

Note: *** $p < .001$, ** $p < .01$, * $p < .05$

The second block in Table 8.5 also shows that age is a strong and consistent predictor of newspaper exposure in all 12 countries except Brazil. The strongest relationships between age and newspaper consumption are found in Canada, China, Germany, Hong Kong, and Switzerland. The observed impact of gender on television exposure is even more prominent for newspaper exposure. Women in Chile, Germany, Portugal, Singapore, Switzerland, Taiwan, and the United States tend to read newspapers less frequently than their male counterparts. However, unlike the mostly insignificant relationships between education and television exposure discussed above, newspaper consumption correlates positively with education in 6 of the 12 nations analyzed here (Canada, Chile, China, Germany, Poland, and Switzerland).

This indicates that newspaper use—at least in some countries—is driven by education, while television news consumption is not. Such findings make sense given the greater amount of effort required to read a newspaper compared with watching television news. These findings are also supported by the fact that income correlates positively with newspaper exposure only in Brazil, Chile, Hong Kong, and Singapore. Thus, newspaper exposure is driven mostly by education, despite the fact that education and income are often related. Overall, demographic variables explain between 2% (Brazil) and 22% (Germany) of the variance in this regression model. Thus, associations between demographics and newspaper exposure are fairly inconsistent across the 13 nations, but also show some strong relationships in nations such as Canada, China, Germany, and Switzerland.

The third block in Table 8.5 shows the associations between respondents' demographics and online news exposure. Unlike the findings discussed above, age correlates negatively with online news exposure in all nations except Chile, Portugal, and Singapore. In other words, older respondents in most nations tend to have less exposure to online news than those who are younger. Similarly, women in all nations except Brazil, Canada, China, and Hong Kong spend less time consuming online news. These findings are hardly surprising, given the age and gender gap that still exists among Internet users around the world. As expected, education correlates positively with online news exposure in all but three nations (Canada, Israel, and the United States).[6] Income is a much less consistent predictor of online news exposure and showed a significant relationship only in Canada, Chile, Germany, and Israel. Thus, both newspaper and online news exposure seem to be driven primarily by education and not income. Overall, demographic variables predict between 3% (United States) and 14% (Portugal) of the variance in this regression model, once again indicating inconsistent but sometimes fairly strong associations between demographics and online news exposure across the 13 countries.

Conclusions

The goal of this chapter was to examine patterns and predictors of exposure to foreign news in television, newspapers, and online news media among citizens in 13 different countries. We were especially interested in finding out more about who the typical foreign news consumers are around the world, how much foreign news they consume, which news media they turn to most frequently, and what reasons they might have for paying attention or not to foreign news.

First, our findings indicate that women spend about as much time with television news as men (36 min. per day), but are slightly less likely to consume newspapers (14 vs. 19 min.) and online news (11 vs. 17 min.). While it is difficult to speculate about the reasons for these differences, it is likely that they are at least partly driven by overly optimistic newspaper consumption self-reports from male respondents and an online gender gap that may still exist in many nations.

One of the most striking findings of this analysis is the fact that age is a strong and consistent predictor of news consumption around the world. Generally, older respondents tend to spend more time watching television and reading newspapers each day. While the youngest age group (18–25 years) in our survey watches about 26 minutes of news per day and spends about 10 minutes with newspapers, exposure among the oldest group (65 years or older) almost doubles for television news (47 min.) and nearly triples for newspaper exposure (27 min.). Thus, the differences in time spent with traditional media between the two groups were substantial. As expected, exposure to online news was found to be negatively related to age. Online news exposure among our youngest group was more than four times higher (26 min.) than in the oldest group (6 min.).

Overall, we believe that these findings spell trouble for the future of traditional news media. Our survey findings show that younger news audiences have turned away from traditional news media and instead devote more and more of their attention to online news. While the average daily television news consumption is still on a par with online news consumption (both about 26 min.) among the youngest respondents in our survey, it is very likely that the observed differences in news consumption between older and younger news consumers will increase with time. While this might be good news for online media, we are concerned that such a move toward customized online news could lead to a fragmentation of news audiences. Such a fragmentation could especially affect foreign news consumption, which almost certainly is driven by individual preferences and therefore an easy target for elimination from one's daily news diet.

Higher levels of education were found to be less consistently associated with more news consumption from traditional media around the world. Generally, more educated respondents spend slightly less time watching television news than audience members with lower levels of education, but are likely to spend more time reading newspapers. However, the differences in time spent with each medium between the groups with the highest and lowest education levels are relatively modest (36 vs. 42 min. for TV news and 16 vs. 10 min. for newspapers). Online news consumption, on the other hand, is strongly affected by education levels. While respondents with the least education on average spend about 5 minutes per day reading or watching online news, those with the highest education levels spend four times that much with online news (20 min.).

Overall then, our findings indicate that there is a significant age and education gap in the consumption of traditional and online news globally. While older and more educated respondents prefer to consume news via newspapers and television, those who are younger and more educated tend to favor online news sources. In addition, there is a slight tendency among women to spend less time than men with newspapers and online news.

Because so little is known about the motivations behind *foreign* news consumption, we also analyzed the possible reasons why people watch television news and why they might not watch foreign news. Our findings show that about 8 in 10 respondents agree or strongly agree that they follow television news primarily to keep up with national (84.1%) or international affairs (78.6%). As expected, respondents in all 13 nations consider keeping up with national events slightly more important than keeping up with international affairs. Less universal agreement was found for the view that television news might provide something to talk about (65.3%) or that it could be entertaining (42.7%). Overall then, it is clear that the majority of our respondents value television news mostly for its information function.

The most important reasons for *not* watching foreign television news are associated with the perception that international news tends to focus on negative events such as violence, wars, or disasters. Almost half (47.5%) of all respondents agree with that view. Surprisingly, almost the same percentage (45.9%) of respondents agrees with the statement that "the same things happen all the time and nothing changes."

Thus, in contrast to the widespread perception that television news helps people keep up with national and local events, when prompted to think about foreign news in particular, a significant portion of audiences around the world either think of negative events or insignificant changes in other nations. At the same time, we did not find strong support for the notion that people believe that they don't understand international events (38.6%) or do not feel affected by them (26.5%). Overall, these findings indicate somewhat more negative perceptions of foreign news as compared to news in general. However, these opinions are not shaped by an audience that feels it cannot follow international affairs, but rather the perception that foreign news is negative and quite possibly boring.

In sum, there appears to be a fairly consistent demand for, and interest in, news in all 13 countries represented in this study, especially news that enables people to keep up with events and affairs in their own countries. The sources of this news differ, however, especially according to age, with older people preferring television and newspapers, and younger people preferring online sources. More educated persons are more likely to prefer newspapers and online news, and the less educated turn more to television. Thus, our findings do not suggest less interest in news overall, especially national news, but rather some differences in preferred sources of news that enable people to keep up with both national and foreign affairs, especially national, and to have something to talk about with other people. In that sense, not so much has changed, but there is a suggestion in these findings that foreign news might have a wider appeal if it did not seem to focus so much on wars, violence, and disasters. And there is also a confirmation that in terms of time spent per day, television is still the main source of both domestic and foreign news for most people.

Summary

This chapter analyzes the findings of a telephone survey that was conducted with more than 10,000 respondents in 13 different nations around the world. The analysis focuses on how much news people in each nation consume, which news media they turn to most frequently, and what reasons they might have for paying attention or not to foreign news.

Generally, our findings indicate that older respondents tend to spend more time watching television and reading newspapers than younger respondents. More educated audiences, on the other hand, spend less time with TV news and more time with newspapers than audiences with lower levels of education. The findings also show that older and more educated respondents prefer to consume news via newspapers and television, while those who are younger and more educated tend to favor online news sources.

Most respondents say that they watch news primarily to keep up with national and international affairs. However, audiences in all 13 countries consider keeping up with national events more important than following international affairs. The most important reasons for *not* watching foreign television news are associated with the perception that international news tends to focus on negative events such as violence, wars, or disasters. At the same time, little support was found for the notion that news audiences believe they do not understand international events or do not feel affected by them.

Notes

1. As noted in Chapter 1, not all 17 countries participated in the survey part of the project.

2. While the overall project is devoted to television news, particularly to foreign news, we took advantage of the opportunity to conduct the surveys and asked the respondents about their exposure to news in other media as well.
3. The survey in the United States was conducted with a representative online panel.
4. About one-quarter of the Israeli population refrain from viewing television on the Sabbath, hence they do not watch the news after sundown on Friday evenings. This may partially explain the relatively low mean number of days of viewing television news in Israel.
5. Income was not measured in Poland.
6. Education was not measured in Brazil.

CHAPTER NINE

Interest in Foreign News

THOMAS HANITZSCH, ABBY GOODRUM,
THORSTEN QUANDT, & THILO VON PAPE

Foreign news on television delivers us the world "outside"; it feeds us with pictures of a world that often lies far beyond the realm of our direct experience (Brewer, Graf, & Willnat, 2003; Ihlen et al., 2010; Perry, 1985; Riegert, 2011; Wanta, Golan, & Lee, 2004). By way of reporting events and occurrences abroad, foreign news contributes to the cultivation of "a sense of belonging in the world," argues the anthropologist Ulf Hannerz (2004, p. 34). The primary importance of foreign news, however, lies in its power to shape our thinking as well as our understanding of other countries and cultures (Ihlen et al., 2010; Shoemaker et al., 2012; Willnat & Weaver, 2003). Large-scale public opinion surveys have shown that foreign and international news can substantially affect the audience's knowledge, perception, and attitude toward other nations (Perry, 1990; Salwen & Matera, 1992). It is exactly for this reason that foreign news is "a prime example of an area where most of us are reliant on what the media report" (Ihlen et al., 2010, p. 31). Indeed, evidence from a large number of empirical studies suggests that greater news exposure and attention to foreign news are associated with increases in knowledge about foreign affairs, international political knowledge, and international engagement (Beaudoin, 2004; Korzenny, del Toro, & Gaudino, 1987; Kwak, Poor, & Skoric, 2006; McNelly & Izcaray, 1986; Perry, 1990; Robinson, 1967; Semetko, Brzinski, Weaver, & Willnat, 1992; Wanta, Golan, & Lee, 2004).

The obvious importance of foreign news withstanding, the proportion of news devoted to events and occurrences from afar seems to be shrinking over time. This has become a matter of concern to media scholars and practitioners in many parts of the world. Emery (1989, p. 151), for instance, has declared the international news hole to be an "endangered species," and a survey of U.S. foreign correspondents conducted in 2001 indicated that the trend toward general neglect of traditional foreign newsgathering is not likely to be reversed in the near future. However, a longitudinal analysis of U.S. newspaper foreign coverage over 7 decades (from 1927 to 1997) suggested that lamentations about the decline of foreign news during the 20th century might be somewhat overstated, as changes in the quantity of international reporting were rather minor (Allen & Hamilton, 2010).

One reason for the rather low proportion of news devoted to international events and occurrences has to do with the economic context of news production. Foreign news is one of the most costly news-gathering endeavors, as Hamilton and Jenner (2004) note; and that, along with other economic considerations, makes declines in traditional foreign correspondence inevitable. Altmeppen (2010) points to the importance of audience ratings, which tend to push foreign news reporting aside when, for instance, the media are preoccupied with popular sporting events. At a time when expense considerations gain relevance in newsrooms and media organizations, news managers consequently raise the question whether the fairly high costs of foreign reporting are justified by the audience's interest in foreign news (Hannerz, 2004). The decline in international news coverage, at least in the United States, is therefore often attributed to the lack of audience interest in news from afar, argue Tai and Chang (2002, p. 254): "The category of 'foreign news' makes it easier for editors to safely assume that most stories from abroad will be as alien to the audiences as the countries involved."

Despite the evidently pivotal role of foreign news in shaping people's perception of the world, and despite the fact that "audience interest" is often used as a justification for the thinning of international coverage, we know surprisingly little about the audiences' desire for foreign news and the reasons why people do or do not pay attention to international reporting (Bilteryst, 2001; Elvestad, 2009). What we do know, however, is that journalists perform quite badly in estimating their audiences' interests (Shoemaker & Cohen, 2006; Tai & Chang, 2002).

Several studies of news consumption indicate that audiences indeed have a relatively small desire for foreign news (Sande, 1971; Sparkes & Winter, 1980; Tai & Chang, 2002; Thurman, 2007), and then only in a limited category of news topics (Weaver & Mauro, 1978), or when linked to domestic issues in some way (Cohen, 2002). A recent study conducted in Norway found that the greater interest was for local rather than foreign news (Elvestad, 2009). One could also argue that interest in foreign news is higher in small countries, as they more strongly depend on foreign relations with their neighbors. Furthermore, people in culturally diverse countries tend to have a higher demand for foreign news than audiences in more homogenous contexts. On the individual level, Elvestad (2009) found interest in foreign news to be related to a number of socio-demographic variables, including gender, age, education, and connections to home.

So far, one can only speculate about the potential reasons for the rather limited or declining audience interest in international coverage. Hannerz (2004) notes that the amount of news space devoted to foreign events is considerably larger in times of war than in times of peace. This thesis has been verified by a longitudinal analysis of U.S. newspaper coverage (Allen & Hamilton, 2010). As a result, argues Hannerz (2004, p. 25), the lack of interest in foreign news can be seen as a "measure of world peace"—a thesis that is probably true for the 1990s, when the world has been a "relatively quiet place," though perhaps not so much for the first decade of the 21st century. Another potential cause for the public's relatively limited desire for foreign news, as Hannerz reasons, is the fact that foreign news just does not fall into the category of what is commonly referred to as "news you can use," as international coverage is of little immediate relevance to individuals' everyday lives.

A third reason identified by Hannerz is that, at least for Americans, "the end of the Cold War had left much foreign news coverage without a major interpretative framework." This idea, however, has been challenged by Wu and Hamilton (2004). They argue that when the United States became the only undisputed superpower, this both increased its potential to be hated and gave it even greater power to shape global politics. American audiences therefore have a vital interest in how the country protects its interests and wields its power around the world.

A potential fourth reason has been suggested by the French sociologist Pierre Bourdieu (1998) who, in his book *On Television and Journalism*, argues that journalism tends to present us a world of war, hatred, violence and crime—"a world full of incomprehensible and unsettling dangers from which we must withdraw for our own protection" (p. 8). This could lead to the assumption that audiences turn away from the news, as it contains too much war and violence. However, empirical evidence suggests otherwise. Audiences appear to be interested mostly in stories of accidents and natural disasters, as well as wars and terrorism, especially when it involves the home country (for example, Chang, Shoemaker, & Brendlinger, 1987; Owens, 2007; Tai & Chang, 2002; Wu, 2000).

In conclusion, we can safely assume that there is a need for systematic analysis of the audiences' interest in foreign news and the reasons why people do or do not pay attention to international coverage. Toward this aim, the present work implemented an audience survey in 13 countries. The comparative survey design allowed us to map public interest in foreign news across different cultural settings, as well as to explain its variation across the individual and societal levels of analysis. This chapter will therefore focus on the following research questions: To what extent are people interested in foreign news? What kind of foreign news

Table 9.1 Interest in foreign news (mean scores)

	Brazil	Canada	Chile	China	Germany	Hong Kong	Israel	Poland	Portugal	Singapore	Switzerland	Taiwan	United States	Total	F	Eta²
General interest in foreign news	3.17	3.83	3.27	3.55	3.43	3.52	3.24	3.42	3.31	3.65	3.47	3.21	3.31	3.39	23.9*	.027
Accidents and natural disasters	3.16	3.69	3.55	3.20	3.13	3.66	3.26	3.30	3.31	3.67	3.14	3.36	3.33	3.34	21.4*	.032
Social issues	3.77	3.36	3.54	2.94	3.09	3.18	2.75	3.26	3.52	3.32	3.28	3.19	3.18	3.23	27.0*	.047
Relations between foreign countries	3.35	3.68	2.81	3.08	3.08	3.25	2.57	3.36	3.03	3.25	3.19	3.02	3.29	3.11	40.0*	.048
Economics, business, and commerce	3.58	3.30	3.03	3.07	3.03	3.30	2.74	2.95	2.98	3.17	3.01	3.32	3.18	3.11	33.8*	.025
Domestic politics of foreign countries	2.64	2.93	2.47	2.75	2.80	3.03	2.27	2.77	2.30	2.67	2.94	2.35	2.94	2.67	41.4*	.049
Crime and violence	2.58	2.68	2.85	2.50	2.60	3.10	2.37	2.72	2.64	2.89	2.65	2.24	2.78	2.64	42.0*	.040
Sports	2.95	2.19	2.59	2.81	2.31	2.99	2.40	2.73	2.51	2.61	2.62	2.96	2.21	2.62	33.9*	.039
N	465	393	1,218	1,114	995	597	755	797	499	496	1,009	1,132	777	10,244		

*df=12; $p < .001$
Scale: 5 = "very interested"; 4 = "quite interested"; 3 = "somewhat interested"; 2 = "not very interested"; and 1 = "not interested at all."

content is most appealing to audiences? How do levels of interest in foreign news compare to the attention people devote to domestic news? Finally: What are the major determinants of interest in foreign news?

Interest in Foreign News

In order to get a sense of the extent to which people are interested in foreign news, we incorporated a question in the survey that addressed the audience's desire for foreign news in a very basic way. The question was worded as follows: "Generally, to what extent are you interested in news about other countries?" Respondents were provided five response choices: "very interested," "quite interested," "somewhat interested," "not very interested," and "not interested at all."

The findings are reported in Table 9.1. It turned out that across all investigated countries, general interest in foreign news was highest in Canada (M=3.83), Singapore (M=3.65), China (M=3.55), and Hong Kong (M=3.52), while it was lowest among the surveyed publics in Brazil (M=3.17), Taiwan (M=3.21), Israel (M=3.24), and Chile (M=3.27). An analysis of variance showed that cross-national variation was significant but not particularly substantial (F=23.9, df=12, $p < .001$). The rather small value for eta-squared indicated that only 2.7% of the overall variance in levels of general interest in foreign news was due to differences between countries.

Several potential explanations come to mind when we look at the differences between country scores. For one, interest in foreign news tends indeed to be higher in smaller countries, as they more strongly depend on foreign relations with their neighbors. This is the case for Singapore, Hong Kong, and Switzerland. These countries may be too small to produce enough domestic news of interest to a national audience. In addition, the three countries incorporate fairly large communities of immigrants who often have substantial interest in news about their countries of origin.

Taiwan and Israel, on the other hand, seem to contradict this pattern. However, this may be resolved when alternative explanations are taken into account: In Taiwan, the fairly low interest in foreign news may be related to the important role China plays in the country's foreign relations and coverage of foreign affairs. Given that Taiwan's independence from China is still a disputed issue in the regional and cultural context, the coverage of China may not be perceived as foreign news by significant segments of the surveyed Taiwanese population. Indeed, news about Mainland China falls into a third category—"news across the Strait" (the Taiwan Strait), which is neither domestic nor foreign. A structural and perhaps even more important reason may be the isolation of Taiwan in terms of its diplomatic relations. Recognized by only a few countries, Taiwan has very few international engagements and therefore commands fairly little media attention.

The case may be similar for Israel, where the conflict-laden Israeli-Palestinian relationship occupies a substantial share of the country's news diet. Coverage of the Palestinian territories might be regarded by many members of the Israeli population as a domestic rather than a foreign topic, perhaps depending on the perception of these territories as belonging to either Israel or the Palestinians. This applies most notably to the coverage of East Jerusalem, but in part also to news on Jewish settlements in the West Bank.

In addition, there is some indication that people in culturally diverse countries with different language communities, such as Canada, Singapore, and Switzerland, have a higher demand for foreign news. At the same time, the fairly high interest in foreign news reported by Chinese audiences may be attributed to the fact that in a party-controlled media system, domestic news may not appear to be appealing to audiences, as most information provided by state-owned media is fairly unsurprising and rather predictable. Foreign news, on the other hand, may have much more to offer in this respect, and the government may actively encourage the media to focus more on foreign issues in order to divert the audiences' interest from domestic problems that might undermine the authority of the government and the party. However, this explanation, as much as it makes sense in the context of the Chinese political system as observed from the outside, is substantially contradicted by another finding that is discussed further below.

General interest in foreign news may be too broad a category to understand the often fine-grained and subtle differences in audiences' desire for news content. Though some people may well be interested in international sports news, they couldn't care less about foreign political affairs. The category of generalized interest in foreign news in these cases may mask some of the more striking cross-national differences. In addition to general interest in foreign news, we therefore asked respondents to indicate their interest in specific subject areas in relation to foreign countries. The subject areas we presented in the surveys included seven broad topics: Domestic politics of foreign countries; Relations between foreign countries; Economics, business, and commerce; Accidents and natural disasters; Crime and violence; Social issues; and Sports.

Table 9.1, however, reveals a fairly similar ranking of topics across the 13 investigated countries. Not surprisingly, accidents and natural disasters attracted the highest scores in terms of audience interest in most of the countries with the exception of Brazil. Social issues also scored high in the audiences' ranking of interesting topics, followed by news concerning relations between foreign countries. Issues related to the economy, business, and commerce seemed to attract only mediocre levels of audience interest. Overall, our study provides further support for Weaver and Mauro's (1978) earlier findings, according to which publics are interested in a rather limited category of news topics.

In most of the countries, the public has fairly little interest in the relations between foreign countries. This is especially true for Chile, Israel, Portugal, and Taiwan. Finally, foreign news that treats crime, violence, and sports ranked lowest in terms of the audiences' interest in specific categories of news content.

Overall, our data revealed a remarkably consistent pattern in which accidents and natural disasters comprise the most interesting foreign news for audiences around the world. This finding is consistent with findings from previous studies, which found publics to be interested mostly in stories of accidents, disasters, war, and terrorism (for instance, Chang, Shoemaker, & Brendlinger, 1987; Owens, 2007; Tai & Chang, 2002; Wu, 2000). The eta-squared values for the seven categories of subject areas range from .025 to .049, indicating that the amount of variance that is due to country differences is fairly small by common standards of survey research—between 3% and 5%. These differences may be small but are not necessarily meaningless. The cross-national differences with respect to interest in domestic politics of foreign countries, relations between foreign countries, and social issues in foreign news are somewhat larger than differences in terms of foreign coverage of economic, business, and commercial affairs, as well as of accidents and natural disasters. This means that there is more disagreement between audiences from the various countries with respect to their interest in the former three subject areas, and that there are more similarities between countries with respect to the latter two topics.

Interest in Foreign vs. Interest in Domestic News

Several studies have shown, almost consistently so, that publics have a rather limited desire for foreign news (Sande, 1971; Sparkes & Winter, 1980; Tai & Chang, 2002), or at least that they are less interested in foreign news than they are in domestic news (Elvestad, 2009). In our study, we therefore also asked respondents to indicate their interest in domestic news, again with respect to the seven broad subject areas indicated above. The findings are reported in Table 9.2; categories are ordered in descending order according to audience interest across all 13 countries.

With respect to the ranking of topics, our findings clearly paint a picture quite similar to the pattern of audience interest in foreign news as reported in Table 9.1. The only substantial difference is that with respect to domestic news coverage, audiences in most of the countries are more interested in social issues than in accidents and natural disasters. Only in the case of Israel did the audience not put social issues among the most-desired news categories, though we should keep in mind that the survey was conducted before Israel experienced the largest social protests in its history. Not surprisingly, domestic crime and violence is a subject area that makes rather interesting news for audiences in Israel, but also for people in Chile, which we believe is due to sharply increasing crime rates in recent years (United Nations Office on Drugs and Crime, 2012).

Table 9.2 Interest in domestic news (mean scores)

	Brazil	Canada	Chile	China	Germany	Hong Kong	Israel	Poland	Portugal	Singapore	Switzerland	Taiwan	United States	Total	F	Eta²
Social issues	4.48	4.12	4.40	3.54	3.83	3.61	3.24	3.94	4.29	3.80	3.72	3.70	3.75	3.86	93.9*	.100
Accidents and natural disasters	3.42	3.71	3.82	3.83	3.34	3.87	3.68	3.49	3.55	3.73	3.34	3.77	3.73	3.64	28.6*	.033
Country's relations with other countries	3.72	3.91	3.76	3.58	3.61	3.53	3.57	3.43	3.38	3.44	3.60	3.24	3.63	3.56	20.09*	.023
Economics, business, and commerce	3.86	3.67	3.38	3.34	3.43	3.53	3.24	3.14	3.38	3.34	3.17	3.43	3.75	3.40	22.0*	.025
Domestic politics	2.85	3.65	2.90	3.43	3.56	3.11	3.20	3.32	2.80	2.86	3.45	2.50	3.58	3.17	75.4*	.081
Crime and violence	2.94	3.41	3.72	3.05	3.06	3.48	3.58	3.17	3.11	3.31	2.90	2.29	3.40	3.15	100.6*	.105
Sports	3.43	2.80	2.93	3.14	2.79	2.82	2.39	3.08	3.00	2.66	2.96	3.05	2.98	2.93	23.30*	.027
N	468	395	1,204	1,123	998	599	757	799	499	499	1,009	1,141	782	10,260		

*df=12; $p < .001$

Scale: 5 = "very interested"; 4 = "quite interested"; 3 = "somewhat interested"; 2 = "not very interested"; and 1 = "not interested at all."

Table 9.3 Differences between interest in foreign and domestic news (mean score differences)

	Brazil	Canada	Chile	China	Germany	Hong Kong	Israel	Poland	Portugal	Singapore	Switzerland	Taiwan	United States
Domestic politics (of foreign countries)	-.21	-.72	-.43	-.67	-.76	-.09	-.93	-.55	-.50	-.20	-.52	-.15	-.64
Relations between foreign (and own) countries	-.37	-.23	-.96	-.50	-.53	-.27	-.99	-.07	-.35	-.19	-.42	-.22	-.34
Economics, business, and commerce	-.28	-.37	-.35	-.27	-.40	-.23	-.50	-.19	-.40	-.17	-.17	-.11	-.58
Accidents and natural disasters	-.26	-.02	-.27	-.63	-.21	-.22	-.42	-.19	-.24	-.05	-.19	-.41	-.41
Social issues	-.71	-.77	-.86	-.61	-.74	-.43	-.49	-.68	-.77	-.48	-.44	-.51	-.56
Crime and violence	-.35	-.73	-.87	-.55	-.45	-.38	-1.20	-.45	-.47	-.43	-.26	-.04	-.62
Sports	-.47	-.61	-.35	-.33	-.48	.17	.01	-.35	-.49	-.05	-.34	-.10	-.77
N	463	390	1,145	1,084	968	583	681	787	462	484	991	1,097	749

While the audiences' priorities in terms of interest in foreign and domestic news topics are relatively similar, there is a strikingly consistent gap in the extent to which people in the 13 countries are interested in domestic news as opposed to coverage of foreign affairs. Table 9.3 shows the findings of a comparison by country of levels of interest in foreign vs. domestic news, reported separately for each of the seven broad subject areas. The evidence speaks a clear language: across the board, mean score differences were generally negative, indicating that audiences clearly have more interest in domestic news than in foreign affairs. Repeated-measures t-tests indicated that mean score differences were all significant at $p < .01$ with only a few exceptions. Differences for interest in news on crime and violence were not significant in the case of Poland; differences in sports news were not significant for Israel and Singapore; and the gap between interest in foreign vs. domestic news about accidents and natural disasters was not significant for Canada and Singapore.

With an average of −.62 across the sample, the mean score differences were largest for interest in news about social issues. This is not particularly surprising, given that people generally care more about social problems in their own countries and communities than about social issues abroad. While foreign social issues leave people mostly unaffected, social problems in their neighborhoods may have a more or less direct effect on their lives. A similar explanation applies to the rather large differences in interest in foreign vs. domestic news on crime and violence (average mean difference: −.52). Here again, Israel clearly stands out because of its specific political circumstances and terrorism-related issues.

The difference between interest in foreign and domestic news is only slightly smaller with respect to coverage of domestic affairs occurring in the home country—or domestic affairs of other countries (average mean difference: −.52). The gap tends to be widest for Western countries, as indicated by the values obtained for Canada (−.72), Germany (−.76), Israel (−.96), Portugal (−.50), Switzerland (−.52), and the United States (−.64). This means that audiences in Western countries have a tendency to prioritize coverage of domestic affairs more strongly than audiences in non-Western countries. Long-established patterns of uneven news flows from the North to the South therefore become evident even in the audiences' interests. The findings indicate that with respect to what is sometimes called "news geography," Western nations are still expected to dominate public debate in the global arena.

An interesting finding, however, is the substantially large difference between interest in foreign and domestic news that we found for China (mean difference: −.67). This result not only contradicts the just-established pattern of Western vs. non-Western countries; it also contradicts the relatively high desire of the Chinese audience for foreign news as reported above. A careful inspection of the data in Table 9.1 hints at a potential explanation for this inconsistency. Although respondents in China reported fairly high levels of interest in foreign news (M=3.55) when asked in a general way, they expressed considerably less interest in all of the seven broad subject areas for which mean scores range between 2.50 and 3.20. It seems that at least in the context of China, the seven specific categories of foreign news topics do not adequately reproduce what Chinese responders have in mind when they refer to "foreign news" The differences between interest in foreign and domestic news on relations between foreign (and one's own) countries is, with an average differential of –.45, still substantial. The difference is highest in Chile (–.96) and Israel (–.99), which means that audiences in these two countries are considerably more interested in news about the relations of their countries with other countries than they are in relations between foreign countries. Generally, the pattern of difference does not seem to follow the common political and cultural divides. In the case of Israel, it might easily be explained by the fairly small size of the country and its heavy dependence on foreign relations, especially on relations with the United States.

The gap between interest in foreign and domestic news on issues relating to the economy, business, and commerce is much smaller, with a mean score difference of –.30 on average. The difference is largest for most Western countries investigated (Canada: –.37, Germany: –.40, Israel: –.50, Portugal: –.40, the United States: –.58), but also for Chile (–.35). Audiences in these countries are therefore more strongly interested in domestic news about economic, business, and financial affairs vis-à-vis foreign news on the subject. A potential explanation for these findings is the relative size of the economy in these countries. Chile is also notable in that it has made remarkable economic progress during the past years.

A similar explanation comes to mind when looking at the differences between interest in foreign and domestic news on sports, which average to a gap of –.31 across all countries. The difference is most pronounced in Brazil (–.47), Canada (–.61), Germany (–.48), Portugal (–.49), and the United States (–.77)—all of which are larger countries that sustain a significant national sports arena, which produces larger numbers of popular and successful sportsmen and sports teams, and which are served by a national media that gives them extensive coverage. This is especially obvious in the case of the United States, which has a long history of commercialized sporting events even to the extent that major finals, such as the National Football League's Super Bowl, have become iconic for American culture. According to Nielsen ratings, the Super Bowl has frequently been the most-watched individual American telecast of the year. In addition, the event marks the second-highest day of food consumption in the United States after Thanksgiving (United States Department of Agriculture, 2009). In Hong Kong, on the other hand, audiences appear to have more interest in foreign sports news than in domestic sports news.

With regard to accidents and natural disasters, the gap between interest in foreign and domestic news is similarly small but, with an average mean score difference of –.30, is still substantial. The gap is largest for China (–.63), Israel (–.42), Taiwan (–.41), and the United States (–.41). Here, the cross-national pattern reflects the extent to which a country is prone to accidents and natural disasters. In countries where these events occur more frequently, audiences tend to be more interested in domestic news on this category than in foreign coverage of accidents and natural disasters.

Using Spearman rank correlations, the respondents' expressed interest in foreign news with interest in domestic news reveals an interesting picture, as can be seen in Table 9.4. As a general tendency, the interest in specific subject areas overrules any generalized interest in domestic vs. foreign news. With respect to the seven broad categories—domestic politics; relations between foreign/with other countries; economics, business, and commerce; social issues; crime and violence; accidents and natural disasters; and sports—there is a fairly strong correlation between interest in foreign news and interest in domestic news (average $\rho=.489$). The relationship is strongest in the subject areas of sports ($\rho=.656$), economics, business, and commerce ($\rho=.563$), as well as accidents and natural disasters ($\rho=.512$).

The correlations between the seven topics of coverage are considerably weaker for interest in foreign news (average $\rho=.266$), and even lower for domestic news (average $\rho=.183$). Substantial correlations between the individual subject areas were found only between domestic politics vs. foreign relations; domestic politics vs. economics, business, and commerce; foreign relations vs. economics, business, and commerce; and crime and violence vs. accidents and natural disasters.

These findings indicate that topical preference is a stronger indicator of interest in the news than the locality of an event marking it as either foreign or domestic news. This means that people who are interested in sports news tend to be attracted by both domestic and international sports reporting, and those who are interested in economics, business, and commerce are inclined to consume both domestic and foreign coverage of these issues. At the same time, however, it is less likely that people interested in international sports news will have an equally strong desire for foreign coverage of international politics or social issues. Likewise, people interested in domestic news on economics, business, and commerce are less likely to be attracted to national coverage of crime and violence.

Explaining Interest in Foreign News

We have noted that there is some variation in the extent to which people are interested in foreign news, mostly at the level of the individual. The question thus remains: Why are some people are more interested in foreign news than others? Since we were not the first to encounter such variation in interest in foreign

Table 9.4 Relationships between interest in foreign news and domestic news (Spearman rank correlations)

	Domestic politics	Relations between foreign/ with other countries		Economics, business, and commerce		Social issues		Crime and violence		Sports		Accidents and natural disasters	
	Domestic news	Foreign news	Domestic news	Foreign news	Domestic news	Foreign news	Domestic news	Foreign news	Domestic news	Foreign news	Domestic news	Foreign news	Domestic news
Domestic politics													
Foreign news	.406**	.481**	.348**	.402**	.267**	.280**	.110*	.308**	.075**	.185**	.093**	.169**	.047
Domestic news		.276**	.383**	.224**	.295**	.097**	.153**	.112**	.173**	.050	.118**	.043	.065*
Relations between foreign/with other countries													
Foreign news			.417**	.454**	.272**	.350**	.184**	.259**	.054*	.181**	.098**	.255**	.094**
Domestic news				.333**	.371**	.257**	.282**	.163**	.167**	.101**	.135**	.182**	.193**
Economics, business, and commerce													
Foreign news					.563**	.324**	.136**	.163**	.004	.212**	.114*	.179**	.067**
Domestic news						.168**	.198**	.065**	.089**	.116**	.142**	.091**	.142**
Social issues													
Foreign news							.408**	.252**	.075**	.123**	.034**	.292**	.128**
Domestic news								.115**	.178**	.003	.028**	.185**	.229**
Crime and violence													
Foreign news									.463**	.149**	.066**	.429**	.293**
Domestic news										.009	.052**	.307**	.373**
Sports													
Foreign news											.656**	.144**	.065**
Domestic news												.076**	.078**
Accidents and natural disasters													
Foreign news													.512**

** significant at $p < .01$

Table 9.5 Predicting interest in foreign news, pooled regression (standardized coefficients)

	Model 1	Model 2	Model 3	Model 4	Model 5	Model 6
Intercept	2.835 ***	1.884 ***	2.613 ***	2.534 ***	1.945 ***	1.673 ***
TV news helps keeping up with current events	.112 ***	.080 ***	.071 ***	.066 ***	.070 ***	.071 ***
TV news gives something to talk	.018	−.002	.009	.011	.017	.021 *
TV news can be entertaining	−.003	−.007	.009	.007	.010	.018
Interested if events concern own nationals		.296 ***	.269 ***	.259 ***	.250 ***	.248 ***
Not affected by events in other countries			−.117 ***	−.119 ***	−.107 ***	−.112 ***
There is too much reporting of violence and disasters			−.005	−.001	.000	.002
Not enough background to follow news			−.103 ***	−.094 ***	−.075 ***	−.081 ***
The same things happen all the time and nothing changes			−.089 ***	−.084 ***	−.074 ***	−.061 ***
Time watched TV news yesterday [min]				.048 ***	.053 ***	.057 ***
Time read newspaper yesterday [min]				.071 ***	.057 ***	.044 ***
Time got news on the Internet yesterday [min]				.060 ***	.045 ***	.045 ***
Years of formal education					.101 ***	.112 ***
Household income					.052 ***	.033 ***
Age					.024 *	.029 **
Gender (1 = female)					−.018	−.021 *
Brazil						.002
Canada						.077 ***
Chile						.051 **
China						.118 ***
Germany						.055 ***
Hong Kong						.066 ***
Israel						.024
Poland						.082 ***
Portugal						.038 **
Singapore						.096 ***
Switzerland						.090 ***
Taiwan						.071 ***
R^2	.014	.100	.145	.158	.172	.187
R^2 change	.014 ***	.086 ***	.046 ***	.012 ***	.015 ***	.015 ***

*** $p < .001$; ** $p < .01$; * $p < .05$

news—or news in general—we can draw on a substantial body of research that already provides us with a few hints as to what may be major determinants of interest in foreign news (e.g., Best, Chmielewski, & Krueger, 2005; Cohen, 2002; Elvestad, 2009; Owens, 2007).

On the basis of this literature, as well as our own modest theoretical reasoning, we built a regression model in a step-wise manner as an attempt to explain interest in foreign news. The findings are reported in Table 9.5. For the regression model we used general interest in foreign news as the dependent variable and added with every hierarchical step an additional set of potential predictors to the model. In this first analysis we included data sets from all 13 countries for which we conducted an audience survey and combined them into a pooled analysis. The resulting pooled sample is by no means meant to be a "sample of the world," as the countries investigated in this analysis were not randomly selected. We therefore need to emphasize that the following interpretations are clearly limited to our country sample and should not be generalized beyond the scope of this study.

The first set of predictors added to the regression model was concerned with motives for watching TV news. A long tradition of uses-and-gratifications research has established that audiences actively use media to satisfy their needs (Blumler & Katz, 1974; Rosengren, 1974b). A variety of taxonomies of media-use motives were proposed, partly in response to a changing mediascape, but in their broadest categorization they still remain reasonably consistent with early classifications of motives put forward by McQuail, Blumler, and Brown (1972), Blumler and Katz (1974), and McQuail (1983). The three broad categories that we found relevant to the use of foreign news were: information (or: surveillance), integration (or: social interaction), and diversion (or: entertainment). For each of these categories we included one indicator in the model: "TV news helps keeping up with current events" for information; "TV news gives something to talk" for social interaction; and "TV news can be entertaining" for entertainment. Of these three variables, only information turned out to be a significant predictor of interest in foreign news. The predictive power of the model, however, was fairly negligible, with only 1.4% of the variance in interest in foreign news explained by viewing motives.

In the second step we included domestication as a potential additional explanation. In this view, domestication holds that people may be more interested in foreign news if nationals of their own countries are involved in the course of those events (Cohen, 2002; Owens, 2007). In the expanded model, domestication turned out to have a very large and highly significant effect on interest in foreign news. The predictive power of the model increased considerably to 10% of explained variance.

The third set of predictors referred to perceived characterizations of news and the personal capacity to follow foreign coverage. We included four variables that have been found to be meaningful characterizations of news in previous research (Pew Research Center for the People and the Press, 2002a): "Events in other countries do not affect me"; "There is too much reporting of wars, violence and disasters"; "I don't have enough background to understand events in other countries"; and "It seems that the same things happen all the time and nothing changes." In a sense, these characterizations could also be seen as motives for *not* watching news. The findings show that with the exception of the item that said "There is too much reporting of wars, violence, and disasters," these perceived characterizations have a significantly negative effect on interest in foreign news. Including the characterizations of news substantially improved the regression model.

We also reasoned that exposure to news may be another dimension that might add to the equation in meaningful ways. The rationale goes as follows: People who generally consume more news regardless of content may have a greater desire for foreign news. The findings in Table 9.5 ("Model 4") clearly show that exposure to TV news, newspaper content, and online news does indeed have a positive and significant effect on interest in foreign news. However, the predictive power of the model, as indicated by the amount of variance explained, increased only slightly from 14.5% to 15.8%.

In the fifth step we added a number of socio-demographic variables to the equation that are known to be related to news exposure and interest (Best, Chmielewski, & Krueger, 2005; Elvestad, 2009), including education, household income, age, and gender. Of these variables, education, income, and age appeared to have a positive effect on interest in foreign news. After controlling for country-level differences in the sixth and last model,[1] however, the effect of gender was rendered significant, indicating that men have more interest in foreign news than women. In a similar manner, the effect of social interaction as a potential motive for watching TV news was also rendered significant.

Overall, we can conclude from this analysis that audiences have more interest in foreign news when they seek information about the world and, to a lesser extent, when they believe that news provides them with topics for social conversation. This evidence lends further support to the assumption that there are rational motives guiding the program selections of television viewers, as hypothesized by proponents of the uses-and-gratifications approach (McQuail, Blumler, & Brown, 1972; McQuail, 1983; Blumler & Katz, 1974). The motivational category of diversion and entertainment, however, has turned out to be of little relevance for the calculus of audience interest in foreign news.

Publics appear to have a greater desire for international reporting when citizens of their own countries are involved in the news from abroad. This finding is also consistent with previous research, for instance by Cohen (2002) and Owens

Interest in Foreign News | 187

Table 9.6 Predicting interest in foreign news, country-wise regression (standardized coefficients)

	Brazil	Canada	Chile	China	Germany	Hong Kong	Israel	Poland	Portugal	Singapore	Switzerland	Taiwan	United States
Intercept	1.118 *	2.213 ***	2.091 ***	2.147 ***	3.179 ***	2.144 ***	2.473 ***	2.284 ***	1.699 **	3.090 ***	1.350 ***	2.225 ***	1.310 ***
TV news helps keeping up with current events	.094 +	.162 **	.104 ***	.129 ***	.079 *	.068	.096 +	-.006	.101 *	.038	.103 **	-.019	.157 ***
TV news gives something to talk	.076	.035	-.017	-.009	.032	-.076	.002	.063 +	.101 *	-.064	.015	-.042	.001
TV news can be entertaining	.047	-.043	-.036	.101 **	-.011	.007	.001	.047	.039	.060	.049	.026	.054
Interested if events concern own nationals	.259 ***	.120 *	.242 ***	.133 ***	--	.234 ***	.070	.380 ***	.253 ***	.087	.359 ***	.263 ***	.355 ***
Not affected by events in other countries	-.018	-.254 ***	-.148 ***	-.156	-.141 ***	-.007	-.094 +	-.080 *	-.132 *	-.047	-.157 ***	-.121 ***	-.030
There is too much reporting of violence and disasters	.068	-.060	.070 *	.044 ***	-.099 **	.030	-.017	-.002	-.171 ***	-.055	-.025	.095 **	-.074 *
Not enough background to follow news	-.058	-.088	-.134 ***	-.094 *	-.097 **	-.113 *	-.081	-.101 **	-.031	-.175 **	-.035	.021	-.063 +
The same things happen all the time and nothing changes	-.108 *	-.033	-.027	-.043	-.089 *	-.058	.004	-.064 +	-.078	.019	-.042	-.084 *	-.061 +
Time watched TV news yesterday	.074	.025	.038	.068 +	.072 *	.047	.042	-.016	.119 *	.080	.099 **	.030	-.042
Time read newspaper yesterday	.022	-.018	-.009	.021	.050	.028	.040	.023	-.015	.036	.043	.006	.062 +
Time got news on the Internet yesterday	.003	.064	.041	.044	.124 ***	.014	.038	-.029	.014	.121 *	.059 +	-.028	.068 *
Years of formal education	--	.132 +	.117 ***	.091 *	.108 **	.170 **	.044	.076 *	.096	.090	.092 **	.080 *	.152 ***
Household income	.057	.064	.007	.042	.064 +	-.052	.173 **	--	-.038	.011	.068 *	.017	.039
Age	-.094 +	.056	.069 *	.129 **	.044	.023	.086	.021	-.037	.068	.021	.069 +	-.194 ***
Gender (1 = female)	.006	-.033	-.069 *	-.149 ***	-.008	.106 *	-.094 +	-.100 **	.009	.012	.016	-.005	-.040
R2	.150	.243	.197	.169	.171	.144	.115	.235	.241	.134	.326	.137	.337

*** $p < .001$; ** $p < .01$; * $p < .05$; + $p < .10$

(2007). Furthermore, higher exposure to news generally has an additional positive effect on interest in foreign news. On the other hand, audiences are less attracted to international coverage when they feel that they do not have enough background to follow foreign news and when they believe that the same things happen all the time and nothing really changes. Likewise, publics tend to be less interested in international reporting when they think that events in other countries do not affect them, which resonates with Hannerz's (2004) hypothesis that foreign news is of relatively little immediate importance to the individuals' everyday lives. The idea that audiences avoid foreign news because it contains too much war and violence (Bourdieu, 1998), however, could not be verified by this study. Finally, older, more educated, and wealthier individuals have a greater desire for foreign news, with men being more interested in news from abroad than women. These findings partly confirm findings from Elvestad (2009), who found interest in foreign news to be related to gender, age, and education.

In order to investigate the more fine-grained differences between countries in the way the various determinants of interest in foreign news play out, we also estimated regressions for each country separately. Table 9.6 shows some variation in the extent to which the various predictors impact on the audiences' desire for foreign news in the 13 countries. While the general picture remains remarkably consistent, there are a few deviations from the pattern. Chinese audiences differ from the publics of the other nations in that it is the only country where the fact that television news can be entertaining positively contributes to interest in foreign news. The feeling that television news contains too much reporting of violence and disasters tends to be negatively related to interest in foreign news in a number of countries, but in Chile and Taiwan, audiences appear to have a greater desire for international news the more they believe that content focuses too much on violence and disasters. A potential explanation here is that domestic news is perhaps so much preoccupied with brutality and tragedy that audiences turn to international coverage that contains less violence.

Socio-demographic predictors do not always point in the same direction if findings are compared across countries. In the pooled analysis, age was weakly but positively related to interest in foreign news—which means that the older people get, the more they are interested in foreign news. This is indeed true of most of the countries, but in the cases of Brazil und the United States, the relationship is actually reversed. In these nations, it is the younger people who have a greater desire for foreign reporting. Perhaps there is some hope, at least for these two countries, that as younger generations tend to be more interested in foreign news, their greater desire for news from afar might be able to convince news managers to expand the international news hole in the long term. With respect to gender, it turns out that while men are generally more interested in foreign news than women, this does not apply to Hong Kong, where it is actually women who have a greater desire for international reporting than men.

Summary and Conclusions

We have learned in this chapter that despite the undeniable importance of foreign news to the public understanding and image of other countries and cultures, we know fairly little about the audiences' desire for international reporting and the reasons why people do or do not pay attention to foreign news. The survey in the 13 countries examined the publics' desire for foreign news, the topics they are most interested in, the level of interest in foreign news as compared to domestic news, and the principal forces that drive audience interest in foreign news. Our findings can be summarized as follows:

1. Publics are significantly less interested in foreign news than they are in the coverage of domestic affairs. This tendency is more pronounced in Western than in non-Western countries.

2. Interest in foreign news seems to be greater among audiences in smaller and culturally diverse countries.

3. Audiences have similar preferences in terms of news topics with respect to foreign and domestic news.

4. In an instance of remarkable agreement, accidents and natural disasters are the most interesting topics of foreign news to audiences around the world.

5. In most of the countries, audiences have fairly little interest in foreign news about international relations, crime and violence, or sports.

6. For both foreign and domestic news, interest in topics is more important than the location of an event.

7. People are more interested in foreign news if nationals of their own countries are involved in the reported events.

8. Information is a strong motivation for watching foreign news, while the motives of social interaction and entertainment are of less relevance in the majority of countries.

9. Negative perceptions of international reporting—such as the notion that foreign news does not affect people, that it is repetitive, and that it is difficult to understand—tend to lower interest in foreign news.

10. Audiences have a greater desire for foreign news when they are generally more exposed to news.

It is interesting to note that the various publics' limited interest in foreign news is contrary to all the talk about globalization, the compression of time and space, de-territorialization, and the growing interconnectedness of the world. Foreign news itself paints a picture of the world as a more dangerous place than ever. From the planetary consequences of human-made climate change, the transnational spread of infectious diseases, and the rising inequalities resulting from international trade to technological failures, networked terrorism, the risks of nuclear warfare, and the battle for dwindling natural resources—existential threats have become more commonplace and globalized in the world of today. One would expect foreign news to assume greater importance as the world becomes more interdependent, but the opposite seems to be true.

Note

1. The United States was used as baseline category.

CHAPTER TEN

Countries of Interest

THILO VON PAPE, THORSTEN QUANDT,
THOMAS HANITZSCH, & JACQUES ALKALAI WAINBERG

Empirical research regarding news geography has focused mainly on content (Golan, 2010), journalistic selection, and construction among professionals (Chang & Lee, 1992). References to the audience serve mostly as distant reminders of the field's normative importance. Journalists are expected to provide the public with valid representations of a wide spectrum of world events and to arouse interest and understanding for other nations and cultures. However, little is known about how interested the public actually is in foreign news from various parts of the world. Although the general consensus among practitioners seems to be that foreign news appears difficult to "sell"—especially with regard to countries and regions that are distant from the average viewer's everyday interests and occupations (Balinska, 2010; Hess, 1996b)—these observations lack a robust empirical basis. This chapter aims to fill this gap with insights derived from our project's representative survey data.

We first provide an overview of the number and diversity of the countries of interest to respondents overall—in other words, across the different country samples. In order to identify patterns at the nation-specific level, this picture of the *overall structure* of the countries' interests will then be refined by comparing the structure of the interests among the various sample countries. The following sections of this chapter describe and explain the amount of interest that was found in the specific countries—that is, which countries had the highest levels of interest across the overall sample and within the specific countries, as well as what might explain the differences in the levels of interest across countries.

Amount and Diversity of Overall Country Interest

The following analyses are based primarily on one open-ended question from the foreign news survey: "In the news about which foreign countries are you most interested?" Participants were allowed, but not required, to name up to five countries. Across the entire sample, respondents named an average of 2.7 countries. The distribution was very polarized, as the largest group of respondents mentioned five countries (25.5%), the second largest did not mention any country (16.7%), and the overall variance in the number of countries mentioned was 3.3.[1]

This finding can be cautiously interpreted as the first indicator of the differences between two types of TV viewers—a group with a wide interest in many countries and the "outside world" in general, and another large group of people who are not interested in foreign news and other countries at all.

Figure 10.1 Distribution of the countries' interest in the overall sample (n=10,347)

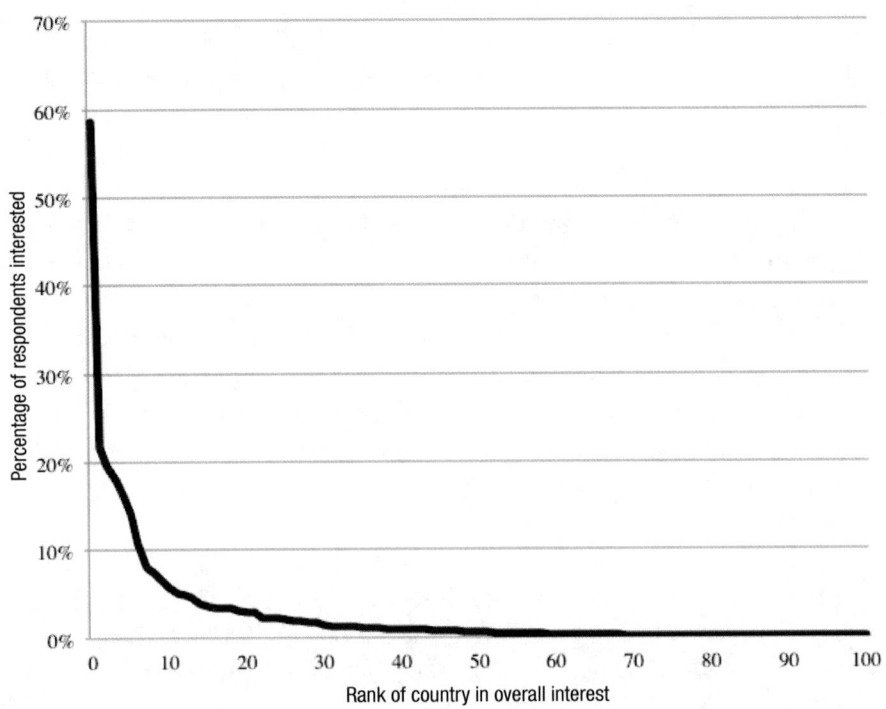

Note: To compensate for varying sample sizes, we weighed the individual respondents so that they were inversely proportional to the respective sample size.

Before going into detail about the specific sample countries, we examine the distribution of the expressed interests in the various countries that our respondents named in the surveys. Figure 10.1 shows the percentage of respondents across the samples that named each of the 100 most often mentioned countries in descending order. Only one country was mentioned by more than half of the respondents as a subject of foreign news: the United States (mentioned by 58.6%). Twelve countries were of interest to at least 5% of the sample, 39 countries were of interest to 1% of the sample, and 87 countries were of interest to at least 0.1% of the sample. The sharp drop in the curve illustrates that very few countries managed to arouse the interest of a considerable number of respondents.

Although the number of countries of interest to a marginal number of respondents appears to be quite large, this is of little quantitative relevance. Taken together, all of the countries that ranked below 30 total only 11% of the interest expressed. In contrast, the United States, which was mentioned more than any other country, was named in 21% of all the responses. Additionally, the top five countries total 48% of all of the responses, and the top 10 countries total 65% of all of the responses. Thus, there is no "long tail" phenomenon, as is found in research regarding e-business (Anderson, 2006), in which one expects the large number of items with a low frequency to add up to a considerable amount of interest, at least in summation. In other words, there is simply a large interest in a very limited number of countries, and the rest of the countries do not really matter to the respondents. This may be viewed as an outcome of the hegemonic structure of the world's economic and political power system as reflected by the news. On the other hand, this division of interest can also be viewed as the result of a media construction that continuously reproduces this hegemonic structure; for example, the logistics of news gathering favor news involving dominating countries (Wu, 2000; Ito, 2009). In any case, the United States, given that it is the single remaining superpower, generates much interest. This is also the case for an exclusive club of elite countries that seem to be the relevant players in the world of TV news.

Structure of the Interest in the Sample Countries

Table 10.1 presents both the number of countries mentioned as being of interest and the diversity among those countries.

The mean number of countries mentioned by the respondents varied greatly among the sample countries, with respondents in the United States mentioning the highest average number of countries[2] (4.28) and respondents from Israel mentioning the lowest[3] average number of countries (1.32).

The countries identified as interesting to the respondents can be compared to the "Country Concentration Index" (CCI) that was presented with respect to foreign news content in Chapter 4. There the CCI was defined as "the percentage of all the foreign news coverage…that is based on the 10 most prevalent countries." With respect to the audience survey, the CCI presents the percentage of the responses referring to the 10 countries mentioned most often by the respondents in each sample country. The CCI for the countries of interest thus indicates the degree of concentration on a few countries in terms of interest and can be considered as a parallel to the CCI of the content.

Table 10.1 Mean number of countries mentioned per respondent and Country Concentration Index per sample country

Sample country	N of respondents	Mean number of countries mentioned per respondent[1]	Country Concentration Index (CCI)[2]	Total number of countries mentioned[3]
Brazil	500	1.75	81.6	875
Canada	395	2.41	81.7	951
Chile	1,220	2.34	75.2	2,862
China	1,134	2.69	86.3	3,056
Germany	999	2.84	84.7	2,835
Hong Kong	600	1.97	88.7	1,184
Israel[4]	760	1.49	99.8	1,103
Poland	800	3.55	82.6	2,840
Portugal	500	2.88	83.6	1,441
Singapore	503	3.91	87.4	1,966
Switzerland	1,010	3.09	88.0	3,117
Taiwan	1,141	1.69	94.9	1,927
United States[5]	785	4.28	62.6	3,359
Overall	10,347	2.68	84.4	27,516

Notes:
1. Weighted by sample size.
2. The index presents the percentage of the responses to the question: "In the news about which foreign countries are you most interested?" referring to the 10 countries most often mentioned by the respondents in each sample country.
3. Theoretical maximum is 5 times the number of respondents in each sample country.
4. Responses were coded into a more narrow range of choices.
5. Survey conducted via Internet using drop-down menu of countries; hence inflated number of countries mentioned and smaller CCI score.

The mean CCI across our sample countries is 84.4%. This means that 84.4% of the countries mentioned by the respondents in the 13 country samples were among the 10 countries that were most often mentioned in the respective samples. This finding should be kept in mind as a general caveat when discussing the degree of diversity of the content of foreign news. Given that viewers' interests with respect to foreign countries is typically concentrated on only a few countries, we can assume that the viewers' horizons are rather limited. News editors should therefore consider the risk of overextending the content with news that is too diverse with respect to the countries presented.

Also, given the fact that the overall calculation is based on all 13 national samples (with each respondent being weighed in a manner that is inversely proportional to the respective sample size), it can only provide a general idea of both the size and diversity of the viewers' interests. It is therefore necessary to examine the extent to which this phenomenon is subject to nation-specific differences within the various audiences studied.

Indeed, the CCI scores for each of the individual countries indicate a substantial range, from an extremely high concentration in Israel (99.8%) and in Taiwan (94.9%) to a relatively low level in the United States (62.6%). Hence, a large number of Israeli and Taiwanese TV viewers were interested in foreign news about narrow sets of countries, whereas the interest of the American audience was more varied. The CCI scores for the remaining 10 countries are in the 75%–89% range.

The parallel with the findings from the content analysis becomes apparent. If one nation's news programs contain a small amount of news about foreign countries, then the diversity of the countries appearing in these foreign news programs is relatively low. In accordance with this link between quantity and quality of foreign news content, we see a general pattern in which the respondents who mentioned a low number of countries also mentioned countries with less diversity. Israel, Taiwan, and Hong Kong were three of the four countries with the lowest number of countries mentioned per respondent and were also among the four countries with the highest concentrations of viewers' interest in foreign countries. The respondents from the United States seem to confirm this pattern, combining an interest in many countries and high diversity. Again, however, both factors can again be attributed to the online mode of the survey in the United States.

Another reason for the higher diversity in the U.S. sample is that the one country that monopolizes interest around the world—the United States—is not a foreign country for the American sample. In other words, although the United States as a foreign country serves as a magnet of interest in all other countries in our analysis, it simply cannot serve the same function in the United States. This explanation is supported by the finding in Chapter 8 that Americans show a strong interest in domestic news (some of which is the same news about the United States that respondents from other countries are interested in). In combination, these findings may put into perspective the old stereotype of the self-centered American (Bloom, 1987), since part of the reason for their self-centeredness is that they actually *are* the center of the world in many respects, even from an outside perspective.

Overall Interest in Specific Countries

Having highlighted the amount and breadth of interest in news about foreign countries in general across the sample countries, we now consider the relative interest in specific countries (see Table 10.2).

To understand the factors influencing peoples' interest in news about different countries, we turn to content-oriented research regarding news geography. In this tradition, the appearance of nation a in the media of nation b is mostly explained through structural factors of the news value, which can be either the prominence as an absolute characteristic of nation a (such as economic prominence as measured by gross domestic product, military power, or cultural indicators) or as a relational characteristic, that is, nation a's proximity to nation b (as indicated by geographic proximity, cultural proximity through common language, or economic proximity through trade links) (Wu, 1998b). Both characteristics—absolute and relational—are often linked. For example, countries with a large gross domestic product (which means high prominence) are also likely to be important trade partners for a large number of countries (which means high proximity to these countries). When taking a global perspective and considering the importance of nation b in the global media, the relational factors becomes less important.

The most frequently mentioned country is the United States, the superpower. The fact that three European countries (the United Kingdom, France, and Germany) are the next most frequently mentioned countries may be partially due to their overall status as important economies and because, in the case of the United

Table 10.2 Interest in countries across the entire sample in percent (n=10,347)

Country of interest	Interest in overall sample (in percent)	Country of interest	Interest in overall sample (in percent)
1. United States	58.6	16. India	3.5
2. United Kingdom	21.7	17. Brazil	3.5
3. France	19.4	18. South Korea	3.4
4. Germany	18.0	19. Argentina	3.4
5. China	16.2	20. Israel	3.1
6. Japan	14.1	21. Mexico	3.0
7. Russia	10.6	22. Indonesia	2.8
8. Italy	8.1	23. Austria	2.3
9. Spain	7.4	24. Thailand	2.3
10. Afghanistan	6.6	25. Haiti	2.3
11. Iraq	5.7	26. Ukraine	2.1
12. Australia	5.1	27. North Korea	2.0
13. Malaysia	4.9	28. Czech Republic	1.9
14. Canada	4.6	29. Peru	1.8
15. Iran	4.0	30. Switzerland	1.8

Note: To compensate for varying sample sizes, we weighed the individual respondents to be inversely proportional to the respective sample size.

Kingdom and France, the countries are strongly linked to other countries around the world through historical ties and language. However, the highly prominent role that these countries play is also partly because Europe is heavily represented in our sample, with four countries. Malaysia is the only example of a country on the top 30 list that is important because of its relevance to one specific sample country (Singapore: 61.5% of the Singaporean audience expressed interest in Malaysia, as opposed to 0.2 % on average for all of the other sample countries).

For some of the other countries, the value of the news associated with a specific country during the time of the surveys may explain their relative importance. This accounts for the importance of Iraq and Afghanistan (because of ongoing military conflicts) and Haiti (because of the devastating earthquake that occurred there in January 2010, when some of the surveys were conducted).

Table 10.3 Interest in continents across the entire sample in percent (n=10,347)

Continent	Percentage of Interest	Variance
North America	60.0	24.0
Europe	48.6	25.0
Asia	37.9	23.5
South America	7.8	7.2
Oceania	5.4	5.1
Africa	4.9	4.6

Note: To compensate for varying sample sizes, we weighed the individual respondents to be inversely proportional to the respective sample size.

Among the countries that raised very little interest are some with huge populations, such as the Philippines (ranked 40th with 0.6%) and Nigeria (ranked 85th with 0.1%). In part, this lack of interest may be explained by their distance from the countries included in the analysis. However, geographical distance is not the only factor; there is also most likely a lack of political and economic relevance or cultural common ground between the countries included in the analysis and the countries of interest.

These findings are also evident when we examine the percentage of interest across the entire sample of 13 countries in the continents of the world (see Table 10.3). Here we clearly see the varying interest levels regarding the different continents. North America is ahead of Europe and Asia, with South America, Africa, and Oceania clearly lagging behind. Given the population sizes of these continents, the lack of interest among our respondents toward Africa is striking. Part of this is certainly due to the selection of countries included in our study, but this is only part of the story. Even geographic and cultural distances are not sufficient to explain this complete lack of interest in Africa, which is practically invisible to TV audiences in our survey. The question "Where in the world is Africa?" that

Table 10.4 Ranked order of each sample country's mentioned countries of interest among the 30 most-mentioned countries overall

Country of interest	BRA	CAN	CHL	CHN	GER	H-K	ISR	POL	POR	SIN	SWI	TAI	USA
United States	1	1	1	1	1	1	1	3	3	1	2	1	x
UK	9	2	12	3	3	2	3	4	4	7	6	5	2
France	3	10	7	5	2	7	2	5	1	11	3	6	11
Germany	7	15	9	7	x	9	–	1	5	12	1	7	7
China	5	3	11	x	5	x	–	10	13	2	7	3	4
Japan	2	13	10	2	14	3	–	19	15	5	11	2	13
Russia	16	14	19	4	4	8	4	2	16	13	8	11	12
Italy	4	16	8	14	6	11	–	8	7	20	4	19	15
Spain	8	–	3	18	8	20	–	9	2	18	9	20	23
Afghanistan	19	4	21	15	7	18	–	13	14	24	14	–	1
Iraq	13	6	15	9	9	12	–	14	11	17	16	17	3
Australia	14	9	13	11	17	4	–	20	17	9	17	8	10
Malaysia	21	–	27	22	–	16	–	25	–	3	–	13	29
Canada	12	x	14	12	20	5	6	12	10	16	18	10	5
Iran	18	7	18	13	12	17	5	16	18	15	13		9
India	11	8	17	10	15	13	–	18	19	8	12	14	18
Brazil	x	20	5	19	19	21	–	21	6	22	15	12	16
South Korea	–	19	–	6	–	6	–	–	–	10	26	4	19
Argentina	6	–	2	–	25	23	7	–	12	–	23	–	21
Israel	15	11	16	17	13	15	x	15	23	19	10	18	8
Mexico	10	12	6	–	24	–	–	23	20	23	21	–	6
Indonesia	–	–	25	23	21	22	–	26	–	4	22	16	28
Austria	–	–	23	24	11	–	–	11	21	–	5	–	20
Thailand	–	21	26	16	22	10	–	24		6	19	9	25
Haiti	23	5	20	21	–	–	–	–	9	14	–	–	17
Ukraine	–	18	–	–	23	–	–	6	24	–	–	–	26
North Korea	20	17	24	8	18	14	–	22	–	21	25	–	14
Czech Republic	–	22	28	–	16	–	–	7	22	–	24	–	27
Peru	22	24	4	25	–	24	–	–	–	–	20	–	24
Switzerland	17	23	22	20	10	19	–	17	8	–	x	15	22

* A – (minus sign) indicates that the country of interest did not appear in the sample country's top 30 list.

Table 10.5 Spearman rank correlations of countries of interest among all sample countries

	BRA	CAN	CHL	CHN	GER	H-K	ISR	POL	POR	SIN	SWI	TAI	USA
BRA	1												
CAN	0.23	1											
CHL	**0.72****	0.15	1										
CHN	**0.68****	0.39	0.35	1									
GER	0.30	**0.58****	0.20	0.42	1								
H-K	0.55*	0.43	0.09	**0.86****	0.43	1							
ISR	0.54	0.50	0.32	0.77	**1.00****	0.71	1						
POL	0.50*	0.27	0.37	0.49*	**0.71****	0.47*	0.54	1					
POR	0.43	0.24	**0.56****	0.23	0.53*	0.14	0.68	0.34	1				
SIN	0.37	0.26	−0.11	0.26	0.22	0.45*	**0.94****	0.01	0.18	1			
SWI	**0.59****	0.51*	0.32	0.32	**0.86****	0.40	**1.00****	**0.75****	0.46*	0.21	1		
TAI	0.51*	0.37	0.28	**0.73****	0.25	**0.81****	0.80	0.26	0.16	**0.61****	0.20	1	
USA	0.21	**0.78****	0.29	**0.61****	0.43*	0.50*	0.31	0.30	0.17	−0.31	0.38	0.32	1

Note: Spearman rank correlation coefficients. Significant values above 0.7 are in boldface.
* $p < 0.05$; ** $p < 0.01$ (two-tailed).

Golan (2008) asked rhetorically with respect to the low levels of news coverage, also applies to respondents' interests.

Specific Interest in Countries in the Various Sample Nations

Finally, we compare the interest levels for news regarding the various countries of interest in the different sample countries. To this end, in Table 10.4 we list for each of the countries in the study its respective ranking among the 30 top countries of interest mentioned by the respondents across all the countries (the same 30 countries as in Table 10.2). For example, in the case of Brazil (the left hand column), the United States was ranked as the top country of interest, Japan was in second place, France in third place, and so forth. In addition, six countries—South Korea, Indonesia, Austria, Thailand, the Ukraine, and the Czech Republic—were not ranked among Brazil's top countries of interest.

Once again, a large proportion of the countries' appearance on the list can be explained by findings from content-oriented news geography, such as the phenomenon of the "next-door giant neighbor," according to which people are interested in nations that border their own. This phenomenon explains, for example, the interest that Singaporeans have in Malaysia (ranked as number 3) and that Poles have in Germany (ranked at number 1) and Russia (ranked at number 2). However, this phenomenon is not explained solely on the basis of geography and the size of the neighboring countries but also by history, economic ties, and cultural proximity. All of these factors contribute to the more general finding that interest in neighboring countries extends beyond what would be expected as a result of a single factor.

Finally, in order to measure the degree of similarity of interest expressed by the respondents in various sample countries, we created a matrix of Spearman rank correlation coefficients based on the rankings in which the 30 countries of interest appear in the respective data sets of each sample country (as presented in Table 10.4). Thus a rank correlation of 1.00 between two countries indicates that the countries appearing in the list of the top 30 mentioned by the respondents in the two respective sample countries were in the same relative position. In fact, the Spearman rank correlation between Israel and both Germany and Switzerland was 1.00, due to the fact that only seven of the top 30 countries were mentioned by the Israeli sample, and their rankings were in the same relative position as the rankings of Switzerland and Germany. The correlation between Switzerland and Germany is only .86, however, because the rankings of some of the top 30 countries that do not appear in the Israeli list differ between the German and the Swiss samples.

With the exception of the correlations involving Israel, the high correlations between three pairs of countries (Chile and Brazil, Canada and the United States, and Singapore and Taiwan) and among two trios of countries (China, Hong Kong, and Taiwan; and Germany, Switzerland, and Poland) can be explained based on their world region and proximity. However, some of the other relatively high correlations cannot be easily explained by region and respective "cultural zones." For example, a high correlation was found between China and Brazil as well as the United States. The similarities between the United States and China might emanate from the political and economic interest that is typical for globally relevant superpowers, and in the case of China and Brazil the common interests may be attributed to the leading emerging economies that may be at play.

In addition to the high correlations between countries, it is important to note the lower or even negative correlations between some pairs of countries. For example, Singapore is a clear outlier given its population's interest in Malaysia, and the two South American countries—Brazil and Chile—are also considerably different from other nations with regard to which countries their populations have an interest in.

Although the economic, political, cultural, and personal circumstances vary among the countries included in our study, one major trend is obvious from the data: the United States emerges as the top country of interest among respondents in practically all of the nations. Portugal, Poland, and Switzerland deviate from this principle because, for these countries, their "giant neighbors," such as Spain and Germany, are placed first. However, even in these countries, the United States is ranked in second place (Switzerland) or third place (Poland and Portugal).

And yet one must be careful with interpretations of these findings, as some of the patterns or explanations might be case-specific and the result of a large number of factors beyond the obvious. Moreover, while considering the interest in other nations among respondents from the various national samples, we must not forget that idiosyncratic and social factors, such as a particular respondent's media habits and knowledge about the world, can promote interest in news about certain nations. The interplay of these micro-level factors with the national level is extremely complex.[4]

Visualization of Interest in Countries

Before setting forth our overall conclusions, we present some of the data another way. Patterns of interest in other countries, world regions, and continents are plainly visible by producing "heat maps" that highlight the "target" countries on a world map according to the interest expressed in the interviews of any given survey country.

Figure 10.2 Top 20 countries of interest for the across-all-sample countries

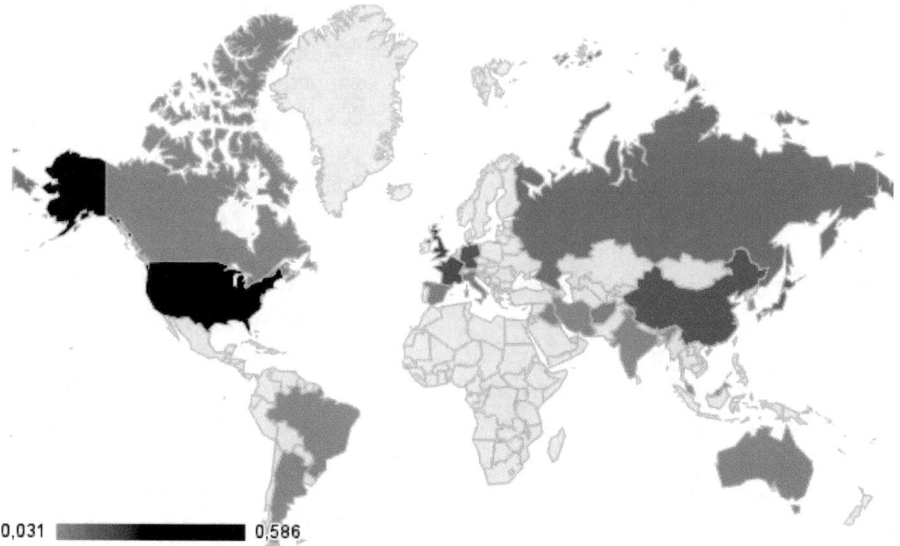

First, we present a heat map of the top 20 countries[5] mentioned as being of interest for the entire sample of 13 countries (see Figure 10.2). Clear differences in the interest levels regarding different countries can be identified with respect to the geographic location of a country in a world region. We also present two specific cases—Portugal and the United States—that clearly illustrate the historical and current connections to the respective countries and regions.

Figure 10.3 Top 20 countries of interest in the Portuguese sample

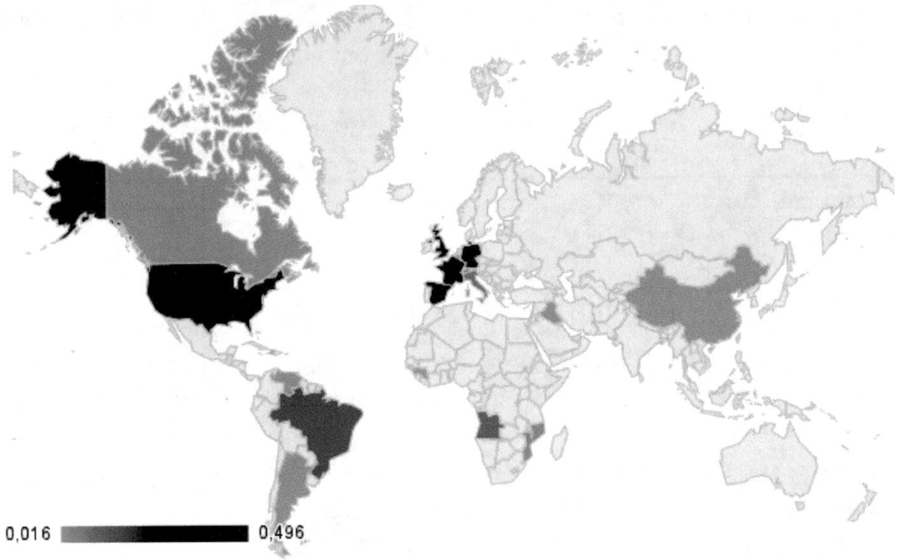

0,016   0,496

In the case of Portugal (Figure 10.3), we identify high levels of interest in the neighboring country of Spain and other economically and politically relevant countries in Europe, such as Britain, France, Germany, and Italy. We also observe high levels of interest in the United States. As an economic and political superpower, the United States dominates the news around the globe and the interest of other countries' citizens. Thus far, these findings are not surprising, and they follow the principles of proximity, as well as economic and political relevance. However, the Portuguese heat map reveals a much more varied pattern, including interest in several world regions from Asia to Africa and South America. As noted above, this is uncommon—especially the interest in Africa, which is usually completely absent from the picture. The most plausible explanation for this varied pattern lies in the historical ties that these regions and countries have, based on Portugal's colonialist history. Naturally, these ties are not solely historical; in many cases, there are also economic and political ties that are expressed in structures (for example, organizations) and regulations (for example, treaties of mutual cooperation and trade). Furthermore, the ties are also personal, as migrants from former colonized countries are also living in Portugal. Thus, these migrants' interests lie in their home country or the home country of their ancestors, which reflects their personal and cultural heritage.

Finally, the heat map for the United States (Figure 10.4) looks very different from that of Portugal. Not surprisingly, it reveals a relevant interest in the neighboring countries of Canada and Mexico. Again, this finding can be explained by proximity, economic and political relevance, and possible personal ties of some

Figure 10.4 Top 20 countries of interest in the U.S. sample

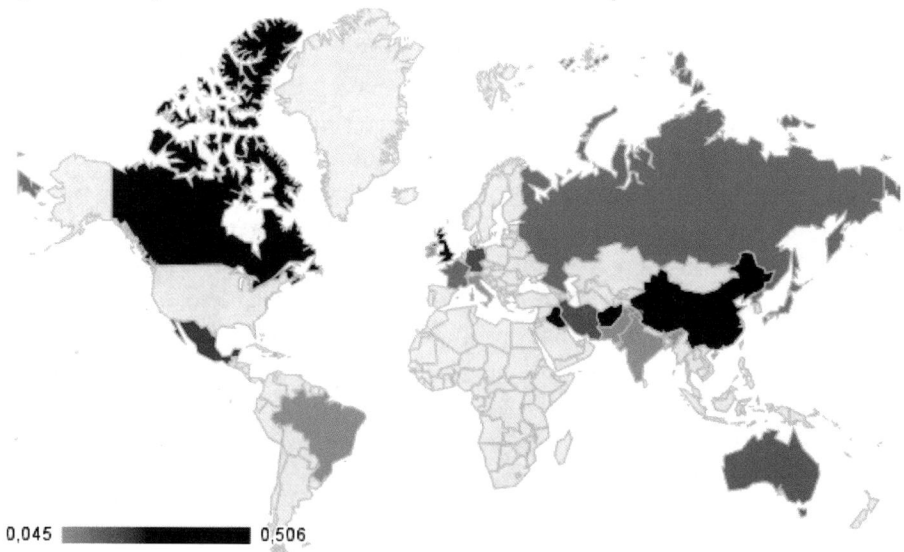

of the respondents in the U.S. sample. The interest in the United Kingdom can be explained by historical ties and because that country is an important ally in some of the military conflicts in which the United States has been involved. These conflicts are also visible in the heat map, as Afghanistan and Iraq are placed in top positions of interest to U.S. respondents. The interest in these countries is both political and personal: the United States had a considerable number of soldiers in these countries at the time of the survey, so naturally there is personal interest in events in these places on the part of relatives and friends of soldiers.

Summary and Conclusions

This chapter has focused on the countries of interest named by the respondents in answer to the question: "In the news about which foreign countries are you most interested?" We first presented the overall structure of interests as it emerged when looking at all sample countries combined. A very limited number of countries turned out to monopolize most of the audiences' interest. We then refined the analysis by comparing the structure of the interests among the various sample countries to identify patterns at the nation-specific level. One general pattern that emerged from these data is that the respondents from country samples such as Israel, Taiwan, and Hong Kong, which mentioned a low number of countries, also mentioned countries with less diversity. In a third step, we explained the degree of interest in specific countries through general, underlying characteristics such as economic, historical, or cultural importance on a global level. This perspective was further refined by differentiation with respect to the ties among sample countries and countries of interest: historical relations dating back to colonization, as well as geographical links such as the effect of the "giant neighbor," all of which turn out to be important factors. Finally, in order to identify differences and similarities between the national patterns of interest, we calculated rank correlations, showing that geographical proximity is often, but not always, the key to common interests in terms of countries appearing in foreign news. A visualization of the country interest through heat maps concludes the chapter, with both a global perspective and two country-specific examples—the United States and Portugal.

Our survey findings reveal several major trends. The United States serves as a focus of interest for all of the nations included in this analysis (except among respondents in the United States, of course). Furthermore, "giant neighbor" effects, a combination of proximity and economic and political relevance, and historical and personal ties appear to explain much of the variation in the data. Systematic data variations can also be noted with respect to the world regions and cultural zones to which countries belong.

In contrast to a common-sense understanding of globalization as a leveling of interests around the globe, we find very specific patterns that mark clear differences between audiences in the countries included in this analysis. Therefore, one could argue that these findings suggest a trend opposite to globalization, according to which countries are segmented into world zones with separate and distinct interests because they have no unifying principle. We suspect that both these developments occur simultaneously. Although there are some powerful relevance systems shaping the interest of specific audiences for news about specific other countries, there are also effects of globalization that allow news from a wide range of other countries to be accessible and relevant to these audiences.

We believe that large-scale longitudinal research is needed to track the direction(s) and strength of these developments over time. Such a project would go beyond the current findings, which are based on a single snapshot in time. Despite this notable limitation, this picture already offers some fascinating insights into the interests of television audiences around the world.

Notes

1. Although the variation here already indicates differences among the countries in the sample, we must point out that some of the variation might be explained by differences and peculiarities of the data-gathering method. Therefore, the variation needs to be interpreted with caution. In this chapter we specifically indicate which analyses we suspect may reflect differences in the sampling procedures and data-gathering method. This is something that could be expected, however, when such a large study was conducted with a considerable number of different countries (despite great efforts to unify planning and research processes).

2. The relatively large number of countries mentioned by American respondents can be at least partially explained by the fact that the U.S. survey was conducted through the Internet and not by telephone. This enabled the respondents to choose countries of interest from a drop-down list of countries rather than being asked to recall the countries freely, as was the case for other countries.
3. Because of a technical mishap, the responses of the Israeli respondents to the open-ended question survey were coded into a limited preset list of countries, including some groups of countries (for example, former USSR countries and Arab countries with the exception of Egypt). For this reason, the number and range of countries mentioned by the Israeli sample appears very limited.
4. We have recently taken a first step toward understanding this complexity with a multi-level analysis of interest in other countries with the German population (von Pape, Quandt, Vogelgesang, & Scharkow, 2012).
5. We present only 20 top countries rather than the 30 that appear in Table 10.2 because of the difficulty in visually discriminating among the various shades of black and gray.

PART FOUR

Gatekeepers

CHAPTER ELEVEN

Gatekeepers on Decision-Making in Foreign News

CONSTANZA MUJICA & THOMAS HANITZSCH

The question of how journalists and news organizations select and process the innumerable events of a given day and squeeze them into a limited number of messages that fit into a newspaper, a newscast, or a more spacious Internet news site, has a long tradition going back to the seminal studies by Lewin (1947) and White (1950). These and subsequent studies tried to analyze not only which news events were selected and processed, but also who selected them and why, what personal traits, organizational processes and routines, political and economic limitations, and cultural considerations affected the shape of the news and thus the "cognitive maps" audiences have about the world (Shoemaker & Vos, 2009).

The investigation of these factors has attracted many researchers throughout the world and ultimately generated a wealth of theories and empirical evidence (see, for example, Berkowitz, Limor, & Singer, 2004; Flegel & Chaffee, 1971; Hanitzsch et al., 2010; McQuail, 2000; Preston, 2009; Shoemaker & Reese, 1996; and Voakes, 1997). The state of research arguably converges toward a structure consisting of five major domains of influence:

1. Influences on the *individual level* originate from the journalists' personal and professional backgrounds and orientations, as well as from their specific roles and occupational characteristics within the news organization.

2. The *media routines level* refers to conventionalized and standardized forms of news production, such as routinized investigation, newsgathering, and presentation of content. Factors on this level can also appear as concrete

limits to the journalists' work, most notably in the form of limited resources.

3. The *organizational level* involves editorial decision-making and management routines and therefore encompasses sources of influence that emanate from multiple levels: from within the newsroom (supervisors and higher editors) and from within the media organization (management and ownership).

4. The *media structures level* refers to the economic imperatives of journalism, which are especially relevant in commercial news organizations. Relevant factors include profit expectations of media companies, advertising considerations, the needs of advertisers, and the influence of market and audience research.

5. The *systemic level* of influence incorporates the relevant social, cultural, and ideological contexts within which journalists work. This includes the political and legal conditions of news making, mostly introduced by the state through means of regulation, codes of ethics, media laws, and possible limitations of press freedom, as well as the nature of professional self-organization and national conventions within the profession.

There is no consensus, however, on the relative importance of these levels of influence. Early gatekeeping research suggested that individual factors reign supreme in the process of news production (White, 1950; Flegel & Chaffee, 1971), while more recent evidence points to a rather modest influence of individual predispositions on journalists' news decisions (Kepplinger, Brosius, & Staab, 1991; Patterson & Donsbach, 1996). There seems to be a growing awareness of the supremacy of systemic influences (Hallin & Mancini, 2004; Weaver, 1998; Zhu et al., 1997), as well as the increasing power of economic criteria and media structures (Bagdikian, 1983; Preston & Metykova, 2009; Whitney, Sumpter, & McQuail, 2004). Organizational factors are also believed to have a substantial impact on the production of news (Cook, 1998; Weaver & Löffelholz, 2008), but the extent to which their effects compare to other sources of influence is largely unknown.

In this chapter we highlight the media routines level, focusing especially on the newsworthiness criteria shared by gatekeepers, in addition to organizational-level considerations, in particular the newsroom structure and size and the training required for working on foreign news. The following research questions will be the focus of this analysis: How do journalists and editors select foreign news? What are the organizational conditions within which foreign news is being produced? How do journalists and editors perceive, interpret, and apply newsworthiness criteria in the case of foreign news? How are foreign news events processed for local audiences?

Gatekeepers, Newsworthiness, and Foreign News

Much research on the gatekeeping process has examined the criteria used by journalists and editors in the selection of news. From White's (1950) study on news selection, in which he focused on a single editor, to Shoemaker's extensive work on gatekeeping and newsworthiness (Shoemaker & Reese, 1996; Shoemaker & Cohen, 2006; Shoemaker & Vos, 2009), researchers have focused on the characteristics an event must have to be selected as news. Despite considerable variation in terminology, most of these studies identified similar criteria for newsworthiness.

Deviance and social significance of the events

Studies focusing on deviance and social significance draw on the work of Shoemaker (1996). His theory proposes that journalists are most interested in two general pieces of information about an event: how intensely deviant and socially significant it is. In their comparative study *News Around the World: Content, Practitioners, and the Public* (2006), Shoemaker and Cohen argue that "the intensity of these dimensions is positively related to how prominently a news item is presented in the mass media" (p. 7). Even though the study did not analyze foreign and domestic news separately, it demonstrated that both were important factors in the news selection process. However, while they found a significant amount of agreement between gatekeepers and the public in terms of newsworthiness, the most newsworthy events were not necessarily those most prominently published in the media.

Prominence of the country of origin within a geopolitical hierarchy of nations

The political, economic, and military power of a country has been found to constitute an important factor in the selection of news in many studies since Galtung and Ruge's (1965) groundbreaking research, in which they named this factor "reference to elite nations." The validity of this criterion has been confirmed by Kim and Barnett (1996), Chang (1998), and Golan (2003), among others.

Cultural affinity

In 1973, Hester observed that the media give more coverage to nations with which they share cultural characteristics. Factors such as religion (Shoemaker, Danielian, & Brendlinger, 1991), language (Kariel & Rosenvall, 1995), migration and ethnic origins (Golan & Wanta, 2003), and press freedom (Van Belle, 2000) have been found to influence the coverage of foreign news. This kind of proximity can be considered an inherent characteristic of the events reported, or as proximity constructed through domestication of foreign events. Domestication is a way of making foreign news more attractive to a domestic audience by making reference to national interests or actors.

Gatekeepers and Their Attitudes toward Foreign News

Within these general criteria, the literature recognizes a variety of attitudinal factors affecting gatekeepers' selection of foreign news. As discovered by Chang and Lee (1992), editors' perceptions of foreign news events help them organize information originating from various countries and news sources, reduce the volume of foreign news flow, and evaluate more promptly the potential newsworthiness of foreign events. They found individual factors such as training, political beliefs, and organizational constraints such as limited space dedicated to foreign news and available sources to be most important in this respect.

Nossek (2004) argues that there is a complex relationship between the coverage of and treatment given to foreign events by journalists and editors: the closer the event is to national interests, the less "professional" the coverage will be. Acknowledging the role of ethnocentrism in news selection, Shoemaker and Vos (2009) note that gatekeepers often use local characteristics as a benchmark against which to evaluate foreign events. Cohen (1993) further adds that larger countries may have a stronger sense of ethnocentrism, which makes their journalists and citizens feel more self-sufficient with their domestic news. Smaller countries, on the other hand, appear to be more interested in what happens around them and how it can affect them.

Methodology and Limitations

Of the 17 countries for which we have content-analytic data, 5 did not conduct the in-depth interviews with the gatekeepers: Egypt, Italy, Japan, Singapore, and the United States. Thus the findings reported in this chapter are based on 49 interviews with editors and journalists responsible for foreign news in public stations (22 interviews) and commercial stations (27 interviews) in 12 of the countries in our study. (For details, see Appendix E.) The interviews were conducted between June 2009 and March 2011. The general outline and scenario of questions was collaboratively developed for all the countries based on the general premises of the study.

Despite the fair number of interviews conducted, it was difficult to establish clear patterns within countries. There were several reasons for this, most notably the variability in the number of interviewees and the depth of the interviews in each country. Translation also posed some difficulties, especially for vernacular expressions and metaphors used by the interviewees. Other reasons were the rather long period of data collection, as well as a lack of response to some questions in a number of countries.

Newsroom as Context

Across the board, the main responsibility of foreign news editors is to select the foreign events that will be covered and to assign reporters to stories. In stations that still have fixed correspondents abroad, foreign news editors are also responsible for coordinating their work. The number of foreign news stories to be included in the newscast and their length and position within the news lineup is decided at the news editorial meetings with the general editor and section editors. However, the influence of foreign news editors in these discussions varies from station to station. While some interviewed gatekeepers felt they were well respected by the management, others were frustrated by their lack of latitude within the newsroom:

> I'm not pleased with the editors who don't understand and don't have the ability to cope with foreign news that doesn't relate at least directly to Israeli discourse. But nevertheless we succeed because the foreign news staff has high standing in the eyes of the news department so somewhere they do listen to us and give us space to report. But it could be much better. (*Israel, IBA*)

The number of people working on foreign news varies with the general size of the newsroom. At China's CCTV, there are 3,000 news people, with 100 dedicated to foreign news alone. Chile's commercial station *Mega*, on the other hand, has a total of 80 journalists, with only one person assigned to foreign news.[1] Some interviewed editors complained that their foreign news staff has decreased over the last few years, mostly because of budget constraints:

> We have serious staff problems. In the entire station we have only three people who deal with foreign news.... We have one correspondent...and he's in Washington. If I compare to what it was like 20 years ago, we had someone in Paris, in Germany, in Moscow, in London, and in New York. (Israel, IBA)

> The cost of having a bureau in Afghanistan is hundreds of thousands of dollars a year. Security, insurance, training, equipment—it's a very expensive process. Moving and traveling internationally to cover other stories is also very expensive. So when the budget squeeze is on it's the first thing [to go]. (*Canada, CTV*)

Maintaining a network of resident correspondents abroad has been a particular casualty of cutbacks in many of the investigated news organizations. A common way to cope with the increasingly scarce resources is the use of flexible "parachute correspondents"—but this, too, seems to be limited to the most essential news events:

> We were the first Belgian station with a full time foreign correspondent. Now we do not have foreign correspondents anymore. It is simply too expensive. If something important happens, we decide to send someone. Only the big moments. A hit and run strategy. (*Belgium, VTM*)

Only two of the investigated television stations described their foreign news service as expanding: China's CCTV and Brazil's Globo. CCTV increased its overseas offices from 20 to 50. It also upgraded the status of several regional offices so that they now have a fully equipped studio. The largest growth for the Brazilian commercial station Globo has taken place in its foreign news operations, including the amount of coverage and the number of permanent correspondents. In addition, it plans to acquire a private airplane for its journalists to travel swiftly to news spots. Editors ascribed this trend to a decrease in transmission costs of live signals from abroad, and especially the perception that the audience welcomes the rise in foreign coverage. The station does not see foreign news as a ratings killer—on the contrary, the editors said that their foreign coverage raised their prestige.

> We are a private company. Our ratings depend on our prestige. Our efforts of spreading our correspondents worldwide therefore offer our telecasts an increasingly international "menu" of topics, helping to strength strengthen our prestige. (*Brazil, Globo*)

Newsworthiness

The literature conceptualizes newsworthiness as being driven by a set of cumulative factors. A presidential election in a powerful country such as Russia, France, or the United States would be newsworthy. If one of the candidates were to propose abandoning diplomatic relations with another major country, it would be a deviation from policy and would potentially cause conflict. If there were pictures of the candidate making an inflammatory speech with his or her followers screaming, this would be considered sensational. The more such elements a given event included, the more newsworthy it would be considered.

During the interviews with the editors, these factors sometimes were considered to be self-evident. The journalists' spontaneous responses to the question about the criteria guiding their news decisions generally reflected the state of the literature. The editors broadly mentioned significance, deviance, proximity, conflict, and strong images. Alternatively, they provided examples of events that they thought were representative of "news," such as elections, wars, diplomatic turmoil, and economic crises. Across countries with different journalistic cultures and different types of television stations, gatekeepers identified the traditional newsworthiness criteria—significance, deviance, conflict, emotion, and proximity.

Several gatekeepers—mostly, though not exclusively, working in public TV stations—reported that significance has always been the primary factor in news selection. Others—mostly, but once again not exclusively, from commercial TV stations—considered audience interest and ratings to be paramount. A third group said that they always tried to reconcile both criteria. The selection of foreign news, particularly news related to politics and economics, was identified as one of the main axes of this dispute, precisely because such news items are identified as highly relevant but less attractive to the public.

Significance

The principal newsworthiness criterion mentioned by most of the interviewed gatekeepers was the significance of the news event. The main consideration is the event's perceived importance for both domestic and foreign news. Most gatekeepers did not elaborate on the meaning of significance, instead referring to it as a self-evident concept.

> If important things happen, we will cover them, like elections in Iran or a speech by the prime-minister of Israel. (*Belgium, Commercial Station, Editor 1*)

> When selecting foreign news topics, VTM emphasizes public issues, such as politics and social issues with significance. (*Taiwan, PTS*)

When conceptualizing significance, gatekeepers usually referred to the real or potential consequences of an event. This was usually linked to economic or political issues.

> You consider how important the event is, what repercussions it might have in a political level. (*Chile, TVN*)

In several TV stations, foreign news coverage is also linked to the stations' role as public broadcasters.

> Viewers who watch us as a public service expect something different; they expect us to be more serious. In the economy, for example, they expect us to deal with pension funds and legislation and not only how the crisis will affect one's pocketbook. The same goes for foreign news. (*Israel, IBA*)

Though the priority of significance over interest is mostly identified as necessary, many gatekeepers recognize that pressure from management to attract audiences and/or increase ratings makes the application of this principle difficult. There seems to be a constant debate within some newsrooms over this issue, and several editors resignedly include "freaky stories" such as hard falls in sports, animals doing funny things, or celebrity news.

Most of the interviewed editors admitted that military and economic superpowers—located in what Chang (1998) refers to as the core of the world system—are covered more frequently and more prominently. The United States was identified as the primary attractor of interest in terms of foreign news, mostly because of its economic and political influence and its military commitments around the world. At a secondary level, the journalists recognized its cultural and technological appeal to audiences. Even in a time of shrinking newsgathering resources, it was conceded that coverage of the United States is unavoidable because its actions have consequences for other countries. As an editor from the

Portuguese public television station RTP aptly put it, the United States is a major locus of foreign news: "everything that Obama does, from his dog to the discourse about the state of the nation." It is interesting that the prominence of the United States is explained as a bias that results from the amount and quality of the images provided by news agencies.

> The USA on the one hand, because the country just has everything to offer. It has global politics, it has oddities, and all of it is perfectly rehashed for the media. If I need another crime report or something, or if I need something funny…in the US networks there will be something—and more importantly…it is made to fit. (*Germany, RTL*)

Ratings/Audience interest

Ratings and the perception of what might be interesting or attractive to the stations' audiences is consistently mentioned as a major consideration in the selection of foreign news. In many stations, mostly commercial ones, it is even the paramount criterion. As a Polish journalist working for a commercial station said, "The viewership index determines the selection of the topics." However, foreign events also compete heavily with local news for space and time.

> Newspapers are different; if there's not enough space you just add a page. Television news is expensive. Time is expensive. You add one more piece of local news and there is one less piece of international news. Because international news does not always affect our audience we would not place it in top positions. (*Hong Kong, ATV*)

Several of the editors see the influence of ratings in journalistic decisions as frustrating pressure from management, and they feel that these influences erode their roles as genuine gatekeepers. The editors believe that this issue causes a decline in journalistic quality and maintain that the selection of foreign news must be left to journalists.

> We've lost the editorial distinction between interesting and important. The public sets the agenda. I think *we* should set the agenda.… The ratings are important. The editor checks the previous day's newscast, how the ratings changed for each item and during the commercial breaks. I think we can package things interestingly. If the information is provided in a good televisual way the audience will stay put. I don't think we need to keep running after things that they say are interesting to them. I would deal more with global processes. I would stress internal politics is some places. (*Israel, Arutz 2*)

Many editors and journalists who were interviewed say that they cope with these influences by emphasizing other newsworthiness criteria over significance, especially proximity, emotional visuals, deviance, and conflict.

So you must have strategies for capturing the audience and not always what one traditionally considers to be relevant and important. There are other things that televisually capture the audience. We are talking about television, the shocking picture, the attractive image. Sometimes it doesn't have much consequence, that's true, and I could say "ok, out, curtain down," but I say "no, curtain up," because I know that with that I am going to capture the audience, and when I have them I can include everything else. (*Chile, TVN*)

Proximity

Proximity was consistently mentioned by the interviewed journalists as one of the top considerations in the selection of foreign news. As a Belgian editor for a commercial television station aptly summed up: "News is always about proximity, even foreign news. You have to connect with the audience: Physical, geographical, emotional proximity. That is what matters. You can present a news item of half an hour about the elections in Dagestan, but nobody cares."

The first and most obvious meaning of proximity—the geographical closeness between the country where events happen and the nation where the news is aired—is frequently mentioned as a factor in news selection. The editors' answers suggest that geographical proximity implies a series of factors that result in higher newsworthiness. Nations are usually more strongly affected by a policy shift in their neighboring countries than by those farther away. It is therefore not surprising that journalists pay more attention to developments in neighboring countries. A Canadian editor even went as far as to consider the coverage of the United States "almost as domestic news."

In the absence of true geographical closeness, gatekeepers often consider cultural and historical affinity as a criterion for news selection. This kind of proximity makes events happening in those countries more attractive and easier to explain to viewers, and thus they have a greater potential to attract audience interest.

> From the rest of the world, I think the Middle East is always a topic. We have the largest Palestine community outside of Palestine, and the conflict in the Middle East is one of the three most important topics in the international agenda, we can't avoid what's happening.... In the European context, Spain is really important because of an historical proximity. (*Chile, Mega*)

It is noteworthy that Portugal, for instance, has a fairly ambivalent approach to the coverage of its former colonies in Africa. Portuguese journalists recognize the cultural and historical links to Lusophone Africa, in addition to economic and migration movements, but they give them relatively little coverage. In the case of Portugal's commercial television station, the neglect of this part of the world is explained by a lack of information supply about these countries from news agencies.

> It's something I don't understand; I mean I understand but it's incomprehensible. I have no doubt that Portuguese people would like to have more news about Angola and Mozambique.... Actually, this is an important gap in our media. Angola is one of the countries on which we economically depend, and it is a country of which we know little. (*Portugal, TV1*)

The involvement of nationals or national interests in foreign issues is perceived as a separate news value. A German journalist working for a commercial television station, for instance, said that "one condition is that Germany is concerned." The involvement of one country's nationals in a foreign event can even provide an opportunity to cover other events taking place in the source country that would otherwise not be reported.

> I believe in emotional closeness or distance, rather than geographic closeness or proximity. I give you only one example: ever since Chile classified to the World Cup, we are much closer to South Africa than ever before. From now on, everything that happens in South Africa, whatever it is, I assure you that it will have more coverage on TV and newspapers. We aired a story about the South African president getting married for the fifth time. Previously we would never have covered it, but now we're thinking about South Africa. A sort of closeness is produced, but we're still at the same geographic distance, but now we're much closer. (*Chile, TVN*)

Finally, proximity can be defined in a broader sense: as an emotional attachment resulting from sympathies with the feelings—especially the suffering—of human beings in other countries. This kind of emotional input has the power to connect people regardless of their location, and it is particularly adequate for television as a medium. Images of other people's suffering, the interviewed gatekeepers say, do not necessarily require explanation or context. The relation of the audience to the covered subjects is primarily emotional, rendering secondary rational considerations.

> Disasters affect human beings. Chinese and foreigners alike are residents on the earth. For example, the explosions in Iraq are terrorist incidents that impact on the emotions of all human beings. Another example is the failure of the American space shuttle *Challenger*. It was controversial in our editing room. One editor argued that some people would be happy about the unfortunate development for countries like America. But it was a common disaster for all human beings in their way of conquering nature. (*China, CCTV*)

Images and emotion

Images are an essential component of television as a medium and are, thus, according to the answers of the interviewed journalists and editors, a major driving factor of newsworthiness in television news. The presence of "good visuals" can very much explain the selection and prominence assigned to events that might not have great value in terms of significance or deviance. And so an Israeli editor in a commercial television station referred to a frequently cited saying: "But the picture, you know, is sometimes worth 1,000 words." "Good" images are defined as those being "spectacular"—footage that contains conflict and intense human emotion.

> Events that produce spectacular images more easily become news, even if there is not that much to say about it, like fires in forests. You can say: so many square kilometers are burnt down, so many people died. And that's it. There simply is not much to say about it. But the images are spectacular, so it becomes news. (*Belgium, VTM*)

> News on TV is basically audiovisual images, and thus anything that satisfies the need for images—catastrophes, accidents, great natural events, hurricanes, a Tsunami where 200 thousand people die—that will enter because of the characteristic of the medium. (*Chile, TVN*)

> I think that, especially on television that is so sensitive, so emotional, the image doesn't speak to people's reason so much as it does to their emotions…. The more human a story is the more attractive it is…. The more face it has, the more attractive it is for television. We can't build a story if there is no face, there are times we reject topics when we don't have images, where we don't know who the protagonist is. (*Chile, TVN*)

Even though editors and journalists across countries agree on the value of images as a factor in news selection, there are differences when evaluating it in contrast to significance. The contradiction between both news factors appeared frequently across countries and news organizations in our survey, many times even without being prompted by the interviewers.

> In fact, according to my own observation, different people have different orientations. Like me, I like visuals, because I think television is dependent on visuals. But there is another editor who thinks that the content of the story is the most important. (*Hong Kong, ATV*)

Several of the journalists interviewed maintained that relevant stories should be aired prominently, even if there are no pictures to accompany them. They describe this as a frequent problem in foreign news, especially in breaking news from distant countries—such as military operations or earthquakes. In cases where no pictures are available, they make use of alternative means of illustration, such as maps, figures, interviews with experts, live comments from correspondents, or archived materials. Other gatekeepers said that significant events could be covered even without images, though they are often shorter and placed less prominently in the newscast.

> A story can be very newsworthy, very attractive, very interesting, but if you don't have an image that shows what's going on in an interesting way—and I add the adjective impacting or attractively—if you don't have attractive images that can illustrate that piece of news it might air or, at the very least, it will lose prominence. This is a new criterion that has been included in the last few years, and that I think that it is awful, but real. (*Chile, TVN*)

Finally, several editors noted that when there are no pictures, the story is not aired. These gatekeepers describe this—sometimes regretfully—to be an almost insurmountable challenge of television journalism. News stories without pictures are covered very rarely, mostly when major events occur, such as declarations of war or major disasters.

> Images are most important for us. Sometimes the editor is interested in some topic but it is impossible to collect images on time, so the topic must be rejected (*Poland, TVN*)

> If we don't have pictures it is difficult to cover the topic. Pictures and videos are very important for foreign news. Certain topics won't be included in the news if we don't have the pictures or videos. If something is very important and we don't have pictures or videos we sometimes work with a map on screen and have a short verbal announcement but usually we just report when we have pictures or videos. (*Switzerland, SF Tagesschau*)

Domestication and Contextualization

When we asked the journalists why they had difficulty doing in-depth coverage of foreign news, they gave two main explanations: foreign news lacks proximity, and it is more complex and more difficult to explain. The lack of closeness and the need for more context information were said to make it less attractive for audiences, leading to less airtime, which in turn makes it more difficult to provide a comprehensive account of these events. In the process of foreign news production, journalists deal with this challenge mainly through two strategies: domestication, or the search for the local point of view through the involvement of nationals or national interests; and contextualization.

Domestication

Most interviewees recognized domestication as a principle in the production of foreign news by which they could make the foreign news appear more relevant and attractive to their home audiences. The editors sought to increase the sense of proximity with foreign events by looking for links with local issues. A journalist from a Chilean commercial television station even went as far as suggesting a "Chileanizing" of foreign news, almost turning it into local news. Overall, editors identified three general models of domestication in foreign news stories.

(1) Locals participating in/or observing foreign events

Here, the interviewed journalists looked for nationals participating in the news events either as subjects (for example, as victims), as sources providing testimonies, as experts providing informed judgments, or as the station's own correspondents.

> But it happens that we add a domestic point of view to a foreign news item to make sure that the public at home will remain attentive. Especially if they are far-away countries where our viewers are not familiar with, we "domesticate" news by looking for Belgian people that live over there or by looking at companies or company leaders that invested in the country. Now, with the earthquake and Tsunami in Japan we clearly chose the perspective of the Belgians living in the area. (*Belgium, VTM*)

(2) Emphasizing local impact of foreign issues or national involvement in foreign events

> This is our baseline for news: News is what is news for our viewers; is the event interesting? Is it important for them? Is it relevant? Can it have an impact on their lives? (*Belgium, VTM*)

(3) Emphasizing similarities or differences with local conditions

> One of the reasons why the conflict in Ireland is interesting in Israel is that many comparisons are made between that conflict and what is happening in Israel.... Or like the Belgian issue, maybe because it's so strange, a country within Europe that may disintegrate: a country about our size with about eight different parliaments. So whenever something develops in that story we try to cover it. When there were concentration camps in former Yugoslavia, we didn't compare them to the Holocaust, but we did show images that are reminiscent of Europe in dark times. (*Israel, Arutz 2*)

Contextualization

Contextualization refers to efforts to put a specific news event into its spatial (geographic, cultural), temporal (causes, consequences), and symbolic (political, economic, etc.) contexts. Given their lack of proximity, providing this sort of background for foreign news is seen by the interviewed journalists as more difficult, more desirable, and more complex. Contextualization is therefore understood as an important strategy for making foreign stories more comprehensible for local audiences and to attract interest in foreign events.

> It is an editorial guideline to make an effort for clarity putting in context these international problems allowing the viewer to comprehend it. This explains long JN broadcast from time to time, as it did recently regarding the millenary conflict in the Middle East after Brazil recognized the Palestinians' pre-1967 borders, prior to the Six Days War. I cannot simply say the statement, "Brazil

has recognized the borders in Palestine." What is that? We presented a full reportage, more than 2 minutes, trying to put in context that situation in order to make sense of the Brazilian attitude. All this is mandatory coverage for JN, even though it is not the topic of the day, but it is our duty to put it in context in order to arouse and renew public interest in the subject. (*Brazil, Globo*)

Even if the interviewed journalists recognized the need and desirability of a more contextualized reporting of foreign events, they admitted that their newscasts are lacking background information and in-depth analysis that could help the audience understand the complexity of foreign events. As a news editor from a commercial TV station in Chile put it, the delivery of context is something that is done when he has the "time to do it." Several gatekeepers, however, said that they did not feel the need for any extensive contextualization of foreign events, as they believe that their publics have the necessary capacity to understand foreign news coverage either because they address a niche of highly knowledgeable viewers or because their audiences habitually follow foreign news.

If we air a story about the tension between Peru and Ecuador, do we have to explain that there was a war and that they are in permanent conflict? I don't really know. I think that since we have aired stories on that topic before, contextualization is less necessary. When stories are totally new, then it is necessary to start from zero and then we talk about it. (*Chile, TVN*)

Conclusions

In terms of the characterization of newsroom structures pertinent to the production of foreign news, it is possible to establish a few trends. Foreign news departments continue to be the main mode of internal organization, but the formality and relevance within the general newsroom has decreased in several stations, and their size has shrunk in most media companies. At the same time, many posts for resident correspondents have been eliminated. Only China's public station and Brazil's commercial station describe their foreign news staff as more relevant and larger than in the past. The interviewed journalists explained this drain of resources flowing into the production of foreign news with low ratings, which in turn seems to be caused by the complexity of foreign news and its distance from the audiences' local realities.

In many of the interviews, the gatekeepers expressed a sense of pessimism about the future of their work, in a way similar to that described by Kim (2002). They seem to think that the high costs of foreign news, together with low ratings, will continue to shrink the news hole devoted to foreign events, with even fewer options to contextualize them, and allow less access to direct reporting through correspondents and parachute reporters.

However, most journalists and editors still consider the coverage of foreign news as necessary and important, especially in the context of a globalized world.

They mostly try to include the events they deem significant—usually linked to political and economic affairs, as well as to major countries such as the United States—which, in the case of public stations, is linked to their public role and social contract. In order to make foreign news more attractive for audiences and more successful in terms of ratings, foreign news editors select stories according to classic criteria of newsworthiness, most notably deviance, emotional value, proximity, and strong visuals. They also consistently resort to domestication and contextualization to bridge the lack of proximity inherent in foreign news.

Summary

This chapter examined various aspects of media routines in the presentation of foreign news on television, including organization-level elements like the structure of the foreign news department, its size, and the training required for working on foreign news. Our primary focus, however, was on the criteria of newsworthiness shared by gatekeepers in their selection of foreign news. In this context, we inquired about how journalists and editors select foreign news; the organizational conditions within which foreign news is produced; gatekeepers' perception, interpretation, and application of the selection criteria; and the ways in which foreign news events are processed and composed for domestic audiences.

The evidence reported in this chapter is based on 49 interviews with editors and journalists responsible for foreign news in public and commercial stations in 12 of the countries in our study. The findings suggest that while the foreign news departments continue to serve as the main arbiter of foreign news in their respective organizations, in all but two of the countries in which these departments have actually grown, the formal status and relevance of foreign news within the overall newsroom has declined in recent years. This has been manifested in shrinking sizes and in the elimination of many resident correspondents in foreign lands. The gatekeepers explain this trend by lamenting the persistent high production costs of foreign news, coupled with lower viewer ratings as compared with domestic news.

However, most journalists and editors still consider the coverage of foreign news as necessary and important, especially in the context of a globalized world. They mostly try to include at least the events they deem significant, which in the case of public stations is linked to their public role and social contract. In order to make foreign news more attractive for audiences and more successful in terms of ratings, foreign news editors tend to select stories according to the classic criteria of newsworthiness, most notably deviance, emotional value, proximity, and powerful visuals. They also consistently resort to domestication and contextualization in bridging the lack of proximity to the domestic audience that is inherent in foreign news.

Note

1. These figures were mentioned by the interviewees, so they may not be precise. Some of them consider within their rank the station's foreign correspondents, some included only the members of the local staff dedicated to foreign news, and in most cases it was difficult to determine which positions altogether were included within these numbers.

CHAPTER TWELVE

Self-Reflexivity of Gatekeepers on Content and Viewers of Foreign News

LARS WILLNAT & AKIBA A. COHEN

The previous chapter analyzed how journalists and editors perceive, interpret, and apply news values in the selection of foreign news. While it is important to understand how journalists decide which foreign news stories to select from the daily flood of events that take place around the world, it is also important to know what and how journalists think about the audience for which they produce these stories. Journalists with much experience and on-the-job training certainly are able to apply news values in a more or less routine fashion, because they have internalized what might be important and which stories their organization tends to focus on. However, how journalists think about their audiences and the foreign news available in their nation might be less dependent on experience and organizational factors. Moreover, journalists in nations that are routinely covered in the news of other nations, such as the United States or Great Britain, might think very differently about what foreign news should focus on and what kind of foreign news their audiences might be interested in. As a consequence, it is important to understand how the work of journalists is influenced by their overall perception of foreign news and news audiences in their respective countries.

In this chapter, we focus on two main questions: How do journalists think about foreign news in their country, and how do they think about their audience for foreign news? Specifically, we ask how journalists and editors evaluate the amount of foreign TV news available in their country, which countries they believe are the focus in foreign news, and how important they think news about their own nation is elsewhere. We also ask how interested they believe their audience members are in foreign news and which countries might be of most interest to them.

Theoretical Approach

Foreign news coverage in many countries has declined significantly in recent years, due largely to corporate demands for larger profits and an increasingly fragmented audience. Worried about declining ratings and profit margins, media executives argue that their audiences show little interest in foreign news and clamor instead for more lifestyle and celebrity stories, more consumer and health news, and more local news. The result is a dramatic decline in foreign news in many countries. In the United States, for example, foreign TV news coverage declined precipitously between 1988 and 2010. While the three main American broadcast networks, NBC, ABC, and CBS, featured more than 4,800 foreign news stories in 1989, the year the Berlin Wall fell, such coverage dropped 56% to about 2,700 stories by 2010 (Tyndall Report, 2010). Seib (1997) noted that because of this, "a self-perpetuating truism has thus evolved: If journalists think their audiences do not want foreign news and therefore do not give it to them, the audiences' appetites for such news will not be whetted.... The result is an under informed public that has a limited agenda" (p. 8).

Ironically, this decline in foreign news coverage occurred when the globalization of commerce, communications, and culture made people of most nations increasingly interdependent. Thus, with the gradual decline of foreign news reporting in most industrialized nations, global news audiences might be growing increasingly ignorant of world affairs.

Despite the importance of the media as information sources about world events—particularly during crisis periods—there has been little empirical research into how journalists think about foreign news in general. The mostly anecdotal evidence suggests that journalists generally lament the decline of foreign news (Hoge, 1997; Randal, 2000; Utley, 1997) or the simplistic and episodic coverage that often dominates U.S. foreign news (Ginsberg, 2002; McClellan, 2001; Parks, 2002). A survey of 218 American editors conducted in 2002, however, found that most editors understand that their readers have a desire for more foreign news than their newspapers provide them with (Seplow, 2002). While 64% of the editors felt that the job that the U.S. media are doing covering foreign news is only fair or poor, most of them also thought their readers were either very interested (36%) or at least somewhat interested (57%) in such news. It is therefore not surprising that the majority of the editors (66%) said their newspapers did not satisfy their readers' interests in foreign news.

As a likely consequence of the fact that there seems to be a clear understanding among practitioners and scholars that foreign news coverage is inadequate, news production research has focused on the values that journalists apply to the selection of foreign news (Chang, 1998, 2010; Chang & Lee, 1992, 1993; Chang, Shoemaker, & Brendlinger, 1987; Chang et al., 2012; Golan, 2010; Wu, 1998b, 2003, 2007). Most of this research shows that the criteria journalists use to select news have remained fairly consistent during the last several decades. This is because the basic considerations that underlie news judgments have not changed significantly over time (Gans, 1979). A recent survey of 318 American newspaper editors, for example, concluded that "the priorities of journalistic values in foreign news reporting appear unchanged in the United States during the past two decades" (Chang et al., 2012). However, the survey also found that news editors have begun to put more emphasis on the domestication of foreign news. According to Chang and colleagues (2012), this "suggests a shift of individual concerns among newspaper editors from the emphasis of foreign properties of events or countries involved to domestic audience orientation" (p. 377).

While the observed consistency of news values among journalists is an important indicator of professionalism, it remains largely unclear how these values have developed into journalistic norms and by what factors they are influenced. According to McQuail (2000), news values have been difficult to define because "value has to be attributed and there are competing sources of perception" (p. 341). Thus, despite the fact that journalists are the most influential judges of value, "the actual perceptions of diverse audiences cannot be ignored, nor can the views of powerful sources and others affected by the news" (p. 341). In short, if we want to understand how journalists select foreign news, we not only need to ask them about which news values they employ, but also how they perceive their audiences.

Journalists and Their Audiences

Studies that have analyzed the production of news have shown that journalists usually consider news about political, international, and economic issues more important than news about other issues (Bennett, 1998; Gans, 1979; Schudson, 2003). In contrast, studies that focus on news consumption have been divided in assessing the public's interests (Boczkowski & Mitchelstein, 2010). While some studies conclude that audiences' interests match those of journalists (Jensen, 1990; Rosenstiel et al., 2007; Stone & Boudreau, 1995), others have found substantial gaps between the news choices of journalists and consumers (Hamilton, 2004; Tewksbury, 2003).

For example, Beaudoin and Thorson's (2002) study of journalists at the *Los Angeles Times* and residents of Los Angeles County found that journalists viewed foreign media coverage more favorably than did the public. Journalists were generally less likely than their audiences to think that foreign news stories in the *Los Angeles Times* mostly focus on disasters, crimes, and wars; that they do not provide enough background to make the story interesting; or that they often rely only on government and military sources. A similar study of journalists and online audiences in Argentina (Boczkowski & Mitchelstein, 2010) found that journalists valued stories about political, international, and economic subjects more than their audiences. During periods of heightened political activity, however, consumers increase their interest in these types of stories, and the gap in news preferences between journalists and audience narrowed.

Media scholars have also claimed that journalists tend to see their audiences as gullible and mostly interested in news about entertainment, crime, and sports. Furthermore, they see journalists as yielding much too easily to the marketing demands of media (Weaver & Wilhoit, 1996). However, studies conducted in the early 1990s showed that journalists generally think more highly of their audiences than previously assumed. Weaver and Wilhoit's seminal survey of U.S. journalists conducted in 1992, for example, found that only a minority (22%) of the journalists thought that their audience was not interested in serious news. In addition, only slightly more than one in ten journalists (14%) thought that their audience was gullible and easily fooled. A majority (69%) did say, however, that their audience was more interested in breaking stories than in analysis. Weaver and Wilhoit (1996) concluded that "this was hardly evidence of elitist attitudes among journalists in general" (p. 237).

How TV Journalists Think about Foreign News and Their Audiences

This chapter, like the previous one, is based on the same 49 in-depth interviews conducted with journalists and editors from 12 nations who were responsible for foreign news in their respective news organizations. Twenty-two of these gatekeepers worked for public TV stations and 27 for commercial stations (see Appendix E).

The interviews dealt with how the journalists thought about the data from the content analysis and the public opinion surveys that we presented in the earlier chapters. In other words, we were interested in finding out whether journalists who select and produce foreign TV news are aware of the foreign news that is shown in their own country and elsewhere, as well as whether or not they are "synchronized" with the opinions of their viewers.[1]

Gatekeepers on Content of Foreign News

The first issue that we compare is what the gatekeepers said about the content of foreign news in the newscasts vis-à-vis the findings of the content analysis of television news around the world. Two caveats must be made here. First, while the content analyses of the news in all the countries were based on the identical sample period in early 2008, the interviews with the gatekeepers were conducted at various points in time significantly later, ranging from June 2009 (in Belgium) to March 2011 (in Poland). Consequently, none of the interviewees could be expected to refer specifically to the content of the sample period. Second, there was much variability in the scope and depth of the interviews with the gatekeepers. In some countries the journalists went into great detail in their responses, while in other countries the responses were very brief, and some questions were not answered at all.

In Chapter 2 we presented the percentage of foreign news for each of the countries. According to Table 2.1, of the 12 countries in which interviews with the journalists were conducted, German television presented the highest percentage (46%) of foreign news (both pure and hybrid). So we begin with Germany and continue with the other countries in descending order of their presentation of foreign television news.

Germany

So what did the German gatekeepers say? The German journalists underestimated the percentage of foreign news in their broadcasts, referring to a range of 20%–30%. After being shown the findings of the content analysis, the chief editor of *RTL Aktuell* commented:

> I am glad that we have such a high percentage…that is a very deliberate choice on our part, because we always ask ourselves when considering foreign news—what can the German viewer take away from that?… I can imagine quite well that this percentage has increased over the last two years, also because we have increased the number of our foreign correspondents and thus the number of our own stories by our own reporters from abroad has risen. Seen from this perspective, we said to ourselves: foreign news is important and we react.

When asked about the relative position of foreign news coverage in Germany compared with other countries, the responses varied considerably. The public service *ARD Aktuell* editor said, "I assume we are a little bit below average." His colleague's view was quite different: "We cover more foreign news than other countries—first position." The RTL journalists, on the other hand, described their position as "in the upper third" and "in the upper midfield."

In Chapter 4 we listed the countries that were covered the most. According to Table 4.4, the top five countries covered by the German stations were the United States, the United Kingdom, Italy, Palestine, Russia, Israel, Norway, Egypt, Sweden, and Spain. Indeed, the German journalists were fairly cognizant of this: all named the United States as the top country, with the United Kingdom and France in second place, followed by Middle Eastern countries and China. Interestingly, China did not appear in the empirical list, while Russia appeared in fourth place but was not mentioned by the gatekeepers.

Canada

The second-ranked country in terms of actually presenting foreign news was Canada (44%). Citing between one-quarter and one-third of the newscast, the Canadian journalists at CBC and CTV were quite close to the findings of the content analysis in their attempt to estimate the percentage of foreign news. It is interesting to note that at several points the interviewees compared Canadian coverage with that of foreign news coverage in the United States and expressed satisfaction that Canadian news contains more foreign news than the news of their U.S. neighbor. As one journalist put it, in making reference to elections scheduled to take place in Haiti (at the time of the interviews):

> In terms of doing international news, I think we perform pretty well. If we look at our American partners, we actually in many cases now have better presence in foreign countries than they do. They tend to be more home-focused. We had a discussion about covering the Haiti election and we, at the moment, are going, but it's getting dangerous and it looks like ABC and NBC may not be going.

As for the countries most covered in foreign news, the content data show that news about the United States appears in 49% of Canadian foreign news items, followed by the United Kingdom, Israel, Afghanistan, Cuba, Pakistan, China, Palestine, Italy, and France. Indeed, the Canadian journalists easily identified the United States as well as the United Kingdom, Israel, Afghanistan, and China.

Switzerland

Switzerland was third in terms of the percentage of foreign news (43%). In fact, Swiss journalists were very accurate in estimating this percentage. Two of the three interviewees guessed between 40% and 45%, even though one, a producer at SF Tagesschau, highly overestimated the correct figure by indicating 60%.

Comparing Swiss television with that of other countries, the journalists all agreed that their country ranks high, stating, "I think we are rather in a top position" and "I think Switzerland has traditionally a focus on foreign nations. Therefore, I think we are rather high with our percentage of foreign news. I don't know the exact rank, but let's say in the upper half."

According to the content analysis, the Swiss television stations presented the United States as the most important nation, followed by several European countries—France, Germany, the United Kingdom, and Italy—as well as Israel, Palestine, Australia, Kosovo, and Serbia. When asked to name the countries that they thought were most covered in Switzerland, two of the three journalists provided almost perfect matches, mentioning the United States and the European countries, as well as Spain and China, while the third mentioned the United States and the Middle East.

Belgium

Belgium, with 36% foreign news, ranked fourth among the countries in the study that included the interviews with the gatekeepers. Both the editor-in-chief and the head of the foreign news desk at the public service VRT station estimated fairly accurately 25% foreign news on Belgian television and specifically mentioned an additional 5% hybrid news. They noted:

> The hybrid type is something special. Especially purposively "domesticating" news items is something we should be careful with. It interprets facts from a strictly Belgian point of view, and that is not always what the situation is about. But it happens that we add a domestic point of view to a foreign news item to make sure that the public at home will keep on being attentive.

When asked to compare Belgian news with other countries, the two journalists at VTM (the commercial station) said:

> I think we do better than other countries, especially compared to other commercial stations. I tend to believe that we are an atypical commercial station with high-quality news. Our newscast is longer. I believe we bring more foreign news than other commercial stations.

His colleague added:

> We offer a much broader window on the world than, for instance, French commercial channels. For them, foreign news means taking an item on a former colony once in a while and covering a state visit of President Obama.

Not unexpectedly, following the United States, 6 of the remaining most-covered countries based on the Belgian content analysis were European. This list also included Australia, as well as Israel and Palestine. When asked about the countries, all the Belgian gatekeepers were fairly accurate, citing the United States, neighboring European countries, and Middle Eastern countries.

Poland

Next in line in foreign news coverage was Poland, with 35%. Two of the three interviewees at Fakty TVN, the Polish commercial station, believed that 15% of the news deals with foreign events, a significant underestimation; the third interviewee could not provide a response. The head of the foreign news department at the public station estimated 20% coverage of foreign news, also an underestimation.

Asked about the comparison to other countries, the gatekeepers in the commercial stations were very indecisive. One of the two journalists said that "it depends" but could not say on what; the other noted that "the same amount of foreign news may be found everywhere," which is obviously not the case. The public service journalist was only able to suggest that "in Poland, the number of foreign news items is similar to the number of foreign news items in such countries as Switzerland, Germany, the United Kingdom, and France."

Poland was one of the few countries in our study in which the United States was not the top country being reported in its foreign news. In Poland, Russia was in first place, followed by the United States and seven European countries: Germany, the United Kingdom, the Ukraine, France, Switzerland, Serbia, and Italy. The three journalists from the commercial station mentioned Russia and the United States, but in reverse order. The gatekeeper at the Polish public station first mentioned European countries—mostly the United Kingdom and France—followed by the United States and Russia.

Israel

Israel was next with 33% of foreign news. Its gatekeepers provided a variety of estimates for the amount of foreign news on Israeli television, ranging from 10%, or 2–3 items per newscast (in one station) or 4–5 items (in the other station). The head of foreign news in the commercial station went into great detail:

> You need to define what you mean by foreign news. For example, some guys saved the Hollywood sign. From my perspective this is foreign entertainment, not foreign news. Entertainment or soccer news, are they foreign? It's totally different. Not like the G-8 or Obama's non-proliferation conference…. I estimate, and I have no empirical evidence, that at least 30% of what is aired comes from me, my department, and if it includes domestic (hybrid) news then you can add another 10%. Thirty percent are foreign-foreign.

Asked about the comparison with other countries, this same interviewee said:

> I guess Israel is not at the bottom of the list. Foreign news is sometimes a refuge of the tyrant. When I lived in South Africa for a while I learned that they broadcast lots of foreign news simply because they didn't want to broadcast domestic news.

His colleague at Channel 2 added:

> Europe is still salient in foreign news. Take countries like France, Britain, Germany, and Sweden; their interest in the world is solid. Japan is also an empire and is interested. They have correspondents everywhere. In the United States, nearly nil; nobody's interested there. I don't know about South America or Africa, but in Europe…foreign news is an integral part of the newscast.

The content analysis showed that Israeli foreign news reports mostly on the United States, followed by Palestine and other Arab countries, the United Kingdom, France, Germany, Australia, and Russia. The gatekeepers all put the United States in first place, but then returned to the prolonged discussion of what constitutes purely foreign or hybrid news, suggesting a mix of countries in Europe, the

Middle East, and some countries such as Turkey and China that they considered important based on their idiosyncratic interests.

Brazil

Brazil's foreign news content was in seventh place, with 32%. The four interviewees—three in the commercial channel and one in the public channel—responded at great length to some of the questions, but seemed reluctant to respond to some of the others.

As for the amount of foreign news aired in Brazil, one gatekeeper spoke in terms of 10%, about 5–6 minutes, whereas another interviewee indicated three or four international stories per day.

Concerning the journalists' perception of how they do in comparison with newscasts in other countries, the editor-in-chief of TV Cultura simply said: "Brazilian international TV news coverage is very good and at the same level of other countries." One of the interviewees at TV Globo expanded a little by saying:

> Our editorial guidelines require us to make an effort to clarify, giving context to international problems, allowing the viewer to comprehend it. This explains long broadcasts from time to time as we recently did regarding the military conflict in the Middle East after Brazil recognized the pre-1967 Palestinian borders. I cannot simply make the statement "Brazil has recognized the borders in Palestine." What is that? We presented a full reportage, more than two minutes, trying to put [it] in context in order to make sense of the Brazilian position.

Finally, Brazilian newscasts covered the United States far more (32%) than other countries such as Colombia, France, Ecuador, Venezuela, the United Kingdom, and Spain. When asked about the countries presented, the journalists only mentioned the United States. One commented by saying: "Our main interest is the United States; it is the greatest nation in the world. Anything it does has effects around and world and vice versa."

Chile

Chile, with 30% of foreign news, including the hybrid variety, was in eighth place. Some of the eight interviewed journalists did not attempt to estimate the amount of foreign news in their newscasts. One journalist said: "In general, the presence of international stories in the newscasts is low and that's something we fight for constantly." Several interviewees believe there is no quota for foreign news. One said:

> I think it's dangerous to manage quotas, because the news agenda is very dynamic and fixing a number of stories might have negative effects. At some point you might have four stories that are worthwhile, and at another you might have none. There is an average. I think that with two stories international news is well covered.

As for the countries most covered by the newscasts, Chile was one of six countries in the study that did not cover the United States most. Specifically, most coverage was found for Argentina (21%), followed by news about the United States (16%), some other South American countries (Brazil, Colombia, and Ecuador), and Spain. In response to the content analysis data, several journalists indicated their veridical perceptions of Chilean newscasts. While the United States was mentioned as the first country by one journalist, several spoke of South American countries as leading the pack. One of the journalists at TVN noted:

> For us there are certain areas of the world that are more important than others. I mean, what happens in Malta is not the same that happens in Paraguay, because the latter is part of our world region, because anything that happens in Latin American can affect us.... [W]e can't stop monitoring Argentina, Bolivia or Peru because we are part of this region, because we belong to a diplomatic alliance, and there is an issue that deals directly with us.... From the rest of the world, I think the Middle East is always a topic. We have the biggest Palestinian community outside of Palestine, and the conflict in the Middle East is one of the three most important topics.... I think the United States has relevance for us because it is one of the few countries that dictates in the world context...in the European context, Spain is really important because of historical proximity.

China

Chinese newscasts presented 27% foreign and hybrid news. The two leading CCTV gatekeepers (who asked to remain anonymous) provided some very detailed responses. Both indicated that about one-third of the items, amounting to 3–5 minutes per newscast, or one-sixth to one-tenth of the total duration, constituted foreign news coverage.

When asked about other countries' coverage of foreign news, both journalists provided references to specific countries. One journalist said: "I think the United States has more domestic news than international news. We have more than them. Japan has less international news, too." The other added: "There are two types of networks abroad, private and public. I have been to NHK in Japan and CBC in Canada. These state-owned networks are responsible to parliament but not to the government under the separation of powers notion. They don't have to listen to specific instructions while we have to. That's enough [for explaining the difference]."

At the time of the content analysis in early 2008, Greece was the country most heavily reported in China. This was due to the lighting of the Olympic torch and controversies concerning the upcoming Olympic Games. The other countries that received high coverage in Chinese news were the United States, the United Kingdom, Japan, Russia, South Korea, Algeria, Germany, Belgium, and Mauritania. The gatekeepers were quite cognizant of this. As the editor-in-chief said:

The United States, it is inevitable as a superpower and is related to so many things. Most are developed countries, like the United States, Europe, and Japan. Others, like Russia, but there is less news about it. It depends on the situation concerning news of North and South Korea. People like news about North Korea, Kim Jong-il and Kim Jong-un. It attracts people.

The other journalists put it similarly, but in greater detail:

> There are more about the United States and England. The United States is a superpower in economics, diplomacy, and news. Issues in Afghanistan, Iran, and Israel are hot, but they are all related to the United States. The U.S. army is always in the Iraq news. A lot of issues are related to American interests. Pakistan and India are related to anti-terrorism of the United States. Japan and the United States are allies. And England is competing with the United States. Belgium, as the EU Headquarters, has a lot of international conferences…. Switzerland is also a center for international activities. Germany is in the top level of developed countries. They are high-ranking countries in the world economy.

Portugal

The average foreign news coverage of the two Portuguese television stations was 26%. Two gatekeepers in each were interviewed. The public service RTP, according to its editors, presents between 10% and 20% foreign news items. The journalists at the private TV1 station provided estimates that ranged from 5% to 15%.

As for their perception of where Portugal stands relative to other countries, there was a consensus that the United States does not cover European nations well. As TV1's foreign news editor said:

> The United States is deeply ethnocentric, and so a newscast in the United States that talks about Europe is something from another world, only if there was a business or an event related to American interests, because they don't know and they don't want to know, they don't give a damn. For them, Portugal should be somewhere between Morocco and Spain.

The content analysis shows that Portuguese coverage of Spain in 2008 was greater than that of the United States, followed by East Timor, the United Kingdom, Kosovo, Iraq, Brazil, Italy, Mozambique, and France. The journalists reinforced some of these findings by estimating that most foreign news coverage in Portugal focuses on Spain, the United States, and European countries. As one journalist in the public station put it:

> We're very dependent on our position in the Western world; we have news mainly from Europe and the United States, and this has a lot to do with the agencies from whom we receive information…so we have a lot of information from Europe, but essentially from countries of Europe, not from the European Union; for example, Italy, Berlusconi, Merkel, Cameron, etc. And the United

States, everything that Obama does, from his dog to the discourse about the state of the nation.

Hong Kong

Next to last among our 12 countries in terms of foreign news coverage is Hong Kong, with 21%. The journalists' estimates of the amount of foreign news were somewhat vague, making reference to the difference between morning and evening newscasts, with one of the four gatekeepers providing no estimate at all. One journalist did say, however, that TVB has an informal rule that the "proper ratio of local news vs. foreign news was 7 to 3," and he pointed out that the ratio never reached 50:50.

As for the comparison of Hong Kong with other countries, three interesting points were made. One journalist said that because resources for domestic news could not be cut, the amount of international news in Hong Kong is low. His colleague at TVB suggested that freedom of speech would affect the proportion of foreign news offered in a given country. He referred to Singapore, arguing that its government would not want people to focus too much on local news, so they would have more foreign news. In Taiwan, he said, the high degree of commercialization led to a very small proportion of foreign news. Finally, an editor at ATV said that foreign news is treated as a "ratings killer," so she was not surprised by the low level of foreign news in Taiwan.

Foreign news in Hong Kong reported on the United States more than any other country (44%), followed by major world and regional powers such as Russia, the United Kingdom, South Korea, and Japan. However, coverage of these nations was low at only 3%–7%. All four journalists clearly identified the United States as the major country of interest in Hong Kong, due to its centrality in world affairs and the fact that the Hong Kong stations rely to a large extent on Western news agencies.

Taiwan

Television stations in Taiwan, with 14%, presented the lowest level of pure and hybrid foreign news than any of the other countries. Unfortunately, the two gatekeepers who were interviewed for this study did not discuss the content of their newscasts.

Summary of Gatekeepers' Views of Foreign News

The preceding analysis of the interviews with the gatekeepers allows for three overall conclusions. First, regarding the amount of foreign news, the journalists in all nations except China and Switzerland, tended to *underestimate* the amount of foreign news compared to the findings of the content analysis. Second, when journalists were asked about how their country compares with other countries, responses varied widely. Some of the interviewees simply declined to make an assessment, while others appeared to be indecisive or contradictory. Other gatekeepers stated correctly that their country either presented more or less foreign news than other countries. Many journalists, however, compared their own country's foreign news coverage with that of the United States, as if the United States represented a yardstick for (scant) coverage of foreign news. Third, when asked which countries were covered the most, most gatekeepers named the United States as the leading country in their respective newscasts—an assessment that matched the findings of our content analysis. In fact, most journalists correctly identified the nations that received the most coverage in their own country as compared to the content analysis.

In sum, while the journalists' ability to estimate the amount of foreign news in their own newscasts (and in comparison with other nations) was moderate at best, they were significantly better at identifying the countries that were covered most in their foreign news.

Gatekeepers on Their Viewers

The second issue that we compare is the gatekeepers' perceptions of the citizens in their respective countries vis-à-vis the surveys. In particular, we wish to determine the gatekeepers' assessments of the general level of interest that viewers have in foreign news and which specific countries they are interested in. One of the 12 countries that conducted the in-depth interviews with the gatekeepers—Belgium—did not do the survey; hence there are only 11 countries in which we can compare the gatekeepers' responses with the survey data. In this analysis we present the countries in descending order, beginning with the country in which there was the highest general level of interest in foreign news according to the surveys

Canada
Based on the 5-point survey question concerning general interest in foreign news (see Table 9.1), the mean Canadian score of 3.83 was the highest of the 11 countries. Asked about their perception of their audience, the journalists clearly indicated that Canadians "...are interested in foreign news if it is breaking news that's relevant.... [W]e take a very populist approach. What are people talking about today? What's the big story today? And that's how we'll approach what we're doing." Another Canadian gatekeeper put it most succinctly: "Yes, big time!"

The journalists were asked how much foreign news their viewers think should be in the newscasts. The CBC interviewee responded: "It would actually depend a bit on how you phrased the question. If you just asked them point-blank, 'should there be more?' they would say 'Yes, there should be more.'" In fact, in the Canadian survey, 22% of the respondents expressed an interest in having more foreign news, 51% thought that the amount of foreign news should be kept as it is, and 27% actually preferred less foreign news.[2]

As for the countries of interest in the Canadian survey (as presented in Table 10.4), the top eight countries[3] were the United States, the United Kingdom, China, Afghanistan, Haiti, Iraq, Iran, and India. Asked what they thought were the viewers' countries of interest, the CBC journalists mentioned the United States and Afghanistan but added that "…our own ratings would speak against what they say. I know sometimes we've asked them, Afghanistan is very high on the list. But we don't know if that actually translates into real interest."

China

China, with a mean score of 3.55 on general interest in foreign news, was in second place among the 11 countries. According to the Chinese journalists, Chinese news viewers are definitely interested in foreign news. The editor-in-chief at CCTV said:

> People I know tell me they prefer international news…. [W]e receive calls asking about some scientific inventions, especially for advanced medical technologies for heart diseases and eye treatment. The first half of the program is about domestic politics, achievement reports, and typical model reports. Although the time is short, there are seven to eight items, sometimes 10 items.

The other journalist said:

> International news is watchable by nature. Both the audience and the producer like international news. The audience likes it mostly for information. News broadcasting is both a window for the Chinese to understand the world and a window for the world to understand China. It's mutual.

Indeed, the survey indicates that while 59% of the Chinese respondents are satisfied with the amount of foreign news, 27% would like to have more, and only 14% said they would like less.

According to the audience survey, the top eight countries of interest are the United States, Japan, the United Kingdom, Russia, France, South Korea, Germany, and North Korea. The Chinese journalists are clearly aware of this, but made no reference to European countries. As one put it:

> The top ones are the United States and Japan. People are interested in news about the United States, maybe because we show them a lot, and the strong power of the United States is also an important factor. People love to see news about North Korea, but we don't have much of it. The ratings are pretty high when North Korea news is on.

The other journalist said:

Most viewers are more interested in the United States and Japan. The economy, diplomacy, culture, and films of the United States have influenced the world. So have their TV and broadcasting programs. On the other side, people are interested in North Korea because information about it is so rare.

Hong Kong

Hong Kong, with 21% pure and hybrid news in its newscasts, was in third place with a mean interest score of 3.52—almost as high as the one found in China. Thus, there was a large gap between what was available and what people in Hong Kong seemed to be interested in. And yet, like their colleagues in Canada, the gatekeepers in Hong Kong felt that if people were asked whether or not they were interested in foreign news, they would reply affirmatively. In fact, the survey data indicate that Hong Kong residents, more than any other group in our study, wanted more foreign news: 48% said they wanted more, 46% felt what was available was adequate, and only 6% preferred to have less foreign news.

The top eight countries of interest among Hong Kong viewers were the United States, the United Kingdom, Japan, Australia, Canada, South Korea, France, and Russia. When presented with the empirical findings, three of the four journalists felt that the peoples' responses made good sense. The choice of the United States was unanimous, as was that of the United Kingdom, given its historical ties to Hong Kong. One journalist, however, expressed surprise that Asian countries (other than Japan) were not mentioned, and another wondered about Thailand not being in a top position (it was in tenth place).

Switzerland

Switzerland's 3.47 score was fourth in the ranking of general interest in foreign news. The three interviewed gatekeepers provided contradictory responses to the question of how much interest viewers have in foreign news. One of the journalists, for example, said: "I think our viewers are very interested in foreign news because our country depends a lot on decisions from big neighbors. We also have a lot of economic relationships with foreign countries, and therefore I think most viewers are interested." Another response was: "I think they are not as interested as in national news." The third response, by a regional broadcaster, was: "I think our viewers are not so interested in foreign news."

Asked about how much foreign news viewers prefer, one interviewee said 40–60%. Another said that he thinks viewers would prefer less foreign news, while the third journalist said, "I really don't know; it's hard for me to say. I think viewers don't want a lot of foreign news in our newscast." These responses coincide with the survey findings: 62% of the Swiss public felt that what was provided was the right amount, 24% wanted less foreign news, and only 14% said they would like to see more.

As for the countries of most interest, the Swiss respondents named the following: Germany, the United States, France, Italy, Austria, the United Kingdom, China, and Russia—all either Switzerland's neighbors or big powers. The nations picked by the journalists matched those mentioned by the public almost perfectly.

Germany

Germany's mean score on the overall interest in foreign news was 3.43. The five gatekeepers presented mixed responses to the question about the level of interest among viewers. One journalist said it is difficult to estimate; three were skeptical and said that although people say they are interested, they really are not. Only the journalist at ARD was semi-positive:

> I think they are very interested in foreign news, especially looking beyond ones' nose. There are countries that are particularly of interest, which might be linked to trivial stories like "I've been on holiday there." People know that the world is more globalized nowadays and that we can't ignore what's happening in Iran or in the Middle East—but sometimes there's also overkill regarding such topics.

The survey data show that Germans were mostly satisfied with the proportion of foreign news available: 71% felt no need for change, 18% wanted more, and 11% wanted less. As for the gatekeepers' perception, an editor at RTL said:

> I think the percentage really desired by the viewers would be somewhere around 30. They probably said 50, because that sounds more international, cosmopolitan, globalized, and socially desirable.

Finally, regarding the countries of interest, the top choices mentioned by the German public were the United States, France, the United Kingdom, Russia, China, Italy, Afghanistan, and Spain. The gatekeepers, while generally in agreement, provided varying perspectives.

> I would put the United States first, and after that it actually becomes quite hard. I don't believe, for example, that the Middle East would be sought after.

> People are interested in the United States and the Middle East. I guess they are also interested in China and also our direct neighbors—France, Poland, etc.

> I would include the United States, the United Kingdom, and Russia. Probably little interest in the Middle East, little in Africa, and apart from the big nations I named before, Europe.

Poland

Poland, with a mean score of 3.42, came in sixth among the 11 countries. There was no consensus among the Polish gatekeepers about their audience. Three journalists suggested that Polish viewers are interested in foreign news and probably would like to see more such news. However, the editor-in-chief of Facty TVN disagreed, saying:

> I would be very interested in what viewers declare, but I know that they are not interested in foreign news. The data from telemetric measures show that only sudden, important, and emotional foreign news keeps viewers watching the newscast. Once the viewers are not interested in a foreign story they change the TV station.

Similarly, the editor-in-chief at the commercial station said, "I think that viewers do not tell the truth—they simply want to make a good impression." And one of his subordinates said:

> We think and receive some feedback on this that viewers are interested in foreign news and they want more news items dedicated to foreign news. But our editor-in-chief watches data collected by telemetric measures and he convinces us that this is not true.

However, the Polish survey data indicate that some people actually want more foreign news: while 57% said they are satisfied with the amount of foreign news on Polish television, 28% wanted more and only 15% wanted less. The gatekeepers were divided on this issue. Two journalists simply said that the people want more foreign news, without citing figures. On the other hand, the editor-in-chief at the commercial station said, "I think that viewers do not tell the truth—they simply want to make a good impression." One of his subordinates said:

> We think and receive some feedback on this that viewers are interested in foreign news and they want more news items dedicated to foreign news. But our editor-in-chief watches data collected by telemetric measures and he convinces us that this is not true.

The pattern of countries of interest as reported in the Polish survey is different from most of the other countries. First, the United States and United Kingdom were only in third and fourth place, respectively; all the other countries of interest were European—Germany, Russia, France, the Ukraine, the Czech Republic, and Italy. After being presented with the survey findings, the reporters by and large expressed surprise. They expected the United States, Russia, the United Kingdom, Germany, and France to be the top choices, but could not understand why Poles would be interested in the Czech Republic, Slovakia, the Ukraine, and Belarus—all nations that are not much covered by Polish television news.

Portugal
Portugal's mean score on general interest in foreign news is 3.31, the first country below the overall mean score of 3.39 for all the countries. The gatekeepers in Por-

tugal were skeptical about the public's interest in foreign news. A journalist in the commercial station put it this way: "So this is what people say that they would like to see, but we would need to know if people really see it." The foreign news editor in the public stations said: "Perhaps when we ask them they would say they have lots of interest, but audiences show that they don't care."

However, the Portuguese public expressed a fairly balanced interest in foreign news: 55% of the respondents felt that the amount provided is satisfactory, 25% wanted to see less, and 20% would have liked to have more. The gatekeepers seemed to be somewhat ambivalent about this issue. Three of the four interviewees did not respond to these findings. The RTP public service journalist speculated that "it could be that they want more or they think that it is enough, that I don't know; I have no data to talk about that."

The Portuguese survey identified the following eight countries as being of greatest interest to the public: France, Spain, the United States, the United Kingdom, Germany, Brazil, Italy, and Switzerland. The journalists, however, preferred other nations. While Brazil (where Portuguese is the national language) was mentioned by the gatekeepers, they also placed much emphasis on African countries, particularly Angola and Mozambique, two former Portuguese colonies. They also expressed disappointment that the viewers were not interested in these countries.

Chile

The mean score for general interest in foreign news in Chile was 3.27. The Chilean gatekeepers were interviewed at length but were quite reluctant to respond directly to the questions concerning the level of audience interest. Nevertheless, several interesting comments were made. A Chilean journalist at TVN said:

> Ratings are a way to measure.... [W]e evaluate the numbers with one day of delay, more or less. How did we do yesterday? There are topics that give a lot, there are topics that fall, there are topics you had lots of faith in and go to hell, and others you didn't believe in that get results. There you have a notion of what characters people like the most, which are the journalists that write the best and attract the audience, not only considering the information but also the production.

A news editor had this to say:

> Because I don't know if what people say is true, you ask, "do you want TV to show more culture?" and people say "yes, I would," and one sees in the ratings that nobody watches the cultural programs.... I think that with foreign news the same happens. Many people say, because it's politically correct, "I would love that they air more foreign news," but when it's time to actually watch it they prefer topics with a more local connection.

The survey in Chile indicated that 50% of the respondents felt that there is an adequate amount of foreign news, 35% would have liked to see more, and 15% preferred having less such news.

When asked about the countries that are of greatest interest, the respondents mentioned the United States, Argentina, Spain, Peru, Brazil, Mexico, France, and Italy. The Chilean gatekeepers were not directly asked about the countries of interest. However, one of the journalists did make the following comment:

> Chile is a country that has a profound contradiction. It is an open economy, it is open to the world, very integrated, people travel a lot, but it is very closed internally. So the function of foreign news is to tell Chileans that the world doesn't end in Arica or Punta Arenas. Foreign news has the sense of making people understand that phenomena that happen anywhere in the world impact us.

Israel

In ninth place in terms of the overall level of interest in foreign news we find Israel, with a mean score of 3.24. The Israeli gatekeepers went into lengthy explanations regarding what they thought the viewers want. After being shown the Israeli data, the editor in the public station said:

> I'm not a great believer in surveys. People say they want more foreign news so that they would appear as open-minded. On the margins, we could add a bit more but we don't want to reach the point where the editor-in-chief would be reluctant to provide foreign news. A former head of the news department once said, "It's better that you shut up and they ask you to speak than to speak and they tell you to shut up."

The other foreign news editor at the public station said:

> I really don't know how much the public wants to see a daily report on Darfur. When they think about foreign news they think about beautiful pictures from around the world, at least some of the people think so, something that would take our mind off the daily shit.

The head of the foreign news desk at the commercial station said:

> I do believe that people want more. I did several programs that were actually foreign news and their ratings were relatively high. "Specials" always brought good ratings.

The survey findings indicate that Israelis indeed wanted more foreign news. While 49% of the respondents indicated that what is provided is right, 11% wanted less, but an astonishing 40% wanted more. The foreign news reporter at the commercial Channel 2 commented:

> I'll tell you why people want more foreign news. First, they are tired of politics, crime, the Palestinians, corruption, poverty…. People are interested in what is happening elsewhere…to get out of this provincial ghetto…it can be amusing, shocking, but it always provides a prism—it could happen here; it can't happen here. It's relative.

The Israeli survey respondents mentioned the following top countries of interest: the United States, Arab countries (except for Egypt), France, the United Kingdom, Russia, Egypt, and Iran. As it turned out, the journalists were fairly precise in their estimates of which countries the public would be interested in. One journalist, typical of the others, noted:

> I suppose your data will show the United States, Russia, France, Britain—the superpowers—maybe China, too. Well, as for the Arab countries, for us that's not foreign news, that's another specialty.

Taiwan

Taiwan, with an average score of 3.21, was next to last in terms of its overall interest in foreign news. Unfortunately, the Taiwanese gatekeepers were not asked about their perception of audience interest in foreign news or countries of interest.

As for the survey responses in Taiwan concerning the desire for more or less foreign news, a nearly perfect split appeared: 46% of the respondents thought things should remain the same, and 47% expressed interest in more foreign news. Only 7% wanted less foreign news, which makes sense, given the fact that Taiwan was the country that presented the smallest amount (14%) of foreign news.

The journalist in the commercial television station had this to say:

> Taiwan's viewers' expectations regarding foreign news have a lot to do with Taiwan's political and economic status. Because we are not recognized as an independent country in many regions of the world, we have few opportunities to be involved in international events and activities, nor are we important members of international organizations. The sense of "separation from the world" is the main reason that Taiwanese people care less about international issues. As a result, instead of hard and serious news, the main trend of foreign news in Taiwan is soft and interesting news.

A journalist at the public station made a similar point:

> Most news media in Taiwan tend to pick fun, interesting stories, less complicated and less important issues for international news contents. Taiwan has lower economic and political status in the world. People have fewer opportunities to be involved in international events, and care less about the information that barely

has anything to do with our country. Therefore, viewers like to gossip, which has become a popular trend.

Brazil

Brazil received the lowest mean score (3.17) on general interest in foreign news. Asked about the interest of the audience, the journalist at the commercial TV Globo station said, "We believe that the interest in international news is growing, since people want to increase their level of information." His counterpart at TV Cultura, the public station, made a more complex observation:

> Our feedback is possible only through the mail.... The public wants more coverage of Brazil.... [O]ur program is long; therefore we can insert international news in it. I do not see public demand for more international news time. But when there is direct Brazilian involvement as in the case of Haiti, with Brazilian military forces, it gives some familiarity to the subject.

According to the survey, 31% of the Brazilian public would like to have more foreign news, 11% would like less, and 58% indicated their satisfaction with the amount presented. In concert with the above, the public service gatekeeper repeated his complaint about lack of contact with viewers, saying: "Our way of interaction with the public is not adequate. Therefore I cannot know for sure whether the public wants more international news." The journalist at the commercial station, however, stated: "The viewers do not like to hear about an issue they do not understand. People must understand what we are talking about. We have adequate language to make this possible."

The leading countries mentioned by Brazilians in the survey were the United States, Japan, France, Italy, China, Argentina, Germany, and Spain. When asked about this, only one gatekeeper responded with a clear voice, naming only the United States.

Summary of Gatekeepers' Views of Foreign News Audiences

In contrast to the gatekeepers' responses to the findings of our content analysis and their moderately corresponding views of what is covered in their own newscasts, reactions to the survey findings were less consistent. It seems clear that most gatekeepers were more positive about the findings of the content analysis than the findings of the opinion surveys. In fact, many of the journalists said that they distrust surveys that measure audience preferences of foreign news, because they thought that most people exaggerate their interest in foreign news. Other journalists simply said that they do not know how much foreign news their audiences want and what they might be interested in. Overall then, these findings indicate that despite the empirical evidence to the contrary, journalists tend to have a rather dim view of their audiences when it comes to interest in foreign news.

Conclusions

At the beginning of this chapter, we argued that it is important to understand how the work of journalists is influenced by their perceptions of foreign news and their audiences. While the news-making process in each nation is undoubtedly affected by political and organization-level factors, the way in which journalists define foreign news and perceive their audiences ultimately must have a significant impact on foreign news selection. Thus, by interviewing 49 gatekeepers responsible for selecting and producing foreign news in 12 nations, we hoped to shed some light on how journalists and editors evaluate the amount of foreign TV news available in their respective countries, and which countries they believed to be the focus of their newscasts. We also asked how interested they thought their audience members were in foreign news, and which countries they thought would be of most interest to them.

Our interviews with the journalists and editors resulted in a few interesting conclusions that might be general enough to stand on their own, despite the limited sample available in this analysis. First, it became clear that journalists in all nations (except China and Switzerland) underestimated the amount of foreign news in their respective nations. At first glance, this is a surprising finding if we assume that the people responsible for selecting and producing foreign news should also know how much foreign news is shown in their newscasts. However, there could be several explanations for this finding. First, the gatekeepers were asked to estimate the amount of pure foreign *and* hybrid (foreign with domestic involvement) news contained in their broadcasts. However, some of the interviewed journalists might have considered only pure foreign news in their answers. Another possibility is that they preferred to be conservative in their estimates so as not to appear boastful about their work. A third possibility, though highly unlikely, is that in some of the stations the amount of foreign news decreased between the time the content analysis was done (early 2008) and the time of the interviews (mid-2009 to early 2011).

We also found that gatekeepers generally disagreed on how the amount of foreign news in their own country compared to the volume of foreign news in other countries. This finding is less surprising given the fact that most journalists probably have very little exposure to foreign news in other countries. While it is certainly true that they are selecting foreign news from other nations, knowing what kind of foreign news is shown in other countries is an entirely different type of perception. However, it is also obvious that many journalists are aware of the fact that foreign news in the United States is a rare commodity. We cannot be sure where they obtained this insight; however, those who have travelled to the United

States or studied journalism in college should be well aware of how little foreign news is available on U.S. television news.

While agreement on how much foreign news is available in their respective nations was limited, most journalists knew that the United States is the most covered nation on foreign newscasts around the world. In addition, the gatekeepers were fairly accurate in their assessments of which other nations received the most coverage in their own newscasts. Again, this is not a very surprising finding, since foreign news selection is part of the daily routine of the journalists we interviewed for this analysis. After all, selecting foreign news is mostly driven by where the news is coming from, so most journalists should be aware of which nations receive the most attention in their newscasts.

Responses to our survey findings, which focused on what audiences might want to see on foreign news, were somewhat hostile. Many of the interviewed journalists openly expressed their distrust of surveys that measure audience preferences, because they believe that respondents exaggerate their true interest in foreign news. It was also clear that some journalists simply did not know how much foreign news their audiences want and what they might be interested in. These findings seem to contradict earlier studies that concluded that journalists not only have a fairly positive view of their audiences (Weaver & Wilhoit, 1996) but also believe that most people are fairly interested in foreign news (Seplow, 2002). Of course, these attitudes also contradict the findings of our public opinion surveys, which clearly indicate that most people around the world are "quite interested" in foreign news (see Table 9.1).

This leaves the question of what the cause of these perceptions might be. Again, we do not claim that the journalists interviewed for this analysis offer a representative view of how newsmakers regard their foreign news audiences. Our sample of journalists is too small and unrepresentative to make such a claim. However, the observed attitudes are interesting and deserve some consideration.

Overall, we do believe that many of our journalists have been exposed to audience research that has shown relatively low ratings for foreign news. Armed with such knowledge, it seems that many journalists simply do not believe surveys that show that people are, in fact, quite interested in foreign news. Instead, most gatekeepers interviewed seem to believe that people would try to exaggerate their true interest in foreign news in a survey in order to mask their more mundane interests in sports and entertainment.

While we agree that such a built-in "social desirability" bias might be a problem in surveys that try to gauge exposure to and interest in foreign news (as it would be for measuring exposure to and interest in politics or public affairs), recent survey findings also show that people have started to recognize the importance of foreign news in their daily lives (Pew, 2011). Thus, journalists might be overly swayed by the low ratings foreign news often gets when compared with more "exciting" stories that focus on gossip and entertainment news. As mentioned earlier, such perceptions might have the unfortunate side effect that some gatekeepers underestimate the interest of their audiences in foreign news and thus provide them with less foreign news than they would consume if given the chance (Seib, 1997).

We hope that this is actually not the case. However, given the precarious status of foreign news in the current media environment, which favors cheaply produced local news rather than expensive foreign coverage, we worry that the journalists' widespread mistrust and rejection of survey findings could lead to a decline in foreign news in the long run. More systematic and representative research is necessary to better understand the attitudes of journalists and editors toward foreign news and their audiences.

Summary

This chapter investigated how the gatekeepers of foreign news evaluate the amount of foreign TV news available in their respective countries, which countries they believe are the focus in foreign news, and how important they think news about their own nation is elsewhere. In addition, we explored how interested they believe their audience members are in foreign news and which countries might be of most interest to them. The analysis, as in Chapter 11, is based on interviews with 49 gatekeepers responsible for selecting and producing foreign news in 12 countries.

Our findings indicate that the journalists and editors in all nations except China and Switzerland tend to *underestimate* the amount of foreign news in their respective countries. We also found that most gatekeepers were unsure about how the amount of foreign news in their own country as compared to the volume of foreign news in other countries. While some of the interviewees simply declined to make an assessment, others appeared to be indecisive or contradictory. Most of the interviewees, however, knew that the United States is the most covered nation on foreign newscasts around the world and correctly identified the nations that received the most coverage in their own newscasts.

When asked to respond to the fact that most respondents in our 13-nation survey expressed relatively high levels of interest in foreign news, many journalists dismissed this finding with the argument that respondents tend to exaggerate their true interest in foreign news. Others simply did not know how much foreign news their audiences want or what they might be interested in.

Notes

1. Of the 17 countries for which we have content analytic data, 5 did not do the in-depth interviews with gatekeepers: Egypt, Italy, Japan, Singapore, and the United States. Also, 4 countries—Belgium, Egypt, Italy, and Japan—did not conduct the

survey. Therefore, the discussion on how the gatekeepers assessed the content is based on interviews in 12 countries, while the discussion on how the interviewees assessed the country surveys is based on only 11 countries (absent are Belgium, Egypt, Italy, Japan, Singapore, and the United States).
2. This calculation was based on combining two questions from the survey: "According to your view, how much of the newscast that you usually watch is devoted to events about other countries?" and "According to your view, how much of the newscast that you usually watch should be devoted to events about other countries?" For both questions, the possible responses range from (1) less than 20% of the newscast; (2) from 20% to less than 40% of the newscast; (3) from 40% to less than 60% of the newscast; (4) from 60% to less than 80% of the newscast; and (5) 80% of the newscast or more. By separately cross-tabulating the two questions among the respondents in each country, we calculated a measure of "desired" foreign news that indicates the percentage of respondents who would like to have less, more, or the same amount of foreign news.
3. In most cases we refer to the top eight countries, which represent a large percentage of all the countries mentioned.

PART FIVE

Tying the Knots

CHAPTER THIRTEEN

Linking Content and Audiences

Topics in the News

KNUT DE SWERT & AKIBA A. COHEN

In the previous chapters we provided information based on the content analysis and the surveys. In the chapters in this section, we attempt to link some of the content and survey findings using two sets of select variables. In this chapter we do this for the main topics in the news as determined by the content analysis and by what the respondents stated about their interest in the topics. In the next chapter we will do this regarding the countries of location of the news events based on the content analysis, and the countries of interest as reported by the respondents.

In other words, in these two chapters we wish to determine whether the topics in the news correspond with the audiences' stated interest. Are people interested in the foreign news that is provided to them? Alternatively, do people get to see the news they are interested in? Moreover, as we have done throughout the book, we examine whether or not there are overall differences between domestic and foreign news or whether such differences, if they exist, are country-specific. Finally, by way of regression analysis, we look into individual-level factors of the audience members that drive the correspondence between news content and audience interest.

An attempt to link news content data with survey data inevitably brings to mind the notion of agenda setting (McCombs & Shaw, 1972; Scheufele, 2000). However, while agenda setting is more concerned, for example, with the effects of news media content on public opinion—that is, what people think is important—the questions asked in our survey were more directly concerned with the *interest* the people had in various subject areas in television news, both domestic and foreign. Clearly, being in sync with audience expectations and interests is important for television news producers, especially in increasingly commercial news markets (McManus, 1994). Therefore, one might expect both domestic and foreign news topics provided by journalists to address the subjects that their viewers consider to be interesting.

While newsmakers may adapt news content (at least to some degree) according to how they perceive audience interests (see Chapter 12 for a discussion of this issue), viewers may also be subject to some form of influence. Thus, for example, people may become interested in news about a particular topic or country after having seen a news item that prompts them to seek more information about it. This form of "soft" agenda setting (or interest setting) may take place when television journalists choose to present news on topics (or countries)—topics that were heretofore not considered interesting by their audience.

Methods and Data

The analyses presented in this chapter are based on several questions that appeared in the survey questionnaire concerning the degree of interest that the respondents had in seven topic categories of domestic and foreign news on television (see Chapter 9 for detailed responses to these questions). Two sets of seven questions each were asked, one for domestic news and the other for foreign news. The topic categories were: domestic politics (and domestic politics of foreign countries); crime and violence (and crime and violence in foreign countries); sports (and sports in foreign countries); a country's relations with foreign countries (and relations between foreign countries); economics, business, and commerce (and economics, business, and commerce in foreign countries); accidents and natural disasters (and accidents and natural disasters in foreign countries); and social issues such as health, education, culture, and religion (and social issues such as health, education, culture, and religion of foreign countries). The lead-in to the questions was: "Generally, to what extent are you interested in the following topics? You can choose between 'very interested,' 'quite interested,' 'somewhat interested,' 'not very interested,' and 'not interested at all.'"

The content analysis data used in this chapter are similar to those presented in Chapter 3. The topic codes of the content analysis were recoded in the best way possible to correspond with the seven topics used in the survey. This was done by collapsing some of the topic categories.

Comparing Topics in News Content and Audience Interests

The main question in this chapter asks whether the topics most frequently covered in the news are the same topics that people are most interested in. Since we were

Table 13.1 Rankings of domestic news topics and audience interest by country*

Brazil				Canada				Chile			
Content		Survey		Content		Survey		Content		Survey	
Social issues	38.1	Social issues	4.5	Social issues	30.5	Social issues	4.1	Social issues	24.6	Social issues	4.4
Economy	26.1	Economy	3.8	Internal Politics	26.3	Foreign Relations	3.9	Crime	24.3	Accidents	3.82
Internal Politics	18.8	Foreign Relations	3.7	Crime	22.1	Accidents	3.71	Economy	22.2	Foreign Relations	3.76
Crime	16.6	Accidents	3.48	Economy	17.5	Economy	3.67	Sports	21.3	Crime	3.7
Sports	4.5	Sports	3.47	Foreign Relations	14	Internal Politics	3.65	Internal Politics	9.7	Economy	3.4
Accidents	3.8	Crime	3.0	Sports	11.8	Crime	3.4	Accidents	7.8	Sports	2.93
Foreign Relations	2.5	Internal Politics	2.8	Accidents	9.6	Sports	2.8	Foreign Relations	0.4	Internal Politics	2.9
Spearman rank correlation	.29		NS		.21		NS		.14		NS

Hong Kong				Israel				Poland			
Content		Survey		Content		Survey		Content		Survey	
Economy	36.8	Accidents	3.8	Crime	36.5	Accidents	3.7	Social issues	34.3	Social issues	3.9
Social issues	26.7	Social issues	3.6	Social issues	33.0	Foreign Relations	3.58	Internal Politics	32.5	Accidents	3.5
Internal Politics	19.5	Economy	3.53	Foreign Relations	22.2	Crime	3.57	Crime	23.9	Foreign Relations	3.4
Crime	16.5	Foreign Relations	3.52	Internal Politics	16.4	Social issues	3.25	Economy	23.1	Internal Politics	3.3
Accidents	12.4	Crime	3.4	Economy	12.9	Economy	3.24	Accidents	8.1	Crime	3.2
Sports	5.1	Internal Politics	3.1	Accidents	4.6	Internal Politics	3.2	Sports	7.6	Economy	3.14
Foreign Relations	2.9	Sports	2.8	Sports	3.1	Sports	2.4	Foreign Relations	7.1	Sports	3.08
Spearman rank correlation	.29		NS		.32		NS		.32		NS

* Content percentages in news coverage; survey mean scores on 5-point scales. In cases of ties between survey categories based on one-tenth of a point, two decimal points were used to break the ties.

Table 13.1 Rankings of domestic news topics and audience interest by country (continued)

China				Germany				Taiwan			
Content		Survey		Content		Survey		Content		Survey	
Internal Politics	40.8	Accidents	3.8	Economy	42.1	Social issues	3.8	Internal Politics	37.8	Accidents	3.8
Social issues	36.9	Foreign Relations	3.6	Internal Politics	30.1	Foreign Relations	3.61	Social issues	33.5	Social issues	3.7
Economy	26.5	Social issues	3.5	Crime	20.7	Internal Politics	3.56	Economy	19.8	Economy	3.4
Accidents	22.1	Internal Politics	3.4	Social issues	20	Economy	3.4	Crime	12.6	Foreign Relations	3.2
Crime	6.1	Economy	3.3	Accidents	10.6	Accidents	3.3	Accidents	6.5	Sports	3.1
Foreign Relations	3.5	Sports	3.2	Sports	10.1	Crime	3.1	Sports	0.6	Internal Politics	2.4
Sports	2.9	Crime	3.0	Foreign Relations	4.9	Sports	2.8	Foreign Relations	0.5	Crime	2.2
Spearman rank correlation	.21	NS			.04	NS			-.07	NS	

Portugal				Singapore				United States			
Content		Survey		Content		Survey		Content		Survey	
Social issues	40.1	Social issues	4.3	Social issues	48.1	Social issues	3.8	Internal Politics	47.9	Economy	3.8
Economy	31	Accidents	3.5	Economy	41.9	Economy	3.34	Economy	34.8	Social issues	3.74
Crime	28.8	Economy	3.39	Crime	12.9	Accidents	3.7	Social issues	30.3	Accidents	3.73
Internal Politics	28	Foreign Relations	3.38	Sports	7.9	Foreign Relations	3.44	Foreign Relations	5.6	Foreign Relations	3.6
Sports	16.4	Crime	3.1	Internal Politics	4.6	Crime	3.3	Sports	3.4	Internal Politics	3.5
Accidents	3.0	Sports	3	Accidents	2.4	Internal Politics	2.9	Crime	2.8	Crime	3.4
Foreign Relations	2.0	Internal Politics	2.8	Foreign Relations	1.8	Sports	2.7	Accidents	1.4	Sports	3.0
Spearman rank correlation	.29	NS			.11	NS			.32	NS	

compelled to deal with only seven topic categories in both the survey and the recoding of the content analysis topics, we used Spearman rank correlations in order to determine the extent to which the two data sets are correlated.

For each of the 13 countries, Table 13.1 (for domestic news) and Table 13.2 (for foreign news) present side-by-side the seven topic categories of the content analyses and the surveys. The content categories are presented in ranked order from the category most prominent in the news to the category least prominent. The survey topics are presented in ranked order from the topic considered by the respondents to be most interesting (based on the mean score of the 5-point scales) to the topic considered to be least interesting.

For example, in Ttable 13.1 for China, the most prevalent domestic topic in the news was internal politics (40.8%), followed by social issues (36.9%), and in seventh place (the lowest prominence) was the sports category with only 2.9%. In the Chinese survey, the topic considered most interesting by the Chinese respondents was accidents and natural disasters; hence it was put in first place with a mean of 3.8. This was followed by foreign relations (mean of 3.6); in last place was crime and violence (mean of 3.0).

Table 13.1 provides information concerning the correspondence between content and audience interest in the realm of domestic news. The Spearman rank correlation coefficients (which appear below the sets of rankings) provide an indication of the extent to which (if at all) content and interest are correlated. Although none of the Spearman coefficients turned out to be statistically significant, they do provide an interesting observation. Since only a very high correlation can reach statistical significance with just 7 paired rankings (the critical values for 1-tailed and 2-tailed are $\rho=714$ and $\rho=786$, respectively), the direction of the correlation (positive or negative) can be taken as an indication, especially if the coefficient is over $\rho=.20$. For Brazil, for example, we see that for both news content and audience interest, social issues were the topics ranked first, and the economy was ranked second for both domains. Among the remaining topics there were a few differences, mainly due to the relatively low (seventh place) news coverage of foreign relations, whereas Brazilians ranked this topic as third in terms of their interest. Thus the overall correspondence between news content and audience priorities was moderate in Brazil, yielding a (positive) Spearman coefficient of .29.

One overall observation is that in 7 of the 13 countries—Brazil, Canada, Chile, Poland, Portugal, Singapore, and Switzerland—social issues were ranked highest both in content and audience interest. And yet, the rank correlations for the 13 countries were low to moderate, ranging from 0.00 in Switzerland to .32 in three countries (Israel, Poland, and the United States) and one near-zero negative correlation in Taiwan (–.07).

Table 13.2 provides the comparable analyses for foreign news. The patterns obtained were far less coherent, however, compared with domestic news. The

Table 13.2 Rankings of foreign news topics and audience interest by country*

Brazil				Canada				Chile			
Content		Survey		Content		Survey		Content		Survey	
Foreign relations	52.5	Social Issues	3.8	Internal Politics	32.6	Accidents	3.69	Sports	45.3	Accidents	3.6
Economy	24.8	Economy	3.6	Crime	28.0	Foreign relations	3.68	Foreign relations	17.1	Social issues	3.5
Social Issues	15.2	Foreign relations	3.3	Foreign relations	26.0	Social Issues	3.4	Economy	14.9	Economy	3.0
Internal politics	8.0	Accidents	3.2	Social Issues	21.5	Economy	3.3	Social issues	14.4	Crime	2.9
Sports	7.3	Sports	3.0	Economy	9.1	Internal politics	2.9	Crime	13.4	Foreign relations	2.8
Crime	6.0	Crime	2.63	Accidents	8.5	Crime	2.7	Internal Politics	5.0	Sports	2.6
Accidents	2.1	Internal Politics	2.61	Sports	4.5	Sports	2.2	Accidents	1.4	Internal Politics	2.5
Spearman rank correlation	.54	NS			−.07	NS			−.36	NS	

China				Germany				Hong Kong			
Content		Survey		Content		Survey		Content		Survey	
Foreign relations	32.1	Economy	3.3	Foreign relations	26.7	Accidents	3.13	Internal politics	36.1	Accidents	3.7
Economy	17.5	Accidents	3.2	Social issues	23.7	Social issues	3.09	Crime	23.4	Economy	3.30
Social issues	15.6	Foreign Relations	3.1	Crime	23.2	Foreign Relations	3.08	Foreign relations	15.4	Foreign relations	3.25
Sports	14.9	Social issues	2.9	Internal politics	21.7	Economy	3.0	Social Issues	10.2	Social issues	3.2
Crime	12.6	Sports	2.81	Sports	20.3	Internal politics	2.8	Economy	8.9	Crime	3.1
Internal Politics	11.7	Internal Politics	2.75	Economy	10.8	Sports	2.3	Accidents	6.9	Internal Politics	3.02
Accidents	2.9	Crime	2.5	Accidents	5.4	Crime	2.6	Sports	2.6	Sports	2.99
Spearman rank correlation	.36	NS			−.04	NS			−.21	NS	

* Content percentages in news coverage; survey mean scores on 5-point scales. In cases of ties between survey categories based on one tenth of a point, two decimal points were used to break the ties.

Table 13.2 Rankings of foreign news topics and audience interest by country (continued)

Israel				Poland				Portugal				Singapore			
Content		Survey		Content		Survey		Content		Survey		Content		Survey	
Foreign relations	38.0	Accidents	3.3	Internal politics	29.3	Foreign relations	3.4	Crime	39.7	Social issues	3.5	Internal politics	33.9	Accidents	3.7
Internal politics	27.5	Social issues	2.8	Social issues	26.1	Social issues	3.3	Foreign relations	38.6	Accidents	3.3	Economy	21.8	Social issues	3.32
Social issues	18.8	Economy	2.7	Foreign relations	25.0	Accidents	3.30	Internal Politics	19.7	Foreign relations	3.03	Social issues	19.4	Foreign Relations	3.25
Crime	17.5	Foreign relations	2.6	Crime	17.2	Economy	2.95	Economy	18.2	Economy	2.98	Sports	15.7	Economy	3.2
Sports	10.7	Sports	2.40	Economy	10.6	Internal politics	2.8	Social issues	17.9	Crime	2.6	Crime	13.3	Crime	2.9
Economy	7.4	Crime	2.37	Sports	6.7	Sports	2.73	Sports	9.9	Sports	2.5	Foreign Relations	9.7	Internal Politics	2.7
Accidents	1.8	Internal Politics	2.3	Accidents	3.8	Crime	2.72	Accidents	4.7	Internal Politics	2.3	Accidents	6.9	Sports	2.6
Spearman rank correlation	−.50	NS			.09	NS			−.32	NS			−.50	NS	

Switzerland				Taiwan				United States							
Content		Survey		Content		Survey		Content		Survey					
Internal politics	37.7	Social issues	3.3	Social issues	22.9	Accidents	3.4	Foreign relations	55.8	Accidents	3.33				
Social issues	26.0	Foreign relations	3.2	Internal politics	20.1	Economy	3.3	Crime	20.1	Foreign Relations	3.29				
Crime	25.2	Accidents	3.1	Crime	16.1	Social issues	3.2	Social issues	13.9	Social issues	3.18				
Foreign relations	20.0	Economy	3.0	Economy	13.7	Foreign relations	3.02	Economy	8.9	Economy	3.17				
Sports	14.7	Internal politics	2.9	Foreign relations	9.8	Sports	2.96	Internal politics	7.7	Internal politics	2.9				
Economy	12.1	Crime	2.7	Accidents	7.9	Internal Politics	2.4	Accidents	3.6	Crime	2.8				
Accidents	6.1	Sports	2.6	Sports	6.7	Crime	2.2	Sports	1.9	Sports	2.2				
Spearman rank correlation	.04	NS			−.25	NS			.35	NS					

Figure 13.1 Graphic display of Chinese data: percentages of coverage and mean interest scores

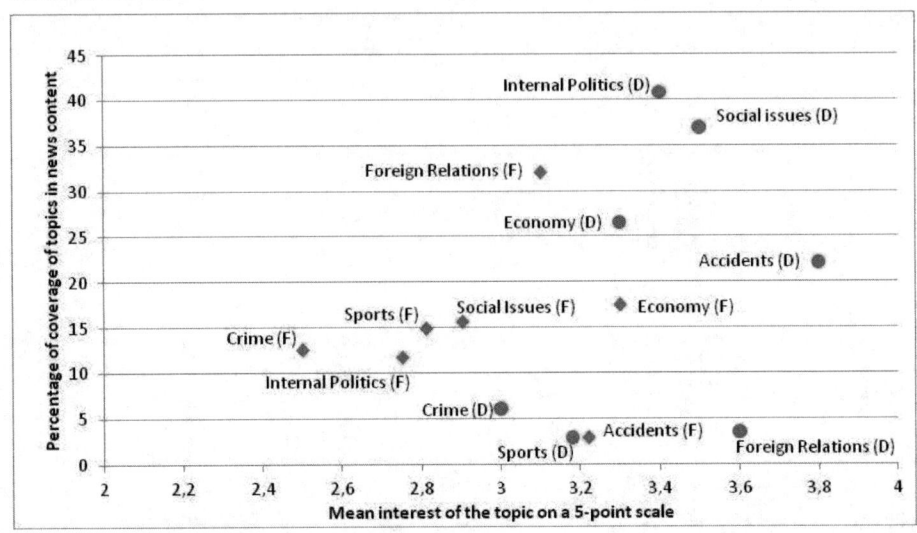

Table 13.3 Percentage of high audience interest in most prevalent topic category of foreign news by country

Country	Most prevalent topic in foreign news content	Percentage of high audience interest in topic category
Brazil	Foreign Relations	42.8
Canada	Internal Politics	22.5
Chile	Sports	23.7
China	Foreign Relations	37.0
Germany	Foreign Relations	32.2
Hong Kong	Internal Politics	30.3
Israel	Foreign Relations	23.3
Poland	Internal Politics	12.8
Portugal	Crime	20.8
Singapore	Internal Politics	23.9
Switzerland	Internal Politics	27.0
Taiwan	Social Issues	32.1
United States	Foreign Relations	38.3
All countries		28.6

dominance of social issues, and to some extent the economy, was gone, replaced only marginally by sporadic perceived interest in foreign relations. Indeed, it was difficult to establish any clear and consistent pattern, and between-country differences appeared to be larger than for domestic news. Also the (tentative) correspondence between content and audience interest that was observed for domestic news was no longer notable for foreign news.

While in the case of domestic news the Spearman correlation coefficients were generally moderate but positive, the pattern for foreign news was inconsistent. In six of the countries, the correlations were negative, ranging from −.21 in Hong Kong to −.50 in Singapore (in Canada and Germany the correlations were −.07 and −.04, respectively, which are essentially zero). In only five countries the correlations were positive, with much variation: from .04 (essentially zero) in Switzerland to .54 in Brazil. It appears that one of the most important reasons for this discrepancy was the notably high interest among the audiences in the different countries in news about accidents and disasters (ranked first in eight countries and ranked second in two countries) but ranked rather low in the content of the newscasts (ranked last in nine countries and ranked next to last in four countries).

The case of Brazil and China is especially interesting in one respect. Brazil, as noted, had a high correlation of .54, and China's correlation was .36. These are the

Table 13.4 Comparison of foreign relations within foreign news content and audience interest by country

Country	Ranking of foreign relations in news content	Percentage of foreign news about foreign relations	Percentage of respondents indicating foreign relations as very or quite interesting
Brazil	1st	52.5	42.8
Canada	3rd	26.0	53.2
Chile	2nd	17.1	22.1
China	1st	32.1	37.0
Germany	1st	26.7	32.2
Hong Kong	3rd	15.4	37.0
Israel	1st	38.0	23.3
Poland	3rd	25.0	40.4
Portugal	3rd	38.6	29.0
Singapore	6th	9.7	43.2
Switzerland	4th	20.0	36.7
Taiwan	4th	9.8	25.4
United States	1st	55.8	38.3
All countries		28.2	33.6

only two countries in which their respective gatekeepers noted a special emphasis that was being placed on foreign news (see Chapter 11). Perhaps this increased attention to foreign news was brought about, at least to some extent, by presenting foreign news items that reflect the interest of the viewers in those countries.

Figure 13.1 presents a visual example for one country—in this case, China—of the placement of all seven topic categories for both content and interest of domestic and foreign news. We chose China as our example because it matches most of the observations noted above. Accidents and disasters, which are of much interest in both domestic and foreign news but rarely reported, appear at the bottom-right corner of the figure, indicating a mismatch between content and audience interest. Domestic social issues and domestic politics, which are heavily reported and are of significant interest to the Chinese people, appear at the top-right corner, in the "matched" zone. The other data points appear in their respective regions of the visual map.

Another way of looking at the correspondence between content and interest is to check if the topic that received the greatest coverage, according to the content analysis, is also of relatively high interest, based on the frequency of responses to the top two categories ("very interested" and "quite interested") of the survey questions. Table 13.3 provides the topic that received the highest amount of coverage in each country, along with the percentage of respondents in that country who indicated a high level of interest.

The first observation based on Table 13.3 is that two topic categories take a clear lead as the most prominent categories in foreign news: in five countries—Brazil, China, Germany, Israel, and the United States—the top category was foreign relations between countries; and in five other countries—Canada, Hong Kong, Poland, Singapore, and Switzerland—the top category was internal politics of foreign countries. In the remaining three countries a different topic was most prevalent: sports in Chile, crime in Portugal, and social issues in Taiwan.

A second observation is that the percentage of people considering their country's top news category being highly important was relatively low. Taking all countries together, only 28.6% of the audience members, on average, claimed to be highly interested in the topic that was most prevalent in their country's foreign news reporting. And yet there was considerable variability among the countries, ranging from as low as 12.8% in Poland to a high of 42.8% in Brazil.

The lack of uniformity might be due to the wide variety of topics that appear in first place in the rankings of the foreign news coverage in the different countries. Across all 13 countries, the topic of foreign relations (that is, relations between foreign countries) was the closest to being the more prevalent topic category. One way to examine this issue is by checking whether, in the countries where the topic of foreign relations is *not* as prominent in coverage, there is also less audience interest in it.

Table 13.5 Logistic regression for correspondence between the most prominent topic in the news content and respondents' evaluation of their interest in the topic

	Exp (B)
Gender (1 = Female, 0 = male)	.797***
Age	.991***
Education	NS
Income	NS
General interest in foreign news	2.428***
Days per week viewing TV news	1.069***
Nagelkerke R²	.179
N	7,839

Note: Entries are standardized regression coefficients. Missing cases were deleted pairwise.
* $p < .05$; ** $p < .01$; *** $p < .001$.

Table 13.4 shows that the topic of foreign relations was the leading topic in the foreign news coverage of five countries (second column of the table): Brazil, China, Germany, Israel, and the United States. Some countries, however, presented quite a different picture—for example, Singapore, where foreign relations was only in sixth place. The third column of the table presents the percentage of the foreign relations topic in the content analysis. Here, too, there was much variability, with very large percentages of foreign relations coverage in Brazil (52.5%) and the United States (55.8%), compared with the very low (and virtually identical) percentages in Singapore and Taiwan (9.7% and 9.8%, respectively). The fourth column of the table presents the percentage of survey respondents who said that this topic is of great interest to them.

Using a Spearman rank correlation to calculate the relationship across the 13 countries between the ranking of foreign relations among the seven topic categories (second column) and the percentage of high interest in foreign relations (fourth column), we found a very weak and insignificant relationship ($\rho=.16$). Also, there was no relationship whatsoever across the countries between the percentage of foreign relations (third column) and high interest in that topic (fourth column) with $\rho=.02$.

Individual-Level Predictors of Audience Interest in Foreign News Topics

A question that still remains is: What could possibly influence audience interest in foreign news topics? Is there any indication to be found in this study that signals an effect of watching television news on the viewer's interests? In this section we tackle this question using logistic regression analyses with individual audience member predictors in an attempt to explain the correspondence between topic

Table 13.6 Summary of significant variables in the logistic regression analyses by country

	General interest in foreign news	Amount of TV news viewing	Gender	Education	Age	Income	Nagelkerke R²
Brazil	+	NS	NS	+	NS	+	.261
Canada	+	NS	NS	NS	NS	–	.221
Chile	+	+	–	NS	–	NS	.188
China	+	+	NS	+	NS	NS	.310
Germany	+	+	NS	NS	–	NS	.295
Hong Kong	+	NS	NS	+	NS	NS	.279
Israel	+	+	NS	NS	NS	NS	.203
Poland	+	NS	NS	NS	NS	NA	.273
Portugal	+	NS	NS	NS	NS	NS	.165
Singapore	+	NS	–	NS	NS	NS	.302
Switzerland	+	NS	–	NS	NS	NS	.150
Taiwan	+	NS	+	NS	NS	NS	.178
United States	+	NS	NS	NS	NS	NS	.450

Note: NA = not available because of absence of variable in the country's data (income variable for Poland);
NS: not significant; + : significant positive relationship at $p < .05$; – : significant negative relationship at $p < .05$.

coverage (the topics that are prominent in the foreign news in the viewer's country) and the viewer's interest. We define correspondence as equaling unity, a situation in which the respondent considered the single most important, prevalent foreign news topic in the news coverage as very or quite interesting to him or her (similar to the analysis presented in Table 13.3).

Table 13.5 presents the results of the logistic regression using all respondents from the 13 countries. Two groups of individual-level predictors are entered in this analysis. First, we included socio-demographics: gender (female = 1, male = 0); age (actual age at the time of the survey); education; and income. In addition, as a measure of news media exposure, we used the average number of days per week that the respondents claim to watch TV news. Finally, we used the response to the question about one's overall general interest in foreign news (as distinct from interest in specific topic categories). This variable, similar to the other interest variables, was based on a 5-point scale.

When we consider the entire data set, as in Table 13.5, age appeared as a negative factor. Older people tended to be less interested in the dominant topic in the foreign news content of their country. As for gender, women were 20% less likely to say that they think the dominant topic in foreign news is very or quite interesting to them. Age and income were not significant.

In this analysis the dominant variable by far is general interest in foreign news. Of course, this does not come as a surprise. When an individual is generally interested in foreign news, there is a greater likelihood that she or he would also indicate interest in all or nearly all the specific topics in foreign news. More interestingly, the extent of watching television news turns out to be a significant positive factor. Accordingly, people watching television news more frequently tend to be interested in the dominant topic of foreign news. The question of causality, of course, still remains open, and it cannot be resolved in this analysis. Is there a phenomenon in television news whereby the news makers provide viewers with much information on certain topics, leading to an increased interest in them? Or, alternatively, have television news makers adapted their content to the interest of their viewers?

Since the general regression analysis does not provide any indication on specific country differences, we present Table 13.6. It provides a summary of the significance and direction of the earlier-mentioned variables in the regression conducted for each country.

As expected, general interest in foreign news is clearly a significant factor across the countries. As for watching television news, while the overall analysis (Table 13.5) indicated a significant contribution, it turns out that this is not universal. Only in China, Chile, Germany, and Israel was there a positive contribution of watching TV news; in the other nine countries the frequency of watching television news did not contribute significantly. The age factor was negatively significant in two countries: Chile and Germany. The gender factor returned the same findings as in the general analysis in Chile, Singapore, and Switzerland, while in Taiwan the finding was in the opposite direction. Taiwanese women are more likely to be interested in the dominant news topic in Taiwanese foreign news, which may be partly explained by the fact that the dominant topic in Taiwan was social issues. Finally, education was a positive factor only in China, Hong Kong, and Brazil. In these countries, the higher the respondents' education level, the more likely they are to find interest in the dominant foreign news topic category.

Conclusions

The main conclusion of this exercise in attempting to link content with attitudes is that with regard to domestic news, there is a meaningful correspondence between the topics that are aired in the newscasts and the perceived interest that viewers ascribe to them. Thus the topics that are prominent in domestic news coverage are, generally speaking, also considered interesting by viewers.

With respect to foreign news, however, the picture is more complex, and the correspondence is not universal. There is relatively much variation in the priorities of the topic categories of foreign news coverage. Also, there is considerable variation in terms of the interest expressed by audiences vis-à-vis the topic categories. While people largely agree on social issues and the economy as important issues for domestic news, they agree much less on which topics are interesting in foreign news. In a large number of countries, accidents and disasters are considered the most interesting topic. Many people feel it is more important that foreign news inform them about disasters occurring around the globe than to learn about significant international political and/or economic events. The foreign television news content does not usually seem to match this interest. Thus, the correspondence between content and interest in foreign news is less pervasive than for domestic news, and country differences are clearly more explicit.

The effort to seek individual factors at the country level that could form the base of correspondence between respondents' interest and extensive news coverage about a dominant topic in foreign news offered some indications that there may be a link between them. In some countries, as well as in the overall picture, there is a significant positive link between the frequency of watching television news and the interest of the audience in the topic(s) that are most heavily reported in foreign television news. However, this raises questions this chapter cannot answer. Who drives these possible links? Do the audiences adapt to the topics presented to them in the news, or do the journalists probe their audience's interest and adapt the (foreign) news content that they broadcast? These are questions that can only be answered by means of longitudinal analyses, which are not likely to be conducted in a broad comparative framework because of the very high cost of such an endeavor. Another approach could be to conduct experimental research on foreign news coverage and interest in news topics.

Finally, what seems to be most important to emphasize and reiterate, as we have done at various other points in this volume, is that the great diversity in foreign news topics across the countries, as well as the different levels of interest, all seem to negate the notion of universality. There can be many reasons for specific idiosyncratic differences in the countries we studied—and these surely would have emerged in other countries as well, if they had been included in our project—but space does not permit this, and it was not our intention to explain each case. This may be left to a different time and place.

Summary

In this chapter we linked content and survey data regarding the coverage of news topics and the interest of the audiences in such topics. The main finding is that while for domestic news coverage the correspondence between audience interest and actual news coverage is quite strong in all countries, in many of the countries the foreign coverage of news topics does not fully converge with the topics in which the audience members have a stated interest. The greatest mismatch that appeared in the finding of this chapter was the high public interest in accidents and disasters, in contrast to the relatively low amount of coverage of them in the newscasts of foreign items. In addition, the differences found among the countries in terms of the correspondence between audience interest and news coverage was larger for foreign news than for domestic news. This provides further evidence for the claim against universality of foreign news. It appears, once again, that neither foreign news content or interest expressed in foreign news by audiences, nor the correspondence between these two data sets, seems to fit a global pattern.

CHAPTER FOURTEEN

Linking Content and Audiences

Countries of Interest

FRANCIS LEE, JÜRGEN WILKE, & AKIBA A. COHEN

For decades, news research has repeatedly told us that the countries of the world are not equally newsworthy. The few countries that are the most powerful in the international political economic system, such as the United States, tend to get the most coverage by news media around the world. Beyond the globally powerful countries, news media of a particular nation tend to cover countries that are geographically, culturally, and/or economically proximate (Chang, 1998; Galtung & Ruge, 1965; Wu, 1998, 1998b, 2000). The analysis in Chapter 4 largely replicated this basic characteristic of foreign news based on the data of the current project. Tuchman's (1978) famous metaphor of the "news net," originally developed to make sense of local news, is therefore equally apt for describing foreign news. Covering the world is like casting a net instead of a blanket; most of the time, only the "big fishes" are caught.

Compared to research on news content, there has been less that addresses audience interests in foreign countries. But the few available studies also point to the limited attention scope of the audience. Sparkes and Winter (1980), for instance, found that Americans were more interested in Europe and much less interested in Asia, the Middle East, and Africa, a finding that can be readily understood in terms of cultural proximity and economic relations. An experimental study by Straughan (1989) also showed that geographical proximity can enhance audiences' interest in foreign news stories. Consistent with these previous findings, Chapter 10 showed that citizens from different countries are indeed interested in different groups of foreign nations. Besides global powers such as the United States, news audiences tend to be most interested in their own "giant neighbors." Regionalism, therefore, seems to be as much a factor in determining audience interests as in determining news content.

If research addressing audience interests in foreign countries is rare, then analysis tying news coverage to audience interests in foreign countries is even more rare. The capability of providing such an analysis is a major contribution of the present research project. Therefore, built upon and extending the analysis in Chapters 4 and 10, this chapter aims to examine the relationship between audience interests in and news coverage of foreign countries. We tackle four research questions. First, are the countries covered most frequently in the news also the countries that the audience members are most interested in? That is, what is the level of content-audience correspondence regarding countries of interest? Second, to what extent do levels of content-audience correspondence vary across countries? And what factors could explain such between-countries variations? Third, Chapters 4 and 10 illustrated that both news content and audience interests can be limited to a few foreign countries. Hence, we may ask: at the country level, is concentration in news content related to concentration in audience interests? Finally, given the fact that some countries are prominently covered in the news and some are not, we may ask whether the factors explaining individual-level interests in these two types of countries differ.

Before the analysis begins, mention should be made of two methodological points. First, as already indicated in other chapters, while the content analyses in all countries were based on the same 4 weeks of newscasts in early 2008, the surveys were conducted at different points in time somewhat later (September–October 2009 and June–July 2010). This may lead to a few idiosyncratic results in the survey responses in some countries, especially where the question of countries of interest is concerned. It also means that some "noises" were introduced when we looked for general patterns in the relationship between the content and survey data. Nevertheless, as we will see below, meaningful patterns in our findings can still be discerned despite these potential lacunae.

Second, while we will be examining the correspondence and association between news content and audience interests, there can be various interpretations regarding the causal relationships involved. For example, when a frequently covered country is also prominent in audience interests, it could be the result of the effects of news coverage on audience interests, the result of the effects of audience interests on news coverage, or the result of certain contextual factors—for example, a close economic relationship between the covered and the covering countries—driving both news coverage and audience interests. Of course, it is also possible for all three causal mechanisms to simultaneously play a role in generating a specific association between news content and audience interests. Strictly speaking, the present data do not allow us to disentangle the causal mechanisms involved. But it should not completely prevent us from providing causal interpretations that are conceptually and contextually plausible. Hence, in the following pages, claims involving presumptions of causality may still be made, but they should be understood as plausible interpretations rather than verified statements.

Comparing Content and Audience Interests

The first research question for this chapter asks whether the countries most frequently covered in the news are also the countries that ordinary people are most interested in, and Table 14.1 provides the basis for addressing this question. The table juxtaposes, for each of the 13 countries in which both content analysis and audience survey were conducted, the lists of the top 15 countries in foreign news and the top 15 countries mentioned by audiences in the surveys. For the top 15 countries in foreign news, the lists used in Table 14.1 are based on countries *reported as involved in foreign news items* rather than reported as the location of the events. This choice is based on the presumption that countries reported as involved in foreign news items are more influenced by journalists' news judgments. Journalists cannot determine where important foreign news events occur. But with many foreign news stories, journalists could determine what other countries to include when covering the event (e.g., Lee, Chan, Pan, & So, 2002). Using countries involved instead of location of events, therefore, can give us a better idea of the correspondence between audience interests and journalists' judgment.

A quick glance at Table 14.1 should give one the sense that the "content list" and the "survey list" for a specific country are often quite similar to each other. The content list for Canada, for example, begins with the United States, the United Kingdom, China, Israel, and Afghanistan, and the audience survey list begins in basically the same way, only with Haiti replacing Israel. Similarly, Chile's content list begins with Argentina, the United States, Spain, Brazil, and Colombia, while the first five countries of the audience survey list also include Argentina, the United States, Spain, and Brazil, though with some reshuffling of positions.

To facilitate a more systematic discussion, the information included in Table 14.1 was transformed into a number of indicators of content-audience correspondence. The indicators are summarized in Table 14.2. The first three indicators of content-audience correspondence simply refer to the number of countries that are shared by the top 5, top 10, and top 15 content and audience lists. Take Canada as an example. The top five content and audience lists share the United States, the United Kingdom, China, and Afghanistan. Hence Canada's score on the first column of Table 14.2 is 4. The top 10 content and audience lists of Canada share eight countries in common: the United States, the United Kingdom, China, Afghanistan, Australia, Iraq, Iran, and France. Where the top 15 lists are concerned,

Table 14.1 Top 15 countries in foreign news and mentioned in surveys

Brazil		Canada		Chile	
Content	Survey	Content	Survey	Content	Survey
United States	United States	United States	United States	Argentina	United States
Colombia	Japan	UK	UK	United States	Argentina
Venezuela	France	China	China	Spain	Spain
China#	Italy	Israel	Haiti	Brazil	Peru
Ecuador#	China	Afghanistan	Afghanistan	Colombia	Brazil
France#	Argentina#	Palestine	Iraq	Italy	Bolivia
Israel	Portugal#	France	Iran	UK	Venezuela
Spain*	S. Africa	Australia#	Australia	Venezuela	Mexico
UK*	Germany	Iraq#	India	Mexico	France
Argentina#	Spain	Iran*	France	Ecuador	Germany
East Timor#	UK	Pakistan*	Israel	France	China
Italy#	Mexico	Germany#	Mexico	Peru	Italy
Germany	India	Kenya#	Greece#	Israel	UK
Russia	Uruguay	India*	Japan#	Cuba	Japan
Australia	Bolivia	Nepal*	Germany	China	Colombia

China		Germany		Hong Kong	
Content	Survey	Content	Survey	Content	Survey
United States	United States	United States	United States	United States	United States
Japan#	Japan	UK	France	Japan#	UK
UK#	UK	France	Russia	UK#	Japan
Russia	Russia	Russia	UK	Russia	Australia
Greece	France	Israel	China	India	Canada
Pakistan	S. Korea	Italy	Italy	Australia*	France
France*	Germany	China#	Spain	S. Korea*	S. Korea
Germany*	N. Korea	Norway#	Afghanistan	Israel#	Germany
Switzerland*	Iraq	Palestine*	Austria	Palestine#	Singapore
Belgium#	India	Spain*	Switzerland	France*	Thailand
S. Korea#	Australia	Austria#	Iraq	Iraq*	Russia
Iraq*	Canada	Sweden#	Poland	Afghanistan#	Italy
Serbia*	Iran	Japan	Iran	Egypt#	Iraq
Israel#	Italy	Egypt*	Turkey	Germany#	India#
Italy#	Afghanistan	Iraq*	Israel	Greece#	Israel#

Note: The list is rank-ordered such that the most frequently covered/mentioned country is listed first. In any list, consecutive countries designated either by # or * are "tied," i.e., they received the same amount of coverage in the news or were mentioned equally by the audience in the survey.

Israel, Germany, and India would be added to the picture. Hence Canada scores 11 in the third column of Table 14.2.

Focusing on these three indicators, we can indeed see a generally substantial level of content-audience correspondence in the 13 countries examined. In 8 of the 13 countries, the top five content and audience lists share four countries in common. Only in the United States and Brazil does the figure drop to only two. When the top 15 content and audience lists are considered, the number of countries shared can be as high as 13 (Singapore). Israel has only six. But Israel is an exception, because its audience list actually contains only 10 countries (hence

Table 14.1 Top 15 countries in foreign news and mentioned in surveys (continued)

Israel		Poland		Portugal	
Content	Survey	Content	Survey	Content	Survey
Arab	United States	United States	Germany	United States	France
United States	Arab	Russia	Russia	Spain	Spain
Egypt	France	Ukraine	United States	East Timor	United States
UK	UK	UK	UK	UK	UK
France	Russia	Germany	France	Australia	Germany
Australia#	Egypt	Italy	Ukraine	France	Brazil
Germany#	Turkey	Belarus#	Czech	China	Angola
China	Canada	China#	Italy	Iraq	Italy
India*	Argentina	France#	Slovakia	Serbia	Switzerland
Russia*	Ethiopia	Switzerland	Belarus	Brazil#	Haiti
Switzerland*		Czech*	Netherlands	Italy#	Mozambique
Italy#		Vatican*	Spain	Kosovo#	Belgium
Turkey#		Belgium	Lithuania	Mozambique*	Canada
Greece*		Georgia	Ireland	Russia*	Iraq
S. Korea*		Iraq	China	Colombia	Argentina

Singapore		Switzerland		Taiwan	
Content	Survey	Content	Survey	Content	Survey
China	United States	United States	Germany	United States	United States
United States	China	France	United States	China	Japan
Malaysia	Malaysia	China	France	Hong Kong	China
UK	Indonesia	Germany	Italy	S. Korea	S. Korea
Japan	Japan	UK	Austria	UK	UK
Taiwan	Thailand	Italy	UK	France#	France
Australia#	UK	Israel	China	Japan#	Germany
Hong Kong#	India	Serbia	Russia	Germany	Australia
India	Australia	Palestine	Israel#	Australia	Hong Kong
Spain	Taiwan	Kosovo	Spain#	Russia	Singapore
France	Hong Kong	Russia	Japan	N. Korea*	Philippines#
Thailand	Philippines	Spain	Palestine	Pakistan*	Thailand#
S. Korea	S. Korea	Austria	India*	Belgium#	Vietnam#
Indonesia	France	Australia	Iran*	Bolivia#	Canada
Russia	Vietnam	Egypt	Libya*	Greece#	Russia

United States	
Content	Survey
Iraq	Afghanistan
Israel	UK
Palestine	Iraq
Afghanistan	China
Colombia#	Canada
Venezuela#	Mexico
Ecuador	Germany
China	Israel
Iran*	Iran
UK*	Australia
Egypt	Russia
France#	France
Kenya#	Japan
Australia*	North Korea
Lebanon*	Pakistan

Table 14.2 Summary of content-audience correspondence in countries of interest

	Number of countries in both		
	Top 5 lists of content and audience interests	Top 10 lists of content and audience interests	Top 15 lists of content and audience interests
Brazil	2	5	8
Canada	4	8	11
Chile	4	6	12
China	4	6	9
Germany	4	7	10
Hong Kong	3	6	11
Israel	4	5	6
Poland	4	8	10
Portugal	3	5	8
Singapore	4	8	13
Switzerland	3	7	11
Taiwan	4	9	10
United States	2	6	8

there is simply not a top 15 audience list for Israel). Putting Israel aside, the top 15 content and audience lists for the other 12 nations share at least 8 countries in common.

The generally high level of content-audience correspondence can also be discerned by looking at the number of countries "missing" in one of the lists. By definition, when the top 15 content and audience lists share 11 countries (as in the case of Canada), it means that four countries present in the content list do not appear in the audience list, and vice versa. However, it should be noted that the incomplete correspondence between the content and audience lists could be partly due to some minor variations in the exact positions of specific countries on the lists. Take Taiwan as the example. The top five content and audience lists share four countries in common: the United States, China, South Korea, and the United Kingdom. Hong Kong is the top five content country that goes "missing" in the top five audience list, whereas Japan is the top five audience-interested country that goes "missing" in the top five content list. But in fact Hong Kong ranks ninth on the audience list, and Japan ranks seventh on the content list. In other words, Hong Kong and Japan still rank high in both the content and audience lists. The incomplete correspondence is only a matter of (arguably) inevitable minor variations in the exact positions of the countries on the list.

Therefore, when constructing the scores for "missing countries," we counted the number of top five countries in the content list that do not exist in the top 15 audience list (and vice versa). These missing cases are "real" in the sense that

Table 14.2 Summary of content-audience correspondence in countries of interest (continued)

	Number of "missing countries"	
	Top 5 in news but not in top 15 in survey	Top 5 in survey but not in top 15 in news
Brazil	3	1
Canada	0	1
Chile	0	0
China	1	0
Germany	0	0
Hong Kong	0	1
Israel	0	0
Poland	0	0
Portugal	2	1
Singapore	0	0
Switzerland	0	0
Taiwan	0	0
United States	2	1

they cannot be accounted for by minor differences in the exact positions of the countries on the two lists. As the second half of Table 14.2 shows, when this procedure is adopted, the number of missing countries is very small. In fact, in 9 of the 13 countries examined, the top five countries in the content list would all appear in the top 15 audience list (that is, the number of "missing countries" is zero). Similarly, in 8 of the 13 countries being examined, the top five countries in the audience list would all appear in the top 15 content list, and in the remaining five countries only one top five country in the audience list is missing in the top 15 content list.

Calculated in this way, the second half of Table 14.2 also helps highlight a small number of "special cases" in which a country features very prominently in one list but goes missing in the other. A look at these special cases can help shed light on why news content and audience interests do not completely correspond to each other. First, it is possible that a country would become temporarily prominent in the foreign news of another country because of a special event that ties the two countries together. But the country would fade away in both foreign news content and public consciousness once the special event ends. A good example here is Greece for China. The Chinese news media covered Greece prominently in early 2008 such that Greece ranked fifth on the content list, and this was almost completely due to the 2008 Beijing Olympics (Lee, Chan, & Zhou, 2011). But it can be argued that the Chinese media and public have never been interested in

Greece *per se*. It is actually questionable if Greece would have been high on the audience interests list even if the survey were also conducted in early 2008. What we know for sure from our data is that, when the Chinese public was asked in late 2009 about the countries that interested it, Greece was not in the top 15 list.

Second, an unexpected event can temporarily push an otherwise un-prominent country to the top of people's minds. An example in our current data is Haiti. The Canadian survey was conducted right after the Haitian earthquake in January 2010. As a result, Haiti ranks very high in audience interest in the Canadian survey. But, understandably, the country does not feature in the top 15 content list. The small country of Haiti is usually "invisible" in foreign news, not only in Canada but also around the world.

Third, some countries may occasionally be covered prominently by another country because of special historical, social, or political ties, but the countries may be too small or insignificant to feature constantly and prominently in public consciousness. An example is East Timor for Portugal. In Table 14.1, we see that only the Portuguese media have paid substantial attention to news from East Timor in the sampled period. This, of course, can be readily explained by the countries' ex-colonial relationship. Yet East Timor is, after all, a small and faraway place in Southeast Asia. In fact, the Portuguese did show some interest in some of their ex-colonies, but they tended to pick the countries that are bigger and closer to them—Brazil, Angola, and Mozambique (Table 14.1)—as places of concern.

Fourth, and turning the above situation on its head, it is also possible for a country to feature very regularly in another country's public consciousness because of special historical, social, or political ties, but there may not be important news flowing from that country on a day-to-day basis, and hence the country might not regularly feature very prominently in news content. An example is Canada for Hong Kong. Hong Kong respondents reported high levels of interest in Canada because of the waves of migration from Hong Kong to Canada in the 1980s and 1990s. As a result, many Hong Kong residents have friends and family members living in Canada. However, it does not mean that the Hong Kong media would report a huge amount of news about Canada. Hong Kong media are heavily reliant on international news agencies, and it is plausible that a news item about Canada, when compared to a news item about another country, is more likely to be picked up by the Hong Kong media. But the amount of news about Canada on any given day might be limited to begin with. Therefore, the sheer amount of news about Canada may still be small.

The above findings, when taken together, suggest why complete content-audience correspondence is highly unlikely. What features in news content and what interests the public are both subject to a certain degree of fluctuation, depending on current events, and there can be situations when people are interested in the events happening in a country without being interested in the country itself.

But in one sense, the presence of these factors makes the generally high levels of content-audience correspondence even more remarkable.

Table 14.3 Content-survey correspondence as measured by Spearman rank correlations

	Rank order correlations
Brazil	−.041
Canada	.492**
Chile	.467*
China	.379*
Germany	.521**
Hong Kong	.392*
Israel	.449**
Poland	.611***
Portugal	.105
Singapore	.688***
Switzerland	.671***
Taiwan	.690***
United States	.018

Note: Rank order correlation between most frequently covered countries and most frequently mentioned countries by citizens was calculated based on the top 15 lists. * $p < .10$; ** $p < .05$; *** $p < .01$.

Notably, while Table 14.2 has provided some indicators of overall levels of content-audience correspondence based on counts, the counts by themselves do not provide us with a means of examining whether the correspondence between news content and audience interests is statistically significant or not for each of the 13 countries. To provide a test of statistical significance, we calculated the rank order correlation between the top 15 content and audience lists for each country.[1]

Table 14.3 summarizes the results. It shows that the content and audience lists are indeed significantly and positively correlated with each other in 10 of the 13 cases. Table 14.3, therefore, further confirms the statement that news content generally corresponds to audience interests in most of the countries being examined.

Before moving on to the next section, it should be noted that there are other ways to examine the lists in Table 14.1 that we will not fully explore here. One method of additional analysis would be to look at whether some countries are ranked consistently higher in the various countries' content lists than in the corresponding audience lists, or vice versa. For example, the United Kingdom ranks fourth on the content list of Singapore but only seventh on the audience list. Hence it ranks higher in the former. Across the 13 countries analyzed, the United

Kingdom ranks higher in the content list in five countries (Singapore, Germany, Switzerland, Chile, and Brazil), but it ranks higher in the audience list than in the content list in only two countries (Hong Kong and the United States). In the other six countries, the rankings of the United Kingdom on the two lists are exactly the same. It means that the United Kingdom is more likely to be "over-reported" than "under-reported" among the 13 countries being examined. Even more likely to be "over-reported" is Israel: Putting Israel itself aside, Israel ranks higher in the content list than in the audience list in 8 of the other 12 countries, while it simply does not exist in both the content and audience list in the other 4 countries.

On the other hand, France ranks higher in the audience list than in the content list in 8 of the 13 countries (Portugal, Poland, Israel, Hong Kong, Germany, China, Chile, and Brazil). It ranks higher in the content list than in the audience list in only three countries (Switzerland, Singapore, and Canada). Hence France is more likely to be "under-reported" than "over-reported." In any case, we do not fully elaborate on this issue of under- or over-reporting of various countries partly because of space concerns, and partly because of the focus of this chapter on overall levels of content-audience correspondence. But this is an issue that could be further and more systematically examined.

Explaining between-Countries Variations in Content-Audience Correspondence

While the previous section has emphasized that there is a generally high degree of content-audience correspondence in countries of interest, Tables 14.2 and 14.3 have also shown that there are between-countries variations in levels of content-audience correspondence. In Table 14.3, the rank order correlation is insignificant in Brazil, the United States, and Portugal, and Table 14.2 shows that these three countries also have lower counts in number of countries shared by the top 15 lists and higher counts in "missing countries." At the other end, Singapore, Switzerland, and Taiwan have the highest rank order correlation coefficients in Table 14.3, and they also have higher counts in number of countries shared by the top 15 lists and lower counts in "missing countries."

How can we explain such between-countries variations? One way of tackling this question is to look at each country in-depth and explain how and why it has a high or low level of content-audience correspondence. For example, Singapore, as just mentioned, is one of the countries that exhibit the highest levels of content-audience correspondence. If we take a closer look at the top 15 lists in Table 14.1, we see that both the content and audience lists of Singapore show a very high level of regionalism. If we take "East, Southeast, and South Asia" as the "region" for Singapore, then we can say that 9 of the 15 most frequently covered countries are from the region, and there are 11 countries from the region in the audience list. The importance of regionalism to both news content and audience interests is a key factor contributing to the high level of content-audience correspondence.

Yet this is not the end of the story: the similarity between the content and audience lists for Singapore resides not only in the overall degree of regionalism, but also in how countries from within the region are ranked. If we focus only on countries from the region, the most frequently covered countries in Singaporean newscasts are ranked as follows: China, Malaysia, Japan, Taiwan, Hong Kong, India, Thailand, South Korea, and Indonesia. The countries that Singaporeans are most interested in, meanwhile, are ranked as follows: China, Malaysia, Indonesia, Japan, Thailand, India, Taiwan, Hong Kong, the Philippines, South Korea, and Vietnam. What is notable is the close correspondence between these two lists. With the exception of Indonesia, the ranks of each country on the two lists are highly similar. Vietnam and the Philippines are absent in the top 15 content list, but the two are ranked very low in the top 15 audience list anyway. Also, one should note that some countries, despite being in the same region as Singapore, are *absent* in both lists: Burma, Cambodia, Pakistan, Nepal, and North Korea. In other words, a high level of regionalism does not assure high and equal levels of attention to all countries in the region. The content-audience correspondence in Singapore is also based, therefore, on the fact that journalists and citizens share the same judgment regarding which countries from within the region are relatively more important. This similarity in judgment is arguably rooted in the precise geographical position of Singapore in the region, as well as the ethnic makeup of the country.[2]

In contrast to Singapore, Brazil is one of the countries with the lowest levels of content-audience correspondence. Interestingly, a close look at Table 14.1 shows that the Brazilian media and audience seem to have exhibited relatively lower levels of regionalism. If we take Central and South America as Brazil's region, then the top 15 content list features only Colombia, followed by Venezuela, Ecuador, and Argentina, whereas the top 15 audience list features only Argentina, Mexico, Uruguay, and Bolivia. Besides the fact that only a small number of countries in the region are featured, it is notable that, in sharp contrast to Singapore, the news media and the audience have picked up different countries from the region to be concerned about (except for Argentina). If we do not compare the content and audience lists, the news content's focus on Colombia and Venezuela would have made very good sense, because the two countries border northern Brazil. Also, the audience's interests in Uruguay and Bolivia would also have made very good sense, because the two countries border southern Brazil. But when the two lists are compared and contrasted, the difference in how selective attention within the region was exercised by the media and by the audience becomes apparent, and this difference is one of the sources of the overall low level of content-audience correspondence in the Brazilian case.

While we can continue to present and compare findings among the individual countries, doing so would take up too much space in this chapter. More important, while discussion of each specific country could help generate country-specific and context-sensitive explanations for the findings in Tables 14.2 and 14.3, it might not help generate generalizable explanations for the between-countries variations in content-audience correspondence. Another approach to explaining the between-countries variations is to examine whether levels of content-audience correspondence would associate with certain country-level characteristics.

Without an established theory about what could explain content-audience correspondence, this chapter provides an exploratory analysis that tests three arguments. First, we are interested in the relationship between level of content-audience correspondence and the size of the countries (in geographical and population terms). In general—and with all other things being equal—it might be easier for journalists in smaller countries to understand what their audiences are interested in. Singapore and Brazil may be used again as the contrast. In Singapore, it should be relatively easy for journalists to assess what the four million people in the small city-state want to know and need to know about the world. The population is literally closer to the journalists and is related to the outside world in more or less the same way. On the other hand, it is likely to be more difficult for the news media in Rio de Janeiro or São Paulo to assess the interests of the audience of the entire Brazilian nation. The population is dispersed over a huge area, and as a result it can relate to the "outside world" in quite different ways. Therefore, we contend that the level of content-audience correspondence is likely to be higher in smaller countries.

Second, we suggest that there should be a *lower* level of content-audience correspondence in countries that have a higher percentage of foreign-born citizens. To the extent that a country has a high proportion of migrants, the country's population can be considered more diverse, and it may be relatively more difficult for journalists to understand the concerns and interests of the population as a whole.

Third, we theorize that there would be a positive correlation between content-audience correspondence and the audience's interests in foreign news in general. To the extent that the audience of a country is highly interested in foreign news, the news media are also likely to put more effort into making sure that they cover the "right type" of foreign news. In other words, when audiences' interest in foreign news is higher, the news media would also have stronger incentives to provide the foreign news that people are indeed interested in. Hence there should be a higher level of content-audience correspondence.

To test the three arguments above, information about population and geographical sizes of the 13 countries was obtained from various online archives. The data for percentage of foreign-born citizens and for audience interests in foreign news were derived from the surveys of the present project. Audience interest in foreign news is simply the average score for each country on the item asking people the extent to which they are interested in foreign news in general (see Chapter 9). Percentage of foreign-born citizens was based on the survey question about the respondent's birthplace. The question was not included in the Brazilian survey, though. Hence the correlation between percentage of foreign-born citizens and content-audience correspondence was tested based on the other 12 countries.

For content-audience correspondence, we employ as the measure the rank order correlation coefficients reported in Table 14.3. As noted earlier, presumably all items in Tables 14.2 and 14.3 can be treated as indicators of content-audience correspondence. But we adopt only the rank order correlation coefficient in Table 14.3 partly for simplicity, and partly based on the consideration that, compared with the counts in Table 14.2, the rank order correlation coefficients have taken in more information from the content and audience lists. Hence it should be a more legitimate measure of overall levels of content-audience correspondence.

Table 14.4 Predictors of country-level content-audience correspondence

	Correlation with content-audience correspondence
Population	−.53*
Geographical size of country	−.57**
% born in foreign countries	.04
Audience interests in foreign news	.45

Note: Entries are Spearman rank order correlations. * $p < .07$; ** $p < .05$. N = 13 for all except % born in foreign countries, for which N = 12.

With the measures established, Table 14.4 shows the correlation between content-audience correspondence and the proposed predictors.[3]

There is indeed a significant relationship between geographical size and content-audience correspondence. The direction of the relationship is consistent with our expectation: level of content-audience correspondence is higher in smaller countries. At the same time, there is a similarly negative and close-to-significant relationship between population size and content-audience correspondence. Therefore, our argument about the implication of size on content-audience correspondence is quite strongly supported by Table 14.4.

Meanwhile, the relationship between percentage of foreign-born citizens and content-audience correspondence is close to zero and hence negligible. The relationship between audience interests in foreign news and content-audience correspondence also fails to achieve the conventional level of significance. But given the small sample size, it is difficult for the correlation coefficient to reach the conventional level of statistical significance. Taking this consideration into account, the coefficient is highly suggestive because it is substantial in size ($pho = .45$, $p <$

.13) and is consistent with our expectation in direction: level of content-audience correspondence tends to be higher in countries where the general public is more interested in foreign news.

Concentration of News Coverage and Concentration of Audience Interests

After examining the correspondence between countries covered in the news and countries that attract audience interests, the next research question is concerned with whether level of concentration of news coverage is associated with concentration of audience interests. Utilizing a measure of country-concentration index and focusing on location of events, Chapter 4 shows that the 10 most frequently covered countries could account for between 54% (Germany) to as much as 96% (Japan) of the foreign news reported by the media from a specific country. Likewise, using the same country-concentration index, Chapter 10 shows that the 10 countries that attracted the most audience interest can account for between 62.6% (United States) and 99.8% (Israel) of audience mentions of countries.[4]

If we examine the association between the two sets of figures—CCI (10) for content and CCI (10) for audience interests, we would see that the rank order correlation is merely 0.05. It is negligible and obviously far from being statistically significant.

However, when used to address the present research question, CCI (10) has a limitation: it is arguably more useful in illustrating the commonalities rather than the variations between the countries in terms of their levels of country concentration in news content or audience interests. For example, if we focus only on the 13 countries involved in this chapter, the CCI (10) for content for the 13 countries would range from 54% to 76%, and, actually, 8 of the 13 countries would have a CCI (10) between 71% and 76%. The between-countries variations are very limited. The figures are therefore useful in illustrating the fact that, for most countries, the 10 most frequently covered countries in foreign news would capture about 70% of all foreign news items. But the CCI (10) may not be a good indicator when we are concerned with between-countries variations. The same applies to CCI (10) for audience interests—9 of the 13 countries have a score between 81.6 and 88.7. The indicator is useful in illustrating the fact that, in most countries, the absolute majority of audience mentions would refer to the same 10 countries. But there is little useful between-countries variance for analysis.

It is exactly for this reason that Chapter 7 utilized a CCI (4)—that is, a country concentration index calculated based on the four most frequently covered countries—in its analysis of the difference between public and private television stations in terms of their country concentration. We therefore also recreate a set of CCI (4) for both content and audience interests, and the figures are summarized in the first two columns of Table 14.5. The variances in both columns are relatively more substantial. The CCI (4) for content (based on countries reported as involved in foreign news rather than the countries of location of events) ranges from 31.2% (Germany) to 64.1% (Israel), whereas the CCI (4) for audience interests ranges from 34.5% (United States) to 80.6% (Israel). The correlation between the two sets of figures would become substantially more positive, though it still falls short of being statistically significant because of the limited sample size (rho = .37, p < .22).

Table 14.5 Content-survey correspondence in country concentration

	CCI (4)		No of countries > 5% mention	
	In news	In survey	In news	In survey
Brazil	38.3%	54.9%	9	10
Canada	54.3%	59.1%	6	9
Chile	39.1%	49.1%	10	14
China	31.3%	61.5%	7	11
Germany	31.2%	49.0%	10	14
Hong Kong	46.3%	70.9%	7	8
Israel	64.1%	80.6%	4	6
Poland	50.6%	51.6%	6	12
Portugal	41.0%	55.0%	6	11
Singapore	41.2%	58.2%	8	12
Switzerland	36.3%	67.8%	9	8
Taiwan	56.4%	79.9%	5	6
United States	48.1%	34.5%	9	21

Note: The percentages in the first two columns refer to the percentages of all country mentions (in news coverage or in survey) accounted for by the four most frequently mentioned countries. The figures in the last two columns refer to the number of countries that were mentioned by 5% or more of the foreign news items and respondents in the surveys respectively.

To further explore the possible association between concentration in news coverage and in audience interests, we created one additional indicator related to the concern of concentration in news coverage by counting the number of countries that were reported to be involved in 5% or more of the foreign news items in a country's newscasts. More precisely, this is an indicator of diversity in news coverage: larger numbers mean more countries were mentioned reasonably frequently in the news. Similarly, an indicator of diversity in audience interests was produced by counting the number of countries mentioned by 5% or more of the respondents in a country's survey. The figures are presented in the last two columns of Table 14.5. There are substantial variations among the 13 countries. When news content is concerned, only 4 countries were featured in more than

5% of the news items in Israeli newscasts, while 10 countries were featured in more than 5% of news items in Chile and Germany. Diversity of audience interests varies even more strongly, ranging from as few as 6 countries (in Israel and Taiwan) to as many as 21 (in the United States).

More important, the figures in the last two columns of Table 14.5 are indeed significantly and highly positively related to each other ($rho = .76$, $p < .01$). That is, the larger the number of countries mentioned reasonably frequently in foreign news, the larger the number of countries mentioned reasonably frequently by the general public as countries of interest. The relationship is graphically presented in Figure 14.1.[5]

Figure 14.1 Relationship between concentration in news coverage and concentration in audience interest

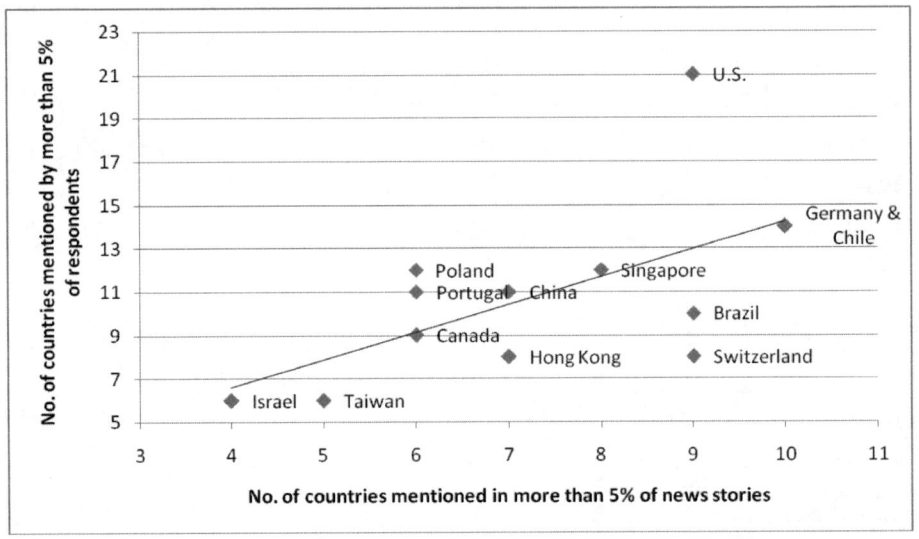

Summarizing the findings, we can argue that there is indeed evidence pointing toward an association between concentration in news coverage and concentration in audience interests, though this association is discernible only when indicators sensitive to between-countries variances are used. As pointed out at the beginning of the chapter, the data would not allow us to ascertain the causal direction involved in an association. To the extent that news coverage of a country can generate audience interests in that country (McNelly, 1962; Wanta, Golan, & Lee, 2004), it is plausible that the narrowness of news coverage has prevented the audience from becoming interested in a wider range of countries. Yet it is also possible that the narrowness of audience interests would lead the news media to follow suit.

Individual-Level Predictors of Audience Interests in Foreign Countries

Our last research question asks what factors would explain audience interests in foreign countries at the individual level. Given the existing data and the discussion in the previous sections, the following analysis is particularly interested in whether the factors explaining audience interests in the most prominently covered countries would be the same as or different from the factors explaining audience interests in less prominently covered countries. Presumably, some factors—such as overall interest in foreign affairs and educational levels—are likely to explain both interests in prominently covered countries and interests in the not prominently covered ones. Highly educated people or people who are highly interested in foreign news in general should be more knowledgeable about the world, and they should simply be more likely to name any country in the world as a country that they are interested in.

However, some factors may explain particular interest in the most prominently covered countries. The clearest example is television news viewing. Given the tendency of television news to concentrate on a few prominent countries, viewing television news—if it has an impact on audience interests at all—is likely to lead to interests limited mainly to those few countries.

In contrast, there can also be factors that explain special interest in less prominently covered countries. Recent research on audience interests in foreign affairs has suggested that individuals' connections with the outside world can generate interests in foreign news (Lee et al., 2012). By the same logic, it is likely that personal connections with a foreign country (such as having friends living in that country) would be one of the most important predictors of interest. Indeed, if one has personal connections with a foreign country, then one's interest in that country is likely to be independent of whether the country is in the news or not. On a practical level it is difficult to measure an individual's connections to each and every specific country in the world. But on a more general level, two possible indicators of personal connections with foreign countries are whether the person is a new migrant to his or her current country of residence, and whether she or he has lived abroad for a significant period of time (these two are not redundant, as non-migrants can also have the experience of working or studying abroad for a significant period of time). Migrants and people who have lived abroad are much more likely to have personal connections with certain foreign countries that may or may not be prominent in the news; hence they should be more likely to name a country that is not prominent in the news as a country in which they are interested.

Given the above considerations, a series of multivariate regression analyses were conducted. The dependent variables are the number of most prominently covered countries mentioned by an individual, and the number of not prominently covered countries mentioned by an individual. Here, "most prominently covered countries" refers to the five most frequently mentioned countries in a nation's foreign news, whereas "not prominently covered countries" refers to all countries outside the 10 most frequently mentioned countries in a nation's foreign news. In other words, we did not count countries ranked between 6th and 10th on the content list. This was done in order to create a clearer distinction between what constitutes "prominently covered" and what constitutes "not prominently covered." To use a concrete example to illustrate the operationalization: if a respondent in the Canadian survey named the United States, the United Kingdom, Australia, and Spain as the countries that she is interested in, then based on the "content list" of Canada in Table 14.1, her score on "number of most prominently covered countries mentioned" would be 2 (the United States and the United Kingdom), and her score on "number of not prominently covered countries mentioned" would be 1 (Spain, which is simply not on the list). Australia, which ranks 8th on the content list, is not counted as either variable.

The independent variables in the regression model include four demographics (age, gender, education, and income); general interests in foreign news; days per week viewing television news; a dummy variable representing whether the person has the experience of living abroad for 6 months or longer; and a dummy variable representing whether the person is a migrant who has moved to his or her current home country within the past 25 years.[6]

Table 14.6 Regression on number of most prominent and less prominent countries mentioned (U.S. data)

	Number of most prominent countries mentioned	Number of less prominent countries mentioned
Gender	.04	.05
Age	.16***	−.07
Education	−.05	.05
Income	−.03	−.01
Interest in foreign news	.17***	.20***
Days per week viewing TV news	.06	.05
Lived abroad	−.15***	.10**
Migrant within 25 years	−.09*	.07*
Adjusted R²	8.2%***	8.1%***
N	755	755

Note: Entries are standardized regression coefficients. Missing cases were deleted pairwise. * $p < .05$; ** $p < .01$; *** $p < .001$.

The regression analyses were conducted for each country separately. Table 14.6 summarizes the results of the analysis based on the U.S. data. The first column shows that older Americans tended to specify a larger number of the most prominently covered countries as those they were interested in. And, consistent with the argument made earlier, interest in foreign news in general is positively related to both dependent variables. Television news viewing also has a positive coefficient in both columns, but both fail to reach the conventional level of statistical significance. Most interesting is that experiences of living abroad and being a migrant are significantly related to both dependent variables, yet the relationships are in contrasting directions. In line with our expectation, migrants and people who have lived abroad were likely to have named a larger number of not prominently covered countries as countries they were interested in. At the same time, they were also likely to have named a smaller number of the most prominently covered countries as countries they were interested in.

Rather than presenting the complete results for each country, Table 14.7 summarizes the major findings from the regression analyses on "number of most prominently covered countries mentioned" (age, gender, and income are omitted from the table for the sake of simplicity and clarity). The table shows that interest in foreign news significantly and positively relates to the number of most prominently covered countries mentioned in 12 of the 13 countries. In addition, education is also a significant predictor of the dependent variable in 9 of the 13 countries.

Table 14.7 Summary of regression analysis on number of most prominently covered countries mentioned

	Education	Interest in foreign news	TV news viewing	New migrants	Lived abroad
Brazil	+	+	+	NA	NA
Canada	NS	NS	NS	NS	NS
Chile	+	+	NS	NS	NS
China	+	+	+	NA	NS
Germany	NS	+	NS	NS	NS
Hong Kong	NS	+	NS	NS	NS
Israel	NS	+	NS	–	NS
Poland	+	+	NS	NA	NS
Portugal	+	+	+	NS	NS
Singapore	+	+	NS	NS	NS
Switzerland	+	+	+	NS	NS
Taiwan	+	+	NS	NS	NS
United States	+	+	NS	–	–

Note: NA = not applicable because of absence of variable in the country's data; NS = not significant; + = significant positive relationship at $p < .05$; – = significant negative relationship at $p < .05$.

The findings in Table 14.7 only partly confirm our expectation regarding the impact of television news viewing that is related to the number of most prominently covered countries in only 4 of the 13 countries, but in all four cases the relationship is indeed positive in direction. Finally, being a migrant and having the experience of living abroad do not relate to the number of most prominently covered countries mentioned. In fact, the U.S. findings shown in the first column of Table 14.6 turn out to be the exception. Besides the United States, there is only one significantly negative relationship, in Israel, between being a migrant and number of most prominently covered countries mentioned.

What about the number of not prominently covered countries mentioned? Table 14.8 summarizes the regression analyses. Same as in Table 14.7, interest in foreign news significantly and positively relates to the dependent variable in 12 of the 13 countries. Education, however, is not an important predictor of the number of not prominently covered countries mentioned, as a significant positive relationship exists only in Chile and Portugal. This suggests that while education may lead people to become more interested in "the world," it actually may not lead people to become interested in a more diverse range of foreign countries.

Table 14.8 Summary of regression analysis on number of not prominently covered countries mentioned

	Education	Interest in foreign news	TV news viewing	New migrants	Lived abroad
Brazil	NS	+	NS	NA	NA
Canada	NS	+	NS	+	NS
Chile	+	+	−	NS	NS
China	NS	+	NS	NA	NS
Germany	NS	+	NS	NS	NS
Hong Kong	NS	+	NS	NS	NS
Israel	NS	+	NS	NS	NS
Poland	NS	+	NS	NA	NS
Portugal	+	+	+	NS	+
Singapore	NS	NS	NS	NS	NS
Switzerland	NS	+	−	+	NS
Taiwan	NS	+	NS	NS	NS
United States	NS	+	NS	+	+

Note: NA = not applicable because of absence of variable in the country's data; NS = not significant; + = significant positive relationship at $p < .05$; − = significant negative relationship at $p < .05$.

Not surprisingly, television news viewing does not have a consistently significant and positive relationship with the number of not prominently covered countries mentioned. A significant positive relationship exists only in the case of Portugal. Interestingly, the impact of television news viewing on the number of not prominently covered countries mentioned is even significantly negative in Switzerland and Chile. It should be noted that, in these two cases, the negative relationships are indeed highly statistically significant ($\beta = -.11$, $p = .001$ in both Chile and Switzerland). Hence the possibility of type I error is small. In other words, there is strong evidence suggesting that, at least in some national contexts, viewing television news can actually narrow people's interests in foreign countries.

Lastly, the expectation that migrants and people who have lived abroad are likely to name a larger number of countries not prominent in the news is only weakly supported. The number of significant relationships indicated in the last two columns of Table 14.8 is small—only 5 of 22 tests. But all five relationships consistently point in the same direction.

It should be noted that one reason for the lack of a stronger and more consistent impact of foreign living experiences and migrant status is the fact that, in some countries, the migrants actually come primarily from the countries that are most prominent in the news. For example, while Singapore has a significant proportion of migrants, many of them actually came from Malaysia and China—two of the top five countries in foreign news content. By the same token, Singaporeans who have the experience of living abroad may actually have lived in China, Malaysia, or the United States. In this case, it is reasonable that, in Singapore, being a migrant or having foreign living experience would not lead a person to name a larger number of not prominently covered countries. In other words, migration and foreign living experience have limited explanatory power, partly because the variables are not sensitive to exactly where the respondents had such personal connections. Taking this into account, Table 14.8 can be considered to be highly suggestive of the importance of personal connections to whether people would be interested in a country not frequently covered in the news.

Conclusion

This chapter examines the linkage between news content and audience responses by focusing on countries of interest. The analysis shows a generally high level of correspondence between news content and audience interests. That is, the countries featured prominently in a nation's news content also tend to be the countries that citizens in the nation are interested in. This content-audience correspondence should not be surprising. Decades of agenda-setting research has shown that the media are highly persuasive when telling people what issues to think about; by the same token, the media are likely to be persuasive in telling people which countries to think about as well (Wanta et al., 2004). At the same time, the media and journalists in many countries are likely to have a good sense of which countries their audience members are interested in. This is partly because professional journalists are, after all, members of their society, and partly because some of the most important principles determining audience interests in foreign countries—for example, the fact that people are likely to be interested in countries that are culturally and geographically proximate—are quite well known and predictable.

Accordingly, we may contend that news content and audience interests mutually reinforce each other in generating distinctive "national worldviews." Chapters 4 and 10 have already pointed out that globalization has not led to the homogenization of news content and audience interests when countries of interest are concerned. Here we may add that an important factor leading to the persistence of distinctive "national worldviews" is how media representations and audience perceptions reconfirm each other.

Certainly, this chapter also shows that content-audience correspondence is by no means complete. Both content and audience interests can be subjected to fluctuations based on the prominence of various current events. More important, levels of content-audience correspondence can vary across countries, and our analysis has shown that such between-countries variations in content-audience correspondence are not idiosyncratic. There are country-level factors that can account for the variations. We have shown that content-audience correspondence is higher in smaller countries, where journalists may find it easier to grasp the interests of the audience. At the same time, there is also evidence suggesting that content-audience correspondence is higher in countries where people are more interested in foreign news.

Either way, this chapter's analysis of the factors behind level of content-audience correspondence is only exploratory. Future studies can construct better measures and/or a more systematic theoretical framework to explain country-level content-audience correspondence. As for a concrete example, this chapter posited that the percentage of foreign-born citizens might explain content-audience correspondence, because content-audience correspondence may be weaker in a country that is ethnically more diverse. While the empirical analysis shows that the relationship between percentage of foreign-born citizens and content-audience correspondence is negligible, it nonetheless does not suggest that ethnic diversity does not matter at all. Rather, it is possible that the percentage of foreign-born citizens is not a good indicator of ethnic diversity. As noted, for example, Singapore has a high percentage of migrants, but the migrants often came from China and Malaysia, and Singapore is a primarily Chinese-plus-Malay society to begin with. The same applies to Hong Kong, where non-locally born citizens are mostly Chinese from the mainland. Therefore, a measure that more directly captures a country's ethnic diversity may come up with different results.

In addition, future analyses can also examine whether the level of content-audience correspondence would be affected by characteristics of the media system. For instance, it is plausible that a more commercialized media system in which the media have stronger pressure to cater to audience interests would exhibit a higher level of content-audience correspondence. Besides, it is also possible that content-audience correspondence may be lower when a news media outlet is heavily reliant on international news agencies instead of its own foreign correspondents for foreign news. This is because the foreign news content would reflect the journalists' own judgment to a relatively lesser extent when a news organization relies on international news agencies.

Last, the analysis in this chapter also informs us about certain possible consequences of the concentration of foreign news on a limited number of foreign countries. At the country level, concentration of news content is positively related to concentration of audience interests. Although the causal direction can go both ways, the finding at least suggests the plausibility that a high level of country concentration in news would narrow the range of countries that the audience members would become interested in. In fact, this latter possibility is supported by the individual-level analysis. Television news viewing does not have an across-the-board impact on people's interest in foreign countries. But the few significant findings show that television news viewing, when effective, tends to generate interest mainly in those foreign countries that are prominently covered in foreign news. And in some national contexts, television news viewing could even undermine people's interest in foreign countries that are not prominently covered in the news.

The normative implications of concentration of content and audience interests can be complicated. When television news covers a wide range of countries, it might mean that each of the counties is covered only in a relatively shallow manner. When television news covers only a few countries, more information would be available and people might gain a deeper understanding of those countries. What our analysis shows is that audience interests and content do, in fact, largely correspond to each other. Therefore, those who are concerned with the narrowness of people's interests in foreign affairs should also be deeply concerned with the narrowness of the media's coverage of foreign affairs.

Summary

This chapter linked the data of news content and audience survey responses concerning the countries of interest. The chapter attempted to answer two major questions. First, what is the degree of correspondence between news content and audience interests, that is, within any given nation, are the foreign countries that people are most interested in also the foreign countries that appear most frequently in foreign news? Second, are there variations in the degree of content-audience correspondence across nations and, if so, what factors may explain such variations? The analysis finds that there is indeed a generally high level of correspondence between news content and audience interests. This finding suggests that the content of foreign news and the attitudes and beliefs of the audience can reinforce each other in generating distinctive "national worldviews." And yet the level of content-audience correspondence does vary across countries. The analysis shows that content-audience correspondence is higher in smaller countries, where journalists and editors may find it easier to grasp the interests of the audience. At the same time, there is also evidence that suggests that content-audience correspondence is higher in countries where, overall, people are more interested in foreign news.

Notes

1. More precisely, the calculation was based on a list of countries derived from the top 15 content and audience lists. The list for calculation contains all countries that appear either on the content list or on the audience list. Therefore, the list for calculation would have exactly 15 countries if the content and audience lists completely overlap, and it would have 30 countries if the content and audience lists do not share any country at all. Neither extreme scenario exists in the present case. The actual length of the lists ranges from 17 (for Singapore) to 22 (for the United States, Portugal, and Brazil).
2. Malaysia is the only country bordering Singapore, and the Singaporean population is composed primarily of Chinese, followed by Malays and Indians.
3. Rank order correlations were calculated because of the small number of cases involved.
4. Based on Table 14.1 of the present chapter, the CCI (10) for audience interests for Israel would be 100%. The slight difference between Table 14.1 of this chapter and Chapter 10 is due to a recoding procedure adopted in the present chapter, which includes Syria and Iran in the broader category "Arab (except Egypt)."
5. It should be noted that, because rank order correlation instead of Pearson r was calculated, the fact the United States constitutes an outlier on the vertical axis in Figure 14.1 does not heavily influence the correlation analysis reported here.
6. We counted as migrants only those people who moved to their current home countries within the past 25 years, because a migrant is likely to become assimilated into the new country over time. People who migrated to their current home countries 30 or 40 years ago may not be different from the "natives" at all. On the other hand, the number of migrants in many countries would become very small if we restrict migrants to those who have moved to their current home countries within 10 or 15 years. Hence 25 is chosen as the cutoff point.

CHAPTER FIFTEEN
Overall Conclusions for Individual Countries

ALL PROJECT PARTICIPANTS

In the following pages we present brief summaries of our findings for the 17 countries. As described in the preceding chapters, all the countries participated in the content analysis. Thirteen countries conducted surveys, though in-depth interviews with foreign news gatekeepers were done in only 12 of the countries. Each of the summaries, which are listed alphabetically by country, presents a brief description of the television broadcasting system in the respective country and the main domestic news items that were aired during the sample period of the content analysis. This is followed by highlights, selected by the country teams, of the findings of the content analysis. Finally, the summaries of the countries that also conducted the survey contain some of the highlights. The summaries do not include information obtained in the course of the in-depth interviews with the gatekeepers. Because of space constraints, no references or sources are provided in this chapter.

Belgium (Kunt De Swert & Ruud Wouters)

In this study Belgium refers to Flanders, the largest (northern, Dutch-speaking) community in the country. The majority of the Belgian population lives in Flanders, which has a very distinct media system due to linguistic and cultural differences from the southern, French-speaking community. Thus it would be misleading to treat Belgium as a single country from a media perspective.

News and information on national television in Flanders is based on a duopoly. On one hand, the strong public service broadcaster (VRT) depends mostly on state subsidies, and it must comply with certain requirements set by the Flemish government every 5 years. On the other hand, its single commercial competitor, VTM, has been in the television news market since 1989. The introduction of a national television news broadcast has had an important impact on the content of news and dynamics of public broadcasting. The duopoly has led to a major conversion of both national news programs, and both now closely follow each other's policy and content while maintaining their own profiles. When it comes to resources for producing news, the public broadcaster clearly outweighs its commercial competitor. Although no precise information is available, based on its corps of foreign correspondents and information derived from interviews with the editors in chief, it is clear that the public broadcaster has greater resources.

During the research phase (early 2008), the main general newscast of the public channel VRT had a market share of 40%, which represented about 900,000 viewers on an average weekday. The flagship news broadcast of the commercial broadcaster VTM had around a 28% market share, representing about 630,000 daily viewers. The news audience in Belgium is on the rise, a trend at odds with most international data.

Several major events occurred in Belgium during the content analysis period of the study. The main event was the negotiations to form a government, which lasted 9 months and ended on March 20, 2008. During the process, a leading candidate for new prime minister, Yves Leterme, was hospitalized with health problems. In December 2007, a young female police officer, Kitty Van Nieuwenhuyze, was brutally killed on duty, causing a small media storm in Belgium. Several suspects were arrested in January 2008, with continued news coverage. Another story that attracted media attention was the case of Belliraj, a Belgian-Moroccan terrorist/criminal who was discovered to have been an important informant for the Belgian National Security Bureau for years. And March 27, 2008, marked the beginning of the trial of Michel Fourniret, the French serial killer who was accused of killing many Belgian victims. This event was preceded by several days of pre-trial coverage. Finally, on March 19, 2008, the well-known Flemish writer Hugo Claus chose to end his life through an approved euthanasia procedure. The event sparked controversy, and the coverage included not only his death but also his funeral.

Belgian television news presented approximately 36% purely foreign news, slightly above the average of the other countries. Atypically, Belgian domestic news items are not longer than hybrid news items. On average, foreign news items with domestic involvement were the longest news items in the Belgian television news sample.

Regarding topics covered, Belgian foreign and domestic news differ from each other, aside from a higher-than-average interest in sports. The level of sensationalism in Belgian television news is fairly high, especially in foreign news items. As Belgium is a small European country with several important neighbors, its television news covers a fairly large number of foreign countries. In terms of actors appearing in the news, Belgium distinguishes itself by a relatively large number of actors per news item. Belgian television newscasts, both the private and the public, are typically "sober" and tend not to resort to the use of special formal features.

Brazil (Jacques Alkalai Wainberg)

In large measure, Brazil's television news attraction is the country itself. Its continental territory (over 8.5 million square kilometers) and regional and social diversity provide abundant and rich content for TV newscasts. In other words, as happens with many large countries, Brazilian news programs are self-centered. And yet precisely because of this distinctive geographic feature, Brazilian television viewers have a significant sense of isolation vis-à-vis the rest of the world. This may help to explain not only the prominence of Brazil's domestic news but also the perception frequently expressed by Brazilian respondents that they have difficulty understanding international events.

It is important to note that television news is the main source of information for Brazil's 191 million inhabitants. Therefore, while providing a national agenda for conversation and political life, the 34 private Brazilian TV networks and their 1,511 channels and newscasts perform a central geopolitical role. By linking its regions, this national television system also includes 1,885 public TV stations that help the country to develop a national identity. Globo Organizations, a multimedia, privately owned corporation and currently the second-largest media corporation in the world, is the leader. Its network consists of 340 stations, and its main newscast, *Jornal Nacional* (*JN*), has a rating of nearly 33% in prime time. Globo's newscast is indeed the main storyteller of Brazil, and this role is well understood by *JN* editors. Hence the company has about 12 foreign correspondents and invests much in international news. Accordingly, the main *JN* newscast carries from four to six international stories per day. Without Globo, Brazilians would be, to a large measure, disconnected from foreign events.

In this sense, *JN*'s coverage not only arouses peoples' interest in such events, but also educates them about reality in general. This is a second geopolitical role performed by TV newscasts in general, and by *JN* in particular. Through *JN*'s correspondents (who speak in Portuguese), Brazilian viewers get a taste of foreign news, and by making connections between global topics and Brazilian actors and themes, TV Globo is the main Brazilian gate to the world. In its reporting, *JN* follows Brazilian diplomats, troops, businessmen, sportsmen, and corporations taking part in the new prominence of Brazil in the world arena.

In early 2008 public TV stations provided the Brazilian people with information about events such as the crisis in East Timor, the presidential primaries in the United States, dramatic developments in the Ingrid Betancourt kidnapping affair, and the conflict between China and Tibet surrounding the Beijing Olympic Games. However, *Jornal da Cultura*—the most important Brazilian public TV news program—has a rating of only 1.4% of all viewers in prime time, far behind TV Globo both in audience and number of correspondents.

The main topics on both TV news programs during the sample period were misbehavior of political and other social actors (22.5%), coverage of state bureaucracy and world events (each with 15%), and social problems and general soft news (each with 14%).

Most Brazilians are not devout newspaper readers, and indeed Brazilians seem to be passing over the Gutenberg Galaxy. Large segments of Brazil's new generation are going directly from orality to the new era of telecommunication. When they read, they read on the screen, not on paper. And when they talk about the outside world, they talk about the United States, which is clearly in first place in terms of the countries reported as the location of events in the Brazilian newscasts, as well as among the countries reported as interested in international news. To a large extent, the United States is the "Other" in Brazilians' imagination.

In sum, while television in general helps to reinforce the Brazilian national identity, its newscasts serve to educate people regarding national and international issues. These news programs provide various public alerts about mismanagement of public affairs, crime, social problems, violence, and international conflicts. In this sense Brazilian television is still the most important storyteller in the country, in spite of the fact that the Internet is also becoming a major provider of information.

Canada (Abby Goodrum & Elizabeth Godo)

Canada boasts a hybrid funding system whereby the Canadian Broadcasting Corporation (CBC, launched in 1952) is publicly funded with supplemental revenue from commercial advertisers and operates alongside other commercial networks such as CTV (launched in 1961 as an alternative to the CBC). For our purposes, we have covered only the English-speaking news, although one of Canada's two official languages is French, spoken primarily in the province of Quebec.

Overall, Canadian news possesses an international component that exceeds that of most other nations in this study, as measured by the amount of foreign news and contextualized hybrid items. This is especially true in the case of the public CBC, where the newscasts are a full hour (as compared to CTV's half-hour program), allowing for a more in-depth discussion of events. This is also reflected in the viewer survey, which indicates that Canadians who watch CTV exhibit a tendency toward pessimism with respect to the news as compared to those who watch CBC. The survey also points to Canada's multiculturalism, as viewers report a desire to see coverage of events in their country of origin.

As the larger study has shown, the United States receives the most foreign coverage of any nation, and Canadian news is clearly no exception. Nearly half of foreign items (44.6%) concern events that took place in the United States, a tendency that is the result of a number of factors. First, unlike any other country in this study, Canada shares a border with the United States, as well as strong economic ties and a great deal of common cultural ground. This cultural component is in part a result of the ubiquity of American programming. Despite a century-long history of protectionist policies seeking to define and reinforce Canadian identity, American content has steadily increased alongside the commercialization of Canadian broadcasting, reflected in the higher percentage of U.S. voices on CTV over CBC. Indeed, much of the political-economic environment that produces Canadian news is founded on attempts to limit American cultural and economic influence. Nonetheless, American news is far more common than that of any other nation, and much of it is entirely foreign, with no attempts made to localize events. Gatekeepers go as far as to report that American news is basically considered to be domestic.

The 2008 U.S. primary elections were certainly a contributing factor during the current sampling, as they received wide coverage in Canada and elsewhere. Overall, "elections" were the most common foreign topic on Canadian news in this study, due in large part to this event.

In addition to this relationship with the United States, Canada is also unique in its political ties to the United Kingdom, the second most mentioned nation in Canadian foreign news at 8.3%. The Canadian head of state is the Queen of England, and while Canada's economy is inextricably linked to that of the United States, its history lies with the United Kingdom, with notions of culture and identity falling somewhere in between.

Nations such as China and Tibet, Israel and Palestine, and Iraq are given prominence because of conflicts either among themselves or with Canadian allies such as the United States. Especially in the cases of Israel and Iraq, the prominent coverage reflects Canada's close relationship with the United States. With respect to Canada's direct concerns, Afghanistan, where at the time of the sample and of this writing Canadian military personnel were engaged in extensive operations, was covered in 5.2% of foreign items. In 2008, an inquiry commissioned by the federal government was released to recommend the future course of Canada's military in Afghanistan. National news coverage of this report reflects Canadians' concerns about an ongoing war, whether social, economic, or in terms of national identity, and serves to establish the terms of the public discourse.

This military report was also one of the most prominent domestic news items, although it was frequently contextualized as involvement with Afghanistan. Other widely covered domestic events included a brawl in a junior hockey league (leading to a larger discussion of violence in the sport), preparations being made by Canadian athletes for the upcoming Beijing Olympics, and the effect on Canadians and the Canadian economy of a recent stock market crash.

Chile (William Porath & Constanza Mujica)

Chile has four channels with national coverage, high prestige, and high ratings: Televisión Nacional de Chile (TVN), Canal 13, Mega, and Chilevisión. The historical development of Chile's television system is unique. Traditionally it was a non-profit business run by universities, and commercial endeavors were forbidden until 1990. But government had never provided funding for its development. The state entered the television business through the creation of TVN in 1969, justifying its action by the failure of the university channels to provide education and culture because of what it perceived as "excessive" commercialization. However, because the state did not provide TVN with funding, it resorted to funding by advertising.

TVN's founders emphasized pluralism, especially in its newscasts. It was not meant to be the government's mouthpiece channel, but rather a public service broadcaster attending to the traditional missions of education, informing, and entertaining. However, through the political polarization of 1970–1973 and following the military coup and dictatorship, TVN lost its independence and was taken over by the government. In 1992, its legal character was reformulated, and it was defined as a public state broadcaster, governed and self-funded through advertising.

Private television was authorized in 1989, generating a new paradigm for TV broadcasting: open to any entrepreneurs, with no public-service pretensions, and abiding by a minimum set of standards and values overseen by the National Television Council. This change implied that TVN had to compete with more channels for ratings, so its programs could no longer be elitist. The move was successful and gave TVN the highest average ratings (8.38%) for 2008.

Mega, the commercial station analyzed in this study, was founded in 1990 by a right-wing businessman. In 2008 it attained an overall rating of 9.32. Its newscast in 2008, when the study was conducted, had an average rating of 11%.

The content analysis of the Chilean sample is based on two newscasts: TVN's *24 Horas* and Mega's *Meganoticias*—each running one hour. The leading domestic stories during the sample period were summer vacation destinations and music shows, the national soccer championship, and criticism of the capital city's public transportation system.

Among the 1,506 news stories sampled, 49% were purely domestic, 21% were domestic with foreign involvement, 16% were foreign with domestic involvement, and 14% were purely foreign events. Thus, most Chilean foreign news was of the hybrid variety. Furthermore, about one-quarter of the news time devoted to purely foreign and foreign news with domestic involvement dealt with Chile's neighbors. This phenomenon was somewhat less pronounced in Chile than in some of the other countries in the study.

Sports dominated foreign news with domestic involvement with over 50% of airtime, usually concerning the performance of Chilean athletes. Politics (15.2%), internal order (11.8%), and business, commerce, and industry (11.6%) followed far behind. As for foreign news with no domestic involvement, sports coverage decreased but remains in first place with 26.9% of newscast time; international politics ascended to second place with 20.5%; human interest stories appeared in third place with 17.7%; and internal politics followed with 12.4%.

The Chilean survey indicates that the public was mostly interested in domestic news rather than foreign events: 33.1% of respondents said they were "very" or "quite" interested, and 49.7% were "somewhat interested." (The rest showed even less interest.) The public was satisfied with the amount of coverage dedicated to foreign events (46.3%).

The findings were consistent with those of the content analysis in that the public's interest resides mostly in the United States (45% of spontaneous responses) and neighboring countries (over 15% of responses mentioned Argentina, Peru, and Bolivia).

The survey findings also showed that the public was more interested in foreign events in which Chilean nationals are involved. While only 30% of the respondents said they were "very" or "quite" interested in purely foreign news, the proportion increased to over 50% for foreign events in which Chile was involved.

China (Joseph Chan & Baohua Zhou)

China's TV broadcasting is controlled by two interlocking systems: the administrative system of the state and the ideological-organizational system of the Chinese Communist Party. Both penetrate downward from the central and national level to the provincial and municipal level. For each TV station, the government bureaucracy at the corresponding level controls its personnel, finance, equipment acquisition, and technological expansion. The Party at the corresponding level exercises ideological control over its programming. Local stations also submit themselves to the policy controls of the State Administration of Radio, Film, and Television and the demands of CCTV (Chinese Central Television). In step with the marketization of the Chinese economy since the 1980s, the Chinese TV broadcasting system has been commercialized without privatization. By the end of 2010, the penetration of TV reached 97.6% of China's population, and the revenue of the TV industry reached U.S. $36 billion. In spite of marketization, Chinese TV in general and TV news in particular was still regarded as an important part of the Party's ideological apparatus. CCTV is the predominant national

TV player, especially in the area of news production and distribution. As a key cultural and ideological organ of the Party-/state, it enjoys unmatched privileges such as access to national information and resources in terms of capital, equipment, and talent.

The content analysis is mainly based on CCTV's 30-minute prime-time evening news program *News Broadcast (Xinwen Lianbo)*, which is relayed in full by all local TV stations as required by the state. At the time of this study, it commanded a strong viewership around the country, registering a mean rating of 8.7% and a mean share of 24.1% in 2008.

During the content analysis sample period, the five leading events that were reported in China included annual sessions of the National People's Congress and the Chinese People's Political Consultative Conference, the snow disaster in early 2008, the Beijing Olympic Games, the Tibet riots, and the Chinese Spring Festival.

Among the 784 news stories sampled, 65% were purely domestic news, 7% were domestic news with foreign involvement, 21% were purely foreign news, and 6% were foreign news with domestic involvement. As in many other countries, domestic news items were longer than foreign news items. As for the placement of news in the line-up, China was the only country in this study where all lead items were domestic news, among which 75% were purely domestic stories. The most frequent news topics in China were internal politics and social issues (36% each); foreign news was largely dominated by international politics (31%). The proportion of sensational news was low in both domestic (26%) and foreign (13.8%) news coverage. A total of 58 countries were covered in CCTV's foreign news, among which Greece was ranked first (14%), obviously because of the Olympic torch being lit there. Greece was followed by the United States, the United Kingdom, Japan, Russia, and South Korea. Regarding the actors in the news, only 35% of foreign news items and 43% of domestic news items involved at least one actor. Most of the actors in foreign news were male (91%) and of high status (74%).

Despite the rapid development of online media, television news still represents the most popular source of information for most respondents. The survey showed that the public watched television news about 5 days per week on average, with a daily exposure of about 32 minutes. Most respondents indicated that they followed television news primarily to keep up with national or international affairs. The most important reason for respondents not watching foreign news was their low confidence in their understanding of foreign events, followed by the perception that foreign news is infested with too much reporting of wars, violence, and disasters. The Chinese audience's general interest in foreign news was relatively high. The topic of accidents and natural disasters in foreign news commanded the highest interest, followed by relations between foreign countries and economics, business, and commerce. The countries that the respondents were interested in included, in descending order, the United States, Japan, the United Kingdom, Russia, France, South Korea, Germany, North Korea, Iraq, and India.

Egypt (Rasha Kamhawi)

Since the beginning of radio and television in Egypt, broadcasting has been controlled by the government and by the Egyptian Radio and Television Union. In 2000, private satellite channels were allowed to operate in Egypt; however, they were not allowed to air daily news bulletins. The government's grip on private channels later loosened, and in 2009 they were permitted to present daily newscasts. Terrestrial channels continue under government control. The content analyzed in our study is from Channel 1, the major state-owned and -run television station in Egypt.

The 21:00 newscast on Channel 1 is the main newscast of the day, and it covers the major events in detail. It is also the most watched of all government channels. *Nile News*, a 24-hour news channel, is not a popular source of news for the Egyptian audience compared to the main newscast on Channel 1. An estimated 75% of the Egyptian population has access to satellite television. A number of pan-Arab news stations broadcast from Arab countries, including Al-Jazeera (since 1996) and its competitor Al-Arabeya (since 2003). Western countries entered the scene in 2008 with several Arabic-speaking channels, including BBC-Arabic, Russia Today, France 24, Euronews, Israel's Channel 2, Deutchwelle, and the Alhurra channel, funded by the U.S. government.

The main domestic events reported during the sample period of the content analysis in early 2008—3 years before the "Arab Spring" and the ouster of Egyptian president Hosni Mubarak—were the Israeli blockade of Gaza and the influx of refugees from Gaza to Egypt; the reaction of Egyptian politicians to the Israeli blockade of Gaza; the Egyptian stock market performance; improving higher education; and the reaction to Egypt winning the African Soccer Tournament.

Based on the content analysis, it was determined that Egyptian domestic news emphasizes executive activities of the president and government officials. Such stories usually run longer than others and often, but not always, lead off the newscast. Many times these executive activities include a foreign element, such as diplomatic visits or executive statements about foreign events. Domestic news remains mostly ceremonial in nature.

Most notable, however, is the fact that an unusually large proportion of the news on Egyptian state television is foreign in nature. This may be because of the significance of the country in the politics of the region and the fact that two major regional conflicts existed at the time of the study that threatened the region's stability. Most foreign news focused on the Arab region, with the Israeli-Palestinian conflict and the U.S. occupation of Iraq heading the list. Other countries featured frequently in the news were the United States; Lebanon, where elections were taking place; and Syria, which hosted an Arab League meeting. There exists another possible explanation for the heavy emphasis on foreign news in Egyptian newscasts, namely, that it is meant to divert attention away from social ills and domestic political dissent.

Germany (Jürgen Wilke, Thorsten Quandt, Thilo von Pape, & Christine Heimprect)

Germany has a dual television system. Following World War II, only public service stations were created (ARD and ZDF). They held a monopoly for decades, being funded primarily by license fees, and they still remain very powerful. Private television stations such as RTL and SAT.1, which are financed exclusively by advertising, have only been licensed since 1984.

In 2008, an average of 8.74 million viewers (a market share of 32%) watched the main news broadcast of ARD (*Tagesschau*), and 3.74 million watched RTL (*RTL Aktuell*) (market share 18.2%).

The leading events during the period of the analysis in 2008 were the announcement of a factory shutdown by the Nokia Company, meetings to address the banking-financial crisis, wage negotiations in the public service sector, regional parliamentary elections, and a criminal investigation of a CEO suspected of tax evasion.

Compared to the other 16 countries examined in the international study, Germany has the shortest newscasts in prime time. Because of the brevity of the newscasts, they can only offer a limited number of items.

Germany is a country with a large proportion of international news on television. Other countries are covered often. *Tagesschau* and *RTL Aktuell* reported on as many as 63 countries within 4 weeks. The 10 countries appearing most frequently account for the lowest portion among the 17 countries of the study (54%). In German TV news, the United States is the country most frequently covered. However, this proportion (17%) is much lower than elsewhere. In second place in early 2008 was the United Kingdom, followed by Italy, Palestine, Russia, Israel, Norway, Egypt, Sweden, and Spain. As in other European countries, TV news in Germany focused on Europe more than half of the time (53%).

Four topics dominated international news in Germany (based on the share of total news time): internal politics, the economy, social issues, and internal order. International politics and sports followed at lower levels. As far as other topics are concerned, German TV news is within the range of the other countries

In half of the German newscasts, at least one actor appeared. On average, there were 1.2 actors per item. Thus, the country was slightly below the international average, a finding that can be explained by the succinct nature of the news items.

One characteristic of German television news is the fact that actors (as in no other country) are quoted and speak in TV news. With actors of high (39%), medium (25%), and low status (28%), *Tagesschau* and *RTL Aktuell* were again ranked within the average. The same can be said for the share of male (78%) and female (22%) actors.

Regarding formal features, German TV news does not stand out in any way. *Tagesschau* and *RTL Aktuell* use graphic representations, charts, maps, and logos a little more often than most of the other countries in the study. The German TV stations (along with Canada, Poland, Taiwan, and Singapore) belong to a group in which photos are dominant. Moreover, German and Taiwanese newscasts reflected expected differences between public service and private stations more than in the other countries.

Among the German survey sample of people over 18 years of age, 45.9% expressed a high or very high interest in foreign news on television. When asked if they want to see more or less foreign news on their preferred news program, 18.6% demanded more and only 10.4% demanded less, the large majority expressing satisfaction with the proportion of foreign news presented. Overall, the audience overestimated the percentage of foreign news shown in their TV program. When asked to name the countries in the news about which they are most interested, they mentioned 2.8 countries on average. The countries most often mentioned were the United States (59.7%), France (33.7%), and the United Kingdom (24.1%). Only 30 countries were mentioned by at least 1% of the sample. With respect to continents, 61.2% mentioned at least one European country and 60.0% at least one North American country, but only 2.1% mentioned an African country or a South American country (1.2%).

Hong Kong (Francis Lee)

Up until 2012, the television broadcasting system in Hong Kong was composed of two free-to-air broadcasters—Television Broadcasting Ltd. (TVB) and Asia Television Ltd. (ATV), the two stations studied in this project—and a number of multichannel pay television service providers. All these broadcasters are commercial players. Radio Television Hong Kong (RTHK), the public broadcaster, also produces public affairs programs, but it does not produce regular television newscasts, nor does it have its own television channels.

TVB is the dominant player in the television market for both news and non-news programs. Regarding news programs, the typical rating of TVB's early evening newscast at 18:30 is around 15 (that is, 1.05 million viewers). In contrast, ATV's early evening newscast, at 18:00, typically has a rating of only about 5 (350,000 people).

From January to March 2008, the biggest news event in Hong Kong was a scandal involving the online circulation of sex photos featuring a number of prominent local singers and movie stars. Originally presented as an entertainment-related, sensational, and gossipy story, the event obtained a "hard news" dimension after the handling of the case by the police aroused public concerns about police power. Another salient news event during the period was pre-scheduled: the annual announcement of the government budget in late February. The announcement, which is a conventional hard news event because the budget has direct implications on a full range of government policies, occupied a prominent place in the news agenda for several weeks.

Beyond the city of Hong Kong and in the broader national context, several events in mainland China and Taiwan also attracted much attention from the Hong Kong media: the presidential election in Taiwan; a serious snowstorm that hit the southern part of China; and the various events and controversies surrounding the upcoming Beijing Olympics.

The content analysis shows that 58.5% of the news items were purely domestic, 20.8% were domestic with foreign involvement, 3.0% were foreign with domestic involvement, and 17.7% were purely foreign items. Notably, Hong Kong newscasts feature a relatively high number of domestic news items with foreign involvement, yet there is a very small amount of foreign news with domestic involvement. This is understandable, though. As Hong Kong is a small, yet economically developed international metropolis, its affairs are often connected to or affected by foreign events (for instance, stock market fluctuations). But without being a sovereign nation, Hong Kong does not play a large role in international affairs, and thus it is much less frequently involved in foreign events.

The survey found that the people of Hong Kong exhibited a moderately high level of interest in foreign affairs: 40.3% of the respondents said they were "quite interested" in foreign news, and 9.9% said they were "very interested" in foreign news. Moreover, while 77.5% of the respondents thought that foreign news constituted up to 40% of all news items in television newscasts, only 57.4% thought that foreign news should constitute that little of the news. In other words, for many people the desired amount of foreign news exceeds both their perceived amount of foreign news (based on survey data) and the actual amount of foreign news (based on the content analysis).

One thing that is common to content and audience interests is their focus on a few prominent countries including the United States, the United Kingdom, and Japan. Besides factors such as historical, cultural, and economic ties, the overwhelming focus on these countries should also be understood in terms of the television stations' access to news about them. Television stations in Hong Kong are highly reliant on international news agencies such as the Associated Press and Japan's NHK for foreign news.

Not all journalists and editors interviewed in the project consider the small amount of foreign news and the concentration on a few countries to be a problem, however. In fact, the interviewees varied in their opinions regarding whether the people of Hong Kong really want to watch foreign news or if they were just paying lip service to it in the survey.

Israel (Akiba A. Cohen)

Television broadcasting in Israel began in 1968, quite late by Western standards. Initially there was only one public broadcasting service, the Israel Broadcasting Authority (IBA), funded by license fees. Its Channel 1 was heavily viewed in the early years and served as the "tribal camp file" long before people meters were introduced. Channel 2, a commercially funded station regulated by a public body, the Second Authority for Television and Radio, began broadcasting in 1993 and was joined in 2002 by Channel 2, another commercial channel regulated by the Second Authority. The prime-time newscasts aired by each of the three stations have undergone various changes over the years. At the time of the content analysis in early 2008, Channel 2 led with around 20% of the viewership compared with about 8% for Channel 1.

The domestic events that received the most prominent coverage during the sample period were the continuous shelling by Palestinians of the town of Sderot and other villages along the Gaza Strip; the impact on Israel of the crossing of Palestinians from the Gaza Strip into Egypt; clashes between Israeli settlers and Palestinians on the West Bank; a terror attack in Jerusalem; the Israeli reaction to the assassination in Damascus of Imad Mughniyah, one of the Hezbollah leaders; and the meetings in Jerusalem between Prime Minister Ehud Olmert and U.S. Secretary of State Condoleezza Rice

In terms of news content, the two Israeli channels are fairly similar and appear near the middle of the rankings of the countries in the study. Both channels emphasize domestic news (around 50%). About 19% of news items were purely foreign, while 31% of the news was of the hybrid type. In terms of the topics, on most categories Israeli news was similar to the overall average across the countries. There were some notable differences, however. Regarding domestic news, Israel was highest of all the countries on internal order as well as military and defense issues; as for foreign news, Israel was lowest concerning economic issues. In its coverage of foreign news, Israeli television referred at least once to 63 different countries, which was slightly below Egypt, Switzerland, and Belgium, and tied with Germany. As in most of the other countries, it referred first and foremost to the United States, followed by countries in the Middle East and Europe. On the other hand, its Country Concentration Index for the top 10 countries was 74%, very high in terms of concentrating on a few countries. As for the presentation of actors in the news, Israeli newscasts were slightly lower than the average of the 17 countries, with its actors quoted relatively less but speaking on camera relatively more than the overall averages.

The Israeli survey was based on 760 respondents. In comparison with the other countries, Israelis watched TV news the fewest days per week, probably because of religious restrictions observed by a segment of the population regarding viewing on the Sabbath. While Israelis were similar to the other respondents in offering three reasons for viewing the news, they were the lowest by far in terms of news as entertaining, probably a reflection of the somber news often aired in the country.

Israel was one of the lowest-ranked countries in terms of general interest in foreign news, and the absolute lowest regarding five of the seven topic areas examined: social issues; relations between foreign countries; economics, business and commerce; domestic politics of foreign countries; and crime and violence. As for interest in domestic news topics, Israelis were nearly average regarding five topic areas but lowest regarding social issues and sports.

Finally, because of a problem in recording the countries of interest, the mean number for Israelis was especially low. As in most other countries, Israelis were most interested in the United States (for 58% of respondents it was their first choice, and for 80% it was one of five choices). Of the 30 countries most mentioned by the entire sample of 13 countries, among Israelis the United States was followed by three European countries—France, the United Kingdom, and Russia—as well as Iran and Canada. In addition, Israelis were interested in several Arab countries and, to a lesser extent, in Turkey.

Italy (Paolo Mancini & Marco Mazzoni)

The Italian television system is characterized by a rigid duopoly that still has far to go before it is overcome. This duopoly includes two main commercial players: Radiotelevisione Italiana and Mediaset. In addition, Radiotelevisione Italiana (RAI) is the public service broadcaster. It is primarily funded by license fees, but it also draws a significant part of its revenue from advertisements. RAI's principal competitor is Mediaset, which is one of the main commercial networks in Europe and is owned by the family of Silvio Berlusconi, the former Italian prime minister. In 2008, at the time of our study, RAI and Mediaset together drew more than three-quarters of the total income in the television sector, while their channels reached more than four-fifths of the overall audience share. With regard to TV news, between January and March 2008, *TG1*, the main newscast of RAI, had an average audience of 5,763,000 viewers (a share of 22.3%), while *TG5*, Mediaset's principal newscast, drew an average audience of 5,630,000 viewers (a share of 21.7%). (This scenario has now changed somewhat with the presence of the new DTT technology and the emergence of a new player, Murdoch's Sky Italia, as the main pay-per-view operator in the Italian TV system.)

The following domestic events were most prominent in Italy during the content analysis sample period of the study: (1) the campaign for the 2008 general elections (scheduled for April 2008), which was characterized by continuous discussion among the main political parties about political alliances and strategies; (2) the resignation of the Prodi government (January 2008) led by Romano Prodi, who was appointed prime minister in May 2006; (3) two "grim" stories—the "Erba massacre" trial (a married couple killed three neighbors) and the investigation relating to the murder of a British student, Meredith Kercher, in Perugia in November 2007; and (4) the possible bailout of the Italian national airline, Alitalia. As for foreign news, the most newsworthy event reported in the Italian newscasts concerned the primary elections in the United States, particularly the Democratic contest between Barack Obama and Hillary Clinton.

Not surprisingly, the content analysis of the two Italian stations revealed that the most heavily covered issues were the election campaign, the fall of the Prodi government, and crime news. The strong presence of political news has always been one of the primary features of Italian newscasts. The data from our study indicate, however, a growing trend in recent years of increasing soft news coverage. In fact, during the sample period, soft news reached the same level of coverage as hard news. This is also confirmed by the nature of the identified actors: national candidates, political leaders, and "men in the street." Finally, one difference between the two channels is that in *TG1*, the public broadcasting channel's newscast, foreign news was more dominant and audio-visual features were more often used than in *TG5*, the commercial channel's newscast.

Japan (Youichi Ito)

Japan is an advanced industrialized country whose GNP/GDP is the third largest in the world after the United States and China. Its population of 127 million is the ninth largest in the world. Japan is a parliamentary democracy with an emperor as the symbolic head of state. The country's literacy rate is nearly 100%, and the per capita income and standard of living are similar to that of the major Western powers. The income disparity is small for a capitalist economy; hence, most Japanese consider themselves to be part of the middle class.

Television service is provided by a dual broadcasting system consisting of the public broadcasting corporation NHK (Nihon Hoso Kyokai) and commercial broadcasters. Supported by viewers' fees, NHK broadcasts two channels nationwide through a network of 54 stations. It also conducts satellite broadcasting with three channels. Although NHK is not state run, its annual budget and executive personnel proposal must be approved by the Diet.

Five commercial broadcasters are based in Tokyo, each affiliated with a major national newspaper. Each broadcaster has a network of stations and is affiliated with regional and local stations.

NHK's *News 7* and TV Asahi's *News: Hodo Station* comprised the samples in our content analysis. The average ratings of these two news programs during the sample period (January–March 2008) were 17.4% for NHK and 14.1% for TV Ashai.

Since the Second World War, the percentage of foreign news in Japanese television news has been very low—lower than in the United States—a fact that has been repeatedly confirmed by studies in the past as described in this volume. The reason for this may be that the Japanese have become inward-oriented or isolationist as a result of their bitter experiences in the 1930s and 1940s.

The main domestic news items that were aired during the sample period were: (1) a mass murder committed by a young man at a railroad station using a knife (not a gun); (2) the possible bankruptcy of a relatively new bank that was heavily subsidized by the Tokyo Metropolitan Government; (3) debates regarding the abolition of the gasoline tax; (4) a random murder in which a victim was pushed off a railroad platform; and (5) cases of cheating in welfare subsidies for the poor.

Of the very small percentage of foreign news, as noted above, as many as 40% of the items concerned the United States. Only two other countries in the study presented more news taking place in the United States: Canada (49%) and Hong Kong (44%). In addition to the United States, foreign news in Japan notably dealt with China (21%) and South Korea (5%). These three countries together accounted for 65% of foreign news in Japan.

Poland (Agnieszka Stępińska)

Poland has a dual system of electronic media consisting of two public terrestrial television channels that provide newscasts: TVP1 with *Wiadomości* and TVP2 with *Panorama*. Both channels broadcast three 30-minute editions per day, including a prime-time evening edition. Polish public television also provides one satellite channel for Polish people living abroad (TV Polonia) that retransmits the prime-time edition of *Wiadomości*. In addition, at 17:00 TVP1 broadcasts a 15-minute news program, *Teleexpress*, that is more entertainment oriented than the prime-time evening newscasts. There are also three commercial television stations, each broadcasting at least two newscasts, including a prime-time evening edition: TVN (*Fakty*), as well as Polsat and Polsat 2 (*Wydarzenia*). Finally, there are four TV news channels, one public (TVP INFO, which originates from a previous system of regional TV stations), and three commercial channels (TVN24, Polsat News, and Superstacja) that broadcast 24/7.

According to AGB Nielsen Media Research, during the first quarter of 2008, the public station TVP1 had the highest ratings (around 24% of the market share). The same station was also the ratings leader among the news broadcasts (*Wiadomości* enjoyed around 33% of the market share, followed by *Fakty* of the TVN commercial station with around 30% of the market share), while the ratings for TVN was around 15.5%.

In the first quarter of 2008, the five leading events reported by the Polish media were a crash of a CASA airplane carrying high-ranking Polish air force officers; the presidential elections in Russia; the Russian response to the idea of placing U.S. missiles on Polish soil; Polish troops in Afghanistan; and Easter celebrations.

Polish newscasts of both public and commercial television stations are relatively short, running about 22–23 minutes. Each consists of a small number of longer items; hence the Polish newscasts provided the smallest number of items (540) of all the countries in the study. As for the actors in the news, 84% of the domestic and 95% of the foreign items presented at least one actor, while the average of 4.6 actors per item was the highest among all the countries.

Poland, with 49% purely domestic news, 16% domestic news with foreign involvement, and 18% purely foreign news, was one of the countries with the highest percentage of foreign news with domestic involvement (17%). At the same time, in 53% of foreign news, Poland was mentioned as a country involved. Poland was among the countries broadcasting predominantly hard news focusing strongly on internal politics (both in domestic and foreign news stories), with one-third of the actors in the news being domestic politicians. The number of countries covered on foreign news was relatively low (39), and Polish TV newscasts were the most Eurocentric in the sample (75% of foreign news covered European countries). In particular, television news in Poland was dominated by Russia (23% of its foreign news). This can be attributed to the presidential elections in Russia that were being held at the time and to Russia's negative response to the idea of placing U.S. missiles in Poland.

According to the survey findings, the Polish audience seems to have a moderate interest in foreign news. Of the major topics in foreign news, relations between foreign countries, accidents and disasters, and social issues were the topics that garnered at least some interest among those surveyed. When asked about the countries of interest, Polish respondents mentioned on average more than three countries, with their top choices being Germany, Russia, the United States, the United Kingdom, France, Ukraine, the Czech Republic, Spain, Italy, and China. Most of these countries are European; four are Polish neighbors. These findings also show that TV newscasts share the audience's Eurocentric perspective and, to a great extent, meet the audience's expectations about selection of the countries to be covered (7 of the 10 most frequently covered countries were mentioned by the audience as being of highest interest).

Portugal (António Belo & André Sendin)

Portugal has two national public service channels (RTP1 and RTP2) and two private channels (SIC and TVI). During the sample period of the study in early 2008, the private channels led in audience share. TVI had 29.4%, followed by SIC with 25.9%, RTP1 with 24.4%, and RTP2 with only 5.2%. Cable television, in which each of the principal broadcast channels (RTP1, SIC, and TVI) has a news channel, had a 15.1% share of the audience.

The leading events reported in Portugal during the content analysis sample period were the possibility that the Portuguese football coach, José Mourinho, might be moving to coach Inter Milano in Italy; a national strike by teachers; a decrease of 1% in the Value Added Tax; Portuguese economic growth in 2007; and a corruption scandal in the Portuguese bank BPN.

The Portuguese newscasts are among the longest: 1 hour on the public channel and 77 minutes on the commercial station, inclusive of commercial breaks. In contrast to the newscasts of most other countries, headlines at the beginning of the newscast are less common in Portugal, the anchor is seen in all items, and blocks of items are rarely presented.

Portugal, with only 18% of purely foreign news, is among the countries with the lowest percentage—along with Taiwan, the United States, Japan, Chile, Italy, Hong Kong, Poland, and Israel, all presenting between 12% and 20%.

The most pervasive topic category in the Portuguese newscasts, especially in domestic news, was social issues, with 34% of the entire newscasts. This was followed by internal order (32%), mainly in foreign news (the highest percentage among all the countries in the study). Two events in early 2008 were the primary cause of this high rate of foreign news items related to internal order abroad: the murder of a child in Spain near the Portuguese border and the attempted murder of the Prime Minister of East Timor.

As for countries of interest, among the 10 most frequently mentioned in the Portuguese newscasts were Spain, Portugal's neighbor (cited most often); Brazil (4%), East Timor (11%), and especially Mozambique (35%), all of which are tied to Portugal as former colonies; and countries such as the United States and the United Kingdom, which generally dominate the international scene. In addition, the presence of Kosovo in the "Top 10" list of countries was noteworthy and probably due to the participation of Portugal in the military force in that country.

In terms of actors, Portugal, along with Belgium, Poland, Hong Kong, and Taiwan, has a high percentage of news items "illustrated" with at least one actor. Most of these actors were of high status, although the presence of low-status actors was also prevalent. This is related to the strong presence of ordinary citizens in Portuguese newscasts, with only Brazil having a higher level. Within foreign news, "citizen" was the most frequent actor category, with Portugal being one of only two exceptions to the "dictatorship" of politicians, which in all other countries was the highest-ranked category.

In Portugal, as in most of the other countries in the study, the public had a moderate interest in foreign news, albeit lower than in domestic news. The topic of greatest interest to the Portuguese respondents was social issues, while domestic politics of foreign countries and relations between foreign countries were the topics of least interest.

Among the various countries of interest, the Portuguese are most interested in France, probably because of the large community of Portuguese immigrants in that country. This also explains their high level of interest in Germany and Switzerland, which are also home to significant numbers of Portuguese immigrants. The interest of Portuguese people in other countries is related to geographic proximity, as in the case of Spain, as well as economic and political relevance regarding the United States and the United Kingdom. Finally, as noted above in reference to their presence in the newscasts, the former Portuguese colonies of Brazil, Angola, Mozambique, and East Timor command the interest of the Portuguese people.

Singapore (Xiaoge Xu)

Singapore is a densely populated island state with more than 5 million inhabitants occupying 697 square kilometers. It is a racial and cultural "salad" with 76.8% of its population being Chinese, 13.9% Malay, 7.9% Indian, and 1.4% other. Small in size but large in economic achievements, Singapore has become increasingly global in areas ranging from aviation to investment. Going global has made this island more hungry for foreign news despite the monopoly over the island-wide media industry by two government-linked media giants: MediaCorp and Singapore Press Holdings.

Since its inception in 1963, the television industry has been monopolized by MediaCorp. As tightly controlled by the ruling party of the country as the other media giant, MediaCorp broadcasts news through Channel 5, Channel 8, Channel U, Channel NewsAsia, Suria, Vasantham, and Teletext. Channel 5 serves as a bridge channel for the whole country for English news and entertainment, while Channel 8 is designed to cater to the needs of the Chinese. Channel U is another Chinese channel, while Suria is a Malay channel and Vasantham is a Tamil channel. Channel NewsAsia is a news channel with a regional reach, while Teletext is available on Channels 5 and 8 and Channel NewsAsia. Representative of the television news landscape in Singapore, Channel 8 and Channel 5 enjoyed TV news ratings of 17% and 5.5% respectively during the study period.

Among the leading domestic events during the sample period was a foreign talent debate fueled by the fact that as a multicultural, multiracial, and multilingual country, Singapore has attracted many foreign talents, creating both opportunities for and challenges to the local economy. Another leading domestic event was the escape of Mas Selamat from detention in Singapore in February 2008. Selamat, who was suspected of plotting to bomb Singapore Changi Airport in 2002, was being held in Singapore after being arrested in Indonesia. Also reported were the issue of refinancing house loans, regulations of aesthetic medicine by the Ministry of Health, and taxi fare adjustments.

Among the leading events covered in Singapore's foreign news during the investigation period were the U.S. primary elections, the Malaysian elections, the Beijing Olympics, and the global financial crisis. This focus derives from the fact that as a regional hub on many fronts, including medicine, education, trade, tourism, aviation, and finance, Singapore was closely related to and heavily dependent on the United States, China, Malaysia, and the global market.

In comparison with other countries in the study, Singapore was high in both purely domestic news (46%) and purely foreign news (42%) but low in hybrid news—either domestic news with foreign involvement (3%) or foreign news with domestic involvement (9%). In terms of news topics, Singapore devoted more coverage of internal politics in foreign news than many other countries. It also had less coverage of social issues in foreign news than in domestic news. Although Singapore was low in coverage of international politics, it was high in coverage of financial and economic matters. Singaporean news presented a relatively high number of high-status actors in foreign news and a preponderance of domestic politicians over their international counterparts. In terms of the tone of the newscasts, the two programs differed, although they are both owned by the same company and regulated by the same government. Channel 5's news program was "sober," while Channel 8's was "playful."

TV viewers in Singapore watched less news than respondents in the other countries surveyed. Like the audiences in Hong Kong and Switzerland, the respondents in Singapore tended to show more interest in foreign news and in neighboring trade-connected or culturally proximate countries such as Malaysia, Indonesia, Thailand, India, the Philippines, and China. (Because of its small size and lack of natural resources, Singapore's foreign relations take on added importance.) Singaporeans were also more interested in news about the countries of origin of its larger communities of immigrants. The findings lend further support to the proximity theory, be it geographic, cultural, social, or economic.

Switzerland (Thomas Hanitzsch & Hong Nga (Angie) Nguyen Vu)

With a population of approximately 7.7 million, Switzerland is a small and culturally heterogeneous country. The Swiss media market is subdivided into three language communities, as German is spoken in the north and northeast, French is spoken in the southwest, and Italian is spoken in the southeast. Each of these language-specific sub-markets competes with spillover broadcasting content provided by the three larger neighboring countries with which they share their respective languages, that is, Germany, France, and Italy. Accordingly, the Swiss broadcasting system is traditionally highly decentralized. Only the public service broadcaster SRG SSR Idée Suisse (SRG) produces and broadcasts content in all official languages. The SRG is the only broadcasting institution that provides a variety of comprehensive television programs for the whole country.

Television broadcasting in Switzerland began in 1950. Public service broadcasting was established in 1931, largely modeled after the BBC. Swiss residents pay a license fee for the service. The SRG public broadcasting system runs three national channels for the German-speaking community, three for the French-speaking Romandie, and two in the Italian-speaking southeast. The most popular public television newscasts found in this study were the German-language *Tagesschau* (SF 1) with a market share of 54.1%, and the French-language *Le Journal* (TSR1) (60.1%).

Commercial television has always had difficulty competing with German, French, and Italian TV stations that broadcast into Switzerland. Some of these "foreign" television stations haven even crafted a Swiss version that differs from the original channel only in regionalized advertising. Switzerland nonetheless sustains a number of regional commercial TV stations for the German-speaking and Francophone regions. In addition to the regional stations, there is a variety of local television channels, of which TeleZüri is by far the most successful, attracting a market share of 18.4% for its news program *ZüriNews* in 2007.

During the sample period of our content analysis, the most frequently reported events in Swiss television news were the U.S. presidential primaries, the Tibet conflict in connection with the Beijing Olympics, the global financial crisis, and the enduring Israeli-Palestinian conflict. The focus on the American primary elections may have contributed to a dominance of foreign internal politics in Swiss television news, as well as to less diversity in the news. Another interesting point is that only in Switzerland did the conflict between Serbia and Kosovo occupy a significant portion of foreign news. This may have been because the high number of refugees and emigrants from that region form one of the largest foreign ethnic groups in Switzerland.

While there was less diversity in terms of news topics in Switzerland's newscasts, the country is grouped with those that covered a relatively large number of foreign nations. Among the countries covered in the news, Switzerland's three "giant neighbors"—France, Germany, and Italy—were naturally the center of attention.

A comparison of the two public TV newscasts revealed that the German-language newscast *Tagesschau* appeared to be more international than its Francophone counterpart, *Le Journal*. The latter dedicated significantly more airtime to events taking place in France and those in which France was involved, while this was less prevalent in the German-language newscasts. At the same time, *Le Journal* relied more on French actors than did *Tagesschau*, where German actors were quoted more often. In addition, *Tagesschau* tended to cover events in a more factual and unemotional manner, as indicated by its more frequent use of tables and charts, still photographs, and printed text. *Le Journal*, on the other hand, used more animated representations.

Our survey indicated that Swiss people watch the least television news per day (19 minutes on average) of all investigated countries. This finding is consistent with the relatively low television consumption commonly found for Swiss audiences in comparative studies. Swiss audiences, like their German neighbors, generally spend more time reading newspapers than watching TV news.

Interest in foreign news tends to be higher in Switzerland because the country strongly depends on good foreign relations with its neighbors and because Switzerland may be too small to produce enough domestic news of interest to a national audience. Furthermore, Switzerland is a country in which foreigners constitute more than 20% of the population, and these large communities of immigrants likely have substantial interest in news about their countries of origin.

Taiwan (Ven-hwei Lo & Tai-Li Wang)

Prior to the lifting of martial law in 1987, three broadcast television channels (TTV, CTS, and CTV) monopolized Taiwan's TV market. All three were under direct or indirect control of the government. After 1987, political interference in news broadcasting continued despite the strengthening of the market mechanisms. When cable television was legalized in 1993, the television news media underwent structural changes. As the media became commercialized and more liberal, the number of news channels soared, and 24-hour news channels began to appear. The resulting heavy competition among news channels led the television stations to place greater emphasis on sensationalism, entertainment, and soft news in order to boost ratings and increase revenues. Currently there are five television channels that provide daily news in four time slots, including the channel analyzed in this study, Public Television Service (PTS). There are eight 24-hour news channels, including the wireless satellite television channel TVBS-N, also analyzed in our project.

During the sample period of our study, elections and referendums dominated the scene in Taiwan. They included the seventh (and first "binary-voting") legislative election, the twelfth presidential election, the third and fourth referendums concerning the return of the Kuomintang's illegally acquired assets and anti-corruption issues, and referendums concerning the use of the name "Taiwan" by the United Nations. The final significant story was the severing of diplomatic ties with Malawi.

Overall, Taiwan's foreign news mostly reported on other countries' internal politics (20%), followed by internal order (16%), fashion, human interest, and weather (14%), the economy (12%), and culture, religion, and ceremonies (12%).

In terms of the proportion of domestic and foreign news, Taiwanese television presented the highest percentage of domestic news and the lowest percentage of foreign news among all the countries of the study. This is in line with previous research in Taiwan indicating that foreign news generally has lower ratings; therefore, commercial television stations do not place importance on such news.

As for the news formats, the most commonly used in Taiwan's foreign news were animation (10.4%) and background music (2.7%).

Regarding actors in the news, a comparison of Taiwan with the other countries in the study reveals that Taiwanese news had greater percentages of certain types of actors. In the domestic news of Taiwan's public television programs, the presence of news authorities was higher than the overall (across the 17 countries) average. In foreign news, too, private citizens occupy a larger share than the overall average. As for TVSB, the commercial station, for both domestic and foreign news the percentage of private citizens in news content was also higher than the overall average. In sum, the proportion of private citizens as news actors in TV news in Taiwan was higher compared to the other countries.

The national telephone survey was conducted in October 2009. The results indicate that the respondents watch television news about 6 days per week. The average exposure to television news per day was roughly 48 minutes. In contrast, the Taiwanese spent about 19 minutes per day reading newspapers and 13 minutes viewing online news. Most respondents indicate that they watch television news primarily to keep up with national or international affairs. The survey also indicates that respondents' interest in foreign news is high. More than 83% of the respondents said they were somewhat interested, quite interested, or very interested in foreign news. The foreign news topics of greatest interest are accidents and natural disasters; social issues; reports on the economy, business, and commerce; relations between foreign countries; and sports. The topics of least interest are crime and violence and domestic politics of foreign countries. The countries of greatest interest to Taiwan viewers are China, Japan, and the United States. The most important reasons for not watching foreign news were insufficient background for understanding foreign news and the perception that nothing ever changes.

United States (Lars Willnat & David H. Weaver)

The media in the United States, mostly under private ownership, comprise one of America's largest business groups. Most of the 1,400 commerical television stations operating in the United States are affiliated with one of the four main commercial broadcasters: NBC, CBS, ABC, and the Fox Broadcasting Company. In addition, nearly 400 public TV stations provide "quality" programming in affiliation with the Public Broadcasting Service (PBS), which is funded by a combination of government subsidies and private contributions.

Despite the fact that the audience for network television news programs shrank in 2008, continuing a quarter-century decline, most Americans still got their news from one of the three commerical television networks. In 2008, an average of 22.8 million people watched at least one of the three 30-minute evening newscasts: *ABC World News* (8.1 million viewers; rating: 5.6), *CBS Evening News* (6.1 million; rating: 4.2), or *NBC Nightly News* (8.6 million; rating: 5.8). The *NewsHour with Jim Lehrer*, a 60-minute newscast produced by PBS, attracted an average of 1.1 million viewers (rating: 0.8) each night in 2008.

The main news events in the United States during the period under investigation (January–March 2008) were the kickoff of the U.S. primary elections in early January, a series of winter tornadoes that ravaged the midsection of the United States on January 8–9, a $145 billion economic stimulus package proposed by the Bush administration on January 18 in response to the looming housing and banking crisis, its passage by Congress in early February, and a large-scale intervention by the Federal Reserve on March 11 that provided a $200 billion loan to to the country's largest banks in order to avert a financial panic. As expected, these events dominated the news on American television, with most stories focusing either on the U.S. primary elections (22%) or the imminent collapse of the U.S. economy (15%).

Only a small portion of the television news in the United States is devoted to foreign news. Worried about declining circulation and profit margins, media executives argue that their audiences have shown little interest in foreign news but do clamor for more lifestyle and celebrity stories, more consumer and health news, and more local news. Thus only about one-quarter (27%) of the TV news in the U.S. sample was devoted to the coverage of foreign affairs, several points less than the average of foreign news found in the other 16 nations included in this analysis.

While TV news in the United States focused mostly on domestic politics and the failing U.S. economy, foreign news reports concentrated on international politics and the involvement of the U.S. military in nations such as Afghanistan and Iraq. Overall, American TV news mentioned only 36 foreign nations between January and March 2008, a number that was found to be lower only in Japan's TV news. The five most covered nations were Iraq, Palestine, China, Israel, and Colombia—all nations that reflect U.S. foreign policy interests and therefore become the focus of U.S. foreign affais reporting.

The U.S. survey found that Americans watch about 41 minutes of TV news per day, which is slightly more than the average in the other 12 nations where surveys were conducted. While older Americans tend to watch more foreign news, younger generations showed slightly more interest in foreign news. Almost 8 in 10 U.S. respondents said that TV news helps them to keep up with events in foreign nations. However, only about one-third (37%) said that they were at least moderatedly interested in foreign news.

When watching TV news, Amerians were mostly interested in domestic news that relates to social and economic issues. Among foreign news items, political and economic relations and accidents and disasters in other countries drew the largest interest. The survey also found that Americans were interested in a relatively diverse set of foreign nations. The five countries of most interest were Afghanistan (13.4%), Iraq (8.5%), Canada (7%), China (7.2%), and Mexico (5.9%), again reflecting U.S. foreign policy interests and geographic proximity.

CHAPTER SIXTEEN

Where in the World Is the Global Village?

AKIBA A. COHEN

As stated at the outset of this volume, our main goal was to examine foreign news that is presented on national television in a variety of countries. The context for our study was, on one hand, the ongoing process of globalization, which has been manifest in recent decades in many realms of life, including the media in general and in the increasing prominence of global 24/7 news networks in particular (see, for example, Chalaby, 2009). On the other hand, we have been witnessing a significant decline in the presentation of foreign news on national television in many countries (Seib, 1997; Tyndall Report, 2010). Thus, in a growing state of interdependence among nations, the question is how the medium of television—which is still the undisputed main source of information for most people worldwide—presents events from abroad that are totally unrelated to the country of broadcast, as well as events that may be relevant to the country of broadcast in one way or another. We were also interested in the extent to which people are interested in foreign news and how gatekeepers responsible for providing such news reflect on the content they produce and on what their viewers think and desire. At a higher level, we were interested in the overarching question of the extent to which similarities and differences exist around the world. To put it in a flowery way, our question is: Has the metaphoric "global village" become a reality?

Based on a project involving three stages—a content analysis of a sample of news in 17 countries, a survey of news consumers in 13 of the countries, and a series of in-depth interviews with gatekeepers responsible for foreign news in 12 of the countries—our inevitable conclusion is that we cannot support the notion of a global village.

Although our study was very broad and ambitious—more so than most of which we are aware—we were not the first to reach this conclusion. On November 19, 1991, 118 individuals from 55 countries participated in a global study of television news in which the evening's main newscasts were recorded for the purpose of determining what Malik and Anderson (1992) referred to as the "Global News Agenda." At their request, and through the auspices of the International Institute of Communications (IIC) in London, the participating scholars and practitioners provided videotaped copies—the method used back then to do off-air recordings—of the newscasts and detailed logs of the items therein. A thorough analysis of the logs was done and published in *InterMedia*, the official journal of the IIC. The main finding was that there is very little communality across the globe.[1]

In the same issue of *InterMedia*, the editor asked several scholars to comment on the findings. Everette Dennis had this to say:

> If there is a headline here, it is that global news coverage via satellite is an idea whose time has not yet come. With few exceptions, this global television news survey exposes the parochialism of news in most countries of the world. It also debunks the persistent notion that news flows from the industrialized information societies to the Third World, not the other way round. The story here is that news doesn't flow very far at all. (Dennis, 1992, p. 36)

This writer was also asked to comment and rendered this opinion:

> If the objective of the *InterMedia* survey was to prove that television news shown around the world is *not* the same, then in retrospect the choice of November 19, 1991 must be an excellent one for creating such a collage. Judging from the newscasts recorded by the various collaborators for the *InterMedia* survey, *variability* seems to have been the name of the game. No single news event seemed to capture the imagination of news editors around the world and no story became the headline all over. (Cohen, 1992, p. 35)

The *InterMedia* study and other studies cited throughout this volume lend support to this general conclusion. In the following pages we summarize what we have found in the present study.

Variability of Content

The sheer amount of foreign news in the main newscasts varied considerably across the 17 countries. We suggest that these differences are a function of numerous factors, including a nation's geographic and population size; its geopolitical location, including neighboring countries; its economic and military position in the world scene; its historic and cultural links to other nations; its media system and how it relates to its political system; and, finally, the idiosyncratic predispositions of the individuals who select, produce, and deliver the news as well as their perceptions of their audience. *Ipso facto*, this cannot lead to much similarity among countries.

We believe we can safely assume that only when highly dramatic events take place would all or at least most stations around the world report on them. But on "normal" days—which we were fortunate to have in our 4-week sample period in early 2008—variability would seem to characterize the news agenda.

As for specific topics of news items, while domestic news by definition deals with national and local matters, foreign news is often subject to domestic considerations, which is manifested in two types of hybrid news: domestic news with foreign involvement and, more often, foreign news with domestic involvement. Thus, for example, the extent to which elections in country A are reported in country B is a function of the perceived importance of the former in the eyes of the latter. This makes for differences among countries, and they abound (see Chapter 3). However, when using a tripartite distinction among hard, soft, and sensational news, we found a tendency for more similarity than difference among the countries.

In Chapter 4 we report on countries of location and countries involved. As for the countries of location of the events reported in the newscasts, some exhibited a wide selection, while in others the number of countries covered was relatively small. While a total of 137 countries of *location* of events were mentioned at least once by one or more of the 17 countries in the study, the largest number of countries mentioned in a *single* county was 70 in both Egypt and Switzerland. The lowest number of countries mentioned was the 28 reported by Japan. Comparable figures were found for countries *involved*: 174 countries were mentioned at least once by one country or more, with 107 countries mentioned in the Egyptian news and 32 in news in Japan. Part of this large variability, we learned from the in-depth interviews with the gatekeepers, traces to the fact that some foreign news editors are simply interested in certain (often esoteric) countries, and they try to present at least one item about them from time to time.

Our analysis of the actors in the news appears in Chapter 5. Across the board, actors in the news naturally appeared more frequently in domestic news than in foreign news. However, in most of the countries, politicians—one of the more well-represented categories of actors—as well as other high-status persons, appeared more often in foreign news. What is even more interesting about the way actors appear in the news is that no clear pattern emerged among the countries, suggesting that there is little if any universality in the way foreign news is presented.

Formal features of television news that represent the non-content aspects of the newscasts would conceivably produce the least amount of variance across the countries (Chapter 6). This is because these features are technology based and depend on the equipment available in the television studios. It can be safely assumed that most news studios use similar equipment and that by and large the training of television journalists and technicians is done in a similar fashion in most places. Nevertheless, it turns out that even these potentially common aspects of the newscasts present quite disparate pictures across our countries.

This variability was also evident when examining the differences between public and commercial broadcasters (Chapter 7). In several countries the public service stations used more audiovisual elements in the news, whereas in others it was the commercial stations that used more such features. More generally, the comparison between public service and commercial stations across the countries yielded mixed findings. In some countries expected differences between the two types were found; in others the data failed to show such differences. We suggest that the only way to resolve this seeming confusion is to provide unique explanations for each country that take into account the variety of factors that influence the news production process. Unfortunately, space does not allow for this in the current volume.

Variability among Audiences

Not only did content differ widely across the countries in the study; so did the people's responses in the surveys. Even though we only conducted surveys in 13 of the 17 countries, much variability was detected there, too.

Exposure to news (see Chapter 8) varied greatly across the countries. All questions put to the respondents related to the previous day, which was in all instances a weekday. In terms of time spent watching TV news, the reported overall mean was 36 minutes, with a range of 19 minutes in Switzerland to 55 minutes in Poland. As for reading newspapers, the overall mean was just short of 17 minutes, with a range of 9 minutes in Chile to 25 minutes in Singapore. Finally, our respondents spent a mean time of 14 minutes reading news online, reporting totals as high as 22 minutes in the United States and as low as 6 minutes in Chile. It should be noted that exposure to TV news was greater than exposure to online news in all the countries, whereas in only two countries—Germany and Switzerland—people devoted more time to newspaper reading than to television news.

Much variability was also found in the responses to the questions about reasons for watching and for not watching news. Regarding reasons for watching, based on 5-point scales, the differences between the high and low countries ranged from 0.58 points (low in Hong Kong and high in Brazil) on the reason "To keep up with national affairs in my country," to 0.98 points (low in Israel and high in the United States) on "TV news can be entertaining." Regarding reasons for not watching, the differences ranged from 0.82 points (low in the United States and high in Brazil) on "I don't have enough background to understand events in other countries" to 1.33 points (low in Singapore and high in Brazil) on "It seems that the same things happen all the time and nothing changes."

Finally, in an attempt to predict the exposure to TV news using demographic variables (excluding Brazil, for which there were no data on education), the total percentage of explained variance also covered a considerable range, from a low of 1.1% in Chile to a high of 17.7% in Canada. The corresponding figures for newspaper exposure were 3.2% in Poland and 22.3% in Germany. As for news exposure online, the low figure was 3.4% in Switzerland vs. a high of 14.4% explained variance in Portugal.

Given the growing worldwide concern associated with globalization and its ramifications in many life domains, it might have been expected that citizens in various countries would express significant interest in foreign news, that is, news about other countries and nations. Not unexpectedly, however, our study found that interest in foreign news, across the board, was less than interest in domestic news (see Chapter 9). This tendency was more pronounced in Western than in non-Western countries and among audiences in smaller and culturally diverse countries. On the other hand, comparatively speaking, there was more communality than disparity across the countries of the study. It turned out that interest in topics was more important than the location of events for both foreign and domestic news. Furthermore, audiences had similar preferences in terms of news topics with respect to foreign and domestic news. In a rare instance of remarkable agreement, accidents and natural disasters were the most interesting foreign news topic to audiences around the world. Also, in most of the countries, audiences had fairly little interest in foreign news about international relations, crime and violence, and sports. Finally, people seemed to be more interested in foreign news if nationals of their own countries were involved in the reported events.

Summing up these findings on the interest that people have in foreign news, it appeared that in terms of topics of interest, there was much similarity across countries. This does make good sense if we consider that the appeal of certain topics may stem from curiosity, concern, and empathy that could all be associated with human nature and human interest. Tragedy, triumph, success, and failure could trigger interest no matter where the events take place.

However, while we noted above that interest in topics was more dominant than interest in countries, when it comes to specific countries of interest as the main parameter, people across the globe definitely have their individual preferences. Chapter 10 clearly illustrated two major points. First, the United States was the main country of interest across the board. Second, factors including the "giant neighbor" effect; proximity and economic and political relevance; and historical and personal ties appeared to explain much of the variation in the data. Systematic variations were also noted with respect to world regions and cultural zones to which countries belong.

Thus, while globalization is often viewed as an equalizer of interests around the globe, our findings point to clear differences among audiences in the countries that we studied. These findings conflict with the notion of globalization. People in various countries seem to be segmented into world zones with separate and distinct interests because they lack any unifying impetus. This is not to say that globalization has no effect whatsoever. There seem to be factors that shape the interest of specific audiences for news about specific other countries, while at the same time globalization may be conducive to allowing news from a wide range of other countries to be accessible and relevant to these audiences.

The Position of Gatekeepers

The gatekeepers—editors and journalists—responsible for foreign news were asked about their decision making (Chapter 11) and their perception of the content they produce and the audiences they serve (Chapter 12).

According to the gatekeepers, it seems that in all the countries except China and Brazil the status of foreign news within the newsrooms has declined in recent years. This has been reflected both in terms of the number of staff members at the station and the number of resident correspondents that the stations maintain in various locations around the world. The gatekeepers suggest that this diminution of resources was caused by markedly low ratings for foreign news, possibly due to the complexity of such news and its distance from the audiences' local realities.

Indeed, many of the gatekeepers expressed a sense of pessimism regarding the future of foreign news on television. Several feared that the high cost of foreign news, together with low ratings, will continue to shrink the news hole devoted to foreign events, resulting in even fewer options to contextualize them and less access to direct reporting through correspondents and parachute reporters.

At the same time, however, most of the gatekeepers continue to believe that coverage of foreign news is necessary and important, especially in the context of a globalized world. In order to make foreign news more attractive for their audiences and obtain higher ratings, they select stories according to classic criteria of newsworthiness, most notably deviance, emotional value, proximity, and powerful visuals. They also consistently resort to domestication and contextualization to bridge the lack of proximity inherent in foreign news.

When it comes to the question of how journalists view both the content they produce and their audiences, it turned out that in all cases except China and Switzerland, they underestimated the amount of foreign news in their respective nations. Also, the gatekeepers generally did not agree on the amount of foreign news in their country versus that in other countries. These reflections by journalists may have been caused by confusion about what was meant by foreign news, by their preference for conservative estimates, and by their lack of familiarity with the situation in other countries. On the other hand, the journalists had quite a veridical perception of which countries were most reported on (in most cases the United States) and which were cited less frequently.

As for how much foreign news viewers want, many of the journalists we interviewed expressed general distrust of surveys and of the specific responses to these questions in particular. Some of the journalists admitted not knowing what their viewers want or what they might be interested in. These findings conflict with some earlier research, as well as our own survey findings regarding viewer interest in foreign news.

How do we explain this seeming contradiction? While "social desirability" in some viewer responses may exist, as media scholars we do believe in survey research and feel that there may indeed be indications of increasing interest, albeit slight, among citizens in various nations about what is happening in other countries.

Linking Content and Viewers

After presenting the major findings of the content and the surveys, we examined whether and how these two data sets correspond with each other. We did this separately for the topics (Chapter 13) and for the countries (Chapter 14). These analyses raise the question of causality, that is, does the content influence viewers—along the lines of agenda-setting theory—or do the television stations attempt to cater to their viewers by providing them with information about the issues and the countries they are interested in? In fact, we may also entertain the possibility that news content and audience interests have reciprocal effects.

Our main finding with respect to domestic news is that viewers by and large appear to be interested in the topics of the news that are presented. As for foreign news, however, there seems to be a mixed bag. On both fronts—content and viewers—there is considerable variation across the countries. Moreover, within specific countries we found less correspondence between the prevalence of topics in the news and the interest expressed by viewers. And yet at the country level there are indications that some individual factors could be at work in linking the respondents' interests with the dominant topics in foreign news. In some countries, as well as in the overall analysis, there is a positive link between the frequency of watching television news and the interest of the audience in the topics that are most heavily reported.

Our study has also demonstrated that despite the globalization process there was no homogenization of news content and audience interests vis-à-vis the countries in the news and in people's minds. As in other areas of the study, we found significant differences across countries. Generally speaking, we found greater content-audience correspondence in smaller countries and in countries where people are more interested in foreign news. Our data may also tentatively suggest that content-audience correspondence is weaker in countries that are more ethnically diverse. It may also be that such correspondence depends in part on a country's media system, particularly its level of commercialization, which may lead to greater pressure on television stations to provide viewers with what they presumably want. Finally, we also found that at the country level, concentration of news content was positively related to concentration of audience interests. While television news is clearly not the sole determinant of people's interest in foreign countries, there are nonetheless indications that news viewing does tend to generate interest, mainly in countries that receive prime attention in the news.[2]

Globalization, Cosmopolitanism, and the Global Village

McLuhan's "global village" metaphor first appeared in *The Gutenberg Galaxy: The Making of Typographic Man* (McLuhan, 1962), where he stated: "The new electronic interdependence recreates the world in the image of a global village" (p. 31). Much has been written about the origins and particularly the variety of meanings and interpretations associated with this concept. Space does not permit us to elaborate here. However, in the context of claims regarding the globalization of media in general, and of news in particular, it would be quite natural to think of the "global village" in the sense of the instantaneous dissemination of news around the world that is commonplace today.

And yet, as we discussed briefly at the outset of this volume, there has been considerable criticism leveled against the notion of globalization. With regard to our present endeavor, a leading issue of contention is whether or not the news aired on television around the world is indeed global in its content. By this we mean, how much does it typically go beyond the domestic and the parochial? By now it should be evident that foreign news, which necessitates journalists going beyond national borders, seems to be rather limited the world over, albeit with some degree of variability among countries.

Even the content of global news networks such as CNN International, BBC World News, Al-Jazeera English, and France 24 present considerable news about their respective home bases (or countries of origin) along with varying repertoires of non-home-base countries on which they also report (Cohen & Atad, 2012). In short, although we believe that foreign news ought to be an important component of TV news broadcasts, such news occupies but a modest portion (at best) and a marginal position (at worst) in countries around the world.

Another aspect of what McLuhan may have meant by the "global village" is the psychological feeling of belonging to a global community that can be created by the media. This may be quite true, particularly during so-called "media events" (Dayan & Katz, 1992) that take place in particular locations, are planned and announced in advance, and are staged for television and broadcast around the world (or at least to many parts thereof) in real time, so that one could say that "the whole world is watching." Such events are also reported, of course, as regular news events and as such are presented in newscasts as well as the special live broadcasts, where they would be foreign news except for viewers in the country of location.

From time to time there are also highly dramatic and mostly tragic events—also foreign but to the country of location—in the form of significant natural disasters or accidents, horrific terror events, mass killings by deranged individuals, prolonged (and often violent) political demonstrations, civil wars, and wars between countries, that are reported as they happen or shortly after. But these are not heralded in advance; they are "regular" news fare. While such events are often presented as foreign news and aired around the world, do viewers have the same sense of "participation" as they might have when watching scheduled "media events"?

This sense of participation brings to mind the notion of cosmopolitanism, another concept that has many meanings. Without going into the vast literature in this area, cosmopolitanism in our context refers to people's sense of being part of a world community, sharing values with people of other nations.

Norris and Inglehart (2009) speak of "cosmopolitan communications" as "the degree of information flowing across national borders, which includes the extent to which people interact today within a single global community and the extent to which these networks remain localized and parochial" (p. 136). Furthermore, according to Norris and Inglehart, "Cosmopolitan communications are understood to reflect openness toward ideas and information derived from divergent cultures, as well as a growing awareness of other places and peoples…" (p. 136).

In her recent book *Mediated Cosmopolitanism: The World of Television News*, Robertson (2010) speaks specifically about the role of television news: "The power of television news resides in its potential to engage its viewers, as well as to inform them, to help them to remember as well as to know, and to make it possible for them to recognize and identify with the distant Other who populate their television screens, rather than just to sit back and be a spectator" (p. 31).

We suggest that foreign news, both in its "pure" form as well as its hybrid varieties, is the prime example of the television repertoire that has the potential to bring about some of this global feeling. Unfortunately, given the current state of affairs, its potential may not be realized. As we have seen in our study, foreign news is in decline. Television organizations, including their gatekeepers in both public and commercial stations, do not seem to sufficiently appreciate its importance. Budgets are being cut, the placement of foreign correspondents in strategic locations around the world is rare, and the foreign news hole in many countries is shrinking—all this despite what seems to be a growing interest on the part of citizens worldwide to know what is happening across their borders and around the globe.

Indeed, Riegert (2011) is pessimistic about the future of foreign television news. She claims that the foreign news genre has not changed over the years "…

because it draws on stable foreign policy traditions and cultural myths, and is rooted in a national-political culture that attempts to reassure the viewer that whatever happens, it happens to someone else." Riegert suggests that there are several types of news narratives about the world outside the nation: "generic news stories, domesticated angles coupled with generic stories, and stories sent in from foreign correspondents and freelancers who attempt to create their own narratives." But, she suggests, "even these types of narratives are in the minority of news stories about the world" (p. 1579).

So despite various attempts by broadcasters—either overtly or subtly—to broaden people's horizons and to provide them with a more global view of the world, somehow creating a semblance of a "global village," such attempts seem to have been unsuccessful. Inglehart and Welzel (2005), whose work centers on how world values relate to democracy, note:

> In recent decades, a simplistic version of globalization theory gained widespread currency, holding that the globalization of the mass media and communication networks was producing cultural convergence; we were headed towards a "global village" in which everyone was on the same wavelength. The evidence presented here demonstrates that this view is false—in fact, global trends are moving in exactly the opposite direction. The values of the publics of rich countries are changing rapidly, but those of low-income societies are changing much more slowly or not at all. As a result, a growing gap is opening up between the basic values of the publics of rich versus poor countries. (p. 133)

It thus seems that despite the globalization that is taking place around the world—mostly in the realm of business and commercialization, including, of course, communication technologies—a "global village" has not been created, and this is not likely to happen. Once upon a time there may have been such a village, a community of one culture and one language. In fact, at the dawn of history it may have actually begun that way. The ancient tale of the Tower of Babel serves as an illuminating metaphor juxtaposing globalization with the "global village." As the legend goes:

> And the whole earth was of one language, and of one speech. And it came to pass, as they journeyed from the east, that they found a plain in the land of Shinar; and they dwelt there. And they said one to another, Go to, let us make brick, and burn them thoroughly. And they had brick for stone, and slime had they for mortar. And they said, Go to, let us build us a city and a tower, whose top may reach unto heaven; and let us make us a name, lest we be scattered abroad upon the face of the whole earth. And the Lord came down to see the city and the tower, which the children of men built. And the Lord said, Behold, the people is one, and they have all one language; and this they begin to do: and now nothing will be restrained from them, which they have imagined to do. Go to, let us go down, and there confound their language, that they may not understand one another's speech. So the Lord scattered them abroad from thence

upon the face of all the earth: and they left off to build the city. Therefore is the name of it called Babel; because the Lord did there confound the language of all the earth: and from thence did the Lord scatter them abroad upon the face of all the earth. (Genesis 11:1–9, King James Version)

Over thousands of years, many cultures and languages developed around the world; some disappeared, some were transformed, but clearly no single unified culture exists today as in the ancient Land of Shinar. As Green and Ruhleder (1995) put it: "The lesson inherent in the story of the Tower of Babel reminds us that the ability to communicate universally does not necessarily lead to the development of a 'global village' and all that a village metaphor implies" (p. 60). So even if the news can reach every point around the globe, and even if people all over are interested in what is happening elsewhere and are able to get such information, a united world or "global village" does not seem to be in the cards.

Finally, two decades ago, Cohen, Levy, Roeh, and Gurevitch (1996), in their multinational study of the Eurovision News Exchange (a news service that to this day supplies member countries with foreign news items) also referred to the contrast between globalization and the "global village." In their concluding paragraphs, they made the following observations:

> However mundane its purposes, the Eurovision News Exchange can be seen as a site of intercultural negotiation where understandings and their limits are continuously expressed. At times this negotiation process can even become a harsh struggle. Tugging in one direction is the McLuhanite vision of a global culture—a worldwide village based on shared values and experiences, created by the technology of communication, a utopian vision of equality and equity, an almost primitive communism where the class struggle has been replaced by consensual communication. Pulling in the opposite direction is that sort of human experience often summarized by the metaphor of the Tower of Babel.... Ever since, with or without the Deity as causal variable, and like it or not, the world has been culturally and politically divided. (p. 154)

In conclusion, we believe that our multi-faceted study has shown that foreign news on television, which remains the quintessential mode of providing information about events, people, and issues, is crucial for enlightened societies and for democracy. But the picture we obtained is not uniform. There is much variability across countries in terms of the amount, nature, and formats of presentation of foreign news; there is variability in terms of people's interest in foreign news; and there is variability in terms of how the professionals whose role it is to provide the news think about it. Despite the potential for some communality across nations thanks to globalization there remains much more division than could be hoped for.

Our study presents a one-time analysis of content and opinions. We believe that additional multinational and longitudinal research is needed to track the direction and magnitude of these developments in the near and more distant future. Yet despite this notable limitation, our study offers some detailed and fascinating insights into the interface between foreign news professionals, the content they produce, and the audiences they serve around the world. We are keenly aware of some of the problems that will confront foreign news in the future. Indeed, the situation is precarious, but we can only hope that, in time, media organizations will understand the significance of providing the public with more information of this kind. We also hope that the public will learn to appreciate and value this important genre of news.

Notes

1. A much earlier study, conducted when television news was in its infancy (Kayser, 1953), examined foreign news in 17 newspapers. The findings indicated that of 18 pre-selected foreign stories, only 3 appeared in all the newspapers.
2. Recent research by Segev and Hills (2012) examined the relationship between countries mentioned in online news sites and people's ability to recall the names of countries. Using two of the top three online sources and a sample of respondents in each of four countries—the United States, China, Switzerland, and Israel—the findings indicated that the best indicators of collective memory for any nationality were the news sources common to that nationality.

Methodological Appendixes

The following pages present five appendixes developed for the three phases of the study: content analysis, survey, and interviews with gatekeepers.

Content Analysis

The codebook for the content analysis was designed so that all news items—domestic, foreign, and hybrid—could be coded for all the variables. The codebook consisted of several sections. Appendix A presents the complete list of variables.

The first section (Variables 1–5) identified the items. The second section (Variables 6–8) identified the topics of the item. A list of 25 major topic categories was created: internal politics; international politics; military & defense; internal order; economy; labor & industrial relations; business, commerce, & industry; transportation; health, welfare, & social services; population; education; communication; housing; environment; energy; science & technology; social relations; accidents & disasters; sports; culture; fashion; ceremonies; human interest; weather; and religion. Each topic category also had as many as two dozen subcategories. The coding was done by identifying up to three subcategories for each item. Most of the analyses that appear in the volume, however, were done on the 25 major topic categories.

The third section (Variables 9–35) was concerned with formal features of the items, including the news and non-news persona involved, sources of video materials, and the use of visuals for illustrative purposes. The fourth section (Variables 36–45) consisted of elements of sensationalism in news. The fifth section (Variables 46–49) dealt with three frames: time perspective of the event (past or future), geographic scope of the event, and potential impact of the event.

Variable 50 (Nature of event) defined the item in terms of being domestic, foreign, or hybrid (domestic with foreign involvement or foreign with domestic involvement). The next section (Variables 51–53) consisted of the countries of location of the event being reported, with up to three possible countries being identified (this was done in order to code events taking place in more than one country, such as wars between countries and natural disasters). Variable 54 enabled the coding of whether or not the country (or countries) of location share a common border with the country of broadcast, that is, whether the (foreign) event took place in a neighboring country. Next, up to 5 countries could be coded (Variables 55-59) as being involved in the item, including the country (or countries) of location. The list of countries was based on the United Nations list of countries and territories. Variables 60 and 61 pertain to international organizations that could have been involved in the event. The list was based in part on organizations affiliated with the United Nations as well as other organizations of various types.

The next section consisted of 4 variables (62–65) that relate to the use of certain techniques used to domesticate foreign news events. Another section of the codebook was based on the study of the portrayal of social conflict in the news. Drawing upon Cohen, Adoni, and Bantz (1990), variables 66–80 dealt with the presence of conflict in the items, focusing on three dimensions of conflict: complexity, intensity, and solvability. Complexity is indicated by the number of parties in the conflict; solvability is determined on the basis of negotiations among the parties as well as willingness to compromise and resolve the conflict; and intensity is reflected in the level of aggression and violence depicted by the parties.

The final section of the codebook consisted of variables 81–88, which deal with the actors who appear in the items. Actors were defined as any person or group of people who say something on camera or are quoted in the item (people seen in the item but who do not speak or are not quoted were not considered actors). Each actor was coded separately on eight variables. The roles of the actors were based on the 25 major topic categories, for example, politicians (internal politics), criminals (internal order), teachers (education), and so forth. Each role could have one of three levels: high, medium, or low. For instance, among politicians, a high-ranking person could be a president or prime minister, a medium-ranking person would be a member of a parliament, and a low-ranking person would be a rank-and-file politician. In addition to the roles of the actors, the following variables were coded: single person or group, gender, country or organization, and the nature of the appearance of the actor in the item (language spoken, duration of sound bite, type of quotation, and form of identification).

Reliability of Content Coding

As noted in Chapter 1, the reliability of the coding of content data in cross-cultural research presents what may be considered insurmountable problems. In addition, the broad spectrum of variables in our codebook required the calculation of different coefficients. The reliability of the coding in the 14 countries for which we do have relevant data (as noted in Chapter 1, three of the countries did not provide data) yielded a massive amount of information. Appendix B presents Holsti coefficients for the variables that are reported in several chapters of this volume. The appendix does not include the reliability coefficients for the four sets of variables that allowed for multiple coding: topics of items (Variables 6, 7, and 8 in the codebook) and countries of location, countries involved, and international organizations (Variables 51–53, 55–59, and 60–61 in the codebook, respectively). In fact, many of the variables in the codebook are not reported at all in this book; some appear or will appear in separate publications.

Audience Surveys

An identical questionnaire was used in all 13 countries: Brazil, Canada, Chile, China, Germany, Hong Kong, Israel, Poland, Portugal, Singapore, Switzerland, Taiwan, and the United States. The questionnaire, consisting of 45 questions, appears as Appendix C. It consisted of several parts:

- General interest in foreign news
- Interest in selected topics of domestic and foreign news (politics, crime and violence, sports, relations with other countries, economics, accidents and disasters, and social issues)
- Perceived present and desired amount of foreign news in country's newscasts
- Interest in countries
- General characteristics of foreign news
- Motives for watching television news
- Perceptions of the world
- Exposure to news on television, in newspapers, and on the Internet
- Demographic variables (gender, age, education, and income)

As noted, the surveys were conducted by telephone, except in the United States, where it was done through a web-based questionnaire. The surveys were conducted at different points in time in the various countries, beginning with the survey in Chile, which took place in September–October 2009, and the final survey, which took place in the United States in June–July 2010. Details of the samples and field work appear in Appendix D.

Interviews with Gatekeepers

Face-to-face interviews with foreign news editors and heads of the foreign news desks were conducted in 12 countries: Belgium, Brazil, Canada, Chile, China, Germany, Hong Kong, Israel, Poland, Portugal, Switzerland, and Taiwan. Appendix E presents the list of countries, the number of interviewees, and the dates of the interviews (between May 2009 and March 2011).

A common list of questions was prepared for all the countries. After a number of introductory questions about the respondent's official title, position, or function in the news department, as well as his/her responsibilities in the news production process, interviewers proceeded with the substantial questions. These included:

1. How many journalists work in the newsroom?
2. Is there a special department or section for foreign news?
3. What are your criteria for the selection of foreign news?
4. What sources do you have for foreign news?
5. Does your TV station have its own correspondents in other countries?
6. How important is the availability of visual material for selecting foreign news?
7. What proportion of your channel's news is devoted to foreign and domestic items (as well as the hybrid types of news)?
8. What proportion of the other channel's news in your country is devoted to foreign news (as well as the hybrid types of news)?
9. Where do you think your country ranks among other countries in the amount of foreign news that it presents?
10. What are the main countries about which foreign news is presented in your country?
11. Based on our survey, how much interest do you think viewers have in foreign news?
12. Based on our survey, what percent of the news do you think viewers believe is devoted to foreign news?
13. Based on our survey, how much foreign news (in percent) do viewers think there ought to be in the newscast?

14. Based on our survey, which countries do you think viewers are most interested in?
15. How satisfied are you with the way foreign news is reported by your station?
16. What would you do differently at your station regarding the coverage of foreign news?
17. Do you do anything in order to domesticate the news for viewers in your country?

Following each of questions 7–10, the interviewee was presented with some empirical data from the content analysis pertaining to those points. The respondent was then asked to relate to these data vis-à-vis what s/he had responded previously about those issues. Similarly, following each of questions 11–13, the interviewee was presented with empirical data from the survey and asked to comment on them.

APPENDIX A

Variables in the Codebook

Number	Nature of Variable	Coding Options
1	Country of broadcast	As indicated
2	Station code	As indicated
3	Date of newscast	As indicated
4	Sequence in line-up	1 to n
5	Key word	Unique names for each item
6	Topic 1	List of Topics
7	Topic 2	List of Topics
8	Topic 3	List of Topics
9	In headlines of newscast?	Yes/No
10	In promo during newscast?	Yes/No
11	In re-cap of newscast?	Yes/No
12	Reference to other TV program?	Yes/No
13	Part of block of items?	Yes/No
14	Duration of item	In seconds
15	Anchor seen/heard?	As indicated
16	Reporter/commentator in studio?	Yes/No
17	Anchor interview reporter in studio?	Yes/No
18	Anchor interview reporter on location?	Yes/No
19	Interview with non-journalist in studio?	Yes/No
20	Use of pre-recorded video from location?	Yes/No
21	Live report from location of event?	Yes/No

Number	Nature of Variable	Coding Options
22	Reporter in "stand-up" on locations?	Yes/No
23	Use of archive materials?	As indicated
24	Visuals claimed to be and identified as "exclusive"?	Yes/No
25	Use of footage from global broadcaster?	As indicated
26	Use of footage from news agency?	Yes/No
27	Use of footage from other TV station?	Yes/No
28	Use of tables or charts?	Yes/No
29	Use of still photo?	Yes/No
30	Use of pictorial or graphic representation?	Yes/No
31	Use of animated representation?	Yes/No
32	Use of printed words/text?	Yes/No
33	Use of geographic maps?	Yes/No
34	Use of country flags or emblems?	Yes/No
35	Use of company logo?	Yes/No
36	Use of background music?	Yes/No
37	Use of slow motion?	Yes/No
38	Use of fast motion?	Yes/No
39	Repetition of same visuals over and over?	Yes/No
40	Use of gory pictures?	Yes/No
41	Use of soft/blurred focus?	Yes/No
42	Use of color change?	Yes/No
43	Use of digitization to conceal identity?	Yes/No
44	Use of audio with distorted human voice?	Yes/No
45	Presentation of extreme emotion?	Yes/No
46	Reference to past events?	Time frame as indicated
47	Reference to future events?	Time frame as indicated
48	Geographic scope of event?	City/region/country/world region/world

Number	Nature of Variable	Coding Options
49	Potential impact of event?	City/region/country/world region/world
50	Nature of event	Domestic/foreign/hybrid
51	Country of location 1	List of Countries
52	Country of location 2	List of Countries
53	Country of location 3	List of Countries
54	Borders on country of broadcast?	As indicated
55	Country involved 1	List of Countries
56	Country involved 2	List of Countries
57	Country involved 3	List of Countries
58	Country involved 4	List of Countries
59	Country involved 5	List of Countries
60	First international organization involved	List of International Organizations
61	Second international organization involved	List of International Organizations
62	Domestication—use of maps?	Yes/No
63	Domestication—use of logos?	Yes/No
64	Domestication—reference to country's citizens?	Yes/No
65	Domestication—reference to impact?	Yes/No
66	Conflict in item?	No/Interpersonal/Social
67	Number of parties in conflict?	As indicated
68	Call for resolution of conflict	As indicated
69	Negotiations taking place	As indicated
70	Rejection of negotiations/resolution	As indicated
71	Verbally reported physical aggression	Yes/No
72	Visually shown physical aggression	Yes/No
73	Number of verbally reported people killed	As indicated
74	Number of visually shown people killed	As indicated
75	Number of verbally reported people wounded	As indicated

Number	Nature of Variable	Coding Options
76	Number of visually shown people wounded	As indicated
77	Verbally reported physical damage to property	Yes/No
78	Visually shown physical damage to property	Yes/No
79	Other verbal report of consequences of violence	Yes/No
80	Other visual report of consequences of violence	Yes/No
81	Role of actor	List of Actors' Roles
82	Entity of actor	Individual/group
83	Gender of actor	Female/Male/Both
84	Actor's country or organization	List of Countries and Organizations
85	Does actor speak?	No/Yes—broadcast language/translation
86	Duration of sound bite(s)	In seconds
87	Actor quoted?	Yes/No
88	Actor identified by name and/or role?	As indicated

APPENDIX B

Reliability Coefficients of Major Content Analysis Variables in 14 Countries *

* The data in the table are presented as percentages

Variable	Belgium	Brazil	Chile	China	Egypt	Germany
9 Item in headline	93	97	97	100	92	100
13 Item part of block	78	100	97	100	77	99
15 Anchor seen or heard	87	92	93	100	99	90
20 Pre-recorded video	89	97	99	100	92	76
21 Live from event	94	100	90	100	99	100
23 Archive footage	78	97	81	100	92	73
26 News agency footage	95	97	100	100	90	94
28 Tables/charts	99	92	98	100	97	93
29 Still photos	93	100	84	100	93	92
30 Graphics	97	95	100	100	96	88
31 Animation	98	100	97	100	96	82
32 Printed text	95	100	97	100	97	80
33 Maps	99	100	99	100	99	98
34 Flags	99	100	95	100	96	89
35 Logos	97	100	85	100	96	90
36 Music background	94	100	95	100	96	83
37 Slow motion	100	100	83	100	97	92
50 Nature of event	73	100	85	99	95	87
66 Conflict in item	82	97	87	100	93	86

Variable	Hong Kong	Israel	Japan	Poland	Portugal	Switzerland	Taiwan	United States
9 Item in headline	88	93	98	98	100	96	84	89
13 Item part of block	99	78	67	100	100	95	100	88
15 Anchor seen or heard	96	62	70	98	96	70	94	96
20 Pre-recorded video	99	78	57	35	82	100	100	95
21 Live from event	99	94	96	65	100	100	100	91
23 Archive footage	99	78	84	62	89	75	80	48
26 News agency footage	99	95	90	57	89	100	100	57
28 Tables/charts	99	99	100	100	95	95	93	89
29 Still photos	96	93	88	80	96	91	76	80
30 Graphics	95	97	98	83	91	79	93	75
31 Animation	99	98	91	74	98	93	66	64
32 Printed text	100	95	86	83	100	64	67	30
33 Maps	99	99	95	94	100	99	97	93
34 Flags	98	99	93	86	98	94	85	84
35 Logos	98	97	82	100	98	95	82	89
36 Music background	100	94	80	98	86	95	99	89
37 Slow motion	99	100	96	99	100	95	99	75
50 Nature of event	95	73	84	82	81	90	88	89
66 Conflict in item	97	82	77	66	88	70	70	73

APPENDIX C

Survey Questionnaire

Q1. During a typical week, on how many days do you watch <u>at least some</u> TV news?
[___]

Q2. On which TV channels do you generally watch the news?
[___] [___] [___]

Q3. About how much time <u>in hours and minutes</u> did you spend watching TV news <u>yesterday</u>?
[___][___][___] minutes

Q4. About how much time <u>in hours and minutes</u> did you spend reading a newspaper <u>yesterday</u>?
[___][___][___] minutes

Q5. About how much time <u>in hours and minutes</u> did you spend getting news from the Internet <u>yesterday</u>?
[___][___][___] minutes

Following are reasons some people have given us for watching TV news. For each reason, please tell me to what extent you agree or disagree. You can choose between "strongly agree," "somewhat agree," "neither agree nor disagree," "somewhat disagree," and "strongly disagree."

	Strongly agree	Somewhat agree	Neither agree nor disagree	Somewhat disagree	Strongly disagree
Q6. It gives something to talk about with other people	[5]	[4]	[3]	[2]	[1]
Q7. It helps keeping up with current events and issues in COUNTRY	[5]	[4]	[3]	[2]	[1]
Q8. It helps keeping up with current events in other countries	[5]	[4]	[3]	[2]	[1]
Q9. TV news can be entertaining	[5]	[4]	[3]	[2]	[1]

To what extent are you interested in each of the following topics in the news about COUNTRY? You can choose between "very interested," "quite interested," "somewhat interested," "not very interested," and "not interested at all."

	Very interested	Quite interested	Somewhat interested	Not very interested	Not interested at all
Q10. Domestic politics	[5]	[4]	[3]	[2]	[1]
Q11. Crime and violence	[5]	[4]	[3]	[2]	[1]
Q12. Sports	[5]	[4]	[3]	[2]	[1]
Q13. COUNTRY's relations with other countries	[5]	[4]	[3]	[2]	[1]
Q14. Economics, business, commerce	[5]	[4]	[3]	[2]	[1]
Q15. Accidents and natural disasters	[5]	[4]	[3]	[2]	[1]
Q16. Social issues like health, education, culture, religion, etc.	[5]	[4]	[3]	[2]	[1]

Q17. According to your view, how much of the newscast that you usually watch is devoted to events about other countries?

[1] Less than 20% of the newscast
[2] From 20% to less than 40% of the newscast
[3] From 40% to less than 60% of the newscast
[4] From 60% to less than 80% of the newscast
[5] 80% of the newscast and more

Q18. According to your view, how much of the newscast that you usually watch should be devoted to events about other countries?
[1] Less than 20% of the newscast
[2] From 20% to less than 40% of the newscast
[3] From 40% to less than 60% of the newscast
[4] From 60% to less than 80% of the newscast
[5] 80% of the newscast and more

Q19. Generally, to what extent are you interested in news about other countries? Very interested, quite interested, somewhat interested, not very interested, or not interested at all?

[1] Very interested
[2] Quite interested
[3] Somewhat interested
[4] Not very interested
[5] Not interested at all

Generally, to what extent are you interested in the following topics in the news about foreign countries? You can choose between "very interested," "quite interested," "somewhat interested," "not very interested," and "not interested at all."

	Very interested	Quite interested	Somewhat interested	Not very interested	Not interested at all
Q20. Domestic politics of foreign countries	[5]	[4]	[3]	[2]	[1]
Q21. Crime and violence in foreign countries	[5]	[4]	[3]	[2]	[1]
Q22. Sports in foreign countries	[5]	[4]	[3]	[2]	[1]
Q23. Relations between foreign countries	[5]	[4]	[3]	[2]	[1]
Q24. Economics, business, and commerce in foreign countries	[5]	[4]	[3]	[2]	[1]
Q25. Accidents and natural disasters in foreign countries	[5]	[4]	[3]	[2]	[1]
Q26. Social issues like health, education, culture, religion, etc. of foreign countries	[5]	[4]	[3]	[2]	[1]

Q27. In the news about which foreign countries are you most interested?

[___][___][___]

[___][___][___]

[___][___][___]

[___][___][___]

[___][___][___]

Now I'm going to read you a list of descriptions that some people have used to characterize international news. For each, please tell me to what extent you agree or disagree. You can choose between "strongly agree," "somewhat agree," "neither agree nor disagree," "somewhat disagree," and "strongly disagree."

	Strongly agree	Somewhat agree	Neither agree nor disagree	Somewhat disagree	Strongly disagree
Q28. Events in other countries do not affect me	[5]	[4]	[3]	[2]	[1]
Q29. There is too much reporting of wars, violence, and disasters	[5]	[4]	[3]	[2]	[1]
Q30. I don't have enough background to understand events in other countries	[5]	[4]	[3]	[2]	[1]
Q31. It seems that the same things happen all the time and nothing changes	[5]	[4]	[3]	[2]	[1]

Q32. Generally, to what extent are you interested in news about other countries if the events concern COUNTRY nationals?

[1] Very interested
[2] Quite interested
[3] Somewhat interested
[4] Not very interested
[5] Not interested at all

The following are statements that some people use to characterize the world. Do you agree or disagree with these statements? You can choose between "strongly agree," "somewhat agree," "neither agree nor disagree," "somewhat disagree," and "strongly disagree."

	Strongly agree	Somewhat agree	Neither agree nor disagree	Somewhat disagree	Strongly disagree
Q33. The world is dominated by a few powerful countries	[5]	[4]	[3]	[2]	[1]
Q34. The world is full of violence and conflicts	[5]	[4]	[3]	[2]	[1]
Q35. International organizations such as the United Nations play a very important role in world affairs	[5]	[4]	[3]	[2]	[1]
Q36. Common people don't have any say in world affairs	[5]	[4]	[3]	[2]	[1]

Q37. Gender:
   [1] Female
   [2] Male

Q38. (alternative a) In which year were you born?
   [___][___][___][___]

Or (alternative b) How old are you?
[___][___]

Or (alternative c) Which age bracket includes your age?

[1] 18–22
[2] 23–27
[3] 28–32
[4] 33–37
      Etc.

Q39. How many years of formal education do you have? This includes all kinds of school from primary school to university.

[___][___]

Q40. Which of the following brackets best describes the total monthly income <u>before</u> <u>taxes</u> of <u>all the people living in your household</u>? If you are not sure, please give me an estimate.

[1] Less than [xxx]
[2] From [xxx] to less than [xxx]
[3] From [xxx] to less than [xxx]
[4] From [xxx] to less than [xxx]
[5] From [xxx] to less than [xxx]
[6] From [xxx] to less than [xxx]
[7] From [xxx] to less than [xxx]
[8] More than [xxx]

Each country should prepare the categories for income brackets according to the national standard and replace the [xxx] above with the appropriate figures. This should be done as follows:
x = median household income before taxes in COUNTRY

1. Less than [0.25*x]
2. From [0.25*x] to less than [0.5*x]
3. From [0.5*x] to less than [0.75*x]
4. From [0.75*x] to less than [x]
5. From [x] to less than [1.25*x]
6. From [1.25*x] to less than [1.5*x]
7. From [1.5*x] to less than [1.75*x]
8. More than [1.75*x]

Q41. In which country were you born?

[___][___][___]

Q42. How many years ago did you immigrate/move to COUNTRY?

[___][___]

Q43. Apart from COUNTRY and the country you were born in, have you lived in another country <u>continuously</u> for more than 6 months?

[1] Yes
[2] No

Q44. Have you lived abroad <u>continuously</u> for more than 6 months?

[1] Yes
[2] No

Q45. Day of week of interview

[1] Monday
[2] Tuesday
[3] Wednesday
[4] Thursday
[5] Friday
[6] Saturday

APPENDIX D

Survey Samples

Country	Sample size	Dates of interviews
Brazil	500	January 1–14, 2010
Canada	395	January 11–February 26, 2010
Chile	1,220	September 22–October 9, 2009
China	1,134	March 13–19, 2010
Germany	999	December 2–17, 2009
Hong Kong	800	August 20–September 21, 2009
Israel	760	September 7–15, 2009
Poland	800	November 2–5, 2009
Portugal	500	February 2–19, 2010
Singapore	503	February 2–13, 2010
Switzerland	1,010	November 10–28, 2009
Taiwan	1,141	October 21–28, 2009
United States	785	June 29–July 6, 2010
TOTAL	10,347	

APPENDIX E

Number of Interviews and Dates Conducted

Country	Public/State Stations		Commercial Stations	
	Dates of interviews	Number of interviews	Dates of interviews	Number of interviews
Belgium	6/2009	2	6/2009	2
Brazil	12/2010	1	12/2010	3
Canada	10/2010	2	11/2010	1
Chile	11/2009–1/2010	5	11–12/2009	4
China	2/2011	2	—	0
Germany	9/2010	2	8/2010	3
Hong Kong	—	0	8–9/2009	5
Israel	4/2010	2	5/2010	2
Poland	3/2011	1	3/2011	3
Portugal	1/2011	2	2/2011	2
Switzerland	10/2010	1	10/2010	1
Taiwan	11/2010	2	11/2010	1

References

Aarts, K., & Semetko, H.A. (2003). The divided electorate: Media use and political involvement. *Journal of Politics, 65*(3), 759–784.
Adatto, K. (1990). Sound bite democracy: Network evening news presidential campaign coverage, 1968 to 1988. *Journal of Communication, 31*(3), 24–31.
Albarran, A. (2002). *Media economics* (2nd ed.). Ames: Iowa State University Press.
Allan, S. (1999). *News culture*. Philadelphia: Open University Press.
Allen, C.J., & Hamilton, J.M. (2010). Normalcy and foreign news. *Journalism Studies, 11*(5), 634–649.
Almaney, A. (1970). International and foreign affairs on network television news. *Journal of Broadcasting, 14*(4), 499–509.
Altheide, D.L., & Snow, R.P. (1991). *Media worlds in the postjournalism era*. New York: Aldine de Gruyter.
Altmeppen, K.-D. (2010). The gradual disappearance of foreign news on German television: Is there a future for global, international, world or foreign news? *Journalism Studies, 11*(4), 567–576.
Anderson, C. (2006). *The long tail: Why the future of business is selling less of more*. New York: Hyperion.
Armstrong, C. (2006). Story genre influences whether women are sources. *Newspaper Research Journal, 27*(3), 66–81.
Asp, K. (2007). Fairness, informativeness and scrutiny: The role of news media in democracy. *Nordicom Review, 28*, jubilee issue, 31–49.
Atwood, L., & Buillon, S.J. (1982). New maps of the world: A view from Asia. In L. Atwood, S.J. Buillon, & S.M. Murphy (Eds.), *International perspectives on news* (pp. 102–130). Carbondale: Southern Illinois University Press.
Babe, R. (2000). *Canadian communication thought: Ten foundation writers*. Toronto: University of Toronto Press.
Bagdikian, B. (1989, June 12). The lords of the global village. *The Nation*, pp. 805–820.
Bagdikian, B. (1983). *The media monopoly*. Boston: Beacon Press.
Balinska, M. (2010). A former BBC producer takes a fresh look at foreign news: "It's the audience, stupid!" *Nieman Reports, 13*(3), 16–17.
Baum, M.A. (2003). Soft news and political knowledge: Evidence of absence or absence of evidence? *Political Communication, 20*(2), 173–190.
Baum, M.A. (2005). Talking the vote: Why presidential candidates hit the talk show circuit. *American Journal of Political Science, 49*(2), 213–234.
Baum, M.A., & Jamison, A.S. (2006). The Oprah effect: How soft news helps inattentive citizens vote consistently. *Journal of Politics, 68*(4), 946–959.

Beaudoin, C. (2004). The independent and interactive antecedents of international knowledge. *Gazette, 66*(5), 459–473.

Beaudoin, C. (2008). The Internet's impact on international knowledge. *New Media & Society, 10*(3), 455–474.

Beaudoin, C.E., & Thorson, E. (2002). Journalists, public differ on perception of media coverage. *Newspaper Research Journal, 23*(4), 52–61.

Becker, H. (1967). Whose side are we on? *Social Problems, 14*(3), 239–247.

Bek, M.G. (2004). Tabloidization of news media: An analysis of television news in Turkey. *European Journal of Communication, 19*(3), 371–386.

Bennett, W.L. (1988). *News: The politics of illusion* (2nd ed.). New York: Longman.

Berkowitz, D., Limor, Y., & Singer, J. (2004). A cross-cultural look at serving the public interest: American and Israeli journalists consider ethical scenarios. *Journalism: Theory, Practice & Criticism, 5*(2), 159–181.

Berry, J.M. (2000). *The new liberalism: The rising power of citizen groups.* Washington, DC: Brookings Institution Press.

Best, S.J., Chmielewski, C., & Krueger, B.S. (2005). Selective exposure to online foreign news during the conflict with Iraq. *International Journal of Press/Politics, 10*(4), 52–70.

Bewilogua, J., & Nieland, J.-U. (1996). Von der "Arriflex" zum "Fly-away." Zur Technikentwicklung bei der ARD/ARD-Aktuell und beim ZDF/Redaktion Aktuelles. In P. Ludes (Ed.), *Informationskontexte für Massenmedien: Theorien und Trends* (pp. 51–95). Opladen, Germany: Westdeutscher Verlag.

Biltereyst, D. (2001). Global news research and complex citizenship. Towards an agenda for research on foreign/international news and audiences. In S. Hjarvard (Ed.), *News in a globalized society* (pp. 41–62). Göteborg, Sweden: Nordicom.

Bloom. A.D. (1987). *The closing of the American mind.* New York: Simon & Schuster.

Blumler, J.G., & Katz, E. (1974). *The uses of mass communication: Current perspectives on gratifications research.* Beverly Hills, CA: Sage.

Blumler, J.G., McLeod, J.M., & Rosengren, K.E. (1992). An introduction to comparative communication research. In J.G. Blumler, J.M. McLeod, & K.E. Rosengren (Eds.), *Comparatively speaking: Communication and culture across space and time* (pp. 3–18). Newbury Park, CA: Sage.

Boczkowski, P.J., & Mitchelstein, E. (2010). Is there a gap between the news choices of journalists and consumers? A relational and dynamic approach. *International Journal of Press/Politics, 15*(4), 420–440.

Bogart, L. (1981). *Press and public: Who reads what, when, where, and why in American newspapers* (2nd ed.). Hillsdale, NJ: Erlbaum.

Bourdieu, P. (1998). *On television and journalism.* London: Pluto Press.

Bourdon, J. (2000). A history of European television news: From television to journalism, and back? *Communications, 25*(1), 61–84.

Boyd-Barrett, O. (1980). *The international news agencies.* London: Constable.

Boyd-Barrett, O. (2001). *Final report of the workshop on news agencies in the era of the Internet.* Paris: UNESCO.

Boyd-Barrett, O., & Rantanen, T. (2000). News agency foreign correspondents. In J. Tunstall (Ed.), *Media occupations and professions: A reader* (pp. 127–143). Oxford: Oxford University Press.

Boyd-Barrett, O., & Rantanen, T. (2002). Global and national news agencies: Opportunities and threats in the age of the Internet. In A. Briggs & P. Cobley (Eds.), *The media: An introduction* (2nd ed., pp. 57–69). Harlow, UK: Longman.

Boyd-Barrett, O., & Rantanen, T. (2004). News agencies as news sources: A re-evaluation. In C. Paterson & A. Sreberny (Eds.), *International news in the 21st century* (pp. 31–46). Luton, UK: John Libbey.
Boydstun, A. (2008). How policy issues become front-page news. Unpublished doctoral dissertation, Pennsylvania State University, College Park, PA.
Braman, S., & Cohen, A.A. (1990). Research from start to finish. In J.A. Anderson (Ed.), *Mass communication yearbook* (Vol. 13, pp. 511–518). Newbury Park, CA: Sage.
Brewer, P.R., & Cao, X. (2006). Candidate appearances on soft news shows and public knowledge about primary campaigns. *Journal of Broadcasting & Electronic Media, 50*(1), 18–35.
Brewer, P.R., Graf, J., & Willnat, L. (2003). Priming or framing: Media influence on attitudes toward foreign countries. *Gazette: The International Journal for Communication Studies, 65*(6), 493–508.
Brosius, H.-B. (1990). Bewertung gut, Behaltenschlecht. Die Wirkung von Musik in Informationsfilmen. *Medienpsychologie, 2*(1), 44–55.
Bucher, H.-J., Gloning, T., & Lehnen, K. (2010). *Neue Medien—neue Formate. Ausdifferenzierung und Konvergenz in der Medienkommunikation.* Frankfurt: Campus.
Bullock, C. (2008). Official sources dominate domestic violence reporting. *Newspaper Research Journal, 29*(2), 6–22.
Chaffee, S., & Frank, S. (1996). How Americans get political information: Print versus broadcast news. *Annals of the American Academy of Political and Social Science, 546*, 48–58.
Chaffee, S., Zhao, X., & Leshner, G. (1994). Political knowledge and the campaign media of 1992. *Communication Research, 21*(3), 305–324.
Chalaby, J.K. (2005). Towards an understanding of media transnationalism. In J.K. Chalaby (Ed.), *Transnational television worldwide: Towards a new media order* (pp. 1–13). London: I.B. Tauris.
Chalaby, J.K. (2009). Television for a new global order: Transnational television networks and the formation of global systems. *Gazette, 65*(6), 457–472.
Champlin, D., & Knoedler, J. (2002). Operating in the public interest or in pursuit of private profits? News in the age of media consolidation. *Journal of Economic Issues, 36*(2), 459–468.
Chang, T.K. (1998). All countries not created equal to be news: World system and international communication. *Communication Research, 25*(5), 528–563.
Chang, T.K. (2010). Changing global media landscape, unchanging theories? International communication research and paradigm testing. In G. Golan, T. Johnson, & W. Wanta (Eds.), *International media communication in a global age* (pp. 8–35). New York: Routledge.
Chang, T.K., Berg, P., Fung, A.Y.H., Kedl, K.D., Luther, C.A., & Szuba, J. (2001). Comparing nations in mass communication research, 1970–97: A critical assessment of how we know what we know. *Gazette, 63*(5), 415–434.
Chang, T.K., & Lee, J. (1992). Factors affecting gatekeepers' selection of foreign news: A national survey of newspaper editors. *Journalism and Mass Communication Quarterly, 69*(3), 554–561.
Chang, T K., & Lee, J. (1993). U.S. gatekeepers and the new world information order: Journalistic qualities and editorial positions. *Political Communication, 10*(3), 303–316.
Chang, T.K., Shoemaker, P.J., & Brendlinger, N. (1987). Determinants of international news coverage in the U.S. media. *Communication Research, 14*(4), 396–414.
Chang, T.K., Southwell, B., Lee, H.Y., & Hong, Y. (2012). A changing world, unchanging perspectives: American newspaper editors and enduring values in foreign news reporting. *International Communication Gazette, 74*(4), 367–384.
Clausen, L. (2003). *Global news production.* Copenhagen: CBS Press.
Clausen, L. (2004). Localizing the global: "Domestication" processes in international news production. *Media, Culture and Society, 26*(1), 25–44.
Cohen, A.A. (1987). *The television news interview.* Newbury Park, CA: Sage.

Cohen, A.A. (1992). Comments on survey. *InterMedia*, *20*(1), 35.
Cohen, A.A. (1993). Israelis and foreign news: Perceptions of interest, functions and newsworthiness. *Journal of Broadcasting and Electronic Media*, *37*(3), 337–347.
Cohen, A.A. (1998). Between content and cognition: On the impossibility of television news. *Communications: European Journal of Communication Research*, *23*(4), 425–439.
Cohen, A.A. (2002). Globalization Ltd.: Domestication on the boundaries of television news. In J.M. Chan & B.T. McIntyre (Eds.), *In search of boundaries: Communication, nation-states and cultural identities* (pp. 167–180). Westport, CT: Ablex.
Cohen, A.A. (2012). Benefits and pitfalls of comparative research on news: Production, content, and audiences. In I. Volkmer (Ed.), *The handbook of global media research* (pp. 533–546). Hoboken, NJ: Wiley.
Cohen, A.A., Adoni, H., & Bantz, C.R. (1990). *Social conflict and television news*. Newbury Park, CA: Sage.
Cohen, A.A., & Atad, E. (2012, May). Cosmopolitanism in global news networks: Countries of location and countries involved. Paper presented at the International Communication Annual Conference, Phoenix, AZ.
Cohen, A.A., & Bantz, C. (1989). Where did we come from and where are we going? Some future directions in television news research. *American Behavioral Scientist*, *33*, 135–143.
Cohen, A.A., Levy, M.R., Roeh, I., & Gurevitch, M. (1996). *Global newsrooms, local audiences: A study of the Eurovision News Exchange*. London: John Libbey.
Cohen, A.A., & Roeh, I. (1992). When fiction and news cross over the border: Notes on differential readings and effects. In F. Korzenny & S. Ting-Toomey (Eds.), *International and intercultural communication annual* (Vol. 16, pp. 23–34). Newbury Park, CA: Sage.
Commission on the Freedom of the Press (1947). *A free and responsible press*. Chicago: University of Chicago Press.
Comrie, M. (1999). Television news and broadcast deregulation in New Zealand. *Journal of Communication*, *49*(2), 42–54.
Cook, T.E. (1998). *Governing with the news: The news media as a political institution*. Chicago: University of Chicago Press.
Cooper-Chen, A. (1992). A week of world news: TV gatekeeping in Japan, the United States, Jamaica, Sri Lanka and Colombia. *Keio Communication Review*, *14*, 69–84.
Cooper-Chen, A., & Kanayama, T. (1998). The Pacific distortion: Mutual TV coverage by Japan and the United States. *Keio Communication Review*, *20*, 31–47.
Cottle, S. (2000). Rethinking news access. *Journalism Studies*, *1*(3), 427–448.
Cottle, S., & Rai, M. (2008). Television news in South Africa: Mediating an emerging democracy. *Journal of Southern African Studies*, *34*(2), 343–358.
Crang, M. (1998). *Cultural geography*. London: Routledge.
Curran, J. (2000). Rethinking media and democracy. In J. Curran & M. Gurevitch (Eds.), *Mass media and society* (3rd ed., pp. 120–154). London: Arnold.
Curran, J., Iyengar, S., Lund, A.B., & Salovaara-Moring, I. (2009). Media system, public knowledge and democracy: A comparative study. *European Journal of Communication*, *24*(1), 5–26.
Danielian, L.H., & Page, B.I. (1994). The heavenly chorus: Interest group voices on TV news. *American Journal of Political Science*, *38*(4), 1056–1078.
Dayan, D., & Katz, E. (1992). *Media events: The live broadcasting of history*. Cambridge, MA: Harvard University Press.
Dennis, E.E. (1992). Comments on survey. *InterMedia*, *20*(1), 36.
De Swert, K. (2007). Soft en hard nieuws als kwaliteitskenmerk van het televisienieuws. In M. Hooghe, K. De Swert, & S. Walgrave (Eds.), *De Kwaliteit van het nieuws. Kwaliteitsindicatoren voor televisienieuws* (pp. 131–149). Leuven, Belgium: Acco.

De Swert, K., & Hooghe, M. (2010). When do women get a voice? Explaining the presence of female news sources in Belgian news broadcasts (2003–5). *European Journal of Communication, 25*(1), 69–84.

Desmond, R., & Danilewicz, A. (2010). Women are on, but not in, the news: Gender roles in local television news. *Sex Roles, 62* (11–12), 822–829.

Dìez, P.L. (2005). *Segundo informe representación de género en los informativos de radio y televisión. Secretaria General de politicas de igualdad.* Madrid: Ministerio de Trabajo y Assuntos Socials.

Donsbach, W. (2004). Psychology of news decisions: Factors behind journalists' professional behavior. *Journalism, 5*(2), 131–157.

Drew, D., & Weaver, D. (2006). Voter learning in the 2004 presidential election: Did the media matter? *Journalism and Mass Communication Quarterly, 83*(1), 25–42.

Durante, R., & Knight, B. (2009). Partisan control, media bias, and viewer responses: Evidence from Berlusconi's Italy. Working paper 14762. Cambridge, MA: National Bureau of Economic research.

Elliott, P., & Golding, P. (1974). Mass communication and social change. In E. De Kadt & K. Williams (Eds.), *Sociology and development* (pp. 229–254). London: Tavistock.

Elvestad, E. (2009). Introverted locals or world citizens? A quantitative study of interest in local and foreign news in traditional media and on the Internet. *Nordicom Review, 30*(2), 105–123.

Emery, M. (1989). An endangered species: The international news hole. *Gannett Center Journal, 3*(4), 151–164.

Entrikin, J.N. (1991). *The betweenness of place: Towards a geography of modernity.* Baltimore, MD: The Johns Hopkins University Press.

Epstein, E.J. (1973). *News from nowhere: Television and the news.* New York: Random House.

Ericson, R.V., Baranek, P.M., & Chan, J.B. (1989). *Negotiating control: A study of news sources.* Toronto: University of Toronto Press.

Esser, F. (2008). Dimensions of political news culture: Sound bite and image bite news in France, Germany, Great Britain, and the United States. *International Journal of Press/Politics, 13*(4), 401–428.

Esser, F., & Hanitzsch, T. (2012a). On the why and how of comparative inquiry in communication studies. In F. Esser & T. Hanitzsch (Eds.), *The handbook of comparative communication research* (pp. 3–47). New York: Routledge.

Esser, F., & Hanitzsch, T. (2012b). Organizing and managing comparative research projects across nations: Models and challenges of coordinated collaboration. In I. Volkmer (Ed.), *The handbook of global media research* (pp. 521–532). Hoboken, NJ: Wiley.

Fenby, J. (1986). *The international news services.* New York: Schocken.

Fiske, J. (1992). Popularity and the politics of information. In P. Dahlgren & C. Sparks (Eds.), *Journalism and popular culture* (pp. 45–63). London: Sage.

Flegel, R., & Chaffee, S.H. (1971). Influences of editors, readers, and personal influences on reporters. *Journalism Quarterly, 48*(4), 645–651.

Forgette, R., & Morris, J. (2006). High conflict television news and public opinion. *Political Research Quarterly, 59*(3), 447–456.

Freedman, E., & Fico, F. (2005). Male and female sources in newspaper coverage of male and female candidates in open races for governor in 2002. *Mass Communication and Society, 8*(3), 257–272.

Gallagher, M. (2006). *Who makes the news? Global media monitoring report 2005.* London: World Association for Christian Communication.

Gallagher, M. (2010). *Who makes the news? Global media monitoring report 2010.* London: World Association for Christian Communication.

Galtung, J. (1971). Members of two worlds. A development study of three villages in western Sicily. Oslo: Universitetsforlaget.

Galtung, J., & Ruge, M.H. (1965). The structure of foreign news: The presentation of the Congo, Cuba and Cyprus crises in four Norwegian newspapers. *Journal of Peace Research, 2*(1), 64–91.

Gans, H. (1979). *Deciding what's news: A study of CBS Evening News, NBC Nightly News, Newsweek, and Time*. New York: Pantheon.

Garcia, J.L. Dader. (1992). *El periodista en el espacio publico*. Barcelona, Spain: Bosch.

Gasher, M. (2009). Guest editor's introduction. *Aether: The Journal of Media Geography, 4*, i–ii.

Gasher, M., & Klein, R. (2008). Mapping the geography of on-line news. *Canadian Journal of Communication, 33*(2), 193–211.

Geddes, B. (2003). How the cases you choose affect the answers you get: Selection bias in comparative politics. In B. Geddes (Ed.), *Paradigms and sand castles: Theory building and research design in comparative politics* (pp. 89–129). Ann Arbor: University of Michigan Press.

Gerbner, G., & Marvanyi, G. (1977). The many worlds of the world's press. *Journal of Communication, 27*(1), 52–66.

Giddens, A. (1991). *The consequences of modernity*. Stanford, CA: Stanford University Press.

Ginsberg, T. (2002, January/February). Rediscovering the world. *American Journalism Review*, pp. 48–53.

Gitlin, T. (1980). *The whole world is watching: Mass media in the making and unmaking of the New Left*. Berkeley: University of California Press.

Golan, G.J. (2003). America's narrow window to the world: An analysis of network global coverage. *International Communication Bulletin, 38*(3/4), 2–11.

Golan, G.J. (2008). Where in the world is Africa? Predicting coverage of Africa by US television Networks. *Gazette, 70*(1), 41–57.

Golan, G.J. (2010). Determinants of international news coverage. In G.J. Golan, T.J. Johnson, & W. Wanta (Eds.), *International media communication in a global age* (pp. 125–144). New York: Routledge.

Golan, G., & Wanta, W. (2003). International elections on the U.S. network news: An examination of factors affecting newsworthiness. *Gazette, 65*(1), 25–40.

Gonzenbach, W.J., Arant, D., & Stevenson, R.L. (1992). The world of U.S. network news: Eighteen years of international and foreign news coverage. *Gazette, 50*(1), 53–72.

Grabe, M.E., Lang, A., & Zhao, X.Q. (2003). News content and form: Implications for memory and audience evaluations. *Communication Research, 30*(4), 387–413.

Grabe, M.E., Zhou, S., & Barnett, B. (2001). Explicating sensationalism in television news: Content and the bells and whistles of form. *Journal of Broadcasting and Electronic Media, 45*(4), 635–655.

Graber, D. (2003). The rocky road to new paradigms: Modernizing news and citizenship standards. *Political Communication, 20*(2), 145–148.

Green, C., & Ruhleder, K. (1995). Globalization, borderless worlds, and the Tower of Babel: Metaphors gone awry. *Journal of Organizational Change Management, 8*(4), 55–68.

Gudykunst, W.B. (2003). Issues in cross-cultural communication research. In W.B. Gudykunst (Ed.), *Cross-cultural and intercultural communication* (pp. 149–161). Thousand Oaks, CA: Sage.

Gulati, G.J., Just, M.R., & Crigler, A.N. (2004). News coverage of political campaigns. In L.L. Kaid (Ed.), *Handbook of political communication research* (pp. 237–256). Mahwah, NJ: Lawrence Erlbaum.

Gurevitch, M., & Blumler, J.G. (1990). Comparative research: The extending frontier. In D.L. Swanson & D. Nimmo (Eds.), *New directions in political communication: A resource book* (pp. 305–325). Newbury Park, CA: Sage.

Gurevitch, M., & Blumler, J.G. (2004). State of the art of comparative political communication research: Poised for maturity? In F. Esser & B. Pfetsch (Eds.), *Comparing political communication: Theories, cases, and challenges* (pp. 325–343). New York: Cambridge University Press.
Hagen, L., Berens, H., Zeh, R., & Leidner, D. (1998). Ländermerkmale als Nachrichtenfaktoren. Der Nachrichtenwert von Ländern und seine Determinanten in den Auslandsnachrichten von Zeitungen und Fernsehen in 28 Ländern. In C. Holtz-Bacha, H. Scherer, & N. Waldmann (Eds.), *Wie die Medien die Welt erschaffen und wie die Menschen darin leben* (pp. 59–81). Wiesbaden, Germany: WestdeutscherVerlag.
Hall, S., Critcher, C., Jefferson, T., Clarke, J., & Roberts, B. (1978). *Policing the crisis*. London: Macmillan.
Hallin, D.C. (1986). *The "uncensored war": The media and Vietnam*. New York: Oxford University Press.
Hallin, D.C. (1992). Sound bite news: Television coverage of elections, 1968–1988. *Journal of Communication, 42*(2), 5–24.
Hallin, D.C., & Mancini, P. (2004). *Comparing media systems: Three models of media and politics*. New York: Cambridge University Press.
Hallin, D.C., & Mancini, P. (2012). Comparing media systems: A response to critics. In F. Esser & T. Hanitzsch (Eds.), *The handbook of comparative communication research* (pp. 207–220). New York: Routledge.
Hamilton, J. (2004). *All the news that's fit to sell: How the market transforms information into news*. Princeton, NJ: Princeton University Press.
Hamilton, J.M., & Jenner, E. (2004). Redefining foreign correspondence. *Journalism: Theory, Practice & Criticism, 5*(3), 301–321.
Hanitzsch, T. (2008). Comparing journalism across cultural boundaries: State of the art, strategies, problems and solutions. In M. Löffelholz & D. Weaver (Eds.), *Global journalism research: Theories, methods, findings, future* (pp. 93–105). Oxford: Blackwell.
Hanitzsch, T., Anikina, M., Berganza, R., Cangoz, I., Coman, M., Hamada, S., Hanusch, F., Karadjov, C.D., Mellado, C., Moreira, S.V., Mwesige, P.G., Plaisance, P.L., Reich, Z., Seethaler, J., Skewes, E.A., Noor, D.V., & Yuen, K.W. (2010). Modeling perceived influences on journalism: Evidence from a cross-national survey of journalists. *Journalism & Mass Communication Quarterly, 87*(1), 7–24.
Hanitzsch, T., & Esser, F. (2012).Challenges and perspectives of comparative communication inquiry. In F. Esser & T. Hanitzsch (Eds.), *The handbook of comparative communication research* (pp. 501–516). New York: Routledge.
Hannerz, U. (2004). *Foreign news: Exploring the world of foreign correspondents*. Chicago: University of Chicago Press.
Hantrais, L. (1999). Contextualization in cross-national comparative research. *International Journal of Social Research Methodology, 2*(2), 93–108.
Harcup, T., & O'Neill, D. (2001). What is news? Galtung and Ruge revisited. *Journalism Studies, 2*(5), 261–280.
Hargrove, T., & Stempel, G.H. (2002). Exploring reader interest in international news. *Newspaper Research Journal, 23*(4), 46–51.
Harkness, J.A. (2003). Questionnaire translation. In J.A. Harkness, F.J.R. van de Vijver, & P.Ph. Mohler (Eds.), *Cross-cultural survey methods* (pp. 35–56). Hoboken, NJ: Wiley.
Hart, J. (1963). The flow of news between the US and Canada. *Journalism Quarterly, 40*(1), 70–74.
Haynes, Jr., R.D. (1984). Test of Galtung's theory of structural imperialism. In R.L. Stevenson & D.L. Shaw (Eds.), *Foreign news and the new world information order* (pp. 200–216). Ames: Iowa State University Press.

Heinderyckx, F. (1993). Television news programs in Western Europe: A comparative study. *European Journal of Communication, 8*(4), 425–540.
Heiser, W.J., & Busing, F.M.T.A. (2004). Multidimensional scaling and unfolding of symmetric and asymmetric proximity relations. In D. Kaplan (Ed.), *The Sage handbook of quantitative methodology for the social sciences* (pp. 25–48). Thousand Oaks, CA: Sage.
Herman, E.S., & Chomsky, N. (1988). *Manufacturing consent*. Toronto: Random House.
Hess, S. (1996a). *International news and foreign correspondents*. Washington, DC: The Brookings Institution.
Hess, S. (1996b). Media mavens. *Society, 33*(3), 70–78.
Hester, A. (1973). Theoretical considerations in predicting volume and direction of international information flow. *Gazette, 19*(4), 238–247.
Hester, A. (1978). Five years of foreign news on U.S. television evening newscasts. *Gazette, 24*(1), 88–95.
Hjarvard, S. (2002). The study of international news. In S. Hjarvard (Ed.), *News in a globalized society* (pp. 91–97). Copenhagen: Nordicom.
Hofstede, G. (2001). *Culture's consequences: Comparing values, behaviors, institutions and organizations across nations* (2nd ed.). Thousand Oaks, CA: Sage.
Hoge, J.F. (1997). Foreign news: Who gives a damn? *Columbia Journalism Review, 36*(4), 48–52.
Holtz-Bacha, C., & Kaid, L.L. (2011). Political communication across the world: Methodological issues involved in international comparisons. In E.P. Bucy & R.L. Holbert (Eds.), *Sourcebook for political communication research: Methods, measures, and analytical techniques* (pp. 395–416). New York: Routledge.
Holtz-Bacha, C., & Norris, P. (2001). "To entertain, inform and educate": Still the role of public television. *Political Communication, 18*(2), 123–140.
Hooghe, M. (2002). Watching television and civic engagement: Disentangling the effects of time, programs, and stations. *Harvard International Journal of Press/Politics, 7*(2), 84–104.
Hoskins, C., McFadyen, S., & Finn, A. (2004). *Media economics: Applying economics to new and traditional media*. Thousand Oaks, CA: Sage.
Hoynes, W. (2002). Political discourse and the "new PBS." *Harvard International Journal of Press/Politics, 7*(4), 34–56.
Husting, G. (1999). When a war is not a war: Abortion, desert storm, and representations of protest in American TV news. *The Sociological Quarterly, 40*(1), 159–176.
Ihlen, O., Allern, S., Thorbjornsrud, K., & Waldahl, R. (2010). The world on television: Market-driven, public service news. *Nordicom Review, 31*(2), 31–45.
Inglehart, R., & Welzel, C. (2005). *Modernization, cultural change and democracy*. New York: Cambridge University Press.
International Press Institute (IPI). (1953). *The flow of news*. Zürich, Switzerland: IPI.
Ito, Y. (2004). The grass beneath two bears: News flows in Eastern and Central Europe. *Global Media Journal, 3*(4). Retrieved from http://lass.purduecal.edu/cca/gmj/sp04/gmj-sp04-ito.htm
Ito, Y. (2009). What sustains the trade winds? The pattern and determinant factors of international news flow. *Keio Communication Review, 31*, 65–87.
Iyengar, S. (1991). *Is anyone responsible? How television frames political issues*. Chicago: University of Chicago Press.
Jensen, K.B. (1990). The politics of polysemy: Television news, everyday consciousness and political action. *Media, Culture and Society, 12*(1), 57–77.
Jewitt, C. (2009). *The Routledge handbook of multimodal analysis*. London: Routledge.
Johnson, T., Braima, M., & Sothirajah, J. (1999). Doing the traditional media sidestep: Comparing the effects of the Internet and other nontraditional media with traditional media in the 1996 presidential campaign. *Journalism and Mass Communication Quarterly, 76*(1), 99–123.

Jordan, D.L., & Page, B.I. (1992). Shaping foreign policy opinions: The role of TV news. *The Journal of Conflict Resolution, 36*(2), 227–241.
Jowell, R. (1998). How comparative is comparative research? *American Behavioral Scientist, 42*(2), 168–177.
Kamps, K. (1998). Nachrichtengeographie. Themen, Strukturen, Darstellung: Ein Vergleich. In K. Kamps & M. Meckel (Eds.), *Fernsehnachrichten. Prozesse, Strukturen, Funktionen* (pp. 275–294). Wiesbaden, Germany: VS-Verlag.
Kamps, K. (1999). *Politik in Fernsehnachrichten. Struktur und Präsentation internationaler Ereignisse—Ein Vergleich*. Baden-Baden, Germany: Nomos.
Kariel, H., & Rosenvall, L. (1995). *Places in the news: A study of news flows*. Ottawa: Carleton University Press.
Katz, E., Blumler, J.G., & Gurevitch, M. (1974). Utilization of mass communication by the individual. In J.G. Blumler & E. Katz (Eds.), *The uses of mass communications: Current perspectives on gratifications research* (pp. 19–32). Beverly Hills, CA: Sage.
Kaye, B., & Johnson, T. (2002). Online and in the know: Uses and gratifications of the Web for political information. *Journal of Broadcasting & Electronic Media, 46*(1), 54–71.
Kayser, J. (1953). *One week's news. Comparative study of 17 major dailies for a seven-day period*. Paris: UNESCO.
Kepplinger, H.M., Brosius, H.B., & Staab, J.F. (1991). Instrumental actualization: A theory of mediated conflicts. *European Journal of Communication, 6*(3), 263–290.
Kerbel, M.R., Apee, S., & Ross, M.H. (2000). PBS ain't so different: Public broadcasting, election frames, and democratic empowerment. *Harvard International Journal of Press/Politics, 5*(4), 8–32.
Kim, H.S. (2002). Gatekeeping international news: An attitudinal profile of U.S. television journalists. *Journal of Broadcasting and Electronic Media, 46*(3), 431–452.
Kim, J., Wyatt, R.O., & Katz, E. (1999). News, talk, opinion, participation: The part played by conversation in deliberative democracy. *Political Communication, 16*(4), 361–385.
Kim, K., & Barnett, G.A. (1996, May). *The determinants of international news flow: A network analysis*. Paper presented at the Annual Convention of the International Communication Association, Albuquerque, NM.
Klijin, M.E. (2003). Attention-getting and comprehension-raising attributes in visuals in Dutch and American, public and private television news about violence. *Journal of Broadcasting & Electronic Media, 47*(1), 124–144.
Kohn, M.L. (1989). Cross-national research as an analytic strategy. In M.L. Kohn (Ed.), *Cross-national research in sociology* (pp. 77–102). Newbury Park, CA: Sage.
Kolmer, C., & Semetko, H.A. (2010). International television news: Germany compared. *Journalism Studies, 11*(5), 700–717.
Korzenny, F., del Toro, W., & Gaudino, J. (1987). International news media exposure, knowledge and attitudes. *Journal of Broadcasting & Electronic Media, 31*(1), 73–87.
Kwak, N., Poor, N., & Skoric, M. (2006). Honey, I shrunk the world! The relation between Internet use and international engagement. *Mass Communication & Society, 9*(2), 189–213.
Langer, J. (1992). Truly awful news on television. In P. Dahlgren & C. Sparks (Eds.), *Journalism and popular culture* (pp. 113–129). London: Sage.
Langer, J. (1997). *Tabloid television: Popular journalism and "other news."* London: Routledge.
Larson, J.F. (1982). International affairs coverage on US evening network news, 1972–1979. In W.C. Adams (Ed.), *Television coverage of international affairs* (pp. 15–41). Norwood, NJ: Ablex.
Lee, C.C., Chan, J.M., Pan, Z.D., & So, C.Y.K. (2002). *Global media spectacle*. Albany: State University of New York Press.

Lee, F.L.F. (2010). Banal global imagination: Multi-nation stories and international organizations in television foreign news. *The Chinese Journal of Communication and Society, 13*, 161–191.

Lee, F.L.F., Chan, J.M., & Zhou, B.H. (2011). National lenses on a global news event: determinants of politicization and domestication of the prelude to the Beijing Olympics. *The Chinese Journal of Communication, 4*(3), 274–292.

Lee, F.L.F., Lin, W.Y., Lee, C.C., He, Z., & Yao, M.Z. (2012). Globalization and people's interests in foreign affairs: A comparative survey in Hong Kong and Taipei. *International Communication Gazette, 74*(3), 221–239.

Lehman-Wilzig, S.N., & Saletzky, M. (2010). Hardnews, softnews, "general" news: The necessity and utility of an intermediate classification. *Journalism, 11*(1), 37–56.

Leon, B. (2008). Science related information in European television: A study of prime-time news. *Public Understanding of Science, 17*(4), 443–460.

Lewin, K. (1947). Frontiers in group dynamics II. Channels of group life: Social planning and action research. *Human Relations, 1*(2), 143–153.

Lin, W.-Y., Lo, V.-H., & Wang, T.L. (2011). Bias in television foreign news in China, Hong Kong, and Taiwan. *Chinese Journal of Communication, 4*(3), 293–310.

Liu, H.D., & Gunaratne, S.A. (1972). Foreign news in two Asian dailies. *Gazette, 18*(1), 37–41.

Livingstone, S. (2003). On the challenges of cross-national comparative media research. *European Journal of Communication, 18*(4), 477–500.

Livingstone, S. (2012). Challenges to comparative research in a globalizing media landscape. In F. Esser & T. Hanitzsch (Eds.), *The handbook of comparative communication research* (pp. 415–429). New York: Routledge.

Lo, V., & Chang, C. (2006). Knowledge and the Gulf Wars. *International Journal of Press/Politics, 11*(3), 135–155.

Lo, V.-H., Neilan, E., & King, P.T. (1998). Television coverage of the 1995 legislative election in Taiwan: Rise of cable television as a force for balance in media coverage. *Journal of Broadcasting & Electronic Media, 42*(3), 340–355.

Lobo, P., & Cabecinhas, R. (2008). As mulheres nas notícias televisivas: metodologia para uma análise crítica das representações sociais de. Actas do 5º Congresso da Associação Portuguesa de Ciências da Comunicação, Moisés de Lemos Martins & Manuel Pinto (Orgs.). Braga, Portugal: Centro de Estudos de Comunicação e Sociedade.

MacBride, S. (1980). *Many voices, one world: Communication and society today and tomorrow: Toward a new more just and more efficient world information and communications order.* Paris: Kogan Page/Unipub/UNESCO.

Machill, M. (1999). The effect of the commercialization of Swedish television on journalistic culture. *Harvard International Journal of Press/Politics, 4*(2), 103–111.

Malik, R., & Anderson, K. (1992). TV: the global news agenda survey. *InterMedia, 20*(1), 8–29.

McClellan, S. (2001). Eyes wide shut. *Broadcasting & Cable, 131*(44), 23–24.

McCombs, M., & Shaw, D. (1972). The agenda-setting functions of mass media. *Public Opinion Quarterly, 36*(2), 176–187.

McLuhan, M. (1962). *The Gutenberg galaxy: The making of typographic man.* Toronto: University of Toronto Press.

McManus, J.H. (1994). *Market-driven journalism: Let the citizen beware.* London: Sage.

McNelly, J.T. (1962). Meaning intensity and interest in foreign news topics. *Journalism Quarterly, 39*(1), 161–168.

McNelly, J.T., & Izcaray, F. (1986). International news exposure and images of foreign nations. *Journalism Quarterly, 63*(3), 546–553.

McNelly, J.T., Rush, T.T., & Bishop, M.E. (1968). Cosmopolitan media usage in the diffusion of international affairs news. *Journalism Quarterly, 45*(2), 329–332.

McQuail, D. (1983). *Mass communication theory*. London: Sage.
McQuail, D. (2000). *McQuail's mass communication theory* (4th ed.). Thousand Oaks, CA: Sage.
McQuail, D., Blumler, J.G., & Brown, J. (1972). The television audience: A revised perspective. In D. McQuail (Ed.), *Sociology of mass communication* (pp. 135–165). Harmondsworthm UK: Penguin.
Miller, J.K. (1994). Broadcast news in Japan: NHK and NTV. *Keio Communication Review, 16*, 77–103.
Mindich, D.T.Z. (2005). *Tuned out: Why Americans under 40 don't follow the news*. New York: Oxford University Press.
Moisy, C. (1997, Summer). Myths of the global information village. *Foreign Policy, 107*, 78–87.
Mutz, D., Roberts, D.F., & van Vuuren, D.P. (1993). Reconsidering the displacement hypothesis: Television's influence on children's time use. *Communication Research, 20*(1), 51–75.
Neveu, E. (1999). Politics on French television: Towards a renewal of political journalism and debate frames. *European Journal of Communication, 14*(3), 379–409.
Norris, P. (1995). The restless searchlight: Network news framing of the post Cold War world. *Political Communication, 12*(4), 357–370.
Norris, P. (2009). Comparative political communications: Common frameworks or Babelian confusion? *Government and Opposition, 44*(3), 321–340.
Norris, P., & Inglehart, R. (2009). *Cosmopolitan communications: Cultural diversity in a globalized world*. Cambridge, UK: Cambridge University Press.
Norris, P., & Sanders, D. (2003). Message or medium? Campaign learning during the 2001 British general election. *Political Communication, 20*(3), 233–262.
Nossek, H. (2004). Our news and their news: The role of national identity in the coverage of foreign news. *Journalism, 5*(3), 343–368.
Östgaard, E. (1965). Factors influencing the flow of news. *Journal of Peace Research, 2*(1), 39–63.
Owens, L.C. (2007). International accident, disaster stories generate greater interest among students. *Newspaper Research Journal, 28*(2), 107–113.
Pantti, M. (2010). The value of emotion: An examination of television journalists' notions on emotionality. *European Journal of Communication, 25*(2), 168–181.
Parks, M. (2002). Foreign news: What's next? *Columbia Journalism Review, 40*(5), 52.
Paterson, C. (1998). Global battlefields. In O. Boyd-Barrett & T. Rantanen (Eds.), *The globalization of news* (pp. 79–103). London: Sage.
Paterson, C. (2011). *The international television news agencies: The world from London*. New York: Peter Lang.
Patterson, T.E., & Donsbach, W. (1996). News decisions: Journalists as partisan actors. *Political Communication, 13*(4), 455–468.
Patterson, E.T. (2000). *Doing well and doing good: How soft news and critical journalism are shrinking the new audience and weakening democracy – And what news outlets can do about it* (Faculty Research Working Paper Series, RWP01-001). Cambridge, MA: John F. Kennedy School of Government, Harvard University.
Perry, D.K. (1985). The mass media and inference about other nations. *Communication Research, 12*(4), 595–614.
Perry, D.K. (1990). News reading, knowledge about, and attitudes toward foreign countries. *Journalism Quarterly, 67*(2), 353–358.
Perry, D.K., & McNelly, J.T. (1988). News orientations and the variability of attitudes toward developing countries. *Journal of Broadcasting & Electronic Media, 32*(3), 323–334.
Peter, J., & Lauf, E. (2002). Reliability in cross-national content analysis. *Journalism & Mass Communication Quarterly, 79*(4), 815–832.

Pew (2011). 2011: A year of big stories both foreign and domestic. Pew Research Center for the People and the Press. Press release. Retrieved December 11, 2011, from http://www.people-press.org/2011/12/21/2011–a-year-of-big-stories-both-foreign-and-domestic/

Pew Research Center for the People and the Press (2002a). *Pew Research Center for the People and the Press biennial media consumption survey*. Retrieved December 11, 2011, from http://www.people-press.org/files/legacy-questionnaires/156.pdf

Pew Research Center for the People and the Press (2002b). *2002 biennial media consumption survey. Public's news habits little changed by September 11*. Retrieved December 11, 2012, from http://people-press.org/2002/06/09/publics-news-habits-little-changed-by-september-11/

Pew Research Center for the People and the Press (2008). *Internet overtakes newspapers as news outlet*. Retrieved December 11, 2012, from http://www.people-press.org/2008/12/23/internet-overtakes-newspapers-as-news-outlet/

Pfetsch, B. (1996). Convergence through privatization? Changing media environments and televised politics in Germany. *European Journal of Communication, 11*(4), 427–451.

Powers, A., & Fico, F. (1994). Influences on use of sources at large U.S. newspapers. *Newspaper Research Journal, 15*(4), 87–97.

Preston, P. (2009). *Making the news: Journalism and news cultures in Europe*. London: Routledge.

Preston, P., & Metykova, M. (2009). From news to house rules: organisational contexts. In P. Preston, *Making the news: Journalism and news cultures in Europe* (pp. 72–92). London & New York: Routledge.

Prior, M. (2003). Any good news in soft news? The impact of soft news preference on political knowledge. *Political Communication, 20*(2), 149–171.

Randal, J. (2000). *The decline, but not yet total fall, of foreign news in the U.S. media*. Working paper series #2000–2. The Joan Shorenstein Center on the Press, Politics and Public Policy. Retrieved July 28, 2012 from http://shorensteincenter.org/wp-content/uploads/2012/03/2000_02_randal.pdf

Rantanen, T. (2003). The new sense of place in 19th-century news. *Media Culture Society, 25*(4), 435–449.

Rantanen, T. (2009). *When news was new*. Oxford: Wiley-Blackwell.

Reinemann, C., Stanyer, J., Scherr, S., & Legnante, G. (2012). Hard and soft news: A review of concepts, operationalizations and key findings. *Journalism, 13*(2), 221–239.

Relph, E. (1976). *Place and placelessness*. London: Routledge.

Riegert, K. (2011). Pondering the future for foreign news on national television. *International Journal of Communication, 5*, 1567–1585.

Riffe, D. (1996). Linking international news to U.S. interests: A content analysis. *International Communication Bulletin, 31*(1–2), 14–18.

Riffe, D., Aust, C.F., Jones, T.C., Shoemaker, P., & Sundar, S. (1994). The shrinking foreign newshole of the *New York Times*. *Newspaper Research Journal, 15*(3), 74–88.

Robertson, A. (2010). *Mediated cosmopolitanism: The world of television news*. Cambridge, UK: Polity.

Robertson, R. (1992). *Globalization: Social theory and global culture*. London: Sage.

Robinson, G. (1998). Monopolies of knowledge in Canadian communication studies: The case of feminist approaches. *Canadian Journal of Communication, 27*(1), 65–72.

Robinson, G.J., & Sparkes, V.M. (1976). International news in the Canadian and American press: A comparative news flow study. *Gazette, 22*(4), 203–218.

Robinson, J.P. (1967). World affairs information and mass media exposure. *Journalism Quarterly, 44*(1), 23–31.

Rosengren, K.E. (1974a). International news: Methods, data and theory. *Journal of Peace Research, 11*(2), 145–156.

Rosengren, K.E. (1974b). Uses and gratifications. A paradigm outlined. In J.G. Blumler & E. Katz (Eds.), *The uses of mass communications: Current perspectives on gratifications research* (pp. 269–286). Beverly Hills, CA: Sage.
Rosengren, K.E., Wenner, L.A., & Palmgreen, P. (1985). *Media gratifications research: Current perspectives*. Beverly Hills, CA: Sage.
Rosenstiel, T., Just, M., Dean, W., Belt, T., & Pertilla, A. (2007). *We interrupt this newscast: How to improve local news and win ratings, too*. New York: Cambridge University Press.
Salwen, M., & Matera, F.R. (1992). Public salience of foreign nations. *Journalism Quarterly, 69*(3), 623–632.
Sande, O. (1971). The perception of foreign news. *Journal of Peace Research, 8*(3/4), 221–237.
Sanders, K., & Bale, T. (2000). The symbolic agenda of a British satellite broadcaster's 1997 general election coverage. *Journal of Broadcasting & Electronic Media, 44*(3), 487–502.
Schaap, G. (1998). Research bibliography: Three decades of television news research. *Communication, 23*(3), 331–350.
Schaap, G., Renckstorf, K. & Wester, F. (1998). Three decades of television news research: An action theoretical inventory of issues and problems. *Communications, 23*(3), 351–382.
Schenk, B. (1987). Die Struktur des internationalen Nachrichtenflusses: Analyse der empirischen Studien. *Rundfunk und Fernsehen, 35*(1), 36–54.
Scheufele, D. (2000). Agenda-setting, priming, and framing revisited. Another look at cognitive effects of political communication. *Mass Communication and Society, 3*(2–3), 297–316.
Schlesinger, P. (1987). *Putting "reality" together: BBC news*. New York: Methuen.
Schmidt, D., & Wilke, J. (1998). Die Darstellung des Auslands in den deutschen Medien: Ergebnisse einer Inhaltsanalyze. In S. Quandt & W. Gast (Eds.), *Deutschland im Dialog der Kulturen. Medien—Images—Verständigung* (pp. 167–181). Konstanz, Germany: UVK.
Schudson, M. (2003). *The sociology of news*. New York: Norton.
Schudson, M., & Tifft, S.E. (2005). American journalism in historical perspective. In G. Overholser & K. Hall Jamieson (Eds.), *The press* (pp. 17–47). Oxford: Oxford University Press.
Schulz, W. (1983). Nachrichtengeographie. Untersuchungen über die Struktur der internationalen Berichterstattung. In M. Rühl & H.W. Stuiber (Eds.), *Kommunikationspolitik in Forschung und Anwendung. Festschrift für Franz Ronneberger* (pp. 281–291). Düsseldorf, Germany: Droste.
Schulz, W. (2001, May 24–28). *Foreign news in leading newspapers of Western and post-Communist countries*. Paper presented at the annual conference of the International Communication Association, Washington, DC.
Scott, D., & Gobetz, R. (1992). Hard news/soft news content of the national broadcast networks, 1972–1987. *Journalism Quarterly, 69*(2), 406–412.
Segev, E., & Hills, T. (2012). *When news and memory come apart: A cross-national comparison of countries' mentions*. Working paper, Tel Aviv University, Israel.
Seib, P. (1997). *Headline diplomacy: How news coverage affects foreign policy*. Westport, CT: Praeger.
Semetko, H.A., Brzinski, J.B., Weaver, D., & Willnat, L. (1992). TV news and U.S. public opinion about foreign countries: The impact of exposure and attention. *International Journal of Public Opinion Research, 4*(1), 18–36.
Senokozlieva, M., Fischer, O., Bente, G., & Krämer, N.C. (2006). *Of frames and cultures: A cross-cultural comparison of TV newscasts*. Paper presented at the annual conference of the International Communication Association, Dresden, Germany.
Seplow, S. (2002). Rating coverage. *American Journalism Review*, June/July. Retrieved July 28, 2012 http://www.ajr.org/article.asp?id=2586
Servaes, J., & Tonnaer, C. (1992). *De Nieuwsmarkt. Vorm en inhoud van de international berichtgeving*. Groningen, the Netherlands: Wolters-Noordhoff.
Shanor, D.R. (2003). *News from abroad*. New York: Columbia University Press.

Shehata, A., & Strömbäck, J. (2011). A matter of context: A comparative study of media environments and news consumption gaps in Europe. *Political Communication, 28*(1), 110–134.
Sheingate, A.D. (2006). Structure and opportunity: Committee jurisdiction and issue attention in Congress. *American Journal of Political Science, 50*(4), 844–859.
Shoemaker, P.J. (1991). *Gatekeeping*. Newbury Park, CA: Sage.
Shoemaker, P.J. (1996). Hardwired for news: Using biological and cultural evolution to explain the surveillance function. *Journal of Communication, 46*, 32–47.
Shoemaker, P.J., & Cohen, A.A. (2006). *News around the world: Content, practitioners, and the public*. London: Routledge.
Shoemaker, P.J., Cohen, A., Seo, H., & Johnson, P. (2012). Comparing news on foreign and international affairs. In F. Esser & T. Hanitzsch (Eds.), *Handbook of comparative communication research* (pp. 341–352). New York: Routledge.
Shoemaker, P.J., Danielian, L., & Brendlinger, N. (1991). Deviant acts, risky business and U.S. interests: The newsworthiness of world events. *Journalism Quarterly, 68*(4), 781–795.
Shoemaker, P.J., & Reese, S.D. (1996). *Mediating the message: Theories of influence on mass media content* (2nd ed.). White Plains, NY: Longman.
Shoemaker, P.J., & Vos, T. (2009). *Gatekeeping theory*. New York: Routledge.
Silveira, J., Cardoso, G., & Belo, A. (2010). *Telejornais no início do século XXI*. Lisbon: Edições Colibri.
Smith, F.L. (1985). *Perspectives on radio and television: Telecommunication in the United States*. New York: Harper & Row.
Snyder, L.B., (1993). Attitudes toward the Gulf War and news criticalness. In B.S. Greenberg & W. Gantz (Eds.), *Desert Storm and the mass media* (pp. 259–269). Cresskill, NJ: Hampton Press.
Sparkes, V.M., & Winter, J.P. (1980). Public interest in foreign news. *International Communication Gazette, 26*, 149–170.
Spears, G., & Seydegart, K. (2000). *Who makes the news? Global media monitoring project 2000*. London: World Association for Christian Communication.
Spee, S., & De Swert, K. (2005). De mannelijke norm bevestigd? Vrouwelijke politici in het televisienieuws van TV1 en VTM. In M. Hooghe, K. De Swert, & S. Walgrave (Eds.), *Nieuws op televisie. Televisiejournaals als venster op de wereld* (pp. 39–55). Leuven, Belgium: Acco.
Sreberny, A., & Paterson, C. (2004). Introduction. In C. Paterson & A. Sreberny (Eds.), *International news in the 21st century* (pp. 3–27). London: John Libbey.
Sreberny, A., & Stevenson, R. (1999). Comparative analysis of international news flow: An example of global media monitoring. In K. Nordenstreng & M. Griffin (Eds.), *International media monitoring* (pp. 55–72). Cresskill, NJ: Hampton Press.
Sreberny-Mohammadi, A. (1984). The "world of the news" study. *Journal of Communication, 34*(1), 120–143.
Sreberny-Mohammadi, A., Nordenstreng, K., Stevenson, R., & Ugboajah, F. (1985). *Foreign news in the media: International reporting in 29 countries*. Paris: UNESCO.
Staab, J.F. (1990). The role of news factors in news selection: A theoretical reconsideration. *European Journal of Communication, 5*(4), 423–443.
Stacks, J.F. (2004). Hard time for hard news. A clinical look at U.S. foreign coverage. *World Policy Journal, 20*(4), 12–21.
Staubhaar, J.D., Heeter, C., Greenberg, B.S., Ferreira, L., Wick, R.R., & Lau, T.Y. (1992). What makes news. Western, Socialist, and Third World television newscasts compared in eight countries. In F. Korzenny, S. Ting-Toomey, & E. Schiff (Eds.), *Mass media across cultures* (pp. 89–109). Newbury Park, CA: Sage.
Stevenson, N. (2010). Chatting the news. *Journalism Studies, 11*(6), 852–873.

Stevenson, R.L., & Cole R.R. (1984). Issues in foreign news. In R.L. Stevenson & D.L. Shaw (Eds.), *Foreign news and the new world information order* (pp. 5–20). Ames: Iowa State University Press.
Stevenson, R.L., & Shaw, D.L. (Eds.). (1984). *Foreign news and the new world information order.* Ames: Iowa State University Press.
Stone, G., & Boudreau, T. (1995). 1985, 1994: Comparison of reader content preferences. *Newspaper Research Journal, 16*(4), 13–28.
Straughan, D.M. (1989). An experiment on the relation between news values and reader interest. *International Communication Gazette, 43*(2), 93–107.
Stromback, J., & Dimitrova, D.V. (2011). Mediatization and media interventionism: A comparative analysis of Sweden and the United States. *International Journal of Press/Politics, 16*(1), 30–49.
Tai, Z., & Chang, T.-K. (2002). The global news and the pictures in their heads: A comparative analysis of audience interest, editor perceptions and newspaper coverage. *Gazette, 64*(3), 251–265.
Tewksbury, D. (2003). What do Americans really want to know? Tracking the behavior of news readers on the Internet. *Journal of Communication, 53*(4), 694–710.
Thurman, N. (2007). The globalization of journalism online. *Journalism: Theory, Practice & Criticism, 8*(3), 285–307.
Tuchman, G. (1973). Making news by doing work: Routinizing the unexpected. *American Journal of Sociology, 79*(1), 110–131.
Tuchman, G. (1978). *Making news: A study in the construction of reality.* New York: The Free Press.
Tuchman, G., Daniels, A.K., & Benet, J. (1978). *Hearth and home: Images of women in the mass media.* New York: Oxford University Press.
Tyndall, A. (2008). 2008 year in review. *Tyndall report.* Retrieved March 5, 2011, from http://tyndallreport.com/yearinreview2008/
Tyndall, A. (2010). 2010 year in review. *Tyndall report.* Retrieved March 28, 2012, from http://tyndallreport.com/yearinreview2010/international/
Tyndall, A. (2011). 2011 year in review. *Tyndall report.* Retrieved March 28, 2012, from http://tyndallreport.com/yearinreview2011/
United Nations Office on Drugs and Crime (2012). http://www.unodc.org/unodc/en/data-and-analysis/statistics/index.html
United States Department of Agriculture (2009). http://www.fsis.usda.gov/News_&_Events/NR_012209_01/index.asp
Uribe, R., & Gunter, B. (2007). Are "sensational" news stories more likely to trigger viewers' emotions than non-sensational news stories? A content analysis of British TV news. *European Journal of Communication, 22*(2), 207–228.
Utley, G. (1997). The shrinking of foreign news: From broadcast to narrowcast. *Foreign Affairs, 76*(2), 2–10.
Van Belle, D. (2000). *New York Times* and network TV news coverage of foreign disasters: The significance of insignificant variables. *Journalism and Mass Communication Quarterly, 77*(1), 50–70.
Van Craenenbroeck, W., & De Swert, K. (2005). Harde cijfers over een harde realiteit. Traditionelerolpatronen in de nieuwsberichtgeving. *Samenleving & Politiek, 12*(6), 53–60.
Van Praag, P., & van der Eijk, C. (1998). News content and effects in an historic campaign. *Political Communication, 15*(2), 165–183.
Van Zoonen, L. (1998). One of the girls? The changing gender of journalism. In C. Carter, G. Branston, & S. Allan (Eds.), *News, gender and power* (pp. 33–46). London: Routledge.

Vettehen, P.H., Beentjes, J., Nuijten, K., & Peeters, A. (2011). Arousing news characteristics in Dutch television news, 1990–2004: An exploration of competitive strategies. *Mass Communication and Society, 14*(1), 93–112.

Vettehen, P.H., Nuijten, K., & Beentjes, J. (2005). News in an age of competition: The case of sensationalism in Dutch television news (1995–2001). *Journal of Broadcasting and Electronic Media, 49*(3), 282–295.

Vijver, F.J.R. van de, & Leung, K. (1997). *Methods and data analysis for cross-cultural research*. Thousand Oaks, CA: Sage.

Vilanilam, J.V. (1983). Foreign policy as a dominant factor in foreign news selection and presentation. *Gazette, 32*(3), 73–85.

Voakes, P.S. (1997). Social influences on journalists' decision making in ethical situations. *Journal of Mass Media Ethics, 12*(1), 18–35.

von Pape, T., Quandt, T., Vogelgesang, J., & Scharkow, M. (2012). Nachrichtengeographie des Zuschauerinteresses. Eine Mehrebenenanalyse des Länderinteresses deutscher Fernsehzuschauer. In H. Wessler & S. Averbeck-Lietz (Eds.), M&K-Sonderband Nr. 2: Grenzüberschreitende Medienkommunikation. [Special Issue] *Medien- und Kommunikationswissenschaft, 60*, 159–180.

Vos, D., De Smedt, J., Hooghe, M., & Walgrave, S. (2012). Vrouw gezocht. Vrouwen in de Vlaamse televisiejournaals (2003–2011). *Nieuwsmonitor 9. Berichten van het Elektronisch Nieuwsarchief, 3*(1), 1–8.

Waal, E.D., & Schönbach, K. (2010). News sites' position in the mediascape: Uses, evaluations and media displacement effects over time. *New Media & Society, 12*(3), 477–496.

Wanta, W. (2004). U.S. public concerns in the aftermath of 9/11: A test of second level agenda-setting. *International Journal of Public Opinion Research, 16*(4), 456–463.

Wanta, W., Golan, G., & Lee, C. (2004). Agenda setting and international news: Media influence on public perceptions of foreign nations. *Journalism & Mass Communication Quarterly, 81*(2), 364–377.

Ward, D. (2006). *The assessment of content diversity in newspapers and television in the context of increasing trends towards concentration of media markets*. Strasbourg, France: Final report of Media Division of Council of Europe.

Warren, J. (1988). Foreign and domestic news content of Chinese television. *Journal of Broadcasting & Electronic Media, 32*(2), 219–224.

Weaver, D.H. (1998). Journalist around the world: Commonalities and differences. In D.H Weaver (Ed.), *The global journalist: News people around the world* (pp. 455–480). Cresskill, NJ: Hampton Press.

Weaver, D.H. (2007). Thoughts on agenda-setting, framing, and priming. *Journal of Communication, 57*(1), 142–147.

Weaver, D.H., & Buddenbaum, J.M. (1979, April 20). Newspapers and television: A review of research on uses and effects. *American Newspaper Publishers Association News Research Report, 19*, 1–11.

Weaver, D.H., & Löffelholz, M. (2008). Questioning national, cultural and disciplinary boundaries: A call for global journalism research. In M. Löffelholz & D.H. Weaver (Eds.), *Global journalism research: Theories, methods, findings, future* (pp. 3–12). Oxford: Blackwell.

Weaver, D.H., & Mauro, J. (1978). Newspaper readership patterns. *Journalism Quarterly, 55*(1), 85–91.

Weaver, D.H., & Wilhoit, G.C. (1996). *The American journalist in the 1990s: U.S. news people at the end of an era*. Mahwah, NJ: Lawrence Erlbaum Associates.

Weaver, J.B., Porter, C.J., & Evans, M.E. (1984). Patterns in foreign news coverage on U.S. network TV: A 10-year analysis. *Journalism Quarterly, 61*(2), 356–363.

Westerståhl, J., & Johansson, F. (1994). Foreign news: News values and ideologies. *European Journal of Communication*, 9(1), 71–89.
Whetmore, E.J. (1987). *Mediamerica: Form, content and consequence of mass communication* (3rd ed.). Belmont, CA: Wadsworth.
White, D.M. (1950). The "gate keeper": A case study in the selection of news. *Journalism Quarterly*, 27(4), 383–391.
Whitney, C.D., Sumpter, R.S., & McQuail, D. (2004). News media production: Individuals, organizations, and institutions. In J.D.H. Downing, D. McQuail, P. Schlesinger, & E.A. Wartella (Eds.), *The SAGE handbook of media studies* (pp. 393–409). Thousand Oaks, CA, & London: Sage.
Wilke, J. (1987). Foreign news coverage and international news flow over three centuries. *Gazette*, 39(3), 147–180.
Wilke, J., & Heimprecht, C. (2011). Europe in Europe and Europe in the world. In A. Stępińska (Ed.), *News in Europe, Europe on news* (pp. 85–98). Berlin: Logos.
Willnat, L., & Weaver, D. (2003). Through their eyes: The work of foreign correspondents in the United States. *Journalism: Theory, Practice & Criticism*, 4(4), 403–422.
Wirth, W., & Kolb, S. (2004). Designs and methods of comparative political communication research. In F. Esser & B. Pfetsch (Eds.), *Comparing political communication: Theories, cases, and challenges* (pp. 87–111). New York: Cambridge University Press.
Wix, V. (1996). *Abgrenzung und Angleichung von TV-Präsentationsformen? Haupt Nachrichtensendungen von ARD, ZDF, RTL und SAT1*. Bochum, Germany: Universitätsverlag Dr. N. Brockmeyer.
Woodward, J.L. (1930). *Foreign news in American morning newspapers. A study in public opinion*. New York: Columbia University Press.
World Press Trends (2010). World Association of Newspapers. Paris.
Wouters, R. (2011). The nature of foreign news: Conceptual considerations about analyzing foreign news over time. In A. Stępińska (Ed.), *News in Europe, Europe on news* (pp. 43–62). Berlin: Logos.
Wu, H.D. (1998a). Geographic distance and U.S. newspapers' coverage of Canada and Mexico. *Gazette*, 60(3), 253–263.
Wu, H.D. (1998b). Investigating the determinants of international news flow. A meta-analysis. *Gazette*, 60(6), 493–512.
Wu, H.D. (2000). Systemic determinants of international news coverage: A comparison of 38 countries. *Journal of Communication*, 50(2), 110–130.
Wu, H.D. (2003). Homogeneity around the world? Comparing the systematic determinants of international news flow between developed and developing countries. *Gazette*, 65(1), 9–24.
Wu, H.D. (2007). A brave new world for international news? Exploring the determinants of the coverage of foreign news on US websites. *International Communication Gazette*, 69(6), 539–552.
Wu, H.D., & Hamilton, J. M. (2004). US foreign correspondents: Changes and continuity at the turn of the century. *Gazette*, 66(6), 517–532.
Zelizer, B. (2000). Popular communication in the contemporary age. In W. Gundykinst (Ed.), *Communication yearbook 24* (pp. 297–316). Thousand Oaks, CA: Sage.
Zhang, G., & Zhu, J.H. (2006). What's news in China. In P.J. Shoemaker & A.A. Cohen (Eds.), *News around the world* (pp. 141–146). New York: Routledge.
Zhu, J.-H., Weaver, D., Lo, V., Chen, C., & Wu, W. (1997). Individual, organizational, and societal influences on media role perceptions: A comparative study of journalists in China, Taiwan, and the United States. *Journalism & Mass Communication Quarterly*, 74(1), 84–96.
Zoch, L.M., & VanSlyke Turk, J. (1998). Women making news: Gender as a variable in source selection and use. *Journalism & Mass Communication Quarterly*, 75, 762–775.

Participants in the Project

António Belo is Professor at the School of Communication and Media Studies, in Lisbon, Porgutal, where he served as president for 6 years. He is currently pro-president of the Polytechnic Institute of Lisbon and also a researcher at the Institute of Communication and Media of Lisbon, where he worked on several research projects concerning the media and participated in writing two books about Portuguese television newscasts and one about local radio in Portugal.

Joseph M. Chan is Professor of Journalism and Communication and the director of the Center for Chinese Media and Comparative Communication Research at the Chinese University of Hong Kong. He served concurrently as a Changjiang Chair Professor in the School of Journalism at Fudan University (2006–2009). His research interest lies in the intersection of international communication, political communication, and journalism studies. He was the founding chief editor of the Chinese journal *Communication & Society* and the current chairman of the Hong Kong Press Council.

Akiba A. Cohen is Professor (Emeritus) of Communication at Tel Aviv University and the founding chair of the department. He is currently the chair of the Department of Communication and director of the Research Division of the Yezreel Valley College in Israel. He is a fellow and a former president of the International Communication Association. His main area of interest is the comparative study of news. Among his co-authored books are *News Around the World: Content, Practitioners and the Public* (2006) and *Global Newsrooms, Local Audiences: A Study of the Eurovision News Exchange* (1996).

Knut De Swert received his Ph.D. from the University of Antwerp, Belgium, where he investigated bias and balance in television news. 2. He is currently Assistant Professor Political Communication and Journalism at the University of Amsterdam in the Netherlands and member of ASCOR. His research is mainly situated in the field of comparative political communication, which focuses on political television news content, including actors, topics, and general news quality.

Elizabeth Godo holds a master's degree in Communication & Culture from Ryerson and York Universities. She earned the Board of Governor's Gold Medal in Communication Studies for her work at the University of Windsor and is a recipient of research funding from the Social Sciences and Humanities Research Council of Canada. She is also the founder of Zeto Communications, a Toronto-based research firm that provides strategic insight to start-ups and communications companies.

Abby Goodrum, Ph.D., is Vice-President for Research at Wilfrid Laurier University. She also co-directs the Network Centre of Excellence in Graphics, Animation and New Media. She sits on a number of national and international boards that focus on issues relating to the new media economy. Her work bridges multiple disciplines, and she is highly cited in the area of media informatics, media flows, and media access.

Thomas Hanitzsch is Professor of Communication at the Institute of Communication Studies and Media Research, University of Munich, Germany. A former journalist, he teaches and studies global journalism cultures, war coverage, celebrity news, and comparative methodology. His six books include the *Handbook of Journalism Studies* and the *Handbook of Comparative Communication Research*. He is currently editor of *Communication Theory* and chair of the Journalism Studies Section of the European Communication Research and Education Association (ECREA).

Christine Heimprecht holds an M.A. degree in Communication and is a doctoral student and research assistant as well as an associate of the students' office at the Department of Communication (Institut für Publizistik) at the Johannes Gutenberg-University, Mainz, Germany. Her areas of interest are news flow, international communication, political communication, media reception, and media effects.

Youichi Ito is Dean and Professor at the Graduate School of Akita International University and Professor Emeritus at Keio University in Japan. He obtained his degrees from Keio University, Boston University, and the Fletcher School of Law and Diplomacy at Tufts University. He served as president of the Japan Society of Information and Communication Research from 2004 through 2008 and was elected a fellow of the International Communication Association (ICA) in 2009.

Rasha Kamhawi, Ph.D., is Associate Professor at the Department of Communication, Ain Shams University, in Cairo, Egypt. Her research interests are the cognitive and emotional effects of audio visual media messages, channel studies, and the framing of media narratives. Her research has been published in a variety of journals, including *Human Communication Research*, *Journal of Broadcasting & Electronic Media*, and *Communication Research*.

Francis L.F. Lee is Associate Professor at the School of Journalism and Communication, Chinese University of Hong Kong. He is the lead author of *Media, Social Mobilization, and Mass Protests in Post-colonial Hong Kong* (Routledge, 2011) and has published in *Communication Research*, *International Journal of Press/Politics*, *Discourse & Society*, *Media, Culture & Society*, *New Media & Society*, *IJPOR*, and *JMCQ*, among others. He is currently associate editor of *Mass Communication and Society* and *The Chinese Journal of Communication*.

Wan-Ying Lin is Assistant Professor in the Department of Media and Communication at the City University of Hong Kong. She received her Ph.D. in Communication from the University of Southern California. Her primary research interests include youths and new media, political use and impact of the Internet, media effects, and globalization. Her recent work appears in *Journal of Communication*, *New Media & Society*, *Journalism*, and *The Chinese Journal of Communication*.

Ven-hwei Lo, Ph.D., is Professor in the School of Journalism at the Chinese University of Hong Kong. He previously taught at the National Chengchi University in Taipei. His research interests include news media performance and the effects of mass media. His is the author of seven books and numerous articles.

Paolo Mancini is Professor in the Dipartimento Istituzioni e Società, Facoltà di Scienze Politiche, Università di Perugia. His major publications include *Politics, Media and Modern Democracy* with David Swanson (1996) and *Comparing Media Systems: Three Models of Media and Politics* with Dan Hallin (2004), which won the 2005 Goldsmith Book Award from Harvard University, the Diamond Anniversary Book Award of the National Communication Association, and the 2006 Outstanding Book Award of the International Communication Association.

Marco Mazzoni is Assistant Professor of Public Relations at the Dipartimento Istituzioni e Società, University of Perugia, Italy. His research interests include popularization of politics and the role of public relations practitioners in the decision-making and news-making processes. His major publications include *Le* *relazioni pubbliche e il lobbying in Italia* (Laterza, 2010), and, with Enrico Caniglia, *Nuovi approcci alla comunicazione politica* (Carocci, 2011).

Constanza Mujica is a journalist and received her Ph.D. in Hispanoamerican Literature from the Pontificia Universidad Católica de Chile. She is a full-time academic at the Faculty of Communications of the Pontificia Universidad Católica de Chile, where she teaches comparative journalism. Her research areas are journalism quality, television journalism, and melodramatic genres. She has authored and coauthored publications on journalistic quality, audiovisual language and narration, and on melodrama in television and film.

Hong Nga Nguyen Vu, Ph.D., was a research and teaching associate at the Institute of Mass Communication and Media Research, University of Zurich, Switzerland. Her research activities focus on international and comparative research in media and communication studies, in particular on issues related to journalism and news, political communication, media systems, and media cultures.

William Porath is a journalist and earned a Ph.D. in Political Science from the Johannes Gutenberg University in Mainz, Germany. He is a full-time academic on the Faculty of Communications of the Pontificia Universidad Católica de Chile, where he teaches methodology of communications research. His research areas are public opinion, media agenda, and media content. He is the author and co-author of multiple publications on journalistic quality and on the relationship between media and political campaigns.

Thorsten Quandt is Professor of Communication Studies at the University of Münster, Germany. His areas of interest include online communication, media innovation research, and journalism. He has served as the chair of the Journalism Division in the German Communication Association (DGPuK), and as the secretary of the Journalism Studies Division in the International Communication Association (ICA). He is currently an Executive Board Member of the European Communication Research and Education Association (ECREA).

André Sendin, Ph.D., is Associate Professor of Audiovisual and Multimedia and Associate Dean at the School of Communication and Media Studies (Lisbon, Portugal). He received his Ph.D. in Communication Sciences from Complutense University of Madrid (Spain). He is President of the Portuguese Multimedia Association (APMP). His main research interests are media and television, as well as economics and media management.

Agnieszka Stępińska, Ph.D., is Assistant Professor on the Faculty of Political Science and Journalism at the Adam Mickiewicz University in Poznan, Poland. In 2001–2003 she participated in an international doctoral program at the Viadrina European University in Germany. Her teaching and research interests include international news flow, political communication, and exploring the content of the news media. She is the author of about 100 book chapters, journal articles, and conference papers.

Thilo von Pape, Ph.D., studied communication sciences at the universities of Munich, Zurich, and Paris (II). Following a postdoctoral year in Metz, France, he is currently a research associate at the University of Hohenheim in Germany. As one of the founding editors of the SAGE journal *Mobile Media and Communication*, he conducts research on media innovations in mobile and online communication, as well as international comparative research on media use.

Jacques A. Wainberg received his Ph.D. from the University of São Paulo, Brazil. He is Professor of Communication at the Catholic University, Porto Alegre, Brazil. His main areas of interest are journalism, intercultural communication, political communication, and history of communication. He is the author of seven books and numerous articles. He is a former Fulbright Scholar at the University of Texas and Visiting Professor at the University of Montpellier, France.

Tai-Li Wang is Associate Professor at the Graduate Institute of Journalism, National Taiwan University. Her research focuses on media effects, television news, tabloid news culture, and social and political impacts of new media. She has been published in several journals: *The Asian Journal of Communication, Online Information Review, Issues and Studies, The International Communication Gazette,* and *The Chinese Journal of Communication.* Prior to her academic career she was a television reporter and news presenter.

David H. Weaver is Distinguished Professor Emeritus and the former Roy W. Howard Research Professor in the School of Journalism at Indiana University. He has published 13 books and numerous articles about journalists, the agenda-setting function of media, newspaper readership, foreign news coverage, and journalism education. He is past president of the Association for Education in Journalism & Mass Communication, the Midwest Association for Public Opinion Research, and a fellow of the International Communication Association.

Jürgen Wilke, Ph.D., is Professor of Communication research at the Institut für Publizistik, the Johannes Gutenberg University, Mainz, Germany. He has published numerous books and articles in several areas of interest, including the history and structure of the media, news selection and news agencies, international communication, and political communication. He is Honorary Professor at the Lomonossow University Moscow (Russia) and a corresponding member of the Austrian Academy of Sciences, Vienna.

Lars Willnat is Professor in the School of Journalism at Indiana University. He previously taught at George Washington University and the Chinese University of Hong Kong. His areas of interest include media effects on political attitudes, theoretical aspects of public opinion formation, and international communication. He has published in journals such as *Journalism & Mass Communication Quarterly*, *International Journal of Public Opinion Research*, *Political Communication*, *Journalism*, and *International Communication Gazette*.

Ruud Wouters is a doctoral student in the Department of Political Science at the University of Antwerp, Belgium. He is a member of the Media, Movements and Politics (M²P) research group. His research interests are foreign news and the impact of foreign correspondents on news content. The subject of his doctoral dissertation is the relationship between social movements, protest tactics, and media exposure.

Xiaoge Xu is Associate Professor at the University of Nottingham, Ningbo, China. He received his Ph.D. in 2004 from Nanyang Technological University, Singapore. His major academic interests include news flow, comparative media systems, digital journalism, and mobile studies. He was Assistant Professor at the Wee Kim Wee School of Communication and Information, Nanyang Technological University, Singapore, during the time the Foreign News on Television project was conducted.

Baohua Zhou, Ph.D., is Associate Professor at the Journalism School of Fudan University, China. He is also a research fellow of the Center for Information and Communication Studies and associate director of the Fudan Media and Opinion Research Centre (FMORC) of Fudan University. His research focuses on new media, public opinion, and media effects. His work has appeared in *The Asian Journal of Communication*, *The Chinese Journal of Communication*, *Communication & Society*, and other publications.

Index

Aarts, K., 130
actors
  citizens as, 103–104, 105
  defined, 87, 91
  format of presentation of, 94
  frequency of, 92–94
  gender of, 89, 90, 100–103, 131
  and gender roles, 90–91
  in German newscasts, 302–303
  and identification with viewer, 103, 105
  lack of pattern regarding, 104
  language spoken by, 94
  methods for analyzing, 91–92
  numbers of, 92–93, 96, 97, *98,* 100
  politicians as, 96–97, 103–104, 321
  in Portugal, 310
  previous studies on, 87–90
  research questions regarding, 91
  roles of, 96–97
  speaking time of and gender, 103
  status of, 94–96, *99,* 100
  in Taiwanese newscasts, 315
  variability of, 321
Adoni, H., 26, 332
advertising
  and PC differential, 145–147
  on public service television, 148
affairs, foreign, 6, 154
affairs, international, 6
affairs, national, 6

Africa
  information supply about, 217
  lack of interest in, 197, 199
  role of, 78
age
  and content-audience correspondence, 286–287
  and interest in foreign news, 186, 188
  and media, 154
  and news consumption, 158, *159*
  as predictor of news consumption, 166, 167
  as predictor of news exposure, 163
  as predictor of newspaper exposure, *164, 165*
  as predictor of online news exposure, *164, 165*
  as predictor of television news exposure, 163, *164*
  and reading of newspapers, 158, *159*
agenda, global news, 320
agenda setting, 253
agenda setting research, 289
Almaney, A., 6, 7
Altmeppen, K.-D., 172
analytical depth
  and PC differential, 138–140
  in public service television *vs.* commercial television, 133–134
anchors, 113, *114*
Anderson, K., 320
animation, *120,* 121

Apee, S., 131
archive material, 117–119
Asia, 77–78
　See also individual countries
assembly strategy, 17–18
audiences
　gatekeepers' views of, 226, 228, 237–246
　interest in countries (*See* countries of interest)
　interest in foreign news (*See* interest, in foreign news)
　interests of (*See* interest, of audience)
　variability among, 322–324
audiences, foreign news
　interests of (*See* interest, of audience)
　lack of research on, 153
audio-visual effects, 133, *137,* 138, 147
　See also images
Australia, as country of location in foreign news, 78
authority, 87, 88, 97
　See also actors

Babel, Tower of, 328–329
Bagdikian, B., 43
Bale, T., 132
Bantz, C., 26, 332
Barnett, G. A., 27–28, 211
Beaudoin, C., 154, 227
Becker, H., 88, 97
Beentjes, J., 130
Belgium
　countries covered in, 231
　as country of location in foreign news, 74–75
　percentage of foreign news in, 231
　views of foreign news in, 231
　See also countries of study; Flanders
Belo, A., 89, 309
Bente, G., 89
Berry, J. M., 89
block presentation, *115,* 116
Blumler, J. G., 5–6, 160, 185
Bourdieu, P., 173
Bourdon, J., 107–108
Brazil
　audience interest in topics covered, 262
　content-audience correspondence in, 279
　contextualization in, 233
　countries covered in, 233
　countries of location in foreign news in, 76
　gatekeepers' view of audience in, 245
　gatekeepers' view of foreign news in, 233
　media system in, 295
　newspaper exposure in, 296
　percentage of foreign news in, 233
　public service television in, 296
　television in, importance of, 296
　topics covered in, 296
　See also countries of study
Brendlinger, N., 27
broadcasting, public. *See* public service television
Brown, J., 185

Cabecinhas, R., 104
Canada
　commercial service television in, 296
　countries covered most in, 230
　countries of location in foreign news in, 75–76
　foreign news in, 297
　gatekeepers' views of audience in, 237–238
　gatekeepers' views of foreign news in, 230
　media system in, 296–297
　percentage of foreign news in, 230
　public service television in, 296
　topics covered in, 297–298
　views of foreign news in, 230
　See also countries of study
Cardoso, G., 89
CCI (Country Concentration Index), 68–69, 141, *142,* 194–195
celebrities, 89
Chan, Joseph, 299
Chang, C., 155
Chang, T. K., 27, 172, 211, 212, 215, 227
charts, *118,* 119
Chile
　actors in newscasts from, 97
　audience interests in, 299
　commercial service television in, 298
　countries covered in, 234
　countries of location in foreign news in, 76
　as country involved in foreign news, 82
　coverage of sports in, 46–47, 49, 51
　gatekeepers' view of audience in, 242–243
　gatekeepers' view of foreign news in, 233

media system in, 298
news types in, 298–299
percentage of foreign news in, 233
public service television in, 298
topics covered in, 46–47, 299
See also countries of study
China
citizens as actors in, 105
countries covered in foreign news in, 234–235
countries of location in foreign news in, 77–78
as country of location, 78
coverage of Greece, 71–72
coverage of in foreign news, 69
coverage of topics of audience interest, *260*, 262
foreign news in, 300
gatekeepers' view of audience in, 238–239
gatekeepers' view of foreign news in, 234
interest in foreign news in, 180–181, 238, 300–301
interest in foreign *vs.* domestic news in, 180–181
media system in, 299–300
percentage of domestic news in, 300
percentage of foreign news in, 234
topics covered in, 300
topics in domestic news in, *256*, 257
topics of audience interest in, *256*, 257, *260*, 262
See also countries of study
citizens
as actors, 96–97, 103–104, 105
and identification with viewer, 103
citizens, foreign-born, 280, 281
codebook, 11–12, 19, 64, 336–339
coding
of actors' status, 94
analyzing actors, 91–92
of countries involved, 64
of countries of location, 64
reliability of, 333
of topics, 43
Cohen, A. A., 26, 27, 90, 186, 211, 212, 305, 329
Cold War, 173
collaboration
organization of, 20
in study, 21–22
in theory, 5, 6
colonial relationships
and content-audience correspondence, 276
and coverage of countries of location, 73, 75
and distribution of news items, 36
and interest in countries, 197
and newsworthiness, 217–218
commercial breaks, 110
commercial television (CTV)
in Canada, 296
in Chile, 298
conflict on, *139*
convergence with public service television, 147–148
cosmopolitanism of, 141–143
Curran on, 129
effects of competition on, 132
European News Exchange, 117
expectations of, 130, 132–133
in Flanders, 294
in Germany, 302, 303
in Hong Kong, 303
influence of on public service television, 148
international organizations on, *142*, 143
in Israel, 305
in Italy, 306
in Japan, 307
length of sound bites on, *139*, 140
news selection in, 214
number of countries involved in news on, *142*
personalization by, 134, 140
in Poland, 308
in Portugal, 309–310
preference for, 131
prominence of soft news on, 145
and sensationalism, 133, 136–138
in study, 10–11
in Switzerland, 313
in Taiwan, 148, 303, 314–315
in United States, 315
variability in, 322
See also PC differential
committee approach, 17–18
competition, 131, 132, 135, 149
conflict
in images, 219
and newsworthiness, 214

on public service television *vs.* commercial television, *139*
conflict, social, 26
conflicts, international, 56
content, variability of, 320–322
content analysis, 9–14, 331–332
content-audience correspondence, 271–278, 325
  and age, 286–287
  arguments for, 280–282
  and audience's interest in foreign news, 280
  in Brazil, 279
  and colonial relationships, 276
  and concentration of audience interest, 282–284
  and concentration of news coverage, 282–284
  and Country Concentration Index, 282–283
  and education, 285, 287, 288
  factors in, 290
  and foreign-born citizens, 280, 281
  and globalization, 325–326
  indicators of, 271–272, 274
  and interest in foreign news, 280, 281–282, 287
  levels of, 289
  and living abroad experience, 287, 289
  and migration, 287, 288, 289
  "missing" countries in, 274–276
  and personal connections, 289
  and population, 281
  predictors of, 281, 285–289
  reasons for, 289–290
  regionalism in, 279
  in Singapore, 278–279
  and size of country, 281
  and television news exposure, 285, 287, 288–289
contextualization, 221–222, 233
continental regions represented, 66–68
correspondents, 213
cosmopolitanism, 134, 140–143
Cottle, S., 88, 89, 97
countries
  in comparative research, 4–5
  high-status actors in, 94–95
  interest in foreign news, *174,* 175–176
  interviews conducted in, 15
  involved in foreign news, on public service television *vs.* commercial television, *142*
  newsworthiness of, 134
  PC differential for, 145
  represented in foreign news, 63 (*See also* countries involved; countries of interest; countries of location)
  in study, 9, 16 (*See also* countries of study; individual countries)
  topics in, *44,* 47–49
  as units of analysis, 5, 16
  See also countries involved; countries of interest; countries of location; countries of study; specific countries
countries involved, 79–84, 271, 321
countries of interest
  in Brazil, 245
  in Canada, 238
  and CCI, 194–195
  characteristics of, 196–197
  in Chile, 243
  in China, 238–239
  and colonial relationships, 197
  countries of study as, 197, *198,* 199–201
  diversity of, 192–193, 194–195
  in Germany, 240
  giant neighbors, 270
  in Hong Kong, 239
  in Israel, 306
  and language, 197
  maps of, 201–203
  number of countries, 192–194, 195
  in Poland, 241, 309
  in Portugal, 310, 311
  preferences for, 323
  specific countries, 195–199
  in Switzerland, 240
  in Taiwan, 315
  in United States, 317
  United States as, 193, 196, 269, 323
countries of interest, audience interest in
  compared to content, 271–278 (*See also* content-audience correspondence)
  effect of news coverage on, 270
  indicators of correspondence with content, 271–272, 274
  methodology in study of, 270
countries of location
  compared to countries involved, 83–84

continental regions represented, 66–68
Country Concentration Index, 68–69
coverage of in countries of study, 70–79
    in European broadcasts, 75
    home continent bias, 66–68
    interpretations of, 85
    in Japanese foreign news, 308
    not identified, 65
    number of, 64–66
    and regionalism, 71
    variability of, 321
countries of study
    audience interest in foreign affairs topics in, 261, 262–263
    audience interest in topic categories in, 260, 262
    audience interest in topics covered in domestic news in, 255–256, 257
    audience interest in topics covered in foreign news in, 258–259, 261–262
    as countries of interest, 197, 198, 199–201
    topics covered in domestic news in, 255–256, 257
    topics covered in foreign news in, 258–259, 261–262
    See also specific countries
Country Concentration Index (CCI), 68–69, 79, 282–283
country of origin, prominence of and newsworthiness, 211
coverage
    factors in, 24–29
    professionalism of, 212
credibility
    and actor's status, 94
    hierarchy of, 88, 97
culture
    and characteristics of newscasts, 89
    and collaboration, 21
    and deviance, 27
    and distribution of news items, 36
    and foreign news coverage, 29
    and interest in foreign news, 176
    and newsworthiness, 211, 217
    and reliability, 13
Curran, J., 129, 149

Danielian, L. H., 88
Danilewicz, A., 104

Dayan, D., 89–90
defense issues, coverage of, 46
democracy, and media, 129
demographics
    and exposure to television news, 323
    in study, 18
    See also age; education; gender; income
Dennis, Everette, 320
Desmond, R., 104
De Swert, Knut, 131, 293
deviance, 27, 211, 214
Dìez, P. L., 90, 104
Dimitrova, D. V., 130, 131
displacement theories, 155
distribution, 35–37
domestication, 8, 185, 186, 211, 220–221
    Belgian journalists' views of, 231
    emphasis on, 227
    models of, 221
Durante, R., 43

economic issues
    coverage of, 45–46
    and distribution of news items, 36
    in domestic vs. foreign news, 50
editors, foreign news. See gatekeepers
education
    and content-audience correspondence, 285, 287, 288
    and interest in foreign news, 186, 188
    and news consumption, 158–159, 166–167
    as predictor of news exposure, 163
    as predictor of newspaper exposure, 159, 164, 165
    as predictor of online news exposure, 164, 165
    as predictor of television news exposure, 163, 164
    and topic interest, 264–265
Egypt
    citizens as actors in, 105
    countries of location in foreign news, 76–77
    foreign news in, 301–302
    media system in, 300–301
    topics covered in, 48, 301
    See also countries
elections, coverage of, 56
Elvestad, E., 173, 188
emblems, 122, 123

Emery, M., 172
emotion
　in images, 219
　and newsworthiness, 214, 218–220
　and proximity, 218
　reporting of, 147 (*See also* sensationalism)
England. *See* United Kingdom
entropy, 59–60
Ericson, R. V., 88
Esser, F., 20, 131
ethnicity, and newsworthiness, 211
ethnocentrism, 82, 212, 235
European News Exchange, 117
Eurovision News Exchange, 117, 329
Evans, M. E., 6

features, formal
　in domestic *vs.* foreign news, 125
　duration, 109, 110–111
　emblems, *122,* 123
　flags, *122,* 123
　of German newscasts, 303
　length, 108–110
　logos, *122,* 123
　materials, 117–119
　modes and tools, *118,* 119–121, *126*
　music, background, *122,* 123–125
　overall distribution of, 111–113
　overall use of, *124*
　slow motion, *122,* 125
　sources, 117, *118*
　studies of, 108
　in types of newscasts, 125–128
　variability of, 321–322
field work, 15
Fischer, O., 89
Fiske, J., 57
flags, *122,* 123
Flanders
　commercial service television in, 293
　domestic news items in, 294
　media system in, 292–293
　percentage of foreign news in, 294
　public service television in, 293
　topics covered in, 295
　See also Belgium
"foreign," use of term, 7
foreign affairs, coverage of, *261*
Foreign Images (Sreberny-Mohammadi), 8

France, coverage of in foreign news, 73–74
functional equivalence, 16–22

Gallagher, M., 104
Galtung, J., 26, 27, 211
Gans, H., 24, 25
gatekeepers
　on contextualization, 221–222
　on domestication, 220–221
　influence of, 213
　in international news flow, 28
　interviews with, 15–16, 20–21, 228–229
　on newsworthiness, 214
　position of, 324–325
　on ratings/audience interest, 216–217
　responsibilities of, 212–213
　on significance, 215
　study of, methodology and limitations of, 212
　views of audiences, 237–246
　views of foreign news, 212, 228–237 (*See also* individual countries)
　See also journalists; news workers; individual countries
gatekeeping, factors in, 42
gatekeeping theory, 24
Geddes, B., 16
gender
　and access to media, 89
　of actors, 90, 131
　of actors in foreign *vs.* domestic news, 102
　of actors in German newscasts, 303
　and interest in foreign news, 186, 188–189
　and news consumption, 158, *159,* 166
　as predictor of news exposure, 163
　as predictor of newspaper exposure, *164,* 165
　as predictor of online news exposure, *164,* 165
　as predictor of television news exposure, 163, *164*
　and speaking time, 103
　and topic interest, 264–265
gender roles, and actors, 90–91
geography, 8, 29, 36
geography, news, 6, 63, 180
Gerbner, G., 27, 64
Germany
　actors in, 302–303

commercial service television in, 302, 303
foreign news in, 302
formal features of newscasts in, 303
gatekeepers' views of audience in, 240
gatekeepers' views of foreign news in, 229
interest in foreign news in, 303
media system in, 302
newscasts in, length of, 302
percentage of foreign news in, 229
public broadcasting in, 148
public service television in, 302, 303
topics covered in, 302
globalization
compared to global village, 329
and cosmopolitanism, 134
criticism of, 326
in foreign news reporting, 84
and importance of foreign news, 324
and importance of news, 222–223
and interest in foreign news, 190, 323
lack of in news, 37–38
manifestations of, 319
reality of, 84
and variability in content-audience correspondence, 325–326
See also global village
Global Media Monitoring Project (GMMP), 90, 101
global village
attempts to create, 328
compared to globalization, 329
concept of, 326
existence of, 5
lack of, 320
Tower of Babel, 328–329
See also globalization
GMMP (Global Media Monitoring Project), 90, 101
Godo, Elizabeth, 296
Golan, G., 199, 211
Goodrum, Abby, 296
Grabe, M. E., 43
Great Britain. *See* United Kingdom
Greece, coverage of in China, 71–72
Green, C., 329
groups, interest, 88–89
Gudykunst, W. B., 13
Gunaratne, S. A., 77
Gunter, B., 131

Gurevitch, M., 5–6, 329
The Gutenberg Galaxy (McLuhan), 326

Hamilton, J., 172, 173
Hanitzsch, Thomas, 20, 312
Hannerz, U., 171, 173
Hantrais, L., 16
Harcup, T., 27
Hargrove, T., 103
headlines, foreign items in, 113, *115,* 116
Heimprect, Christine, 302
Heinderyckx, F., 108, 128
H entropy measurement, 59
Hester, A., 211
hierarchy of credibility, 88, 97
Hjarvard, S., 26
Holtz-Bacha, C., 16, 131
home continent bias, 66–68
Hong Kong
audience interest in, 304–305
commercial service television in, 303
countries covered in, 236
gatekeepers' view of audience in, 239
gatekeepers' view of foreign news in, 236
interest in foreign news in, 304–305
media system in, 303
news types in, 304
percentage of foreign news in, 236
in political system, 81
public service television in, 303
topics covered in, 303–304
Hooghe, M., 130, 131
Hutchins Commission, 133

identification, 26
ideology, and foreign news coverage, 29
images, 218–220
See also audio-visual effects
income
and interest in foreign news, 186, 188
as predictor of newspaper exposure, *164,* 165
as predictor of online news exposure, *164,* 165
as predictor of television news exposure, 163, *164*
and topic interest, 264–265
information, sources of, 29
Inglehart, R., 327, 328

interest, in countries. *See* countries of interest
interest, in foreign news
  in Brazil, 245
  in Canada, 237–238
  in Chile, 242
  in China, 238
  conclusions regarding, 189
  and content-audience correspondence, 280, 281–282, 287
  by country, *174*
  and culture, 176
  and demographics, 186, 188, 323
  differences between countries, 175–176
  and domestication, 185
  explanations of, 182–189
  and exposure to news, 186, 291
  factors in, 285
  in Germany, 240
  and globalization, 190
  in Hong Kong, 239
  and interest in topics, 265
  in Israel, 243
  lack of, reasons for, 173
  and perceived characteristics, 186
  perceived lack of, 172
  in Poland, 240–241
  in Portugal, 241
  predicting, *184,* 185–186, *187*
  research on, 172–173
  in Switzerland, 239, 314
  in Taiwan, 244, 315
  and topics, *174,* 176–177
  vs. domestic, 177–182
interest, of audience
  and agenda setting, 253–254
  in Chile, 299
  in China, 300–301
  compared to topics in content, 254–263
  in countries of interest, 269 (*See also* content-audience correspondence; countries of interest, audience interest in)
  in foreign affairs coverage, *261,* 262–263
  in Germany, 303
  in Hong Kong, 304–305
  in most prevalent topic category, *260,* 262
  and newsworthiness, 216–217
  in Poland, 309
  predictors of, 263–265
  in topics, conclusions about, 265–266

  in topics covered in foreign news, *258–259,* 261–262
  in topics in domestic news, *255–256,* 257
interest groups, 88–89
InterMedia, 320
international, use of term, 6, 7–8
International Institute of Communications (IIC), 320
Internet
  age and exposure to news on, *159*
  demographics as predictors of exposure to news on, *164,* 165, 167
  education and exposure to news on, *159*
  and exposure to foreign news, 154
  future of news on, 166
  as source for news, 155
  time spent reading news on, 157
interviews, 15–16, 228–229, 334–335, 351
Israel
  commercial service television in, 305
  countries covered in, 76–77, 232–233
  gatekeepers' view of audience in, 243–244
  gatekeepers' view of foreign news in, 232
  media system in, 305
  news types in, 305
  percentage of foreign news in, 232
  public service television in, 305
  television news exposure in, 306
  topic coverage in, 48, 305
  See also countries
Italy
  commercial service television in, 306
  media system in, 306
  news items in, 306–307
  news types in, 307
  public service television in, 306
Ito, Y., 29, 307

Japan
  commercial service television in, 307
  countries of location in foreign news in, 78, 308
  media system in, 307
  news items in, 308
  percentage of foreign news in, 308
  public service television in, 307
Jordan, D. L., 88, 104
journalism, responsible, 133

journalists
  views of audience, 226, 228
  views of foreign news, 226, 227–228
  See also gatekeepers

Kaid, L. L., 16
Kamhawi, Rasha, 301
Kamps, K., 63, 108
Katz, E., 89–90, 160, 185
Kerbel, M. R., 131
Kim, H. S., 222
Kim, K., 27–28, 211
Klijin, M. E., 131
Knight, B., 43
Kohn, M. L., 5
Kolmer, C., 132
Krämer, N. C., 89

Langer, J., 89
language
  and coverage of countries of location, 73
  and interest in countries, 197
  and interest in foreign news, 176
  and international news flow, 29
  and newsworthiness, 211
  spoken by actors, 94
  in study, 12, 14, 19
  of surveys, 14
Larson, J. F., 7
Lauf, E., 13
Lee, F. L. F., 134, 303
Lee, J., 212
Legnante, G., 26
Lehman-Wilzig, S. N., 25
Levy, M. R., 329
Lewin, K., 24, 209
line-up, placement of items in, 34–35
Liu, H. D., 77
Livingstone, S., 4
Lo, V., 155, 314
Lobo, P., 104
location, 6
logos, *122,* 123

Malik, R., 320
Mancini, Paolo, 306
maps, 63–64, *120,* 121
  of countries of interest, 201–203
maps, cognitive, 209

Marvanyi, G., 27, 64
Mauro, J., 176
Mazzoni, Marco, 306
McLuhan, M., 5, 23, 326
McQuail, D., 185, 227
media
  access to, 89, 94
  and age, 154
  in democracies, 129
  deregulation of, 129, 130
  and foreign news exposure, 157
  future of, 166
  research on audience, 153 (*See also* audiences)
  sources of foreign news, 155
  types of, 153–155
Mediated Cosmopolitanism (Robertson), 327
Middle East, countries of location in foreign news, 76–77
migration, and newsworthiness, 211
military
  coverage of, 46
  and distribution of news items, 36
movie reviews, 110
"Mr. Gates" (White), 24
Mujica, Constanza, 298
Murdoch, Rupert, 43
music, background, *122,* 123–125

nation-state. *See* countries
neighbors, giant, 270
news
  classification of, 24–26
  demand for, 167–168
  exposure to, 156–159, 186
  importance of, 25
  influences on from individuals, 27
  reasons for watching/not watching, 322–323
  selection of (*See* news selection)
  types of, distinguishing, 57–58
  See also television news
news, domestic
  defined, 8
  distinguished from foreign, 6
  distribution of, 35–37
  duration of items in newscast, 31–33
  percentage of in sample, 29–31
  placement of in line-up, 34
  selection of, 24–25

topics in, 50–53
topics of interest in, 325
news, domestic with foreign involvement
　defined, 8
　See also news, hybrid
news, foreign
　amount of, 23, 24, 226, 319, 320, 324
　attention to, 154
　and competition, 24
　concentration of on limited countries, 291
　concept of, 6–8
　cost of gathering, 172, 213
　decline in coverage of, 226, 319
　defined, 8
　desire for, 325
　distribution of, 35–37
　domestic influences on, 28–29
　duration of items in newscast, *32,* 33, 37
　exposure to, 154, 163–165
　future of, 222, 324, 327–328
　gatekeepers' views of, 222–223
　importance of, 171, 190, 324
　in-depth coverage, 220
　interest in (*See* interest, in foreign news)
　media sources of, 155 (*See also* Internet; newspapers; television)
　motivations behind consumption of, 167
　percentage of in sample, *30,* 31, 37
　perceptions of, 161, 162, 163, 167, 173, 186
　placement of in line-up, 34, 37
　predictors of exposure to, 163–165
　proportion of news devoted to, 171–172
　relationship with gender balance, 90
　selection of, determinants of, 24–29
　staff for, 213–214
　topics in, 50–53, 321 (*See also* topics)
　types of, 321 (*See also* news, types of)
　variability of content, 320–322
news, foreign with domestic involvement
　defined, 8
　See also news, hybrid
news, general, 25
news, hard, 25–26
　coverage of, 58
　defined, 136
　prevalence of, 56–57
　on public service television, 130
　standardized roles in, 89

news, hybrid
　Belgian journalists' views of, 231
　defined, 8
　distribution of news items in, 36
　duration of items in newscast, *32, 33*–34
　percentage of in sample, *30,* 31
　placement of in line-up, 34
news, light, 25
news, online. *See* Internet
news, sensational
　coverage of, 57–58, 59
　defined, 136
　prevalence of, 56–57
　See also sensationalism
news, soft
　by country, *137*
　coverage of, 58
　defined, 136
　prevalence of, 56–57
　on public service television *vs.* commercial television, *137,* 145
　standardized roles in, 89
news, tabloid, 57–58
news, types of, 8, 29–31, 307
news agencies, 28, 29, 117, *118,* 329
News Around the World (Shoemaker), 211
newscasts
　dates of, 18–19
　development of genre, 107–108
　formal features of (*See* features, formal)
　manner of presentation of, 113–116
　selection of for study, 9–11, 18
newscasts, playful, 127
newscasts, sober, 127
news characteristics, arousing, 130
news flow, international, 26, 27–28, 29, 180, 320
　See also gatekeepers
news gathering, and countries, 193
news geography, 6, 64, 180, 196
　See also countries involved; countries of location
news items
　duration of, 31–34
　foreign, number of per country, *65*
　length of, 110
　live from location, *115,* 116
　number of per newscast, *109,* 110
　pre-recorded on location, *115,* 116

type of and actor status, 95
news judgments, and countries involved, 271
news net, 269
news organizations, studies on, 209
newspapers
  age and reading of, *159*
  demographics as predictors of exposure to, *164,* 165, 166
  education and reading of, 159
  exposure to in Brazil, 296
  exposure to in Switzerland, 314
  foreign coverage in, 172
  time spent reading news in, 157
news production, 26
news reception, 26
news selection, 24–27, 42, 43
  in commercial service television, 214
  and contextualization, 221–222
  criteria, 227
  and domestication, 220–221
  and gatekeepers' attitudes, 212
  influences on, 209–210
  and media owners, 43
  and media routines, 209–210
  and news workers, 42, 212 (*See also* gatekeepers)
  and newsworthiness, 211 (*See also* newsworthiness)
  organizational influences, 210
  in public service television, 214
  See also gatekeepers
news theory, 24
news values, difficulty in defining, 227
news workers
  and news selection, 209 (*See also* gatekeepers)
  staff for foreign news, 213–214
newsworthiness
  and cultural affinity, 211
  and ethnic proximity, 211
  factors in, 211, 214
  and images, 218–220
  and prominence of country of origin, 211
  and proximity, 217–218
  and ratings, 216–217
  and selection, 211
  and significance, 215–216
  See also countries of interest; gatekeepers; news selection

New World Information and Communication Order, 63
Nguyen Vu, H. N., 312
Nguyen Vu, Hong Nga (Angie), 312
Norris, P., 6, 131, 327
Nossek, H., 212
Nuijten, K., 130

Obama, Barack, 216
O'Neill, D., 27
On Television and Journalism (Bourdieu), 173
Östgaard, E., 26
Owens, L. C., 186
owners, media, 43

Page, B. I., 88, 104
Palmgreen, P., 160
Pantti, M., 147
Patterson, E. T., 25
PC differential (public-commercial differential)
  analytical depth, 138–140
  contextual factors, 149
  cosmopolitanism, 140–143
  defined, 130
  for each country, 145
  effects of commercialization on, 135
  method and data in analysis of, 135–136
  and reliance on advertising revenue, 145–147
  research questions regarding, 133–135
  and sensationalism, 133, 136–138
  studies of, 130–131, *132*
  summary of, 143–145
  in Taiwan, 148
  variations across countries, 148–150
Peeters, A., 130
personalization, 133–134, 140
Peter, J., 13
Pfetsch, B., 131
photos, still, 119, *120*
Poland
  actors in, 309
  commercial service television in, 308
  countries covered in, 232
  countries of interest in, 309
  gatekeepers' view of audience in, 240–241
  gatekeepers' views of foreign news in, 231
  interest in foreign news in, 309
  media system in, 308

news items in, 309
news types in, 309
percentage of foreign news in, 231
public service television in, 308
political system, global, 81
politicians, as actors, 96–97, 103–104, 321
politics
coverage of, 45, 49, 54–56
coverage of in domestic news, 50
coverage of in foreign news, 51–53
coverage of in United States, 47
and distribution of news items, 36
and foreign news coverage, 29
population, and foreign news coverage, 29
Porath, William, 298
Porter, C. J., 6
Portugal
actors in newscasts from, 97, 310
audience interest in, 310
commercial service television in, 309–310
countries covered in, 235
countries of interest in, 310, 311
gatekeepers' view of audience in, 241–242
gatekeepers' view of foreign news in, 235
interest in former colonies, 217–218
media system in, 309–310
news items in, 310
percentage of foreign news in, 235, 310
public service television in, 309
topics in, 310–311
PRAM (Program for Reliability Assessment of Multiple Coders), 13
presentation, manner of, 113–116
press freedom, and newsworthiness, 211
production, and news workers, 42
project. *See* study
proximity, 214, 217–218
public-commercial differential. *See* PC differential
public service television (PTV), 8
advertising on, 148
in Canada, 296
in Chile, 298
coexistence with commercial television, 129 (*See also* PC differential)
commercialization and, 149
and competition, 131, 135, 149
conflict on, *139*

contributions to Eurovision News Exchange, 117
convergence with commercial television, 131–132, 147–148
cosmopolitanism of, 141–143
in democracies, 129
expectations of, 130, 132–133, 215
in Flanders, 294
foreign news on, 3–4
gender of actors on, 131
in Germany, 302, 303
hard news on, 130
in Hong Kong, 303
influence on commercial television, 148
international organizations on, *142*, 143
in Israel, 305
in Italy, 306
in Japan, 307
length of sound bites on, *139*, 140
mission of, 36
news selection in, 214
number of countries involved in foreign news on, *142*
personalization by, 134, 140
in Poland, 308
in Portugal, 309
preference for, 130–131
sensationalism in, 133, 136–138
soft news on, 145
in study, 10–11, 18
in Switzerland, 312
in Taiwan, 146, 148, 303, 314
in United States, 315
use of audio-visual effects by, 147
variability in, 321

Quandt, T., 302
questionnaire, 14–15

Rantanen, T., 6
Reese, S. D., 27, 42, 43
regionalism
in Asian foreign news, 77
in content-audience correspondence, 279
and countries of interest, 270
in coverage of countries of location, 71
in Singapore foreign news, 77
in South American foreign news, 76
in U.S. foreign news, 76

regionalism, universal, 37
Reinemann, C., 26
reliability, 13–14, 333
reliability coefficients of major analysis variables, 340–341
religion, and newsworthiness, 211
representation, pictorial and graphic, *120*, 121
  See also images
research, comparative
  "country" in, 4–5
  theory in, 5–6
  See also study
research, comparative media, 3–4
Riegert, K., 327–328
Riffe, D., 29
Robertson, A., 327
Robinson, G. J., 28
Roeh, I., 329
roles, standardized, 89
Rosengren, K. E., 160
Ross, M. H., 131
Ruge, M. H., 26, 27, 211
Ruhleder, K., 329
Russia, as country of location in foreign news, 78

Saletzky, M., 25
samples, 15
Sanders, K., 132
Scherr, S., 26
Schmidt, D., 8
Schulz, W., 7, 37, 63
Seib, P., 226
selection, of news. *See* news selection
Semetko, H. A., 130, 132
Sendin, André, 309
Senokozlieva, M., 89
sensationalism, 26
  and emotions, 147
  expectations of, 132–133
  and newsworthiness, 214
  and PC differential, 136–138
  See also news, sensational
Shanor, D. R., 24
Shoemaker, P., 24, 27, 42, 43, 211, 212
significance, social, 27, 211
  gatekeepers on, 215
  and newsworthiness, 214, 215–216
  vs. images, 219–220

Silveira, J., 89, 104
simplification, 26
Singapore
  content-audience correspondence in, 278–279
  countries of location in foreign news, 77
  foreign relations in, 312
  media system in, 311
  migrants in, 289
  news items in, 311–312
  news types in, 312
  in political system, 81
  topic coverage in domestic news in, 50
  topics covered in, 312
  See also countries
slow motion, *122,* 125
social issues
  actors in, 96
  coverage of, 45
  in domestic *vs.* foreign news, 50
sound bites, length of, 138–140
sources. *See* actors
South America, countries of location in foreign news in, 76
Soviet Union, 78
Sparkes, V. M., 28, 269
sports
  actors in, prevalence of, 97
  coverage of, 46, 49, 51, 54–56, 299
  interest in news regarding, 181–182
  time assigned to, 110
  in United States, 181
Sreberny-Mohammadi, A., 8
staff, for foreign news, 213–214
"stand-up," *115,* 116
status, and identification with viewer, 103
Stayner, J., 26
Stempel, G. H., 103
Stępińska, Agnieszka, 308
stories, "interesting," 25
stories, people, 25
Stromback, J., 130, 131
study
  assembly strategy in, 17–18
  audience surveys, 14–15
  coding of newscasts, 11–14, 19
  collaboration in, 20, 21–22
  commercial stations in, 10–11, 18
  content analysis, 9–14, 331–332

countries in, 9, 16 (*See also* countries of study)
demographics in, 18
design of, 9–22
functional equivalence in, 16–22
funding of, 21
interviews with gatekeepers, 15–16, 20–21 (*See also* gatekeepers)
languages in, 12
public service stations in, 10–11, 18
reliability in, 13
selection of newscasts for, 18
surveys, 19 (*See also* surveys, audience)
synchronization of, 20–21
Super Bowl, 181
surveys, audience, 14–15, 19, 333–334
description, 155
exposure to news, 156–159
questionnaire, 342–349
reasons for watching/not watching television news, 160–163
translation of, 19
in United States, 195
using to map interest in foreign news, 173 (*See also* interest, in foreign news)
See also interest, of audience
survey samples, 350
Switzerland
commercial television in, 313
countries covered most in, 230
countries of location in foreign news in, 74–75
exposure to television news in, 314
foreign relations in, 314
gatekeepers' view of audience in, 239
interest in foreign news in, 314
media system in, 312–313
news items in, 313
percentage of foreign news in, 230
public television in, 312
topics covered in, 313
views of foreign news in, 230

tables, *118*, 119
Tai, Z., 172
Taiwan
actors in, 315
commercial television in, 303, 314
countries of interest in, 315
countries of location in foreign news in, 77
gatekeeper interviews with, 236
gatekeepers' view of audience in, 244–245
interest in foreign news in, 315
media system in, 314
news items in, 314
PC differential in, 148
percentage of domestic news in, 314
percentage of foreign news in, 236, 314–315
public service television in, 146, 303, 314
television news exposure in, 315
topics covered in, 315
television, and exposure to foreign news, 154
television news
consumption of, 156–159
and content-audience correspondence, 285, 287, 288–289
as main source of foreign news, 154–155
motives for watching/not watching, 160–163, 167, 185
television news exposure
and age, *159*
demographics as predictors of, 163, *164*, 166, 323
and education, 158–159
and gender, *159*
and interest in foreign countries, 291
and interest in topics, 265
text, printed, *118*, 119
theory, gatekeeping, 24
theory, in comparative research, 5–6
Thorson, E., 227
topics
coding of, 43
in content, compared to audience interest, 254–263 (*See also* content-audience correspondence)
correlations between, 53–54
by country, *44*
coverage of, 47–49
diversity of, 59–60
in domestic news, *255–256*
in domestic *vs.* foreign news, 50–53, *55*
foreign affairs, *261,* 262–263
in foreign news, 321
and gender of actors, *101,* 102
hard *vs.* soft news, prevalence of, 56–57 (*See also* news, hard; news, soft)

interest in, *174,* 176–177, *183, 260,* 262, 265, 323 (*See also* interest, of audience)
   of interest in foreign news, 323
   of interest in foreign *vs.* domestic news, 177–182
   most frequently identified, 54–56
   and numbers of actors, 96, 97, *98,* 100
   overview of, 43–49
   predictors of interest in, 264–265
   reasons to compare, 41
   recoding of, 43
   and status of actors, *99,* 100
Tower of Babel, 328–329
Tuchman, G., 25, 43, 269

United Kingdom
   as country of location in foreign news, 78
   coverage of in foreign news, 72–73
United States
   commercial television in, 315
   countries of interest in, 317
   countries of location in foreign news in, 76
   as country involved in foreign news, 82
   as country of interest, 193, 196, 269, 323
   as country of location in foreign news, 75, 77, 78
   coverage of in foreign news, 69–70, 229, 230, 231, 232, 233, 234, 235, 236
   decline in foreign news coverage in, 226
   exposure to television news in, 316
   lack of interest in foreign news in, 173
   media system in, 315
   news items in, 316
   percentage of foreign news in, 316
   perceptions of foreign news in, 161, 162, 163
   public television in, 315
   as role model, 108
   significance of in foreign news, 215–216
   sports in, 181
   topic coverage in, 47
   views of, 235–236
unit of analysis, 5, 16
Uribe, R., 131

Vettehen, P. H., 130
victims, 89
viewer
   identification with, 103, 105
   See also audiences
Vilanilam, J. V., 29
violence
   perceived, in foreign news, 173
   visuals of, 133, 138
visual material, *115,* 116, 218–220
von Pape, Thilo, 302
Vos, D., 90
Vos, T., 42, 212

Wainberg, J. A., 295
Wang, T., 314
Ward, D., 104
weather forecasts, 110
Weaver, D. H., 176, 228, 315
Weaver, J. B., 6
Welzel, C., 328
Wenner, L. A., 160
White, D. M., 24, 42, 209, 211
Wilhoit, G. C., 228
Wilke, J., 8, 23, 302
Willnat, L., 315
Winter, J. P., 269
witnesses, 89
women
   appearance of in news, 90
   See also gender
Woodward, J. L., 63
worldviews, national, 290
Wouters, R., 293
Wu, H. D., 28, 173

Xu, X., 311

Zhou, B., 299